VOICES OF WOMEN HISTORIANS

VOICES OF WOMEN HISTORIANS

THE PERSONAL,
THE POLITICAL,
THE PROFESSIONAL

EDITED BY

EILEEN BORIS AND NUPUR CHAUDHURI

INDIANA UNIVERSITY PRESS
BLOOMINGTON AND INDIANAPOLIS

This book is a publication of

Indiana University Press
601 North Morton Street
Bloomington, IN 47404-3797 USA

http://www.indiana.edu/~iupress

Telephone orders 800-842-6796
Fax orders 812-855-7931
Orders by e-mail iuporder@indiana.edu

The paper used in this publication meets the minimum requirements of American National Standard for Information Sciences—Permanence of Paper for Printed Library Materials, ANSI Z39.48-1984.

Manufactured in the United States of America

Library of Congress Cataloging-in-Publication Data

Voices of women historians : the personal, the political, the professional / edited by
Eileen Boris and Nupur Chaudhuri.
p. cm.
Includes index.
ISBN 0-253-33494-2 (cloth : alk. paper). — ISBN 0-253-21275-8 (pbk. : alk. paper)
1. Women—United States—History—20th century. 2. Women historians—United States—Biography. 3. Feminism—United States—History—20th century. I. Boris, Eileen, date. II. Chaudhuri, Nupur.
D13.5.U6V65 1999
907'.202273—dc21 98-51191

1 2 3 4 5 04 03 02 01 00 99

TO ALL WOMEN HISTORIANS
PAST, PRESENT, AND FUTURE

E. B.
N. C.

CONTENTS

ACKNOWLEDGMENTS

We conceived of this project over lunch with Joan Catapano in a Montreal cybercafe during the Eighteenth International Congress of Historical Sciences in 1995. Without Joan's vision and support, this book would have remained a dream. We would like to thank officers of CCWH—Executive Directors Peggy Renner and Sarah Larson; Presidents Judith Bennett, Peggy Pascoe, and June Hahner; Newsletter Editor Susan Wladaver-Morgan; and Graduate Student Coordinator Regina Lark—for their encouragement and willingness to defray some of the expenses involved with a collection of twenty authors. Ann J. Lane and Judith Zinsser offered cogent comments on the original proposal, while Lisa Lindquist read the manuscript from the standpoint of the current generation of graduate students in women's history. We benefited from their wise counsels even if we could not accommodate all their suggestions. Jeff Ankrom and the rest of the staff at Indiana University Press produced the book in time to celebrate the thirtieth anniversary of CCWH at the Berkshire Conference in 1999; we are grateful for all their effort. Rachel Vorberg-Rugh saved us with her professional index.

Finally, we would like to acknowledge the creativity and cooperation of our authors. Without their generosity, we could not have left this legacy to the three decades of advocacy for women in the historical profession and promotion of women's history for which CCWH stands. We wish we could have included the stories of all the women and men who have served this organization. "Thank you for your contributions" will have to suffice. Of course, we would like to recognize each other for sustaining this project over the last two years. E-mail gets deleted, but memories remain—especially of our Australian adventure after the 1998 meeting of IFRWH. Even historians sometimes play.

INTRODUCTION: STANDPOINTS ON HARD GROUND

Eileen Boris and Nupur Chaudhuri

We are makers of history, both as individual subjects and as professional generations. This is no grandiose claim coming after the recovery of those once "hidden from history"[1] by those whose own entrance has helped to transform the academy. Think of the double meaning of "making." Claiming the title "historian," we craft tales about the past; some of us also try to uncover "the truth about history."[2] Despite our varying chronological ages, many of us came of age during the 1960s and early 1970s when political activism—civil rights, peace, student, women's movements—swept through the academy, no less than the society. "The feminist desire to 'make history' entangles the desire to effect significant and lasting change with the desire to be the historian of change," critic Susan Stanford Friedman has contended. "The narrative act of assigning meaning to the past potentially intervenes in the present and future construction of history."[3] In that spirit, we offer this collection, which looks back, past the 1969 founding of the Coordinating Committee on Women in the Historical Profession (CCWHP) [now the Coordinating Council for Women in History (CCWH)], through the lives of some of the women who have served on its board.

CCWH developed out of the activist ferment that marked a new cohort of women in the profession who turned their scholarly gaze toward the recovery of women's experiences. CCWH brought an independent feminist voice to debates within the American Historical Association (AHA), of which it is an affiliate organization. As one of the first women's caucuses in the academy, it addressed issues in the larger society as well, including the Equal Rights Amendment and other civil rights measures (like the Civil Rights Restoration Act); reproductive rights (like the historians' brief for the *Webster* case); and child care. It also considered the connection between home and work (such as the tenure clock for mothers/parents), and academic freedom and the structure of academic life (such as adjunct and contingent workers).[4] It has supported a more inclusive profession and a more expansive understanding of history.

This collection tells some of the stories of the women behind CCWH. While commemorating three decades of feminist activism and scholarship, it contributes to the emerging historiography of women's history and the literature on women in the professions. In the spirit of CCWH, all royalties from this book go to scholarships offered by the organization to women who write and study history. The number of women receiving PhDs in history rose from 14.3 percent in 1977 to 21.3 percent in 1995. Still, women compose the largest numbers of temporary, non–tenure-track historians.[5] By recognizing women scholars, we seek to enhance their place in the profession.

These reflective essays combine the autobiographical with the analytical to forge personal narratives that reflect on the myriad connections between the personal, the political, and the professional. Emerging from individual lives, they serve as markers of where the authors have been, where they are, and where they might be going. They record the many paths taken to becoming a historian in the middle to late twentieth century: how some women during that time confronted the pulls of being a woman, a professional, and an activist. They suggest the power of the modern women's liberation movement and varieties of feminist thought on individual lives and academic careers. They stand as offerings to a new generation that can witness how others made personal, political, and professional decisions as it embarks upon its own journey.[6]

Through personal narratives, we weave together the past and present of women's history and women in the historical profession to leave a record for those who would shape the future. We are mostly white and middle class, but some of us are women of color, immigrants, and working class. Perhaps a disproportionate number are Jewish. We are single, married, divorced, heterosexual, lesbian, mothers, and other nurturers. A cluster comes from New York City, but we represent all areas of the country: the South, New England, the Midwest, far West, and California. We live in small towns, suburbs, and cities. We are associated with a range of academic institutions. We span in age from our mid-twenties to over seventy. Some of us are just starting out, while others have retired from teaching, but not scholarship. Many are in mid-career, in our forties and early fifties, with another cluster ten years older. We embrace different feminisms.

Only recently have historians joined the chorus of self-reflective voices that mark "the Memoir Boom."[7] Gerda Lerner, for one, has produced powerful essays reflecting on what it meant to be a Jewish refugee, an outsider, "living in translation." A number of historians of "race" have commented on "the significance of the personal for the professional," as Mark D. Naison has explained. Other collections, which come out of English departments, emphasize the working-class origins of academics.[8] Dominated by literary critics and creative writers, this turn to the autobiographical has developed just as a "postpositivist" social science disrupted the fictions of objectivity that had separated researcher from researched.[9] Indeed, the heightened self-consciousness of the storyteller stems from the deconstructive project even as it subverts the post-structuralist dismissal of the subject. In a recent review, Nancy K. Miller calls attention to "a renewed urgency to add the story of our lives to the public record." She names this genre as "the canonical chronology of the curriculum vitae: the life course of an education . . . the bildungsroman of a *feminist* professor."[10] These personal narratives spill outside the groves of academe to represent the bildungsroman of the *feminist* as historian and the historian as *feminist*. These voices move from the personal to the political to the professional. Though some speak in unison, we compose a multivocal chorus, whose distinct sounds blend together as we represent not only different fields within history (and within women's history) but contrasting approaches to history itself.

THE ORGANIZATION

In celebrating the thirtieth anniversary of CCWH, we look back to the work we have done "to change the profession of history, to change historical scholarship, and to change the direction of our own history."[11] Here we focus on organizational changes and CCWH accomplishments.[12]

During the 1960s and the beginning of the 1970s, when many women historians actively participated in social movements, AHA remained a "'gentlemen's protection society' . . . openly supporting practices of sexism, racism, classism, heterosexism, and antisemitism."[13] In this context, CCWHP was founded in December 1969 to encourage the recruitment of women into the historical profession, to oppose discrimination against women in the profession, and to encourage research and instruction in women's history. During the first decade, it spent much of the time lobbying for advancing the status of women in the profession and the status of women's history, then almost entirely neglected. The enormous growth of women's history led to the creation of the Conference Group on Women's History (CGWH) in 1974. Instead of becoming a separate affiliate of AHA, CGWH stayed with CCWHP. It shared memberships, newsletters, and many activities but separated the promotion of women's history from advocacy for women in the profession. During the presidency of Barbara Penny Kanner in 1984, for example, CGWH published course outlines in its newsletter to facilitate the teaching of women's history as well as scholarship in the field.

During the second decade, new hostile forces outside the profession threatened to wipe out whatever little the community of women historians had achieved. CCWHP/CGWH spent much of its time and energy defending these gains. Still it continued strengthening the field of women's history. Through the efforts of Claire Moses, Karen Offen, and Phyllis Stock, CGWH became the US representative to the International Federation on Research on Women's History (IFRWH). However, in the second decade, the organizational character of CCWHP/CGWH went through a major change. It became mature, more stable financially and structurally. In 1989, it was incorporated and received tax-exempt status, which still permitted lobbying for legislation which might affect the community of women historians.

About twenty-five years after the inception of CCWHP, AHA and the Organization of American Historians (OAH) appeared more responsive to the needs and interests of women historians because of the critical interventions of CCWHP over the years. In addition, CGWH easily could claim partial responsibility for the growing acceptance of women's history. At this juncture many members and the executive board desired to reevaluate our goals, chart new directions, and prepare to face the challenges of the 1990s and beyond. Some members objected to the bifurcation of our work into activist (CCWHP) and academic (CGWH) components.[14] And then there was the name! Many new members found it "klutzy," definitely not user-friendly. After a lengthy discussion, the executive board proposed changing the name to the Coordinating Council for Women in History (CCWH) to more accurately reflect the reality of one organization; to provide a name that is more memorable and understandable; and to present ourselves in a more effective manner.[15]

In 1995, the membership voted to accept the new name. To assure members that the new name signified no change in the values and goals of the organization, then co-president Nupur Chaudhuri wrote: "We have changed our name. But my commitment and that of our board members has not changed. The values and goals of CCWH remain what they have been. As always, we will act as the conscience of the historical profession with respect to women's issues. . . . Our activism will be closely tied to scholarship in women's history."[16] During these thirty years the contour of our organization has shifted. In the words of Mary Elizabeth (Betsy) Perry, "What had begun as a caucus of protest has been transformed into a lasting national organization of programs and policies."[17]

As part of its initial democratizing impulse, CCWH has focused on graduate student access to the profession. From 1972, CCWHP had appointed two graduate students to its executive board. In December 1988, it established a graduate student fund in honor of our twentieth anniversary and past presidents. Soon the Berkshire Conference on Women Historians joined CCWHP/CGWH in this effort and created the CCWH[P]/Berkshire Dissertation prize. Recently, we have had sufficient money to offer a second graduate student dissertation prize, the CCWH/Ida B. Wells Prize. In addition, CCWH sponsors a drop-in room for graduate students and organizes a graduate students' reception at AHA. To provide practical help, for a number of years CCWH has co-sponsored with the AHA Professional Division a workshop on job interviewing. Furthermore, each year CCWH promotes women's history among schoolchildren. In 1989, it established a Women's History Day Prize for fifth- to twelfth-grade students who participate in the National History Day competition.

Following an emphasis on the needs of part-time/adjunct faculty, the main theme of Catherine M. Prelinger's presidency from 1979 to 1982, CCWH has organized panels at various conferences to discuss the status of such faculty. An anonymous donor recognized our efforts on this front by contributing $50,000 to establish an award so that nontraditional scholars could carry out research. To honor Catherine (Kitty) M. Prelinger's memory, and her contribution to the profession, the CCWH board named this award after her. We honored the first recipient at the 1999 AHA meeting, part of our thirtieth-anniversary activity.

With our growing maturity as an organization has come the inevitable, though at times premature, loss of other key members through death. In 1984 graduate student representative Elizabeth (Beth) Weisz-Buck died of breast cancer. On August 15, 1982, we lost Joan Kelly, a founding member of CCWHP, an inspiring teacher, scholar, and role model for many, including a number of contributors to this volume, who mention her in their essays.[18] In honor of Kelly, in 1982 CCWHP/CGWH established an endowed fund for a book award in women's history and feminist theory. On May 21, 1983, the AHA council voted to approve the Joan Kelly Memorial Prize in Women's History, with CCWHP/CGWH as official sponsor.

The CCWH board has never forgotten its activist roots. In the mid-1990s, it wrote letters protesting the proposed closure of various feminist research centers, such as the Canadian Simone de Beauvoir Institute. In 1996 it passed a resolution in support of unionizing Yale graduate students who attempted to bargain collectively. Thanks to a strong letter from Judith Bennett and Nancy Hewitt, the AHA Council agreed to change its meeting place from Cincinnati, which had passed anti-gay regulations. Our AHA panels addressed timely topics, such as *Roe v. Wade* (1989), welfare reform (1997), and affirmative action (1998). In 1997, an anonymous donor gave funds to facilitate the provision of childcare at the annual AHA meeting. That service had stopped when the price of liability insurance skyrocketed, so that a new generation of mothers—and fathers—found themselves faced with the same dilemma that CCWHP founders faced thirty years ago. Peggy Pascoe and other board members hoped to convince AHA to take on again the responsibility for offering childcare. During the last thirty years, our organization has continued to act "as the conscience of the historical profession's stance on women's issues," as Mollie Davis explained.[19]

Members and officers held leadership positions in other history organizations, which further helped to democratize AHA. We have co-sponsored sessions on women outside of Euro-America with the World History Association, thanks to its past president and CCWH member Judith Zinsser. June Hahner, co-president of CCWH beginning in 1998, helped to strengthen ties with the Conference on Latin American History (CLAH) by proposing sessions with it for AHA.

We have worked hard within AHA to create a supportive feminist space. Susan Lebsock, one of the first CCWHP graduate student representatives, did her best to humanize the association. She wrote the first survival manual for women graduate students. The appointment of Noralee Frankel, another graduate student representative in the mid-1970s, as AHA Assistant Director of Women and Minorities helped CCWHP to be heard at AHA. The elections of Natalie Davis, Louis A. Tilly, Carolyn Bynum, and Joyce Appleby—all members of CCWH—as presidents of AHA aided in the empowerment of women historians. Elections of other members and officers to important AHA offices—Mollie Davis, Nancy Hewitt, Frances Richardson Keller, Claire Moses, Betsy Perry, Barbara Ramusack, Peg Strobel, Gerhard Weinberg, and Robert Zangrando, to name only a few—also facilitated our objectives. Consider this the strategy of infiltration from below.

We attribute success to our networking system, about which Sally Gregory Kohlstedt commented: "CCWHP performs an important task by maintaining the network to be mobilized."[20] Past officers, especially early ones Jordy Bell and Joanna Zangrando, worked hard to set up this network system. Though some women have gained power within the formal institutions of the profession, we want to maintain "outsider" status because it "is very important," as Claire Moses once wrote. "When everything feels calm, the differences are not great. It's when there are tensions that our capacity to lobby the organization or distance ourselves from them that our position most matters."[21] As we proceed toward the next century, we like to believe with Frances Richardson Keller that "as an organization, we represent the very center of a national, now an international, effort to nurture and to explore a broader comprehension of our origins as they contribute to the development of our future."[22]

THE VOICES

The twenty essays in this collection illuminate threads; they are illustrative rather than representative. We see the forces of marginalization and discrimination retreat before active struggle and resistance. We witness the process of professionalism and a simultaneous transformation of the profession. Written by survivors, these are narratives of success and achievement, tales of triumph. The most-used word throughout must be "heady." "We met resistance each step of the way, but in the end we prevailed," Gerda Lerner contends. But these are also cautionary tales that credit circumstances as much as talent. As Linda Kerber notes, "the structural changes we envisioned that would make the academy a more hospitable site have been only fitfully accomplished." Sandi Cooper's continual struggle at City College serves as only one indication of how success is always conditional, never absolute, always subject to renegotiation.

The essays do not speak for the many other women who entered graduate school from the 1960s into the 1980s, when sexual discrimination and then a weakened job market further curtailed their choices; their voices became silent. Nor do these essays speak for those who benefited from the impact of feminism on the academy but were not active or chose other organizational forms for their activism. In 1979 African American women established their own group, the Association of Black Women Historians (ABWH), which has brought a black women's perspective to professional and scholarly issues. Given the antiracist commitment of many within CCWH, as expressed in a number of these essays, beginning in the 1980s CCWH sought a closer working relationship with ABWH. "Race" then marks these essays but in a conscious manner, no less for "white" women than for the women of color—Nupur Chaudhuri, Nancy Raquel Mirabal, and Crystal Feimster—whose lives as outsiders complicate other outsider identities, as Joan Hoff's working-class origins or Betsy Perry's adjunct status.

That so many who received degrees in the 1970s constructed their own careers and have followed nontraditional paths as independent historians and adjunct teachers suggests that activism in CCWHP/CGWH functioned as an alternative professional route. Because of their gender, outsiders thus became insiders of the networks they wove. Networks became safety nets. But these networks among women historians continue to be porous, inviting new women into the web. Community and network represent key words in these stories; some of them have overlapped not only in terms of CCWH or women's history but also in terms of peace, student, trade union, socialist, or feminist politics. Nancy Hewitt's "Emma thread," for example, stretches to Lynn Weiner, who wrote her senior thesis on Goldman, and Eileen Boris, who locates Emma as part of the feminist pantheon.

History and activism intertwined in the lives of these historians, as seen in the stories of Berenice Carroll, Renate Bridenthal, and Mollie Davis. While some began by keeping their writing of history separate from their antiwar or civil rights politics, for others "women's history became my means of addressing women's issues," as Karen Offen confesses and Barbara Penny Kanner demonstrates in her trajectory. Barbara Winslow and Peg Strobel have turned to documenting the women's liberation movement itself. The women's movement led some to women's history; for others, particularly those who entered graduate school in the 1960s, overt discrimination as mothers and as women catapulted them into the study of women.

These essays suggest that many women academics have undergone a life cycle different from that of their male counterparts. Motherhood could restrict, delay, or transform career paths. So could the cultural construction of woman as mother. A number of the essays refer to the opening that higher education offered in the 1960s to undergraduate women of talent. As young women without children, they could act like "men" in their career choices, an option that Frances Richardson Keller never could consider, entering graduate school as a single mother in her late forties. When she took time off from courses while having her child, Hilda Smith had to fight expulsion from student housing. Marriage too could limit job searches and other professional decisions.

In assembling this collection, we have refrained from editing out the distinctiveness of each woman's voice. Thus we decided to keep individual renditions of the same story, such as the founding moment of CCWHP. Neither have we insisted on personal confessions over intellectual portraiture. Authors interpreted in their own ways the assignment to link the personal, the political, and the professional. They disagree. Some embrace postmodernism; others find its influence pernicious. Some have turned to gender history; others consider themselves women's historians. In problematizing the categories "woman historian" and "women's history," they explore the construction of identity in telling about the self. We have let contributors stand in dialogue with each other and with you, our readers.

NOTES

1. Shelia Rowbotham, *Hidden from History: Rediscovering Women in History from the 17th Century to the Present* (New York: Pantheon, 1973).

2. Joyce Appleby, Lynn Hunt, and Margaret Hunt Jacobs, *Telling the Truth About History* (New York: Norton, 1995).

3. Susan Stanford Friedman, "Making history: reflections on feminism, narrative, and desire," in *The Postmodern History Reader*, Keith Jenkins, ed. (New York: Routledge, 1997), 233.

4. Hilda Smith, Nupur Chaudhuri, Gerda Lerner, and Berenice A. Carroll, eds., *A History of the Coordinating Committee on Women in the Historical Profession—Conference Group on Women's History* (Chicago: CCWHP-CGWH, 1994) summarizes the first and second decades of the organization.

5. Betty D. Maxfield et al., *Science, Engineering and Humanities Doctorates in the United States: 1977 Profile* (Washington, DC: National Academy of Sciences, 1978), 39 (table 2.3); Linda Ingram et al., *Humanities Doctorates in the United States: 1995 Profile* (Washington, DC: National Academy Press, 1997), 30 (table 2). See also, Committee on Women Historians of the American Historical Association, prepared by Carla Hesse, with the assistance of Katharine Norris and Gail Phillips, *Report on the Status and Hiring of Women and Minority Historians in Academia*, 4th edition (Washington: AHA, 1995).

6. For earlier in the century, see Jacqueline Goggin, "Challenging Sexual Discrimination in the Historical Profession: Women Historians and the American Historical Association, 1890–1940," *American Historical Review* 97 (June 1992), 769–802; for a version that carries the story through the early 1980s, see Joan Scott, "American Women Historians, 1884–1984," in her *Gender and the Politics of History* (New York: Columbia Univ. Press, 1988), 178–98.

7. "The Memoir Boom," editorial, *Women's Review of Books* 13 (July 1996), 5.

8. Gerda Lerner, *Why History Matters: Life and Thought* (New York: Oxford Univ. Press, 1997), 33; Mark D. Naison, "Conclusion: The Significance of the Personal for the Political," in *Historians and Race: Autobiography and the Writing of History*, Paul A. Cimbala and Robert F. Himmelberg, eds. (Bloomington: Indiana Univ. Press, 1996), 131; C.L. Barney Dews and Carolyn Leste Law, eds., *This Fine Place So Far From Home: Voices of Academics from the Working Class* (Philadelphia: Temple Univ. Press, 1995); Michelle M. Tokarczyk and Elizabeth A. Fay, eds., *Working-Class Women in the Academy: Laborers in the Knowledge Factory* (Amherst: Univ. of Massachusetts Press, 1993). For a project similar to our own, see Barbara Laslett and Barrie Thorne, eds., *Feminist Sociology: Life Histories of a Movement* (New Brunswick: Rutgers Univ. Press, 1997).

9. Camilla Stivers, "Reflections on the Role of Personal Narrative in Social Science," *Signs: Journal of Women in Culture and Society* 18 (Winter 1993), 408–25.

10. Nancy K. Miller, "Review Essay: Public Statements, Private Lives: Academic Memoirs for the Nineties," *Signs: Journal of Women in Culture and Society* 22 (Summer 1997), 981–1015, esp. 982–83.

11. Berenice Carroll, "Scholarship and Action: CCWHP and the Movements," *Journal of Women's History* 6 (Fall 1994), 79.

12. For our history, see Smith et al., *A History of the CCWHP*; see also, Carroll, "Scholarship and Action," 79–96; Nupur Chaudhuri and Mary Elizabeth Perry, "Achievements and Battles: Twenty-five Years of CCWHP," *Journal of Women's History* 6 (Fall 1994), 97–105; Judith M. Bennett and Nancy A. Hewitt, "The Future of the CCWHP/CGWH," *Journal of Women's History* 6 (Fall 1996), 106–11; Judith Zinsser, *History and Feminism: A Glass Half Full* (New York: Twayne, 1993), 95–112.

13. Berenice Carroll quoting Jesse Lemisch, "Scholarship and Action," 80.

14. Bennett and Hewitt, "Future of the CCWHP/CGWH," 106.

15. *Conference Group on Women's History Newsletter* 26 (March 1995), 2.

16. "Message from CCWH Co-President, Nupur Chaudhuri," *The CCWH Newsletter* 26 (August/September 1995), 4.

17. Mary Elizabeth Perry, as quoted in *The CCWH Newsletter* 28 (December 1997), 9.

18. Joan Kelly, *Women, History, and Theory: The Essays of Joan Kelly* (Chicago: Univ. of Chicago Press, 1984). Kelly (1928–1982) was Professor of History at City College of New York. She had co-directed the Women's Studies Program at Sarah Lawrence College and was a specialist in Renaissance history.

19. Mollie Davis, "Interim Report: CCWHP Civil Rights Zap Action Committee," *CCWHP Newsletter* 17 (December 1986), 4.

20. Kohlstedt response to CCWHP questionnaire, Spring 1989, quoted in Nupur Chaudhuri, "CCWHP—CGWH: The Second Decade," in Smith et al., *A History*, 25.

21. Moses' response to CCWHP questionnaire, in ibid., 32.

22. Frances Richardson Keller, "Message from CCWHP President," *CCWHP Newsletter* 19 (February 1988), 1.

VOICES OF WOMEN HISTORIANS

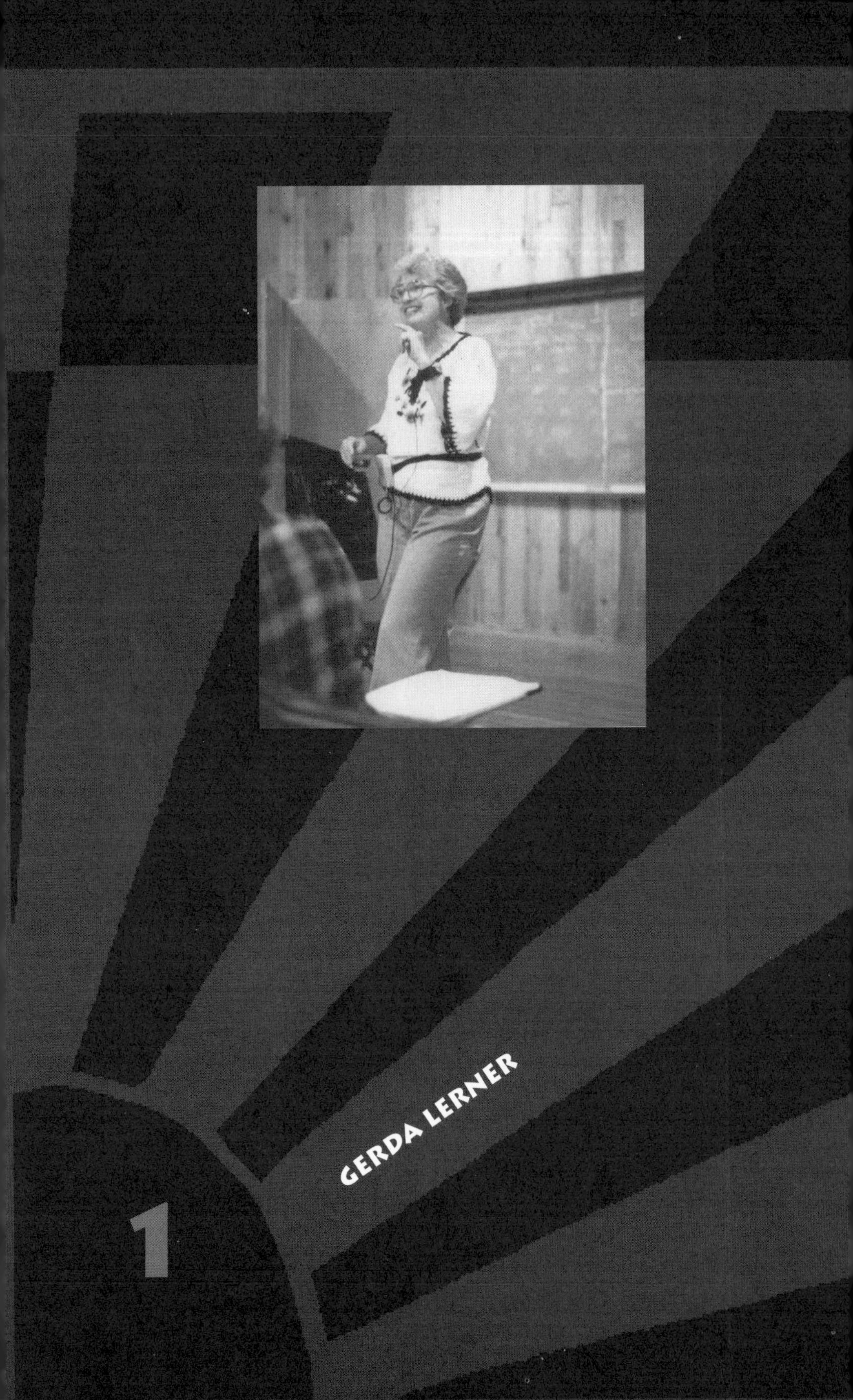

1

GERDA LERNER

WOMEN AMONG THE PROFESSORS OF HISTORY: THE STORY OF A PROCESS OF TRANSFORMATION

As I look back to the beginnings of feminist organization among historians in the late 1960s, I am aware of the fact that I entered the field with an unusual background.[1] I came to academic life as a mature woman, having been a committed political activist since age fifteen. A refugee from Hitler, I had experienced fascism, racism, imprisonment, and persecution. Raised in an upper-middle-class family in Vienna, Austria, I became stateless and totally impoverished after my forced emigration. As an immigrant in the United States I worked in typical unskilled women's jobs, from domestic work to file clerk, and it took me years to work my way up to becoming a medical technician. I had long worked with women in their community organizations and I knew in my bones that women build communities. But as I entered academic life as a student, I encountered a world of "significant knowledge," in which women seemed not to exist. I never could accept that patriarchal mental construct and resisted it all through my training. My commitment to women's history came out of my life, not out of my head.

I first attended a convention of the Organization of American Historians (OAH) in 1963, the year I entered graduate school at Columbia. It was a discouraging experience: I knew no one there and there seemed to be no way of getting to know anyone. The group was overwhelmingly male; there were

Gerda Lerner teaching at the Summer Institute on Women's History for Leaders of Women's Organizations, July 13–31, 1979 at Sarah Lawrence College. Photo by Vivian J. Scheinmann.

so few women and so very few female graduate students, that one noticed each woman in the room. Yet no one seemed to want to be the first one to speak to a stranger. The social highlights of the convention were something called "smokers," organized by various prominent schools. The Columbia smoker, true to its name, took place in a smoky room without chairs, in which men, each carrying the obligatory over-priced drink, milled around trying to connect with others they knew. The few women present usually turned out to be wives. The famous professors were surrounded by a few nervous and eager young men whom they had chosen from among their graduate students to be introduced to other important professors who might further their careers.

At that time there were no accepted ground rules for hiring and interviews. Most jobs were never advertised, but were announced informally through the old boys' network. When a job opened, a professor from that department would call his friends and contacts in other schools and elicit the names of their favorite and preferred students. The job search then took place privately, at the convention or on campuses, as a sort of competition between the pre-screened chosen few. Less favored students or those whose professors were not well connected in the network simply lost out. Women and minorities tended to be among the losers. At the "smoker" one could stand in a corner and watch the ballet of eminent professors introducing their favorites to other eminent professors or one could try to stand on the outer rim of a group and catch the professor's eye in hopes of being included. It was a dismal form of social interaction.

I also remember taking a number of lonely meals at these conventions and feeling miserable, until I finally decided to make my own contacts. At first, I just walked up to one or more of the nuns present and asked if I could have lunch or dinner with them. The nuns were always friendly and cheerful and I made some splendid contacts and lifelong friendships. From this I branched out to introducing myself to other women, but many of them were busy socializing with men they knew and hanging around the important professors. It took several years before I had built up enough contacts so that I would not pass the convention in misery and loneliness.

I may have been particularly inept socially or, as I then believed, I was enough of a misfit among the Columbia students (too old, a married mother of teen-agers, and interested in Women's History) to account for my isolation. In the sixties very few women over forty pursued graduate training. Those who did faced discrimination not only in admission to graduate programs, but especially in access to the informal networks which sustain professional development.

The ways for graduate students to become professionally known, by participating in conference sessions, offering papers or commentary, and getting articles published, were deep mysteries that students found accessible only through their mentors. If one leafs through the programs of the conventions of the major historical professional organizations in the fifties and early sixties, if one looks through their journals, the absence of women as participants and contributors is glaringly obvious. Women were not on the boards of editors of journals; they were not among those elected to the boards and offices of the professional organizations. The same was true for members of minority groups, only their exclusion was more total.

All of this changed with the organization of the Coordinating Committee on Women in the Historical Profession (CCWHP) at the 1969 convention of the American Historical Association (AHA). Although only seventeen people attended the first meeting, which Berenice Carroll had organized, a public meeting held later during the convention drew a large crowd and generated a list of over one hundred who wished to participate in the new organization. We drew up a statement of purpose, a set of immediate demands, and elected officers: Berenice Carroll and Gerda Lerner, co-chairs; Hilda Smith, treasurer; and a steering committee of five members. Our program was threefold: to encourage the recruitment of women into the profession and advance the status of women at all levels; 2) to oppose discrimination against women; and 3) to encourage and develop research and instruction in the field of Women's History. Other specific demands were quickly formulated: the formation of special "women's committees" to investigate the status of women in the profession; the provision of childcare at the conventions; changes in hiring practices, and the appointment of a special assistant to oversee the transition to open hiring practices; the establishment of a roster of women historians to facilitate the hiring of women; equal access of women to all committee appointments of the professional organizations; and equal participation in the formation of convention programs. In one form or another all of these demands were implemented over the next five years.

Responding to women's petitions the AHA, at its December 1969 meeting, appointed an ad hoc Committee on the Status of Women, which soon became a permanent committee, with Professor Willie Lee Rose as chair. A year later, this committee presented the organization with a report on the status of women in the profession, which proved the under-representation of women in every aspect of the professional society's work and provided the factual foundation for a massive effort launched by CCWHP to improve the status of women historians. Soon after, the OAH established a similar committee. Unlike other committees of the two organizations, the "women's committees" had a lively constituency that prodded them along and supported their recommendations. One of the significant features of our work was the close cooperation between women appointed to the two committees, women in CCWHP, and those in the "Berks." We managed to advance a broad-spectrum program for women historians and Women's History, regardless of institutional boundaries and constraints, and to work together effectively. This was something other groups, for example Radical Historians, had great trouble doing. I am proud of the fact that we did not have any problem with factionalism in thirty years of our work.

One of our earliest goals and one in which we were most spectacularly successful was to change the undemocratic structures and practices of the professional historical associations. We demanded, and eventually succeeded in gaining, the setting up of an employment roster and the mandatory advertising of jobs. It took a number of years of fact-finding, lobbying, and constant pressure, before we could prove the results of discriminatory practices in OAH and AHA. The Rose report and several follow-up reports quantified and systematized a story of long-term discrimination against minorities and women in salaries, in advancement, and in their representation on journals and organizational boards and committees. We supported all efforts to make the hiring process open, equitable, nondiscriminatory and accessible to all, and with some support from government affirmative action rules and from some male historians, we succeeded.

We set out also to systematically demystify the process of becoming a professional historian. A few of us found out how the professional organizations worked, how program committees formed their programs, how one got to suggest a panel proposal, how one got appointed to a committee. Whatever we found out, we immediately shared with everyone. We organized graduate students workshops, issued survival manuals, organized and proposed our own panels and fought to get them accepted by program committees. The AHA Committee on Women Historians issued several helpful leaflets which became popular with male and female historians: "Survival at Interviews," "How to Apply to Graduate School," "How to Get on a Program at a Meeting of Professional Associations," "How to Publish," and "How to Apply for Grants and Fellowships" were some of the most important titles.

Panels and workshops on each of these subjects began to be featured at succeeding conventions. They provided contacts for networking, forums for airing grievances and planning future actions, and they became models for open democratic process. The CCWHP cocktail hour, which we started in 1973, quickly became an institution and soon it was THE social event of the conventions, a good antidote to the old boys' smokers. For women, for graduate students, and for many men, we transformed the social climate during conventions, simply by modeling other possibilities. For me, from 1970 on, the two professional conventions and, of course, the revitalized Berks, have become warm social occasions, not only for learning what's new and current in scholarship, but also for meeting an ever-widening circle of close friends and co-workers.

At the time, changing the social climate of the conventions was not high on our priority list, but it proved to be an important side effect of the work of CCWHP and the "women's committees." Creating an alternative to the hierarchical model of the old boys' network not only made the conventions more pleasant and more inclusive, but it helped to involve a far broader group of people in the work of the organizations.

The two "women's committees" quantified the glaringly unequal representation of women in articles published in journals and in reviewing assignments. We monitored the articles submitted and the rejection letters; we set up meetings with editors of the journals to discuss these issues. I remember participating in several very unpleasant meetings of this kind with editors and various gatekeepers in which our efforts to gain access for women scholars and Women's History scholarship were rebuffed. The usual first response was denial: nobody ever had rejected articles by women or treated them in any way differently than articles written by men. The second response was more maddening: it was a sad "fact" that no good articles by women were being submitted to journals. If such quality articles were to be submitted, they would undoubtedly be accepted. CCWHP proposed that OAH and AHA might try publishing separate journal issues focusing on scholarship by women. Such proposals were rejected with disdain by editors of historical journals. Were we afraid of fair and open competition? Did we wish to lower standards?

It may be difficult for younger historians to imagine the extent to which male historians' resistance to our efforts took the form of disparagement. It is, of course, an ancient tactic by those resisting change to accuse those advocating change of lowering standards. The same response greeted educational reformers in the 1840s and again at the turn of the century who wished to include the study of American history and literature in college curricula. They, too, were accused of wanting to lower standards and dilute the value of higher education. The same accusations are, of course, made today against those advocating affirmative action and multicultural curricula. The assumption of the gatekeepers was and is that education is a zero-sum game. If new groups were to be included, it must mean that old groups would be slighted. The other, and more galling assumption, was that by definition scholarship by women was and would be inferior to scholarship by men. These objections vanished in the face of the solid scholarly work of the women and minority scholars who finally succeeded in gaining representation on the advisory boards of the journals and as members of program and executive committees.

Petitions, lobbying, and the introduction of resolutions by and about women at each of the conventions became staples of our organizing work. It was a slogging, slow, and often utterly frustrating process. We met resistance each step of the way, but in the end we prevailed. For example, the practice of CCWHP interviewing candidates for election to OAH and AHA offices regarding their views on a number of organizational issues was considered divisive, unprofessional, and terribly threatening when we first started it. By now, it has become an accepted feature of OAH and AHA elections and has certainly contributed to making candidates for office more accountable to the voters. I think that our shattering of the old boys' network and transforming the hierarchical, mystified way of running the professional organizations was one of the best and most useful things CCWHP did for everyone in the profession, not just for women and minorities.

If, in 1969, the status of women in the profession was marginal and hedged around by discriminatory practices and an androcentric tradition, the status of Women's History was nonexistent. At a time when political and institutional history was the measure of significance and social history had only recently been elevated to legitimacy, the subject "women" was defined as doubly marginal. Women's History was not recognized as a legitimate field and to admit that one worked in it was considered the kiss of death professionally. In 1970, there were only five scholars in US history who defined themselves primarily as historians of Women's History: Janet James, Anne Firor Scott, Elizabeth Taylor, Eleanor Flexner (a non-academic historian), and myself. Carl Degler, Clarke Chambers, and Christopher Lasch had done significant work in Women's History and Degler and Chambers were instrumental in furthering the establishment of the field. Christopher Lasch told me, probably in 1971, when I asked him what his next project in Women's History would be, that he had "taken the field about as far as it would go," and was now working on other subjects. A younger generation of graduate students was, of course, already working on Women's History topics and would shortly emerge as a self-conscious force, but there was a vast gap between them and the generation of Mary Beard, Elizabeth Schlesinger, Eugenia Leonard, and Elizabeth Massey who had, mostly outside the academy, worked to establish Women's History in the 1920s and '30s.

I was very much aware of lack of support for Women's History during the founding period of CCWHP. A questionnaire answered by 72 CCWHP members in 1970 regarding what should be the focus of the organization's work, revealed that 45 percent wanted it to focus primarily on the professional status of women and only 25 percent wanted to focus on Women's History.[2] My commitment was then already clear—for me the promotion of Women's History as a field had primary importance. Accordingly, I concentrated in 1970 on getting several panels sponsored by CCWHP into the programs of both AHA and OAH. After lengthy negotiations I succeeded in organizing a panel, "Feminism—Past, Present and Future" for the 1970 AHA convention

(Chair, Anne Firor Scott; papers by Alice Rossi, Jo Freeman, and myself, with William O'Neill as commentator). During the same convention the innovative chairman of the Program Committee, Professor Raymond Grew, accepted a panel discussion, "Women's Experience in History: A Teaching Problem," organized by the AHA Committee on the Status of Women. What a triumph—out of 100 sessions, two concerned women. These path-breaking sessions were lively and well attended. As a mark of progress, the 1971 AHA convention featured five Women's History panels. The 1971 OAH convention featured a panel on Mary Beard, and two panels on professional concerns of women historians. I served as the single woman member of the 1972 OAH program committee and wrote more than fifty letters trying to get several panels on women organized, but succeeded only in getting two on the program (or perhaps three, if one wants to consider a paper on the "marriage market" as representing women's history). One of these sessions, "The Case of the Missing Ladies," which dealt with a study of the leading college textbooks and the near-total absence of references to women in them, proved to be quite sensational, with an overflow audience and reporters present. It was written up in the New York Times the next day. So it went, step by step, six steps backward for every two steps gained. Yet, since 1972, at each convention, there have been panels and workshops pertaining to the professional interests of women and to Women's History.

In the summer of 1970 CCWHP reported that, nationwide, 22 members were offering at least one course on Women's History and that four Women's Studies programs were then being developed. That was only 27 years ago. Today women's history courses number in the thousands. In 1972, when with the help of a Rockefeller Foundation grant, I launched the MA Program in Women's History at Sarah Lawrence College, which I co-directed with Joan Kelly, ours was the first graduate program of its kind in the US and to my knowledge, in the world. Today students can earn an MA or PhD with a Women's History specialization at over seventy colleges and universities.[3]

The process of gaining acceptance for this new field of scholarship was slower and even more labor-intensive than that of promoting the status of women historians. We had to advance on three fronts all at once: we had to show that there were adequate and interesting sources available in Women's History; we had to produce first-rate work based on these sources; we had to train teachers, develop bibliographies and syllabi; and convince administrators and our colleagues that there was student demand for these courses.

Just as we had often been told by traditional historians that Women's History was insignificant, so we were constantly met with the unproven but widespread belief that there was a lack of sources for this field. This was disproven once and for all in a project I helped to conceive, organize, and finance. In April 1971, a small group of scholars who had worked in women's history sources got together at the OAH convention to discuss what might be done to make sources on women more readily accessible to scholars. All of us who participated in this meeting—Anne Firor Scott, Carl Degler, Janet James, Clarke Chambers, and myself, had done primary source research in the archives. Janet James, with her husband Ed James and Paul Boyer, was then still editing the first three volumes of *Notable American Women,* the first modern reference work on the subject. We all knew that one of the difficulties for researchers on women was the fact that archives and libraries did not catalogue their material on women in a coherent way. Women's diaries, letters, and writings were lost in family correspondences catalogued under male family members' names. The records of women's organizations were not systematically collected or identified. It was a common experience to go into an archive, ask the archivist what they had on women, and be handed one or two items, when in fact the archive contained hundreds of items by or about women. The five of us decided that we needed to do a survey of archives and of items by or about women. What we needed was a reference work, a sort of union catalogue of holdings on women. Clarke Chambers offered his state, Minnesota, as a testing ground and recommended that we bring in Andrea Hinding, curator of the Social Welfare History Archives, to take on the project and do a state survey to test the feasibility of a national project. With the help of Dorothy Ross, who chaired the AHA "women's committee," we secured the cooperation of both AHA and OAH in drafting a grant proposal for such a project. We also organized a workshop for historians and archivists at the 1972 OAH meeting, which enthusiastically supported the project.

Meanwhile, in the fall of 1971 I had been invited by Peter Wood, then an officer of the Rockefeller Foundation, to consult with him about how to advance work in Women's History and Women's Studies. I recommended the convening of a small planning conference to designate priorities in the development of Women's History. As a direct result of this conference at the Rockefeller Foundation, held April 8, 1972, we were able to secure grant support for the test run of the Women's History Sources Survey, which afterward was funded by NEH and the University of Minnesota. The final project, which took four years to complete, resulted in two volumes: Andrea Hinding (ed.), *Women's History Sources: A Guide to Archives and Manuscript Collections in the United States* (New York: R. R. Bowker, 1979).

Of all the projects I have ever been involved in, this, I think, was the most effective and important. Not only did we show that there were vast, and mostly unused, primary sources available virtually in every major community in the US, but we made these sources easily accessible. The informal networks of Women's History scholars, which were then being established, helped greatly to spread the effect of this work to the broader community. Further, in the process of conducting the survey, most archives and libraries decided to reclassify their items on women in such a way that they could be easily identified. In fact, we transformed the way archives were cataloguing their holdings in Women's History.

The production of monographs, essays, collections, documents, and books in Women's History was greatly aided by this archival project. In 1960, one could find thirteen books in print in Women's History. In 1987 I published a *Bibliography in US Women's History*, which listed 291 titles. There were then hundreds of dissertations in the field still in progress.

The professional organizations of women historians contributed to this development from 1970 on. We began by publishing lists of "Research in Progress in Women's History," and we systematically distributed course syllabi and bibliographies in Women's History to all interested. Beginning in 1972 the "women's committees" and CCWHP agitated for the commissioning of a pamphlet on Women's History, to be sponsored by AHA in its series of teaching pamphlets. Typically, the editor of the series refused us with the information that such a pamphlet was not high on the AHA's priority list. When we persisted, he changed his mind. I was asked to write this pamphlet, which, when it was finally printed, turned out to be the best-selling pamphlet in the series for many years.

Networking and the sharing of work in progress was another way in which we helped to build the field. In the fall of 1969, Patricia Graham (Columbia University) and I organized New York Metropolitan Area Women Historians, which soon affiliated with national CCWHP. By December 1970 the national organization had three affiliates: the NYC group, the West Coast Association of Women Historians, and Committee on the Status of Women of the Southern Historical Association. Today, with twenty-four CCWHP affiliates, it is probably hard to realize how triumphant we felt then at our swift growth. The New York City group quickly organized a campaign, securing 600 signatures to a petition in support of the demands made by CCWHP on the professional organizations: 1) support for the office of a special assistant on the rights of women by AHA; 2) urging history departments to increase the number of women graduate students; and 3) affirmative action in the hiring of women faculty and the setting up of time tables to effect equal ratios of men and women in departments.

It took several years longer before we could persuade Columbia University to make room among its 232 faculty seminars, which were organized by fields of historical scholarship, for ONE seminar dealing with women. Pat Graham, Marcia Wright, Annette Baxter, and I cooperated on this project. When, at last, the seminar "Women and Society" was established it quickly became one of the most popular and best attended seminars of all. Similar work was, of course, being done all over the country by women historians trying to promote the new field.

When I graduated from Columbia in 1966 my specialty, Women's History, did not really exist. I was advised to hide my interest in this "exotic subject" and to market myself as a good social historian. I did not take that well-meant advice, but I was aware of the fact that my special interest was a professional liability. We have come a long way since then. We have disproven the skeptics, persisted in the face of disparagement, ridicule, and tenacious resistance to change. CCWHP and the "women's committees" staffed in succeeding years by new and enthusiastic advocates of women and Women's History deserve a large part of the credit for the advances the field has made.

As for myself, looking back on sixty years of organizational work, mostly for lost causes, the past thirty years tell a story of spectacular, and often unexpected, success. The quest for restoring the interpreted past of half of the world's population has been richly rewarding, exhilarating, and energizing. We have proven, over and over again, that women make history and have always made history. In so doing, we have had to challenge the exclusionary and outdated patriarchal structures of academic institutions. Life and thought have merged; transforming knowledge has led us to transform institutions. It has been my privilege to be part of the most exciting intellectual movement of the century.

NOTES

1. Copyright Gerda Lerner, 1997. All rights reserved.

2. *CCWHP Newsletter* 1 (Summer 1970), 6.

3. Accurate accounts of graduate training in Women's History are elusive. The figure mentioned was derived from a hand count of programs listed in Karen Kidd and Ande Spencer, eds., *Guide to Graduate Work in Women's Studies,* 2d ed. (College Park, MD: National Women's Studies Association, 1994). It is likely the figure somewhat understates the number of such institutions.

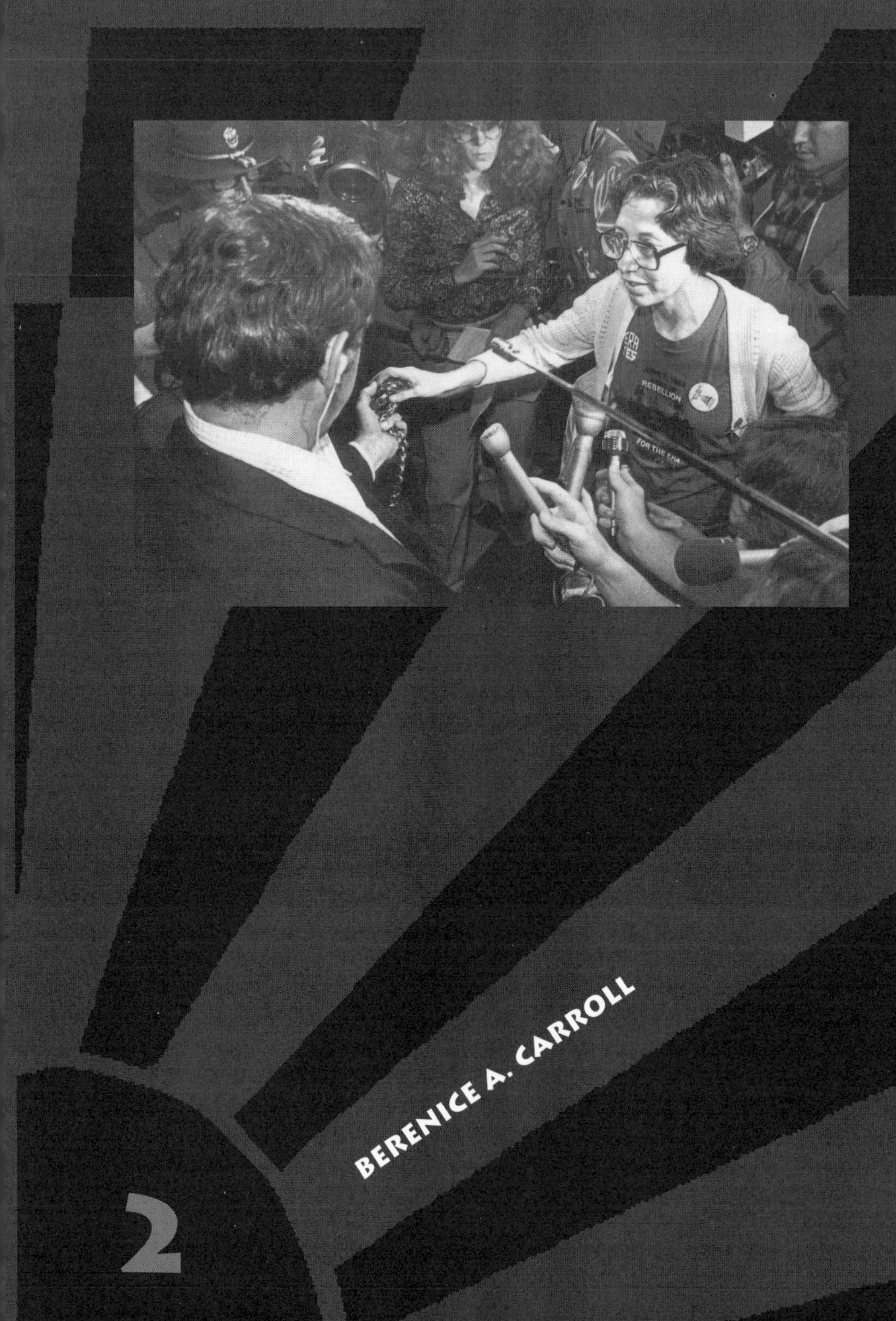

2

BERENICE A. CARROLL

THREE FACES OF TREVIA: IDENTITY, ACTIVISM, AND INTELLECT

> The line between "activism" and "scholarship," if there is such a line at all, is difficult to discern . . . , and perhaps it would be better to use instead an image favored by the women's peace movement, the web. Our activism and our scholarship were woven together to create the strength of both action and intellect that we brought to history.[1]

On the twenty-fifth anniversary of the founding of the Coordinating Committee on Women in the Historical Profession (CCWHP), I wrote these words in a memoir of that quarter century. This association has been a vital thread of my life, and I am tremendously grateful to all the wonderful women who were co-founders or later sustained and enhanced its work. This essay addresses how I reached the place and time of that founding, and how it relates to other threads of my life and work. I want also to extend the notion of the unity of theory and practice to embrace a third dimension, that of identity.

On a theoretical level, I always have been puzzled by the assumed separation or even opposition between "theory and practice," "scholarship and action." Activism and intellectual engagement have been intertwined and

As part of the Grassroots Group of Second-Class Citizens, Berenice A. Carroll hands over chains to a reporter at a demonstration for the Equal Rights Amendment on June 3, 1982 in the Capital Rotunda, Springfield, Illinois. From the Collection of the St. Louis Mercantile Library, University of Missouri at St. Louis.

inseparable in my life for some fifty years. The focus, the content, the balance, and the modes of interweaving have changed dramatically over time, but not the underlying sense that who I am, what I think, what I do, are like the three faces of Trevia. As in ancient images of this three-faced goddess, no one aspect could exist without the others; identity is interwoven with intellect and action.

I claim some labels of political and intellectual identity: pacifist, feminist, anarchist-socialist, and nonviolent direct activist. Labels are, of course, problematic. Gloria Anzaldúa wrote in *This Bridge Called My Back*: "Only your labels split me." Virginia Woolf wrote in *Three Guineas*, fifty years ago: "In our age of innumerable labels, of multi-colored labels, we have become suspicious of labels. They kill and constrict." But labels are of two kinds: those imposed by others and those freely chosen. Today the very concept of "freely chosen" is under challenge, but I cling to a belief in conscious human choice and agency. The labels imposed by others split, kill, and constrict. But those freely chosen give voice to identity, commitment, webs of sharing, and solidarity with others.

Identity, action, and intellect are all woven together in our "multi-colored labels." How this is so, however, is often difficult to see.[2] Intellect, especially, may seem to stand aloof from identity and action. But as I think about my own intellectual work, I see it both driven by and driving the others. If there is a central theme in my scholarship, it is the discovery, recovery, and understanding of the "powers of the 'powerless,'" and rejection of the mystiques of dominance that bind our attention and our loyalties—even against our will—to those conceived as "powerful." The central ideas embedded in this theme came from many sources, from books and protest marches, from consciousness-raising groups and spontaneous mass action, from speaking and listening, from "serious organizing" and "guerrilla theater," from family, children, and friends, from collective living and feminist collectives, from writing and thinking. How this theme appears and reappears in my work will be touched on in some examples below. But in retrospect, I see my labels and my ideas nestled in each other: my pacifism, my feminism, my anarchist-socialism, and my nonviolent activism all embrace and are shaped by my ideas about the "powers of the 'powerless.'"

I came to my current chosen labels rather late. My parents were liberal democrats but not politically activist, though as I later learned, my paternal grandfather had fled Russia as a Bolshevik in 1905, my maternal grandfather was an active Zionist, and my maternal grandmother supported woman suffrage. My mother, Margaret Segall Jacobs, was a teacher in the New York public schools, a proponent of progressive education. My father, Morris B. Jacobs, was a public health scientist, a proponent of science for the public interest. But I had aunts and uncles who were strongly committed on the left and I remember many a heated argument at family gatherings. Pacifism was not among those arguments. Through exclusion, victimization, and cultural forces over centuries of exile and dispersion, Jews have not had a strong military tradition between ancient times and the creation of the state of Israel, and there are pacifist strains in Judaism. But the Jewish community in the US, though not fully informed of the dimensions of the Holocaust until the end of World War II, knew enough to believe it necessary to support the war against Hitler. As a child my head was filled with images of war movies and terrifying enemies, and at twelve years of age, as my scrapbooks attest, I was an enthusiastic supporter of the Allied war effort.

In 1946, at age thirteen, I was recruited into a socialist Zionist organization, Hashomer Hatzair (The Young Guard), that was affiliated with the far-left Kibbutz movement, Kibbutz Artzi, and after the establishment of the state of Israel, with the political party Mapam. My education in Hashomer Hatzair (HH), from 1946 to 1952, was rather unusual. Hashomer Hatzair had been among the leaders of the active Jewish resistance to Nazism and its recent past and heroic figures offered a strong model of revolutionary struggle. Committed to a socialism of practice in the kibbutz movement, to an intellectual politics of Leninism and Stalinism in the early Cold War era, and to support of clandestine resistance to British imperialism, HH followed a self-protective policy of relative isolation from US politics and an insular but sweeping education of its youth members. It opposed the jingoistic nationalism, expansionism, and terrorism of the Irgun Zwai Leumi and the Stern Gang, and advocated a secular, bi-national state with complete separation of religion from the state and a democratic polity with full equality for all citizens (Arabs, Jews, and others). The youth movement was seen as both a source of recruits for Kibbutz Artzi and an opportunity for alienated youth in capitalist society to find meaningful and useful activities and goals. It gave its young members exceptional responsibilities and the prospect of "an unparalleled opportunity to live out their ideology on a kibbutz."

"The movement," as we called it, demanded daily total involvement: frequent meetings, study groups, creative and cultural activities collecting money for the Jewish National Fund and the Histadruth (labor federation), scout training at movement camps, and leadership of younger members. It taught (if it did not always live up to) an egalitarian, androgynous, antiracist, anti-elitist, and pro-labor ethic. It encouraged formation of a new identity, taking a new Hebrew name, rejecting make-up and "bourgeois" fashions in dress, abstaining from sexual intercourse and even from forming couples while in the youth movement, and accepting the commitment to emigrate with one's age collective to a kibbutz in Israel designated by Kibbutz Artzi. Even as teenagers, we pooled and redistributed our limited income, and experienced socialist living directly at the movement's cooperative farm. No physical coercion enforced these encompassing demands, but group approval and disapproval, the example and encouragement of admired older leaders, and the ultimate possibility of expulsion, were powerful forces of attraction, instruction, and persuasion. Altogether, it was an extraordinary education in cooperative living and politics and in the inseparability of the intellectual, the personal, and the political. At age sixteen, the excitement and exhilaration of jumping on and off subway trains in pairs with collection cans and one-minute speeches merged with the intellectual challenges of studying Ber Borochov and Karl Marx, the intensity of debates on sexual mores and Israeli party politics, and the joys and pains of dance, song, friendship, and love.

In 1949, several of my most admired mentors in Hashomer Hatzair left the organization following the decision to subordinate the youth movement to the Mapam party line. Though I felt too uninformed to take sides in this debate in 1949, I remained in touch with some of the defectors and various new associates, including an obscure group called "CI" that published the journal *Contemporary Issues*. CI held that the Soviet Union was a state capitalist formation, that is, neither a socialist state, as the Communist Party held, nor a "deformed workers' state," as Trotsky had held. This made a great deal of sense to me and, as I learned, much later, it was also the view of Raya Dunayevskaya. But CI was inclined to a conspiratorial outlook that portrayed the Cold War as an Orwellian hoax to maintain capitalist hegemony both east and west, and while I could conceive that it functioned in that way, the particular character of this conspiracy theory was not persuasive. The views of CI added, however, to my skepticism and alienation even from the politics of the left.

I visited Israel in the summer of 1952 and left Hashomer Hatzair immediately afterward, in circumstances too complex to detail here. I was then still fairly uncritical of the state of Israel and the incipient militarization of the institutions and consciousness of the Jewish communities both there and at home in the US. At the time, the armed status of the border kibbutzim I visited, the armed patrols on the walls then dividing the new and old cities of Jerusalem, the military convoys with which I hitchhiked rides to Elath (the southernmost point in Israel, then completely undeveloped)—all seemed to me benign and even hopeful of a better future. The informal, revolutionary style of the military seemed egalitarian and focused on self-defense and economic development, not conquest and repression. I now recognize that its increasing militarization has turned Israel into a garrison state internally and an oppressive, colonizing force externally. How to work to change this, from the problematic site of identities that I inhabit today, is a gnawing conundrum that I have not yet been able to untangle.

I left Hashomer Hatzair feeling confused, disoriented, and uprooted. After years of battling my parents for my freedom to choose a future in the kibbutz rather than in a middle-class American profession, the new peace at home felt strange and empty. In 1953 I completed my undergraduate degree in history at Queens College of New York. I might have been happier in English, anthropology, sociology, political science, or even mathematics, but I chose history because it was "hard" and I was still enmeshed in an internal debate over historical and dialectical materialism. Jack Hexter was teaching at Queens College at the time, and he helped me to secure a scholarship for graduate study at Brown University. Hexter epitomized the historian's dedication to "the sources," to rigorous analysis, and to elegant prose; but the history he taught, as he himself later acknowledged, was of institutions and events that were "pretty much stag affairs." So was the history taught at Brown University.

Though not yet conscious of that particular deficiency of my education, I found Brown University an intellectual and political desert. Certainly I learned a great deal from my courses, though I was told that I did worse on my qualifying oral exam than anyone who had ever passed. I suspect that had to do with my inability to see "the point" (in terms of the intellectual-political training and values I had received in "the movement") of most of what was presented. I was cut off from my closest friends and struggled through a series of miserable relationships that added little to my good cheer. On social occasions, all the faculty talked about was who was better than whom, and who had gotten an appointment at Harvard or Yale (shades of Mr. Ramsay and Charles Tansley, in *To the Lighthouse*). Compared with the intensity of life, struggle, politics, and intellect in Hashomer Hatzair, graduate study at Brown seemed pale and barren.

The habit of disengagement from US politics established in HH was hard to break. I was imbued with disdain for bourgeois politics in general and skepticism that anything but a revolutionary politics could bring society closer to the ideals I still held. I did not think much then about "the unity of theory and action," but in a way I was living it still, since alienation from theory underlay my alienation from political action. But I began to seek a theory and practice that would be meaningful. In 1956 I received a Fulbright scholarship (for which I gave up an AAUW fellowship) to study in Germany. My intended dissertation was a project in the history of science, but I abandoned that and decided to embark instead on a study of "big business" in the Third Reich. This was to be a test, for me, of Marxist theories of the relationship of capitalism to fascism. My new thesis advisor was Sinclair W. Armstrong, a European historian who had worked for the OSS during World War II and in the last stages of the war engaged in assembling captured German official records. Armstrong sent me to Washington, DC, to talk with

Gerhard Weinberg, who was in charge of an American Historical Association project to microfilm the large collection of captured records deposited in Alexandria, Virginia, a project for which I worked after my return from Germany. In later years, Gerhard remained a mentor, a friend, and later a dedicated supporter of CCWHP.

In the still-wounded Europe of the mid-fifties, I found much that was dark and perplexing, but returned to the US engaged to a mathematician, Robert Carroll. Bob, then ending two years of service in Army intelligence, was probably the most antimilitary person I had ever met, though not an active pacifist. We were married in early September, 1957, and moved to Maryland, where Bob entered the PhD program in mathematics at College Park and I commuted to the Federal Records Center in Alexandria.

In 1959 Bob Carroll completed his PhD at Maryland and I completed the writing (and he the typing) of my dissertation that summer (the degree was awarded in 1960). We spent 1959–1960 in France on Bob's postdoctoral fellowship, then moved to New Jersey, where Bob took a position at Rutgers, while I taught first at the Baruch School, and then at Douglass College, where I first met Sandi Cooper. At Douglass, however, the same Margaret Judson whose egalitarian principles led her to seek gender "balance" in the Douglass history faculty informed me that I would not be allowed to apply for an opening in my field because they had decided to hire a man.

The long period of withdrawal from active political engagement after I left Hashomer Hatzair ended rather suddenly in 1960. I had become increasingly concerned about the problems of nuclear weapons and atmospheric testing. In 1960 attending a lecture by Dr. Spock, addressed to a packed and volatile crowd, I joined SANE (Committee for a Sane Nuclear Policy) on the spot, and soon became active in the Raritan Valley chapter. I served as the New Jersey State representative to the national board of SANE, 1962–64. At the height of the fallout shelter craze in 1961, I joined with H. H. Wilson of Princeton University in circulating to our respective faculties an anti-shelter statement published with many signatures of academics around the country in the *New York Times.*[3] In 1962, while Kennedy was proclaiming the unity of the nation in the Cuban Missile Crisis, our little band of SANE protestors was demonstrating on the streets in New Brunswick.

Despite deepening involvement in antinuclear and antiwar action, I did not yet identify with the label "pacifist." In 1961, however, I had two encounters with nonviolent direct action that marked a new direction.

In the spring of 1961, I had the exceptional experience of housing members of the Committee for Nonviolent Action (CNVA) when they stopped in the New Brunswick area on the route of their precedent-setting peace walk from San Francisco to Moscow. I was deeply impressed by the walkers and for the first time gave serious consideration to the idea of a conscious, organized, nonviolent movement for social or political change. The idea was profoundly attractive, and the personal commitment of the walkers was powerful. I began to read about nonviolence and found myself amassing peace movement literature: *Peace News, Liberation, CNVA News.* At this time I first heard of Elise Boulding, who in 1962 was editing a *Women's Peace Movement Bulletin* to document women's peace actions nationwide and internationally.

On January 15, 1961, Women Strike for Peace held their first action at the White House. I was moved by the spontaneous power of the WSP actions and their wildfire spread around the country to other women's groups. The guerrilla theater tactics adopted by Dagmar Wilson and others in WSP when HUAC subpoenaed them in December 1962 were mind-bending. "Peace Women Baffle HUAC's Masculine Minds," proclaimed one story, recounting among others the following exchange: Alfred Nittle, HUAC counsel: "If a group has no organization and has no members, how in the world does it function?" Dagmar Wilson: "It's quite remarkable. Sometimes I wonder myself." Though I laughed, the image and the reality of anarchist process, egalitarian collective action by the "powerless," defying and indeed forever undermining the dominance of the "powerful," was etched in my mind. In December 1963 a local newsletter profile quoted me as saying: "If we believe that events in history are produced by the many thousands of actions and inactions of many thousands of individuals, we are obliged to recognize that each of us must shoulder responsibility for what takes place in our society."[4]

In 1964, Bob received an offer from the University of Illinois, and we moved to Urbana. We had two children: David, born in 1963, shortly before the assassination of John Kennedy (of which I learned from the diaper deliveryman!) and Malcolm, born in 1971, at a peak time of my engagement in antiwar and feminist activism. The marriage ended in divorce three years later. In the same year, 1974, Clinton Fink, former editor of the *Journal of Conflict Resolution*, came to live with my children and me, and we have been partners ever since, collaborating closely in life, research, and activism.

I spent most of the first year in Illinois working on *Design for Total War: Arms and Economics in the Third Reich* (The Hague: Mouton, 1968). I was wrestling with the theoretical issues of arms, economics and "total war" in Germany before and during World War II. The book took up the theme of the powers of the allegedly "powerless" in this context, without formulating the idea in explicit terms. But I was not yet attuned to women's history and feminist analysis, and the book generally ignored the roles of women and issues of gender.

In fall 1965, I was hired by the chair of the history department at Illinois to teach and supervise a large-enrollment, multisection course in the history of civilization, taught through another unit, the Division of General Studies (DGS). In 1969, when DGS was dissolved, the dean offered my line to several departments. The history department declined to take it, presumably because, as the department chair had told me earlier, "they did not hire faculty wives." But the political science department accepted the line, finding my work appropriate. And so I became a political science professor, teaching courses on war and peace, medieval political theory,[5] socialist theory, theories of peace and nonviolence, and women and politics.

Meanwhile, opportunities had emerged to move to a peace agenda in my scholarship and teaching. From about 1960, Arthur Waskow, a former student of Merle Curti, was working at the new Peace Research Institute in Washington, DC, to initiate peace research associations in the major disciplines. Waskow succeeded in drawing together a group of prominent historians who met in 1963 to establish the Conference on Peace Research in History (CPRH). In 1964 I saw a meeting announcement in the *American Historical Review* for the December convention. I had not until then thought that academia would allow me to join the activist and research components of my life as one. The idea was liberating and exhilarating. I attended the meeting and was hooked. The following year (1965) I presented a paper drawing on my previous work with more direct application to a specific current problem—inspection for disarmament. In 1967 I succeeded Arthur, the first secretary-treasurer of CPRH, in that capacity. Through CPRH I met Blanche Cook, and worked closely and joyously with her and Sandi Cooper for many years.

After President Johnson sent ground troops into Vietnam in 1965, the immediate urgency of war led me to found with Jacqueline Flenner and others the Ad Hoc Faculty Committee on Vietnam.[6] This activist engagement had another face in scholarship. Peace research had focused on the causes of wars in the past, but had given little attention to ending wars already in progress. I began to work on this topic and to call for others to do so, organizing sessions or conferences on war endings, sponsored by CPRH. In 1969 I edited a collection on war endings as a special issue of the *Journal of Peace Research*.[7] That spring, I had visited the Peace Research Institute, Oslo, where I first met Johan Galtung, Marek Thee, and other leading European peace researchers, and was challenged to examine peace research and practice from an interdisciplinary perspective bridging history and social sciences. My own paper in that collection, "How Wars End," reflected this effort to reach across disciplines; it also reflected Bob Carroll's interest in applying mathematical methods to social research. With his encouragement and assistance, this was actually one of the first efforts to use mathematical modeling, particularly partial differential equations, in peace research.[8] Nevertheless, the article explicitly recognized the problems and limited value of such an approach. In fact, I soon turned to a critique of game theory and other abstract methods in conflict theory.[9]

Meanwhile, echoes of feminism were beginning to dance in my head. News of the radical feminism of the late 1960s came to me not only through the media but by word of mouth from friends and colleagues at home and in peace research. In 1967 I offered an informal course on women's liberation through the local "Communiversity," learning more than teaching, through the reading and discussions the small group did together—much more a consciousness-raising group than a class. In 1968 I began to receive materials from the New University Conference, including early radical feminist documents. I attended the NUC conference in Chicago that year, met Florence Howe and others in the women's caucus, and took in their critique of sexism in the leadership of the left. Robin Morgan's "Goodbye to all that" came into my hands in the original *Rat* version (February 6–23, 1970) and hit me like a revelation. Kate Millett's *Sexual Politics* also had that revelatory character; I began to devour other women's liberation literature. Nancy DiBello, Cheryl Frank, and others in the student Women's Liberation Cadre pressed me to offer a course on campus, and in 1970 I taught the first women's studies course at the University of Illinois at Urbana: "The Politics of Women's Liberation."

The participation of women of color and the issues of racism were prominent from the beginning of my engagement with the antiwar movement and feminism. Celestine Ware's *Woman Power* was one of the foundations of my understanding of feminism. Toni Cade's *The Black Woman*, and the writings of Frances Beale, Pat Robinson, and others were among core readings for my courses. The campaigns for justice for Angela Davis and Joanne Little were an integral part of the radical activism of the time; a powerful poster from a fundraiser for them hung in my office for over fifteen years. Community campaigns around such issues as housing, healthcare, police brutality, and representation on the city councils were ongoing activities of the informal progressive coalition in the Champaign–Urbana area. Nevertheless, not until the Common Differences conference in 1983 (below) would I come to understand more of the complexities and power of racism in the peace and feminist movements.

The rending national events of 1967 and 1968—assassinations, burning cities, mass demonstrations, police riots and killings at Jackson State and Kent State—also had impact on my consciousness and life. By 1969 I was connected to a network of antiwar, feminist, and radical groups that increased my engagement in organizing and direct action. With something like the exhilaration of jumping on and off subway trains with collection boxes at the age of sixteen, I found myself at the age of thirty-six jumping on and off airplanes with stacks of organizing literature, often writing speeches and papers en route. In the years 1969 to 1971 I was engaged in co-founding and organizing the Women's Caucus for Political Science (WCPS), CCWHP, the Women's Caucus of the American Association of University Professors (later Committee W), the Consortium on Peace Research, Education, and Development

(COPRED), the University Women's Caucus at the University of Illinois, and a crisis shelter for women, A Woman's Place in Urbana. Of these, COPRED has had the most continuous place in my life, a thread I cannot follow in this essay.

In early September, 1969, at the annual convention of the American Political Science Association in New York, I attended a crowded meeting at which the recently appointed Committee on the Status of Women presented a report. At the following discussion, a number of younger women, including Jo Freeman, raised questions and demands for action. I joined with several other women to form the founding committee of the WCPS, of which Kay Klotzburger was the first chair.

While in New York, I met with Carl Schorske on CPRH business, and asked his advice on what might be done to raise at the American Historical Association (AHA) some of the issues that I had just heard debated in APSA. Schorske, a member of the AHA Council, suggested a petition to the council as the way to proceed. On September 18, I sent a letter to a number of friends and prominent historians asking for their support for a petition I had drafted the previous day, calling upon AHA to appoint a Committee on the Status of Women charged to undertake studies and make recommendations relating to the status of women in the historical profession; to give active support for recruitment of women and expansion of opportunities for women in the profession; to provide for more active participation of women in offices and programs of the association; to take action against discrimination against women in the profession, and to continue these programs "until some reasonable parity between men and women in the profession is achieved." On the same date, I circulated a call to women historians declaring: "It's clearly time for women in the historical profession to get organized, to oppose both discrimination against women in the profession itself and the 'feminine mystique' in historical writings."

The response to both calls was gratifying. On October 28, 1969, I sent AHA executive director Paul Ward sixteen copies of the petition signed by both men and women historians.[10] The council met on October 30 and agreed to appoint a committee on the status of women, and to refer the remaining points in the petition to that committee. Meanwhile I was receiving a large number of enthusiastic responses to my call to women historians, and about twenty-five met on December 27, 1969, to form CCWHP.[11] Two days later, we held an open forum, organized by Hilda Smith, on "Women in the Historical Profession." Hilda was then still a graduate student at the University of Chicago; we have worked very closely together through many projects and struggles in women's history and women's studies over the years since then. The meeting on December 29 was packed, and a large number of those present signed up to keep in touch. As I have argued in "Scholarship and Action,"[12] the "activist" CCWHP initiated the current wave of academic work in women's history, not only by demands and pressure, but by direct scholarly activities. I served as co-chair with Gerda Lerner in 1970 and as chair from 1970 to 1971.

In those same years, I committed a deep part of my affective life to the collective that founded and built a crisis shelter for women. The idea for the shelter was born in 1970 in a series of conversations between Jacqueline Flenner and Cheryl Frank, Binnie Williams, Fran Friedman, me, and others. No shelters for battered women existed anywhere, the issues of domestic violence and incest were hardly recognized, and our idea was to open the shelter to women in various crisis situations who could go to stay for a time, until they could recover and get established independently. The women who came for shelter taught us about the dimensions of domestic violence in the community.

In 1971, Jackie took the major step of buying a duplex house in Urbana, which could house four permanent residents, their children, and a number of women in crisis. Jackie, Cheryl, Chris Rich, Alice Ann Kingston, and their children were the first permanent residents. I was a founding member of the group of community women committed to supporting the shelter through volunteer time, contributions and fund-raising, personal support, and, in my case, emergency housing for women in crisis when A Woman's Place was full. For several years we operated as a feminist collective, adopting consciousness-raising techniques at meetings and helping to work through the problems of sharing and collective living at the house.

Two of the residents soon formed a couple, and the personal and political issues of sexuality became a central part of the work, the joys, the conflicts, and the mind-expanding struggles of this period of my life. Though it was not until many years later that I read Adrienne Rich's "Compulsory Heterosexuality and Lesbian Existence," I was already living in what Rich called "the lesbian continuum." When *Liberating Women's History* appeared in 1976, I dedicated it to Jackie Flenner and A Woman's Place, expressing the bonds of connection I felt between exploring the theory and force of women's history and living the everyday experience of women's struggles and creative power in the community.

In the midst of all this, I was embarked on co-founding a journal of peace research in history. This came into being in 1972, largely through the efforts of Han-sheng Lin (a former student of CPRH chair Hilary Conroy's) and Robert Brown at Sonoma State College. Brown and I were the first co-editors of *Peace and Change*, named to emphasize its commitment to a conception of peace embodying social change. I remained articles editor until 1980, and am gratified that it flourishes today, co-sponsored by the Peace History Society

(PHS, formerly CPRH) and COPRED. We conceived of the journal as above all else uniting scholarship and action, and the spirit, if not the letter, of that goal has carried over through the years.

Radical student demands for change at the university and protests of racism and militarism, both on campus and in the community, were then a growing force in society. At the University of Illinois in Urbana, student activism escalated to mass demonstrations, sit-ins, strikes, blockades, window-breaking in campustown, and the bizarre atmosphere of a campus bristling with armed National Guardsmen. The day after National Guardsmen at Kent State University killed four protesters in May 1970, fifteen members of the political science department signed a statement called "Faculty for Resistance," declaring our intention to circulate in each other's classes to address "the problem of political repression and resistance to the abuses of official authority."[13] The *Chicago Tribune* attacked our statement in an editorial titled "Why the Crazies Get That Way" (May 30). The Board of Trustees obligingly followed the lead of the *Tribune*, demanding that we retract the statement or be summarily fired for propagandizing in the classroom. The university administration was less than courageous with regard to our rights of academic freedom, but pointed out to the board that university statutes prohibited summary dismissal of tenured and tenure-track faculty. Eventually the board not only backed off this demand but even approved the promotions of a number of us who were coming up for tenure that year.

In 1972, as the war dragged on and campus protests escalated, I found myself more directly confronted with various forms of police repression. In a demonstration at the Illini Union Building, visiting political science faculty member Michael Parenti was clubbed by local police, who alleged that he had hit one of them with a rock, though numerous witnesses testified that he had done no such thing. In April 1972, I was arrested with others in a symbolic blockade of Chanute Air Force Base, about thirty miles north of Urbana. We were arrested by County Sheriff's police after a burlesque but dangerous scene in which the sheriff tried to have us pushed onto the base itself while the base police were firm in keeping us out. The charges were eventually dropped, but the experience gave us an instructive view of police behavior and the inside of local prisons.

The 1972 paper "Peace Research: The Cult of Power" presented the first explicit formulation of my ideas on the powers of the "powerless." It challenged the preoccupation with the "powerful" in the field of peace research, and argued that to break out of the "cult of power" we must turn attention, admiration, and loyalty away from those with the powers of dominance and search for the powers of the allegedly "powerless." (Perhaps it says something about my relationship to motherhood that I was debating my classification of those powers and proofreading stencils of the paper with Jackie Flenner in the labor room just before the birth of my son Malcolm in 1971.) In later years, I attempted to apply the powers of the "powerless" in a variety of contexts, such as the weaknesses of "victory" and the powers of "the defeated" in "Victory and Defeat: The Mystique of Dominance."[14]

In the mid-1970s my teaching and scholarship turned to a focus on the history of women's political thought and theoretical work. I had first addressed this in an essay on Mary Beard (1971, 1972), and subsequently in work on the ideas of Ellen Key and other women peace theorists.[15] In 1974 I started teaching the history of women's political thought, and was overwhelmed by the magnitude and the brilliance of the works I began to discover. That fall I lectured on Virginia Woolf, reading her work with new eyes, appalled by what I had been mistaught as a student, and comprehending her words for the first time with the knowledge and theory I had learned in those heady years of activism and organizing. I now saw the powers of the "powerless" in her "poor college," her "Outsiders' Society," her "four great teachers," and her images of secret, unarmed resistance in *Three Guineas*. In 1976 I gave "'To Crush Him in Our Own Country': The Political Thought of Virginia Woolf" at the Berkshire Women's History Conference, published in 1978 in *Feminist Studies*.[16] In the same year I presented, at the Purdue University American Studies Symposium, an early version of the "The Politics of 'Originality': Women and the Class System of the Intellect."[17] These studies of women's intellectual work are closely tied to the theme of the powers of the "powerless" in multiple ways, especially as an exploration of the intellectual powers that have been obscured and devalued to deny their real power.

In the early 1980s, two major events stood at the intersections of activism and theory. One was the campaign of the Grassroots Group of Second-Class Citizens in Springfield, Illinois in June 1982, when I joined Mary Lee Sargent, Kari Alice Lynn, Jane Mohraz, and others in a series of direct action protests of the refusal of the Illinois legislature to ratify the Equal Rights Amendment. The actions opened on June 3, 1982, with a colorful, ceremonious demonstration by about 200 supporters of our group in the Capitol Rotunda. Our group's actions included chain-ins, occupation of the Capitol Building for four days and nights, sit-ins, disruptions of legislative sessions, and writing in blood on the marble floors. In "Direct Action and Constitutional Rights" I reflected on the complexity of the actions and of the political and theoretical issues they raised.[18] They led me, in any case, to seek a deeper knowledge and understanding of women's nonviolent direct action, reflected in my article "Women Take Action!" and the special January 1989 issue of *Women's Studies International Forum*, co-edited with Jane Mohraz.

The other major turning point was my participation in the "Common Differences" Conference at the University of Illinois in 1983. Two graduate students, Chandra Mohanty and Ann Russo, initiated the conference, which was planned by a fairly diverse collective of students, faculty, and staff. The conference was an unprecedented success in bringing many women of color together both as speakers and as participants to confront openly issues of feminism and racism, class, and—less openly—sexuality. There were over 900 registered participants and many more who came and went without registering—a highly diverse group of whom the overwhelming majority were women of color, from across the US and abroad. For many white women present, myself included, the experience of intense listening and dialogue in this atmosphere was truly transformative.[19]

A major part of my life and work over several decades has been devoted to building women's studies programs at the University of Illinois and Purdue University, and to regional and national women's studies associations. Despite—or perhaps by virtue of—the intense intellectual and political conflicts in the field at large, in the National Women's Studies Association (NWSA), and within many individual programs, women's studies remains one of the most important sites of intellectual vitality and transformational politics in the academy today. A certain distancing has existed between the NWSA and many women historians, and there is a need to bridge the distance. I see that as a goal of my own in coming years.

These long years of intense and constant activity have been intimately intertwined with my intellectual work. My mind did not check out while I marched and organized against the war in Vietnam—on the contrary, it processed both my experiences and my widening understanding of the dynamics of the war and wove them into my scholarly work on war endings and critique of conflict theory. Engagement in women's liberation led to the theoretical questions on women's history posed in my study of Mary Beard and the introduction to *Liberating Women's History*. In turn these questions, as well as my experiences of both organized and unorganized mass action, led me to theorize the "powers of the 'powerless'" and the mystique of dominance associated with concepts of victory and defeat. Such efforts to analyze the powers of the "powerless" pressed upon me the need to direct attention to those who are seemingly without "power," who, as Virginia Woolf put it, are continually "finding new words and creating new methods." And the interweavings of identity, intellect, and action in my past experience allow me to hope that we may go forward to continue to develop those creative powers.

NOTES

1. Berenice A. Carroll, "Scholarship and Action: CCWHP and the Movement(s)," *Journal of Women's History* 6 (Fall 1994), 83.

2. In this essay, I do not deal with the interrelationships between several identity labels. One attempt to do so is my "Feminism and Pacifism: Historical and Theoretical Connections," in Ruth R. Pierson, ed., *Women and Peace* (London: Croom Helm, 1987), 2–28.

3. The *New York Times* advertisement appeared on November 10 and December 19, 1961; our statement appeared with 130 signatures in the *Newark Evening News* on January 15, 1962.

4. *The Kendall Park News*, December 1963, 7.

5. Medieval history had been one of my doctoral fields. My experience in teaching medieval political theory is probably what emboldened me, in the 1990s, to undertake a study of a medieval writer: "Christine de Pizan and the Origins of Peace Theory," in *Women Writers and the Early Modern Political Tradition*, Hilda L. Smith, ed. (Cambridge: Cambridge Univ. Press, 1998), 22–39.

6. Jacqueline Flenner, a native of Little Rock, Arkansas, and a veteran of the 1964 Freedom Summer, was working at that time as a computer programmer at the university; later she worked for the Champaign County Mental Health District and it was in that period that she became the founder of the first shelter for battered women in the country (see below).

7. Special issue on "How Wars End," *Journal of Peace Research* (Oslo) (December 1969).

8. "How Wars End: An Analysis of Some Current Hypotheses," *Journal of Peace Research* (December 1969), 295–320.

9. "War Termination and Conflict Theory: Value Premises, Theories, and Policies," *The Annals of the American Academy of Political and Social Science* 392 (November 1970), 14–29.

10. The signatories were Charles A. Barker, Berenice A. Carroll, Jean Christie, Blanche Wiesen Cook, Sandi E. Cooper, F. Hilary Conroy, Merle Curti, Natalie Zemon Davis, Samuel Haber, Sondra Herman, Gerda Lerner, Virginia McLaughlin, Jo Ann McNamara, Louis Morton, Dagmar H. Perman, and Carl E. Schorske. Several additional signatures were sent later, including those of Peter Filene, Robin C. Man, Joan W. Scott, Kathryn Sklar, Gerhard L. Weinberg, and Marilyn B. Young.

11. Twenty-two women signed a list of interested participants: Betty Chmaj, Bernice Rosenthal, Susan Resnick, Barbara Morgan, Mimi Lowinger, Hilda Smith, Edythe Lutzker, Natalie Zemon Davis, Phyllis Stabbe, Ellen DuBois, Gerda Lerner, Carol Bleser, Elisabeth Israel, Charmarie Webb, Marian Low, Marjorie Gesner, Constance Myers, Lucille O'Connell, Jane De Hart Mathews, Jo Tice Bloom, Gillian Townsend Cell, Sandra Keen, and Berenice Carroll. I later recalled that Blanche Cook, Nancy Roelker, and a number of others were present.

12. "Scholarship and Action: CCWHP and the Movement(s)," *Journal of Women's History* 6 (Fall 1994), 79–96.

13. The text of the statement was published in *The Summer Illini*, Thursday, July 30, 1970, 5.

14. "Victory and Defeat: The Mystique of Dominance," in Stuart Albert and Edward Luck, eds., *On the Endings of Wars* (Port Washington, NY: Kennikat Press, 1980), 47–71.

15. "Mary Beard: A Critique," Organization of American Historians, 1971; "Mary Beard's *Woman as Force in History*: A Critique," *Massachusetts Review* (Winter–Spring 1972), 125–143, reprinted in *Liberating Women's History* (Urbana: Univ. of Illinois Press, 1976), 28–41. Introduction, Ellen Key, *War, Peace and the Future* (New York: Garland Press reprint edition, 1972).

16. "'To Crush Him in Our Own Country': The Political Thought of Virginia Woolf," *Feminist Studies* 4 (February 1978), 99–131.

17. Published in the *Journal of Women's History* 2 (Fall 1990), 136–163. I have been reminded that when I visited Purdue for this lecture in 1978, I met with women interested in starting a women's studies program, and they liked my advice, which I'm told was: "Just do it!" I am proud to be directing today the program that they founded that year.

18. "Direct Action and Constitutional Rights: The Case of the ERA," in *Rights of Passage: The Past and Future of the ERA*, Joan Hoff-Wilson, ed. (Bloomington: Indiana Univ. Press, 1986), 63–75.

19. See Chandra Talpade Mohanty, Ann Russo, and Lourdes Torres, eds., *Third World Women and the Politics of Feminism* (Bloomington: Indiana Univ. Press, 1991).

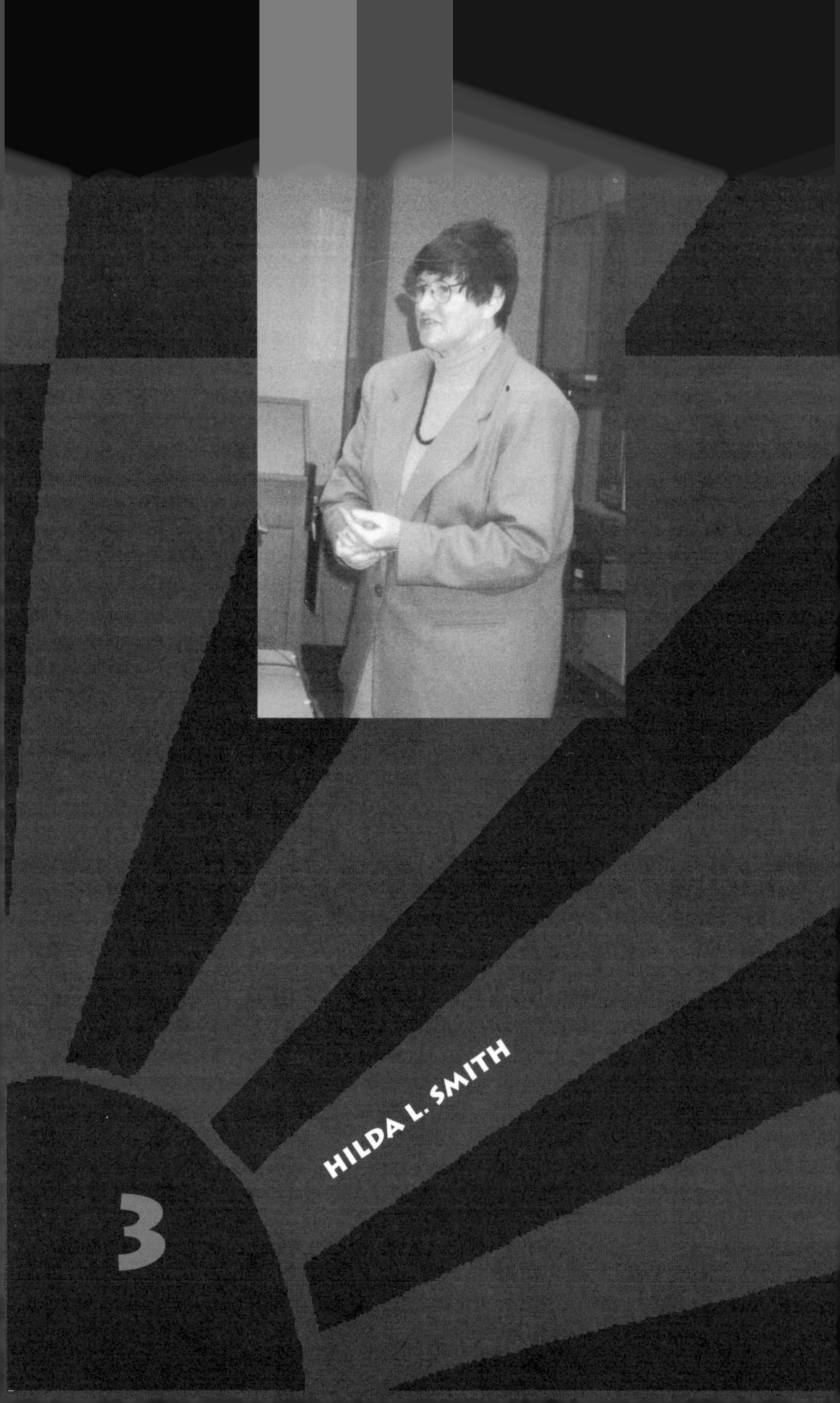

3

HILDA L. SMITH

REGIONALISM, FEMINISM, AND CLASS: THE DEVELOPMENT OF A FEMINIST HISTORIAN

My intellectual interests in women's history, my career as a woman academic, and my involvement in feminist professional organizations have been intertwined since I entered the University of Chicago as a graduate student in the fall of 1966. I had previously received degrees in education and history from Southwest Missouri State University and the University of Missouri and had taught high school English and history in Granite City, Illinois. I was unsatisfied with the intellectual possibilities I found in secondary teaching and had spent the two summers prior to enrolling at Chicago at the University of Missouri taking more graduate training following my MA in 1964.

At the time I had some inkling that a young married woman who had come from poor hillbilly parents from the Missouri Ozarks was entering a career path not intended for her, but I was naive and ill informed about what lay ahead for me. As we learn more about the distinctions between the 1960s and the present, I now realize that while what I was able to do was extraordinary, the economic climate and opportunities of that decade greatly aided me. I completed a doctorate wholly on NDEA (National Defense Education Act) loans at a prestigious private university—something impossible today. During my childhood my parents had been migrant farm workers in California for brief periods. They had owned a small farm north of Springfield, Missouri, and after I was nine years old we moved to Springfield (then a small city of 100,000), where my father worked digging ditches for the city utility com-

Hilda Smith.

pany. My mother, who had contracted a serious heart condition from incorrectly diagnosed rheumatic fever as a child, died when I was a senior in high school.*

As with many poor people, I had inadequate counseling as a student, and although I received a curator's scholarship for undergraduate tuition at the University of Missouri, no one encouraged me to take it or explained how I could survive through a combination of loans and work-study. I rather entered Southwest Missouri State to prepare to become a teacher, and from that point began an academic career that ultimately led to my studying women's history and being involved with the founding of the Coordinating Committee on Women in the Historical Profession/Conference Group on Women's History (CCWHP/CGWH). Other than the greater opportunities of that period, the single most important factor in my success was having a husband who was supportive both financially and professionally—who allowed me to study for the PhD before he completed an MBA and who worked full time and went to school in the evening while I went to school full time and worked part time to supplement our income.

When I entered the history department at Chicago in 1966, I joined a large cohort of female graduate students who were encouraged to go to graduate school (nearly 100 new graduate students in total entered with me) because of concerns over declining enrollment numbers because of the loss of men to the draft for the continuing Vietnam War. It is difficult to imagine a place better situated to involve a person in the great social and political movements of the late 1960s and early 1970s. There had previously been student protests over submitting registration information and grades to the Defense Department. In the years I was at Chicago there were antiwar protests, the riots following the assassination of Martin Luther King, the Democratic Convention of 1968, the killing of Black Panther leaders, the underground Weatherman movement, student protests leading to the occupation of the Administration Building, and the beginnings of a feminist movement on campus. I was among those who (hesitantly at first) joined public protests against the war; my first public action was a protest march on campus against Dow Chemical for its role in making napalm. I was at the university during the 1968 riots when National Guard troops surrounded the campus, and a large section of the western part of the city had been burned. (The following anecdote reflects the confusions of that time: the night of the riots my then husband and I and two friends drove up Lake Shore Drive to Northwestern University while the city was burning to the west because we had Simon and Garfunkel tickets.) I was in Grant Park

*I might add that I was a "black-market baby" (in my case, given rather than sold) whom my parents acquired through a letter from my mother to a local radio program, "Hillbilly Heartbeats"; I was not legally adopted until age eighteen, following my mother's death. I do not know the identity of my birth mother.

along with many others trying to avoid the police and listening to Dick Gregory and Eugene McCarthy (for whom I had been a campaign worker, traveling to Wisconsin and Indiana). During these years I also earned extra income substituting in Southside high schools and learned from my black students opinions about the city and society I never could have gained at the university.

Most significant for my later intellectual interests and career, the sit-in at the University of Chicago was triggered by university officials' refusing to answer student inquiries concerning the dismissal of Marlene Dixon (the lone woman in the Department of Sociology). It was the only sit-in in the country with feminist origins, and it had a lasting impact on how I view history and the historical profession.[1] The university had had a progressive and leftist past, but it was being transformed into a conservative institution that many today associate with the conservative "Chicago School": game theory, market-driven economic theory, and skepticism over, and lack of support for, social programs at home and human rights issues abroad. Marlene Dixon stated that she had been fired because she was a woman; I wondered at the time what that could mean. Like many growing up in the 1950s and early '60s, I did not think about women as a group. But as the protests expanded, and as I spoke with Jo Freeman, who was a graduate student in political science (as was Nancy Hartsock), I came to understand the unfolding events from a feminist perspective.[2]

The sit-in and its aftermath had a profound impact on my intellectual interests and professional concerns. The reputation of Chicago has emerged more unscathed from the sixties than the reputations of institutions such as Berkeley and Columbia, but more students were suspended or expelled at Chicago than all the other schools that experienced student protests combined. I went in with the initial group to occupy the Administration Building (but left when the mother of a friend with whom I entered—a U of C administrator—came down the stairs to identify students, and told him to leave). Hardly a brave act. A police official said we were trespassing and would be arrested, but the university never called in the Chicago police, and this meant that when students were called before disciplinary hearings there was no due process and no recourse to the court system. They could be arbitrarily suspended and expelled by a faculty committee, and they were.

A few years later, when then–University President Edward Levi was appointed Attorney General, I wrote a letter to the Chicago *Maroon*, the student newspaper, about how one of the most unjust men I had known had now been made head of the Department of Justice. The university was clever, though, to refer loftily to the "life of the mind" (something over which it claims a proprietary interest) to keep out legal authorities, and to remove students who were considered politically suspect. As a part of the street theater of the time, law students came to the disciplinary hearings dressed as kangaroos, and sociology graduate students used their training to prove that the "crimes" involved—sitting in, spending time in the building, or holding leadership positions—did not warrant punishments meted out. What correlated were membership in radical student organizations and offering serious political justifications for protesting, rather than being contrite and saying one stayed in the building to have fun or sleep with one's boy/girlfriend.

A number of things converged in 1969–70 to influence my intellectual and professional direction. I had previously been encouraged in a graduate seminar to write a paper on the militant suffrage movement; while the professor saw the movement as exemplary of comic relief, my reading of the Pankhursts' speeches and the newspapers of the WSPU encouraged insights into the interaction of class and gender that has henceforth influenced my work. As one from a poor background, my life supported Emmeline Pankhurst's response to a Labor heckler when asked why she wasn't addressing the needs of the poor. When she replied, "And who are the poor; who are making 6, 7 pence a day," the hands of many women shot up. That research also led me to disagree with the current negative feminist view of the WSPU. I came into open dispute with the professor over the nature of the paper and my intention to do a dissertation on the topic, something he opposed. Given the opposition to my militant suffrage topic, two months before leaving for England to do research on my dissertation I switched topics and centuries, ultimately completing a thesis on seventeenth-century English feminism.

As a part of the sit-in, and my involvement in the student movement more broadly, I picketed classes at the university, investigated the distribution of fellowships within the department to discover possible gender bias and got the department to base graduate fellowships on need, co-founded the Radical Students Association, and founded Graduate Women in History, in which I organized an initial meeting (with our two women faculty, Hannah H. Gray and Joan W. Scott, as speakers) on "From the Apple to the Archive: Women in the Historical Profession." I found organizing especially difficult; the first time I called women graduate students cold to ask them to attend this meeting was one of the more difficult moments I have faced. I would have likely not accomplished it had not Jo Freeman been putting pressure on me and others to organize women in our disciplines.

I became pregnant in the winter before I went to England for dissertation research, and this led me to take up an unexpected cause. I was one of few married women students whose husband was not a student at the university, so that when I did not register for classes the quarter my elder son was born I received a notice saying we would be evicted from married student housing. Many couples were having children in our building; but it was always the nonstudent wife who was having the baby, and thus they were not asked to leave due to nonregistration. I took my complaint to the U of C housing office and claimed that this was discrimination against women graduate students, for no men were forced to leave married student housing because of a birth in their family. The university made an exception and allowed us to stay, and I believe changed its policy based on my experience.

In the fall of 1969 Joan Scott passed to me a letter she had received from Berenice Carroll soliciting assistance to organize a new group to focus on the status of women in the profession. She wanted to hold an organizing meeting at the American Historical Association (AHA) convention that December. I called Berenice and suggested that we have a panel on the status of women. She thought it was a good idea, and I organized the panel, which included Hannah Gray, Christopher Lasch, Emiliana Noether (then president of the Berkshire Conference), Jo Tice Bloom (research director for the Women's Business and Professional Clubs), and myself. The attendance was so great that we had to open one of the folding dividers that the convention hotel had installed between rooms. Unable to get into the AHA program in time, we were forced to inform people about the panel and the organizing meeting through the mail and by putting up posters around the hotel. Out of these efforts, CCWHP (CCWH) was born. Berenice, Gerda Lerner, and I were the organization's first three officers, and I produced its newsletter at the national headquarters of the National Organization for Women (NOW), which was then in Chicago. One of my fonder memories is of my elder son as a baby sleeping on mailbags in the NOW headquarters while we were producing the newsletter. It was a cooperative effort on the part of NOW officials (who knew how to operate the printer), my husband, and a number of U of C graduate students, both male and female. While in Washington, Berenice Carroll and I appeared on a noontime public affairs television program about the founding of CCWHP; I remember a Chicago radio program with myself, Ellen DuBois, and Ann Firor Scott just after publication of *The Southern Lady*. I also appeared on educational television programs run by the University of Chicago. It was a heady time for a third-year graduate student.

Following the research on my dissertation, which I believe was the first one written on women at Chicago following the establishment of the field of women's history, I taught part time at nearby George Williams College. I was hired at the University of Maryland in 1973 to teach 100 percent in the area of women's history, where I gave comparative US–European courses, established an MA in women's history (I believe the second, after Sarah Lawrence's program), but did not ultimately get tenure. Being denied tenure had complex causes, as is often the case, but certainly a part of the denial was tied to my teaching field and my feminist activism, as I was the first person with a book contract and articles to be denied tenure by the history department. When I filed a state EEOC complaint, which was unsuccessful, the final determination said that I had demonstrated that I had been discriminated against on the basis of teaching women's history; but that field, rather than sex, was not a category covered by EEOC guidelines, and thus the university had not broken the law.

While my years at Maryland were not unpleasant, I do remember an incident that may offer some clue to my later difficulties. In the fall of 1977, I was about 6½ months pregnant with my second son, Christopher, when school began; I was teaching full time and organizing an international conference in women's history. The academic year always began with a departmental picnic that included a volleyball game. I volunteered to play as I usually had in the past, but I noted my colleagues were acting rather strange. One noted that it was unfair because two people were playing my position and balls seemed to be directed my way with some force. My suspicions were confirmed when my elder son (then nearly seven) said after the game, "Mommy, why don't those men like you?" I thought it one example of where male academics didn't accept women who tried "to do it all."

After leaving Maryland I worked as an administrator in public humanities programs until 1987, when I was hired as director of women's studies and associate professor of history at the University of Cincinnati. Over the years, I continued my organizing efforts. I founded the Chesapeake Area Group of Women Historians and organized the first international conference in women's history in 1977 in College Park. The conference, which was funded by the Rockefeller Foundation and the Maryland Committee for the Humanities, drew scholars from a range of European countries, Canada, and Australia, as well as from the United States. After coming to the University of Cincinnati, I organized a National Women's Studies Association (NWSA) conference for women's studies program directors in the early 1990s. I continued organizing and grant activities and directed a number of summer institutes incorporating feminist scholarship, funded by NEH and FIPSE.

Returning to my intellectual career, when I went to England to research my dissertation in 1970, I wasn't sure of my topic, but I thought I'd do something on Puritan attitudes toward the family. I began my research by reading everything under the heading "women" in the index to the Thomason tracts of the mid-seventeenth century held at the British Library. Through this broadly directed reading, I discovered gynecological texts, feminist works, household guides, Puritan sermons on proper sex roles, etc. When I began my reading, I was not aware of Margaret Cavendish or Mary Astell or any of the feminists I later wrote about, and I was amazed to find that women during the 1600s wrote works systematically critical of the status of women in English society. I read tracts by midwives who criticized men's displacing them in the delivery of babies. I read poets who castigated men for monopolizing the art of writing while infantilizing women through trivializing and sexist images. Through this work, and follow-up readings over the years, I became both knowledgeable of and excited about the way women had analyzed and defended themselves in the past.[3] This has led me to concentrate on women's intellectual history as my field of primary interest. It has not always been a popular choice.

In the early 1970s, when I was studying seventeenth-century feminist writings, social historians overwhelmingly dominated the field of women's history. It was acceptable to study working-class women, but not middle- and upper-class women intellectuals from the past. The importance of techniques such as oral history encouraged the view that the closer one's topic was to the present the more authentic and inclusive its nature. Over the years, those in other fields have come to dominate or influence the direction of women's history: family historians, historians of sexuality, cultural historians. Intellectual history, though, has never been seen as a field that meshed easily with women's history, either in scholarly or political terms. The transition from one set of historical emphases to another has continued with little attention to the past writings of women. Efforts by women thinkers to explain gender structures and power relationships have had little impact on current scholarship in women's history. When such thinkers have been incorporated, they have been studied as historical subjects, seldom as individuals with theories and insights to aid in understanding gender relationships at other points in time, or as offering synthetic analyses of their own age.

Realization of these intellectual trends came to me first during the 1974 Berkshire Conference, at which I appeared on a panel on comparative feminism. After presenting the ideas of the feminists from the 1600s who were the subject of my dissertation, a young woman in the audience asked me, "Why do you study these elite women?" After trying to answer her, it struck me that these women intellectuals and writers who had been kept out of universities, whose works had for the most part been shunned and ridiculed during their lifetimes, were now being rejected by young feminists who believed that they were being more purely feminist by identifying with working-class women, with whom most had little in common. Theory, in women's history and feminist scholarship more broadly, has been appropriated most readily from male theorists, or from women who have applied the work of those theorists to the topic of gender. Women over the centuries have offered systematic and impressive explanations for the power of men within their societies, for the standing of their own sex, and for both heter/homosexual and social relationships. Yet their insights, for the most part, have been ignored, and the ideas of men like Foucault, Habermas, and Bakhtin, theorists for whom women were seldom the subject, have been privileged. And one can virtually find no theorist who writes from a woman-centered perspective.

In other words, why have we moved from those writers who wrote specifically about explaining women's lives to ones who seldom treated them but have a more respected intellectual standing? It is difficult for me to imagine a more sophisticated and complex analysis of the ideological and power realities that separate men and women in society than Virginia Woolf's *Three Guineas*. In addition, I don't know of feminist insights that have emerged over the last two decades that were not first suggested or argued in the underground or published works emerging from the women's liberation movement during the late 1960s and early 1970s. One of the results of this intellectual trend has been to universalize the qualities of an age (such as the Enlightenment) and ignore the women of that age who were both outside of and critical of many of its values.

My attraction to intellectual history comes from a number of sources: excitement about ideas as a poor hillbilly girl who had little previous contact with philosophy or ethics as a child, pleasure at a number of high-quality courses in the history of political theory taught at Southwest Missouri State, and training at the University of Chicago that emphasized original intellectual sources as the best way to understand the nature of a particular age. I remember, as a college freshman, first reading Plato's *Republic* and being encouraged to discuss the ideas that already meant a great deal to me: the nature of goodness, of truth, of government. While I later came to realize both the basic conservatism of Plato's message and its exclusion of women, foreigners, and slaves from Greek citizenship, that never led me to discount the importance of ideas in framing everyday decisions and human possibilities. My training was not limited to intellectual history, and Peter Stearn's modern European history class introduced me to the social history critique of traditional political history. (I can still remember his lecture on how Dennis Mack Smith's history of modern Italy focused on irrelevant parliamentary majorities and ignored the country's social and economic realities.) That course had a significant influence, as did William H. McNeill's history of the Balkans that incorporated topography and a broad comparative view of social structures and relationships. While I continue to have strong differences with the academic structure and politics of the University of Chicago, I realize that the breadth of its training directed me to some of the more fundamental questions I have raised in women's history—even though those who taught me, with the exception of my advisor Charles Gray, likely would not approve of such questioning. And it was, above all, Charles Gray's tolerant encouragement of my interests that furthered my interests in women's history. A graduate student does not write, as I did, a paper on "Feminism and the Methodology of Women's History" without being encouraged to question the fundamental assumptions of a discipline. It's one of the reasons I regret the current over-specialization of graduate training.

My publications and conference organizing have emphasized the importance of women's intellectual contributions to the past, as well as creating resources in women's intellectual history. Through focusing on women's writings beyond the feminist canon, I, along with others (especially Berenice Carroll), have demonstrated the range of women's general social and political works and tried to undercut the assumption (even among feminist scholars) that women only had something significant to say when writing about themselves.

Since the integration of gender analyses into women's history, I have concentrated on questions of masculinity and citizenship, especially how advice to men on all aspects of life has prepared them for an adulthood and social and political standing unavailable to women. While some women always wielded economic and political authority at all levels, the conceptual frameworks delineating full membership in a society have been much more exclusive. While others have focused on qualities traditionally associated with masculinity, my work has been directed more to the conflation of the adult man with the characteristics of the modern individual. I have attempted to demonstrate that basic human functions (such as the aging process) have been explained and exemplified in stages of life, moments of educational attainment, and occupations and family standing open only to men. These "false universals" again point to the power of intellectual concepts, as distinct from daily realities or supposedly inherent social and sexual differences, to help determine one's choices.[4]

My work has often been as strongly at odds with the direction of women's history, and later gender studies, as with traditional historical scholarship. In "Women's History and Social History: An Untimely Alliance," which appeared in the newsletter of the Organization of American Historians (OAH) during the early 1980s, I argued that women's history and social history had distinct intellectual goals and distinct origins. Social history worked to bring into historical narrative men, especially members of the working class, who had been traditionally ignored. But women as a whole had been omitted from the past; thus women did not need to be included simply "from the bottom up," but from all social standings. In addition, I differed with those who saw the "new women's history" as a branch of, or closely allied with, the "new social history," and rather noted that social history was as apt to be male-centered as was traditional political history. It has always seemed more important to me to incorporate gender analysis and the experience of women into all fields of history rather than to valorize some fields over others.[5]

Moreover, while the concept of gender has been a useful analytical tool, it too has serious drawbacks in helping us understand the nature of women's history. Gender replaced sex as a category in historical scholarship in the late 1970s and early 1980s to distinguish the socially constructed nature of the sexes from the sex of the bedroom or from the Male/Female spaces on application forms. It had, and continues to have, a valuable role in clarifying our definition of sexual characteristics and behavior. However, it has not emerged without a number of drawbacks. First, it has a pseudo-scientific and inappropriately precise ring. One of the problems, but also one of the values, of continuing to use the word "sex" is that most people continue to confuse and conflate biological, social, and sexual qualities when discussing the qualities of women and men. Gender was to distinguish the broad-based uses of the term "sex," but now newscasters and political commentators speak regularly of the "two genders" just as they did in the past of "two sexes." Even forms often call now for one's gender. What have we gained?

The use of "gender" hardly has led to avoiding essentialist analyses, and, with its grounding in the social sciences, rather has often seemed to spur one-dimensional analyses of gender difference based on a single sexual or cultural paradigm. One of the most interesting qualities of women's history is its representation of women in all aspects of society, so that issues of class, religion, politics, sexuality, popular culture, and a range of prescriptive and autobiographical or analytical literature comes under scrutiny when one studies women's history. When women are studied only in the family, or through their sexual qualities, or economic position, one misses the complexity of women's lives and their concomitant analyses.

Finally, while I recognize the significant intellectual insights and advancement in the field of women's history over the last decade, I also worry that those who study women's past only through the lens of one theoretical paradigm drawn often from a field other than history may miss the feminist lessons embedded within women's history itself. To study the history of women as a group offers its own feminist insights. Sometimes it feels as if younger scholars believe that they alone have integrated the feminist meaning and content into their subject, and those speaking from the past offer little feminist analysis themselves, either through their actions or their words. Not only do I think this is inaccurate, but I also think it is another way to disempower women in the past—to turn them into individuals who serve our purposes of scholarly analyses, but are seldom seen as our teachers as well as our subjects.

At a brief summer institute on teaching, I presented to faculty in other departments a computer-based slide presentation on "Aristocratic Women and Politics in Early-Modern Britain." I sought to show that these women understood the importance of their political standing, and it was not simply historians bestowing such standing upon them. A sympathetic faculty member regretted that I had had to use a graphics software package entitled, I believe, "Dad.tie" for a feminist presentation. I, however, had not seen the presentation as solely feminist, but rather as women's history. While I understand that the kind of questions I posed and the materials I selected emphasized a feminist analysis of the past, still the feminist insights came as much from the realities and words of the people I studied, as from myself.

If we have lost anything from the early days of women's history, I think it is trust in the "stuff" of the past to teach the lessons we need to learn. The excitement of first encountering both visual and literary images from past women still remains one of the most important intellectual motivators for our scholarship in the field. It should never be lost for the thrill of imposing our own insights, or for applying in a new and sophisticated fashion those of male theorists, to understanding the lives of real women in the past. And this excitement should include recreating the whole of that past: the gender assumptions affecting both sexes, the class and racial interactions and assumptions of all women, and the comments of the women at the heart of our research, the analyses of contemporary women intellectuals, and the work of women in later periods who have studied similar phenomena.

In my current work on the gendered nature of seventeenth-century individualism and an intellectual biography of Margaret Cavendish, Duchess of Newcastle, I have been consistently struck by the degree to which interceding years of historical scholarship have worked as much to obscure the realities of these subjects as to illuminate them. The history of the English Revolution has been so little concerned with issues of gender, so overwhelmingly concerned with class divisions and radical politics (and more recently parliamentary compromise), that it is necessary literally to start over in reading documents and formulating questions if one is to discover the gendered aspects of the subject. And, in grappling with the nature of Margaret Cavendish, I have also been struck by the long reach of her contemporaries' appellation, "Mad Madge" and the constraints imposed by historians and literary critics who analyze her through a royalist framework that only partially characterized her work.

It is thus essential, I think, for those studying women's history that we come to our research intellectually open-minded, ready to learn from as wide a range of representative documents and materials about our topic as possible. Such an approach will enhance our intellectual excitement and push us to listen more thoroughly to the voices and contexts of those we study.

NOTES

1. There has been less treatment of the Chicago sit-in than of events at Columbia or the earlier free speech movement at Berkeley. The best accounts today remain in the student newspaper, *The Chicago Maroon*, but Chicago is also included in general treatments of the student movement.

2. Jo Freeman, who had been an undergraduate at Berkeley and had been involved in both student and civil rights actions in California and elsewhere, became increas-

ingly interested in women's issues and is the author of *The Politics of Women's Liberation: A Case Study of an Emerging Social Movement and Its Relation to the Policy Process* (New York: McKay, 1975) and editor of *Women: A Feminist Perspective*, Fourth Edition (Mountain View, CA: Mayfield Publishing Co, 1989); Nancy Hartsock has been an important feminist theorist and is the author of *Money, Sex, and Power: Toward a Feminist Historical Materialism* (New York: Longman, 1983).

3. My research on women's intellectual history and the early evolution of feminist thought has led to the publication of *Reason's Disciples: Seventeenth-Century English Feminists* (Urbana: University of Illinois Press, 1982), an annotated bibliography (with Susan Cardinale) entitled *Women and the Literature of the Seventeenth Century* (Westport, CT: Greenwood Press, 1990), and the recent edited collection, *Women Writers and the Early Modern British Political Tradition* (Cambridge: Cambridge Univ. Press, 1998), along with a range of essays on the topic.

4. The views delineated here appear in the introduction and the essay "Women as Sextons and Electors: Kings Bench and Precedents for Women's Citizen" in *Women Writers and the Early Modern British Political Tradition*, in an unpublished essay, "Reconsidering the Freeborn Englishman: Gender and the Disruption of Social Categories," as well as in the book manuscript, "'All Men and Both Sexes': The False Universal in England, 1640–1832." Emphases of these works are on the gendered nature of male citizenship.

5. One of the problems with the growth of gender analysis over women's history is the ignorance of younger historians about the early scholarship in the field. In a review to appear in the journal *Albion*, I note the lack of knowledge of the origins of women's history expressed in the introduction by editors Hannah Barker and Elaine Chalus to *Gender in Eighteenth-Century England: Roles, Representations and Responsibilities* (London: Longman, 1996): "The study of gender in its own right developed in the 1980s, as women's historians began to appropriate ideas about the construction of meanings and identities put forward by French poststructuralists, especially Michel Foucault, Jacques Derrida, and Jacques Lacan. As women's historians began to incorporate these ideas, they focused attention on gender as an alternative explanation for historical inequalities. Instead of seeing sexual differences between men and women as a reflection of purely biological differences, they accepted the notion that these distinctions were socially constructed and, therefore, varied with time, place, culture, class and ethnicity" (p. 6). Such a statement ignores the analyses made by Joan Kelly and many others in the mid-1970s and does not bode well for an accurate memory of the origins of women's history.

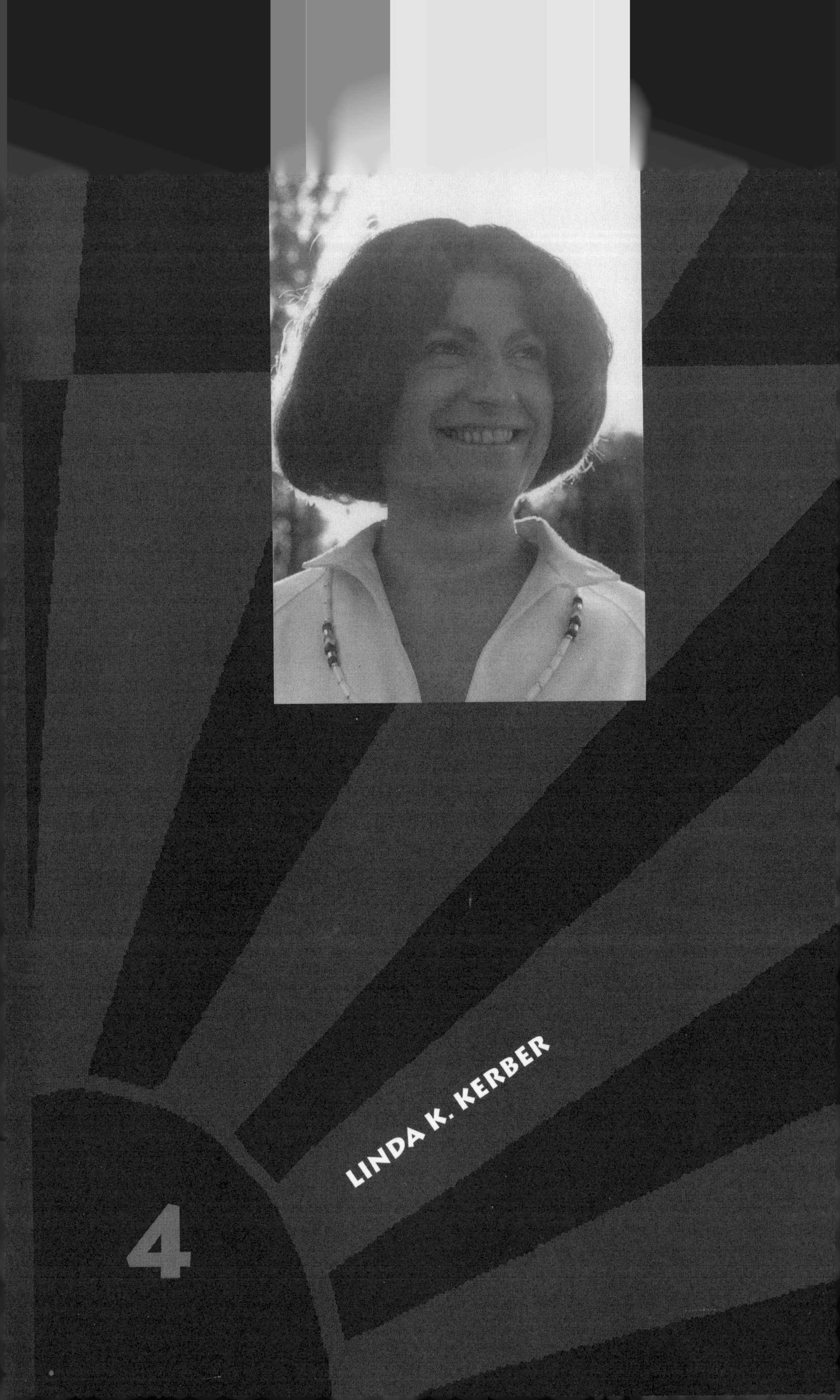
LINDA K. KERBER
4

ON THE IMPORTANCE OF TAKING NOTES (AND KEEPING THEM)

In the early 1970s, when I was beginning to consider writing and teaching women's history, a friendly but unadventurous colleague tried to warn me off.[1] "Women's history is a topic, not a subject," he said gently. I knew he was wrong: Mary Beard's *Woman as Force in History* (1946) and Eleanor Flexner's *Century of Struggle* (1959) sat rock solid on our shelves; Gerda Lerner had already begun a series of major interpretative essays in 1969. But I also knew he was right: gender was not yet, in Joan Scott's felicitous phrase, understood to be "a useful tool of historical analysis." Throughout my graduate student years at Columbia University, my colleagues and I had read virtually no books by women historians, no biographies of women activists, and, with the exception of abolitionists, no primary source materials testifying to women's experience. This would have been less true had we been medievalists. Columbia historians took great pride in public speaking, and during my years there, from 1961 to 1968, I heard many dazzling lectures. But none were by women faculty members. There were, in fact, no women faculty members among the Americanists at Columbia, although I had been taught by women at Barnard, the women's college of the university, whose faculty had courtesy privileges at Columbia and occasionally served as graduate examiners or on dissertation committees. No lecture in graduate school that I remember focused clearly on women's historical experience—as workers, teachers, educators, politicians, criminals. None of the books that I was expected to read in preparation for examinations were written by women.

Linda K. Kerber, 1975.

I am no longer surprised. I was in school during the Cold War, in the long 1950s which stretched until 1967. The constraining politics of the time was accompanied by an ideology which undermined the ambitions of women to shape careers outside the home, and which rewrote history to deny that they had ever done so. When women figured in historical narratives they were an odd and disruptive force, from the witches of Salem in the eighteenth century to Communist sympathizers in the present. My parents' politics were progressive, but they had been too frightened by the witch-hunts of the 1950s—which in New York City had reached into classrooms, humiliating teachers sometimes literally before the eyes of their astonished students—to permit their daughter to explore the left publications where some concern for women's history still flourished. I was thirteen years old when Ethel Rosenberg was executed, and I can still remember the ominous emptiness of the Manhattan streets that day, as if Yom Kippur were being observed. When Judith Coplon, a bright Jewish graduate of Barnard College, was arrested as a spy, my mother was shocked enough to worry about the risks of sending a bright daughter to one of the few elite colleges which no longer had a Jewish quota.

But if I had learned no women's history in the Cold War years, why had I taken all those unused notes—on Mary Wollstonecraft, on women's fashions—in that era before photocopiers when notes were laboriously copied by hand and retyped? While I had been writing my dissertation, which I thought was a history of political thought, my subconscious had been playing identity politics. Perhaps more precisely, my subconscious was driven by the academic feminism it had absorbed as an undergraduate at Barnard College in the 1950s, where the feminism of the 1930s persisted, and where my teachers had made sure that the women's March on Versailles in 1789 was part of what we learned about the French Revolution and where Edith Wharton was central to the American literature survey course. In my freshman English class, the obligatory Shakespearean play we read was neither *Hamlet* nor *Julius Caesar* but *Anthony and Cleopatra*; the complexities of a woman's choices were central to our introduction to the western literary tradition.

That English class was taught by John Kouwenhoven, a man of patrician bearing and sly wit, who taught first-year students with great dedication—he was fond of saying that he wanted to get hold of students *first*—and who had initiated Barnard's American Civilization program. He had recently published *The Columbia Historical Portrait of New York*, a book that remains unusual for its construction of a narrative history in which images—prints, maps, portraits—are used as visual evidence for the substantive arguments, not merely illustration. (Years later, when I used visuals in a similar spirit in *Women of the Republic*,[2] his influence was surely at work.)

In the 1950s there was an inchoate but pervasive sense that American Civilization—which I chose for my major—was an exciting place to be.[3]

Nowadays as global studies, African-American studies, women's studies and other interdisciplinary programs flourish, it is useful to remember that it was the American Civilization programs of the 1940s and 1950s which challenged departmental boundaries by juxtaposing literature and politics, art and social history, architecture and foreign relations. (One friend wrote a memorable senior thesis on the ideologies of design that informed American embassies abroad.) American Studies programs at least suggested—as did virtually no other element in the standard college curriculum of the 1950s—that African Americans and women were central to understanding American culture. By the variety of cross-disciplinary choices they offered, American Studies programs first surrendered to undergraduates substantial power for innovation in the planning of a personal academic career. Eleanor M. Tilton's American literature classes offered a window into the excitement of precise textual scholarship, and Annette Kar Baxter, who had already written about Henry Miller and Elvis Presley as important contributors to American culture, shaped an undergraduate program full of surprises.

I could not tell that the intellectual excitement of American Civilization in those days was greatly facilitated by the substantial amounts of federal and foundation money going into it. I did not then understand myself to be living in a postwar, Cold War world, where American Civilization was one way among many of making a defensive claim for Our Side against theirs. The American Civilization curriculum involved a strident validation of American exceptionalism.

The organizing analytical question of the 1950s was "What's American about America?" Its answer, brilliantly framed in an essay by John Kouwenhoven with that subtitle, written by Kouwenhoven and published in *Harper's* only two months before I met him, stressed interchangeable and endlessly extendable structures of the sort found in an infinitely amendable Constitution, an expandable grid town plan, the poetic forms of Walt Whitman (as contrasted to the sonnet) or the musical forms of jazz (as compared to the sonata). To approach American culture in this way, however, was necessarily to drain it of political content or political responsibility. To search for American culture in processes that had shape but not closure was necessarily *not* to search for power, for hierarchy or for structure. I have been greatly indebted to what I learned at Barnard, but I did not learn much about the exercise of power.

I have often wondered whether had I been a history major I would have focused more clearly on those issues. On the other hand, had I not chosen an interdisciplinary major I would have written books of a different character. In *Federalists in Dissent*[4] I wrote chapters juxtaposing political and scientific thought, political and literary satire, ideas about education and ideas about government, the language of legislation and the language of the polemic: all juxtapositions which had been common to our discussions in Barnard seminars and which drove the major books in American Studies, like John William Ward's *Andrew Jackson: Symbol for an Age* and Henry Nash Smith's *Virgin Land*, but which never to my recollection filtered into graduate work in history at Columbia. By the late 1960s, there was wide recognition that the term "Civilization" itself made a polemical claim to authority and distinctiveness. The learned society in the field had always been called the "American Studies Association," and by the 1970s most college and university programs had been renamed to reflect their goal of engaging in critical inquiry rather than mere celebration—which, of course, the best work in the field always had done.

I graduated from Barnard in 1960, at a commencement in which the college president assured our parents that over half the class was married or engaged. (Since I was to be married the following week, the words seemed to me at the time only the common sense of the matter, but decades later there remain dozens, maybe hundreds of my classmates who have never forgiven her for intruding this reminder of what was perceived to be their inadequacy into a day which was supposed to be dedicated to a celebration of their academic accomplishments.) We emerged into a world in which most women who worked outside the home did so in occupations that were traditionally female, and the average woman earned 61 cents for every dollar earned by a man. I would learn from bitter experience not to convey at fellowship interviews that my plans for graduate school would be adjusted to my plans for marriage. Women were regularly asked openly why they were taking up a space that could be held by a man. Professional schools generally maintained informal quotas on race, gender, and ethnicity. Although Jewish quotas were eroding, no one denied that they still existed. As David Hollinger has lucidly explained, if by the 1990s Jews have "long since come to be perceived as part of an empowered white, or European-American demographic bloc," that had not been true in 1940, or 1950, or 1960.

But there were in 1960 competing understandings of what women were and might become. My parents—my mother was a public school teacher in New York City; my father, trained as a lawyer, was the manager of a camera store and a superb amateur photographer—were unambivalently committed to supporting professional aspirations. They never needed persuasion. I landed luckily in a college full of women like myself—only years later did I learn that Barnard administrators had for generations felt uneasy about their necessary hospitality to the Jewish and Italian girls of New York City—where we were simultaneously instructed that we were to marry and also that we were to put our educations to serious, preferably professional use. The models were Eleanor Roosevelt, who had five children, and our distinguished college president Millicent McIntosh, who had four. At the first Freshman Luncheon, Mrs. McIntosh was introduced with a brief biographical sketch, which made a point of telling us that she had all her babies in the summer. I was sixteen years old and I thought that was a curious point to make so publicly. Only many years later, when my friends and I found it not so easy to accomplish a pregnancy while simultaneously maintaining a career, did we realize what the message had been. So long as a woman accepted her role as the center of home and family life there was much that she might attempt; problems came when professional identity competed with the demands of the nuclear family. (At that point, even powerful minds confessed themselves at a loss.)

After a year at New York University, I returned to Columbia, then one of the very few elite universities reasonably hospitable to women students and authentically hospitable to Jewish men. The first generation of Jewish men to receive tenure were among its most distinguished faculty—Lionel Trilling, Richard B. Morris, Richard Hofstadter—although, *naïf* that I was, I could not read the signs of ethnicity if they were unaccompanied by a New York accent, and was surprised and moved to tears when the *Kaddish* was recited at Richard Hofstadter's memorial service in 1970.

In the years when I was in his seminar, Richard Hofstadter was publishing a substantial book roughly every three years. He taught by the dazzling example of his own work that ideas as well as economic relations matter and are often deeply intertwined; that historical knowledge can link to political understanding; and that historians should be confident that if they can write simultaneously sharply and gracefully their work will claim its audience. I am not sure what drew me to the inquiry that shaped my dissertation, Federalist opposition to Jefferson, but I now think it was compounded in roughly equal measure of an urge on the part of a descendant of immigrants to say something original about the Founding generation and of an authentic admiration, in the early stages of the Vietnam War, for a political faction that had resisted the War of 1812.

I did not find it particularly difficult to be a graduate student; it seemed not very different from the life my husband Dick was living as medical student—we worked equally long hours, although I had much more flexibility—and when we decided to have a child it was not impossible to mold the final stages of dissertation writing around the last months of pregnancy and the first months of Ross's life.

I was lucky to find a teaching appointment while working on my dissertation; the women's college of Yeshiva University accepted me although I was not an observant Jew. The dean asked only for assurance that I respected what his students believed. The intensely serious environment of Stern College was the safest of spaces; only when I went outside of it, onto the coed, secular job market, would I find that I was virtually unemployable.

Of the next few years I find it still almost impossible to write. Dick was drafted into the army after his second year of residency. Anxious anticipation of my dissertation defense evaporated in the face of the authentic panic I felt during the year he was in Vietnam. I still cannot remember a single question I was asked at that defense in the early spring of 1968. Not long after, the Columbia campus erupted in resistance to university authority and a generalized opposition to the war; we joked that I was sending photographs to Vietnam from the New York battlefront. When Dick returned in the summer we moved to California, where Justin was born in 1969; we lived through the next intensely political years in Palo Alto, then the most intensely political of places.

If I somehow had known that it was wise to take notes about women in the mid-1960s, I had not known what to do with the notes I had taken. In *Federalists in Dissent* I wrote three paragraphs—of which I am still very proud—on the women and children who served as the first American proletariat in the primitive cotton mills of the early republic. I had a hunch that there was more to be said but I could not think how or where to push the research. My advisers never prompted me; I didn't know how to ask for help. Not until the revitalized feminist movement of the turn of the 1970s could I see what I already had done, did I have the courage (I take no credit; stronger spirits than mine had done this long before) to intrude into a manuscript library to ask what women's collections they had without feeling like a fool. In 1968 it was a dumb question, revealing that the asker was on a fishing expedition and need not be taken seriously; in any event a woman's manuscripts were generally absorbed into her father's or husband's papers and many curators had no idea what their own collections held. But in 1972 the same question was in many libraries a welcome one, which could be counted on to elicit sparkles in curatorial eyes, compliments on one's perspicacity and not infrequently an invitation to ramble in closed stacks. Women's history has regularly flourished in times of progressive and feminist politics and regularly declined in periods of repression; activists are hungry for their history. Elizabeth Cady Stanton and Susan B. Anthony saved the records of the suffrage movement and regularly commissioned historical essays recording the work that was done, decade by decade, state after state, country after country, until they and their successors had filled six indispensable volumes with their *History of Woman Suffrage*. The revitalized feminist movement of 1969 and thereafter sustained its own demand and its own audience for women's history, and my own work has been done in response to and sustained by the feminism of my own time.

By 1971 we were in Iowa City. Dick was appointed to the faculty of the medical school and I was made welcome by the history department. After the years at Stern there had been a year without a job, then a part time appointment at San Jose State College, then a temporary but glorious year at Stanford, replacing a professor on sabbatical leave, and then Iowa. But there had been absolutely no options in each transition; there had been lots of rejection letters, and had the single job not appeared—and if Dick, who as a smart young cardiologist had many choices, had not also seen opportunity in the University of Iowa faculty—I would have been unemployed.

Women of my graduate school cohort at Columbia had much the same experiences, different only in the details; one of my fellow students, now a senior professor at a major university, holds the record for our cohort of nine consecutive temporary appointments. Another, who currently holds a chaired professorship, spent nearly a decade marginally employed or dependent on grant money. Looking back now, comparing us to what graduate students in the humanities now face, the rickety early years of finding a job don't seem so outrageous. But those were years of enormous growth in the size of colleges and universities, and the men of our cohort were likely to emerge from graduate school into tenure-track positions. We knew we were as smart—or smarter—than they were.

What I could not see was that I was one of the lucky ones. My gender and ethnicity may have made me marginal, but my skin color did not. When I received my PhD only 2 percent of the nation's university, college, community college and staff members were African American. Columbia was almost as segregated as if it had been in the deep South. Had I been born ten years earlier, the professions would have been even less merciful. My generation mostly escaped the political tragedies of the McCarthy era. Supreme Court Justice Ruth Bader Ginsburg has not forgotten the petty humiliations to which she and her women colleagues were subjected at Harvard Law School in 1956. Janet Wilson James, who completed a brilliant dissertation on women in the early republic at Harvard in 1954, could not find a stable job until 1971, when she was 53 years old. Her dissertation went unpublished until 1981. When I wrote *Women of the Republic* I had no idea that it had a predecessor in Janet's dissertation until my own book was nearly complete. Scores, hundreds, thousands—no one has counted—of women started graduate school in the 1940s and 1950s and were deflected. I have lived my professional life in an academic world from which women ten and twenty years older than I have been virtually absent. The very few who seem to fit the category—Gerda Lerner, Anne Firor Scott—in fact had interrupted careers and took their PhDs or entered the job market only a few years earlier than my own generation did. They only appear to be significantly older than we are. The few of us who managed to hang on into the transitional years of 1971–75 were those whose timing was right, although, in the exhaustion of our struggle, we rarely appreciated it.

In 1970, an unemployed historian and new mother—our younger son Justin had been born eight months before—I watched in awe as Professor Willie Lee Rose of Johns Hopkins University told the business meeting of the American Historical Association (AHA) that women historians faced discrimination because of their sex. In effect she was explaining why there were no older women historians. In the 1980s it would be common for patronizing men to observe that the new generation of women academics was *sui generis*; since the generation of the 1930s women just hadn't had the smarts and the gumption of the liberated women they knew. But that was false history. Rose presented a modest statistical report that revealed the severe under-representation of women historians in all history departments in 1970 except those in women's colleges (where, nevertheless, their proportion had declined in the previous twenty years). On behalf of a distinguished committee of historians—which included Carl Schorske, Page Smith, Hanna Holborn Gray (who some years later would serve as president of the University of Chicago) and Patricia Albjerg Graham (who would a decade later be dean of the Harvard School of Education, and subsequently president of the Spencer Foundation) —Rose called upon AHA to establish a permanent committee charged with working actively to enlarge the number of women in the profession and to deal with cases of discrimination against them; to ensure greater representation of women on the programs and in the committees of AHA; to work with history departments to eliminate nepotism rules; to support more flexible part-time employment; and to develop policies of maternity leaves. They called the situation "urgent" and in need of "prompt action."

To acknowledge that women historians faced "discrimination" from their own mentors and colleagues was to name publicly a situation that had theretofore been understood to be "normal," "natural," and permanent. The Rose Report spoke directly to my own confusion as a woman who claimed a professional life that was intellectual at its core and to which many thought no woman was entitled. The atmosphere in the Boston hotel ballroom—standing room only, some five hundred historians—was almost as charged as it had been in Washington, DC the year before, when radical historians had demanded that AHA take a position against the Vietnam War.

The Rose Committee had its own history. It had been formed in response to a petition drafted and signed by Berenice Carroll and twenty-two women who shortly thereafter would organize themselves as the Coordinating Committee on Women in the Historical Profession (CCWHP). The signers were themselves involved on their own campuses in demands for reports on the status of women modeled on the pioneering report produced at Berkeley in 1969 which showed, among other things, that in some departments no woman had been appointed since the 1920s and that some departments had never had a woman member.

Instead of the permanent committee which the petitioners demanded, AHA had established a temporary one, instructed to "commission studies and collect statistics," to gather information about discrimination, and to publish what they had learned. The temporary committee was given no money to spend and AHA was unused to data-gathering. But the committee could be clever, and the brilliance of the Rose Committee lay in its decision to collect rapidly a set of statistics that everyone could understand. With the help of Helen Astin, the Rose Committee focused on the previous ten years—that is, the decade of my own graduate work—in three strategic groups of ten institutions each: ten major public and private research universities, ten selective coeducational colleges, and ten women's colleges. They found that only in women's colleges did women account for nearly half the faculty, and in those colleges the proportion of women in the history faculties had declined in the decade of the 1960s. Although some 15 percent of the PhDs in history awarded in the decade of the 1950s had gone to women, not a single woman was a full professor in the ten most distinguished graduate departments of history in the early 1960s. By the end of the 1960s, a decade in which the size of these departments roughly doubled, and the numbers of full professors went from 160 to 274, only *two* women became full professors in those ten large departments, which numbered forty to sixty men each. When Willie Lee Rose called upon AHA to establish a permanent committee on the status of women, the ten history departments at major research universities which had been awarding between 10 and 15 percent of their PhDs in history to women for decades employed a total of seven women in tenure-track or tenured positions. There were no women in *any* rank at Cornell, Stanford, or Wisconsin between 1959 and 1967.

The Rose Report frankly and explicitly said that these statistics were no accident, that they were the result of intention, and that intentions were shaped by prejudice, misjudgment, and perverse ideology. It found that despite the widespread assumption that women married and substituted caring for children for scholarship, "91 percent of the women receiving doctorates in all fields in the mid-fifties were employed in some type of work seven years later"; married women PhDs who were employed full time published *more* than their male counterparts. The report concluded: "Those who practice discrimination against women in academic employment also hold general views concerning female inferiority."

As luck would have it, I had already been drawn into the circle of feminist historians organized as the Berkshire Conference of Women Historians. Jeannette Nicols and Mary Beard had organized the Conference in 1929 at a time when women historians were unwelcome at the "smokers" to which male historians repaired in the evenings at conventions. In the late 1960s the "Berks," at which attendance had declined in the 1950s and 1960s—perhaps a dozen historians actually came to the annual informal meetings in the Berkshires or at country inns elsewhere—was greatly invigorated by a younger generation that found it to be, in effect, a profession-specific consciousness-raising group.

I had gone to my first Berks meeting around 1965, drawn there by Doris Goldstein, who had had the faith to hire me at Stern and who herself had become part of the Berks years earlier, when she had taken her PhD at Bryn Mawr. I believe she intended to recruit a younger generation—Molly Rosenhan and Sandi Cooper were also at my first Berks meeting at the Red Lion Inn in Stockbridge. Although I found some of the older women intimidating, I also understood myself to be in stunningly interesting company.

By 1968, when Dick and I moved to California, where I knew no historians, it was Berks people who made sure I would not be lost. Mary Dunn introduced me to Grace Larsen, a former member of the Berks who now taught at the College of the Holy Names in Oakland. I believe it was Mary who remarked that perhaps Grace and I might draw together a Berks-like group in California; perhaps the idea emerged out of our own need for comradeship. Grace knew that the state-supported conference center at Asilomar would be hospitable (an old letter says it cost less than $28, room and board, for the weekend). I, pregnant and unemployed, had plenty of time to construct a mailing list. I settled down in the Stanford University Library to make up a list of women historians on the West Coast and was stunned to find 30-man, 40-man, 60-man departments.

To that first weekend at Asilomar (designed by pioneer woman architect Julia Morgan) came eleven women, most of whom already knew Grace; they taught at Holy Names or Sacramento State College. Just as we were about to conclude that we could have saved a lot of money by having a long lunch in the Bay Area, Sister Agnes Murphy from San Diego College for Women arrived dusty and tired; she had come all the way by bus. Her wisdom and enthusiasm convinced us that there was a real role for a West Coast Association of Women Historians (WCAWH) to play; as I write the WCAWH celebrates its thirtieth birthday.

When the Rose Report was being debated on the floor of the AHA annual meeting I felt myself a part of a national community of feminist historians. Along with CCWHP, Berks people were mobilized to make sure that the Rose Report passed. We were prepared to take to the floor microphones ourselves to speak in its favor. But without our prompting, historians crowded the floor to speak in support, including, much to our surprise but as the Report itself had predicted, elderly men (among them Chester McArthur Destler) who rose to address the meeting on the barriers faced by their granddaughters.

When CCWHP decided to accompany its newsletter with a *Bulletin of Current Research and Courses in the History of Women*, I, still unemployed, welcomed the opportunity to handle it. Palo Alto felt a long way from New York, but the flow of mail to my home from women all over the country told me quickly and emphatically of a new world of scholarship coming into being. I edited the *Bulletin* as long as I could, through a temporary job at Stanford and then for the first year or two at Iowa, after which Arnita Jones took it up. (I would not meet her until more than a decade later, when she began her long service as executive director of the Organization of American Historians [OAH]). I still don't know whom I have to thank in CCWHP for floating my name for AHA positions—I was a write-in candidate for the Nominating Committee in 1971, and I understand I lost by ten votes—but I have always suspected their hand in encouraging my selection to replace Adrienne Koch on the AHA Committee on Women Historians (CWH) after her death. A year after my appointment I served as the committee's chair. I would thus be given a ringside seat for the controversies and changes that were to come and a crash course in the sociology, politics, and academic culture of the historical profession.

The first chair of the permanent committee was Patricia Albjerg Graham, who had drafted much of the Rose Report. It was unlike any committee AHA had ever seen. Created with the power to choose its own paid full-time Special Assistant, a role first played by Dorothy Ross, its male members were feminists and its women members were young. It was the first AHA committee to have a graduate student member (Suzanne Lebsock). We were an expensive committee. We kept proposing projects which the Washington office staff said couldn't be done. I sent in an expense account for my first meeting that included a bill for childcare.

Most importantly, CWH had a constituency, organized as CCWHP, to which most of its members belonged and which, though it was full of old friends and colleagues, let us know both formally and informally when they thought we were not moving fast enough or far enough. We were warned against the dangers of being co-opted. CCWHP had its own meetings at AHA, and it commented frankly on what we did. It monitored the number of women who offered papers or comments at the annual meetings of AHA and OAH (when hundreds of men were on the program in 1970, the numbers of women were in the single digits). When the AHA Council decided to cut the funding for the Committee's Special Assistant to half-time, CCWHP joined with CWH in the unsuccessful fight against the decision. When, in 1972, the draft of the new constitution for AHA made no room for a continuing permanent committee on the status of women, CCWHP and CWH successfully defended it.

The most significant sentence of the Rose Report, I have always thought, read "The discrepancy between women's professional status and performance is thus not grounded in any lack of commitment to the life of learning." Its description of the demography of the profession was shocking but also reassuring; we were not unemployed because our scholarship was weak or because we had made fools of ourselves at interviews. We were unemployed because a profession that prided itself on its commitment to the life of the mind measured its colleagues by nonintellectual criteria. (Long before, in 1947, John Hope Franklin had made much the same point regarding the bar against black men in academia.) In the interludes between the working sessions of the permanent Committee, we talked endlessly about whether it would be possible to improve the status of women as professional historians without simultaneously constructing for women a history that professional historians would have to respect.

In that context I returned to the unused dissertation notes—responding to a new sense that not only was I myself newly situated, but that the professional situation in which I lived had long been politicized, had I only had the wit to see it. By 1972 I was not only chairing the AHA committee but I was also teaching my first course in the history of women in the United States. In those days junior faculty rarely invented new courses; they taught the standard ones—the American Revolution, the Progressive Era, the New Deal—and the changes they made were relatively minor. But the demands of women students for women's history courses opened the curriculum to us. For me, as for my colleagues across the country, this experience came as a revelation. There turned out to be no dearth of material to teach. Even in those early years there was more than enough available in paperback to sustain many different courses—emphasizing work, or culture, or politics, or family life. Once we attacked the archives, looking for documents, they sprang out at us as if alive. There were diaries, there were letters, and there were acts of legislation and public reports. There were artifacts of women's making, like quilts. There were institutions women had populated: girls' schools and colleges, women's prisons, textile factories, and garment shops. In this embarrassment of riches, my colleagues and I made our choices for our next research projects.

There was continuity in my own work. I had once insisted that the Federalist objection to the Jeffersonians was not fully explained by different economic self-interest, as traditional progressive historians would have had it, and had taken the position that Federalist *ideas* deserved to be taken seriously and evaluated on their own terms. Now I took the position that the founding generation, which had such complex ideas about so many other things—the relation between ruler and ruled, the appropriate power of masters over servants, the natural history of the continent—must also have had ideas about women and the social order. Wherever I looked, that turned out to be so.

In 1974 or 1975, Joseph Ellis, then and now a professor of history at Mount Holyoke, had undertaken to edit a special issue of the *American Quarterly* scheduled to appear for the bicentennial of the Declaration of Independence. When Joe's invitation flattered me into the project, I was fresh from writing "Daughters of Columbia" as a memorial tribute to Richard Hofstader. I had a hunch that I had not exhausted the subject, and indeed was already committed to a book, but I had not yet thought through how I would develop and extend the ideas in the original essay. Joe was not in a hurry for his essay, but because of the bicentennial, the special issue was going to be advertised well in advance of its appearance. Long before the essay was due, Joe needed a title. Like many writing people, I usually write titles last, after everything else is in shape. I put Joe off. He wrote pleading notes. I didn't answer. Finally he tracked me down on the phone, and refused to hang up until we had come up with a title for the preliminary table of contents. Desperate, I offered Joe "The Republican Mother" more in the hope of bringing the conversation to closure than because I was certain of the theme of the essay.[5] Yet nothing I have written, before or since, has been so instantly useful for my own thinking or, it turned out, to other historians, as the essay that I developed on that theme. I have been reflecting on why this should be so.

While I was writing "Daughters of Columbia" and "The Republican Mother," I was less conscious of actively seeking a new interpretation—whereas years later, writing "The Paradox of Women's Citizenship"[6] I was consciously trying for a new interpretation—than I was desperately trying to make sense out of a confused mass of note cards. There were few interpretative schemes with which I could connect. Everyone knew that Abigail Adams had written to John "Remember the ladies" and thought they knew—inaccurately—that Betsy Ross had sewn a flag. When I found women's verses against drinking tea, or Rachel Wells bringing food to soldiers under fire on the battlefield at Yorktown, or Judith Sargent Murray calling for "a new era in female history," what was I to make of them except a few more anecdotes?

In "The Republican Mother" I tried to move from anecdote to meaning, and to argue that those who thought about the future stability of the new republic *necessarily* considered the role of women in it. A few of the shrewdest members of the founding generation understood that the status of married women gave the lie to claims of government by the consent of the governed. In a culture that solidly associated intellect with masculinity—"women of masculine minds have generally masculine manners" one Federalist minister confidently asserted—some who did not have the stomach for radical disruption found a compromise position by envisioning mothers as playing a political role in the socializing role they played in their own families. By refusing to marry unpatriotic men, by raising their sons to be the next generation of virtuous citizens, women could play a meaningful political role, assuring the future stability of the fragile republic. Political virtue, a revolutionary concept that has troubled writers from Edmund Burke to Hannah Arendt, could be safely domesticated in eighteenth-century America; the mother, and not the masses, could be the custodian of civic morality.

By politicizing private behavior, the concept of "republican motherhood" pulled women's agency and the relations of men and women into the narrative of the American Revolution, suggested further questions about the transmission of republican ideology to the next generation, and challenged other historians to ground it more firmly in social experience. It supported the understanding that even when women were absent from legislatures and had not yet organized large-scale political movements, gender was of central significance to the great questions of the relationship between law and liberty. Everywhere I turned, ideas about what women were, what relations between men and women should be, seemed to infuse contemporary understanding of major problems: in political theory, in the new law for an independent nation, in educational institutions, and in the substance of what men and women should study and should write. To search for the revolutionary generation's own understanding of women meant to work toward a new narrative of intellectual history grounded in gender as well as in other elements of American political and cultural life.

But if the concept of "republican motherhood" is deployed without the ironic, double-sided implications I meant to convey, if it is taken to mean unambivalent progress—from the Revolution white men get a more democratic polity and white women get republican motherhood—then it is silly and misleading. In this unnuanced sense, the term started turning up in textbooks (and, no doubt, in student examination papers), making me edgier and edgier over the years.

After the publication of *Women of the Republic* in 1980, I continued to be asked to speak or to write on the themes of the book. I accepted these invitations as occasions to restate what I thought in different contexts than my own book had provided. This work, in turn, kept me pondering what I had once said, re-examining the notes and documents I had once used, until, turning them around and around like crystals before the light, I disengaged from the irony and decided that republican motherhood was the ideological result of the gendered deployment of the old law of social relations. It had been a strategy middle-class women adopted to enter political conversation despite the bitter laws of coverture, which when they married denied to them power over their bodies, their property, and their children. I would now say—as I would not have said in 1972 when I was pondering the problem of women in American revolutionary thought—that the founding generation understood clearly that they were sustaining the power of husbands over wives, parents over children, masters over servants and slaves while simultaneously undermining the power of the king over his subjects. American revolutionaries stabilized the radical changes they were making in conceptions of sovereignty by keeping the hierarchies of domestic relations intact. The subordination of women was not unintentional; it was an essential ingredient of the Revolution and the republican polity that followed. That is why it has taken more than two centuries and much bitter struggle to change it.

By the mid-1980s Women's History was firmly established as a field of inquiry. Virtually every history department supported at least one course (although most history majors still graduate without having taken even one), prizewinning books had been written, and the scope of investigations continued to expand. Distinctive to the revitalized women's history of the 1970s—as contrasted to that written by previous generations, which had tended to focus on women's own experiences—was the confidence that "the social relations of the sexes," in Joan Kelley's graceful term, had a history as well as a sociology. The effort transformed the field of history.

But the structural changes we envisioned that would make the academy a more hospitable site have been only fitfully accomplished. When we instituted childcare at annual meetings I do not think we intended it to be an end in itself but rather a token of our hope to invent a profession which embraced rather than denied the private responsibilities of its members. We are far from our goal. We have not yet figured out how to navigate between the Scylla of antinepotism rules (with which in principle we generally agree) and the Charybdis of favoritism, to chart a pattern for partnerships of two equally accomplished and challenging careers. The racial and ethnic diversity of our departments rarely mirrors the diversity of the history we try to teach. Not until the late 1980s did we see the first substantial cohort of children born to tenure-track faculty women, but pressures in the academy still signal young women to postpone, and postpone again, their childbearing choices. Despite some minor modifications, the tenure clock and the biological clock are still in conflict.

I have found myself wondering whether the academy has not been more vulnerable to downsizing and to the attacks of the "culture wars" in part because we have been feminizing the academy, and we live in a social culture in which work is still largely sex-segregated and in which high-status, high-paying professions have few women in them. Those of us with tenured positions have a special responsibility to use our power in faculty governance to halt the erosion of the profession into part-time and insecure positions. Sustaining and supporting the work of the humanities in the coming generation will demand energy and creativity at least equal to that brought to bear in the early 1970s. In 1920, when suffrage was accomplished, the great feminist Crystal Eastman wrote, "Men are saying, thank goodness that everlasting women's fight is over. Women are saying, 'Now at last we can begin.'" Now, at the turn of the twenty-first century, with feminist historians solidly located in positions throughout American academic life—as tenured professors, college and university presidents, deans, provosts, museum directors, executives in learned societies and private foundations—now we too, at last, can begin.

NOTES

1. This essay is an adaptation of the Introduction to *Toward an Intellectual History of Women: Essays by Linda K. Kerber* (Chapel Hill: University of North Carolina Press, 1997). Copyright © 1997 the University of North Carolina Press. Used by permission of the publisher.

2. Linda K. Kerber, *Women of the Republic: Intellect and Ideology in Revolutionary America* (Chapel Hill: Institute of Early American History and Culture, Univ. of North Carolina Press, 1980).

3. I have discussed the field in "Diversity and the Transformation of American Studies," *American Quarterly* 4 (Fall 1989), 415–31.

4. Linda K. Kerber, *Federalists in Dissent: Imagery and Ideology in Jeffersonian America* (Ithaca: Cornell Univ. Press, 1970).

5. Linda K. Kerber, "The Republican Mother—Women and the Enlightenment: An American Perspective," *American Quarterly* 28 (1976), 187–205.

6. Linda K. Kerber, "The Paradox of Women's Citizenship in the Early Republic: The Case of *Martin v. Massachusetts*, 1805," *American Historical Review* 97 (1992), 349–78.

SANDI E. COOPER

5

THE SHAPING OF A FEMINIST HISTORIAN

Coming of age in Cold War America meant, above all else, conformity to middle-class norms, which privileged masculine sovereignty as the natural law of daily life. Among the handful of women who slipped into graduate school from college, and, then, accidentally or incidentally into college teaching, none imagined a reason to challenge the prevailing scholarly culture. Indeed, we often felt like trespassers. Professional life—the structures of academic departments, conventions, classroom relationships, the content of journals—was molded by gentlemen's agreements.

At the annual meetings of the American Historical Association (AHA), women—a marginal category—occasionally met for breakfasts sponsored by the quiet, well-mannered, little-known Berkshire Conference of Women Historians. This modest society of *soi-disant* dowager historians from northeastern women's colleges had been formed in 1927 as a protest against women historians' exclusion from the (long-defunct) New York State Historians Association. Berkshire members usually convened in springtime at the Red Lion Inn in Stockbridge, Massachusetts to socialize, take walks, discuss their work, host an occasional visiting scholar who wore sensible shoes and did British history, and award a free drink to the woman who found the first trillium. At the national AHA, it hosted breakfasts.

In 1969, the first jolts of a revolutionary cultural challenge to established routines impacted American scholars, including historians. At the Washing-

Speaking in Central Park, Sandi E. Cooper supports the ERA at a New York NOW rally, August 26, 1979.

ton convention of AHA, a posting invited women to an open discussion of their status as historians. From the enthusiastic group that assembled arose the original Coordinating Committee on Women in the Historical Profession (CCWHP), co-chaired by Berenice Carroll and Gerda Lerner. (Berenice Carroll had already helped launch a similar group in political science.) Women's activism, which had mobilized in the 1960s, began its long march into the professions. The two-pronged attack, on women's (limited) presence in the profession and general absence in historical literature, was launched.

In 1969, I missed the birth moment of the women's caucus in history because my doctor advised against a trip to Washington with a week-old daughter. However, Berenice Carroll very quickly inveigled me—infant and all—into an active role, and in 1971, I became the national co-chair. From 1971–73, I worked to generate visibility for CCWHP, organizing regional affiliates similar to the New York City organization which had been independently established; connected with newly emerging groups of women historians such as the West Coast Association which seemed to be growing from the model of the older Berkshire Conference; struggled to get daycare at conventions; campaigned for CCWHP's agenda wherever I could get a hearing—and, simultaneously, tried to run a house, be a decent mother, teach four courses a semester, and do some publishing. Life in the early 1970s was heady, exciting, full of possibilities, a moment when retrograde ideas appeared to have disappeared. (They hadn't.) It was also exhausting. Sundays were for sleeping.

I also was involved with the Berkshire Conference because Margaret Judson, chair of the Department of History at Douglass College, where I taught (1961–67), had invited me to come along. Margaret was trying to bring in a younger generation but we were very few—until some of us had the idea of bringing our own friends. Somehow it clicked . . . Mary Maples Dunn of Bryn Mawr, Emiliana Noether from U Conn (Storrs), and I drove carfuls of young women up the roads to the Berks, forging links that still connect. Early in the 1970s I was asked to organize a weekend program for a mini-Berks. Sheila Tobias, then at Wesleyan, Claudia Koonz at Holy Cross, and Renate Bridenthal at Brooklyn College agreed to present their very early work on German women's history. Following this meeting, Louise Dalby (Skidmore) and Emiliana Noether thought we might put together a larger conference on women's history—something none of us had ever done. This impulse was realized at Douglass College, where Lois Banner and Mary Hartman persuaded the history department to host a meeting in 1971. About 200 participants were expected; over 700 came. Despite the fact that a misogynist, Lionel Tiger, gave the after-dinner speech—rebutted by several gifted women—the meeting was a smashing success. None of us had ever left an AHA convention with quite that feeling of intellectual stimulation, camaraderie, and a sense of adventure about opening an entirely new frontier.

Everyone wanted another meeting. We held the second at Radcliffe, expecting 700; over 2,000 came. The newly reconfigured Berkshire Conference —with a major meeting devoted to the history of women—was off to a start. For years, we preserved the smaller meetings as well, but these lost their sense of intimacy with growth. Though I did not begin to do research in women at that point, I served on every program committee throughout the 1970s, chaired the committee in 1978 at Mt. Holyoke, and then chaired the Berks itself. My service on the committee lasted through the early 1980s, when Carroll Smith-Rosenberg and I were unceremoniously dumped by a new generation who wanted a larger, professional organization and the removal of the "mothers" who had set the thing in motion. The limits of sisterhood were very clear.

One of the ideas which I remain proud of was to take the conference revenue of the big Berks, invest it, and create a nest egg to underwrite book prizes, article prizes, and a summer research stipend at the Schlesinger Library, Radcliffe. Wonderfully expansionary interest rates in the 1970s helped us take modest sums and turn them into magically larger amounts.

In the 1970s, my ability to serve as national president of a new women's caucus and later, of the Berkshire Conference, was made possible, frankly, by the fact that I had been awarded tenure by 1970–71 at a (then) new, experimental branch of the City University of New York. My colleagues and even the administration were open to a variety of new approaches to higher education—interdisciplinary programs, collaborative teaching, and a willingness to substitute openness for traditional barriers. Older students—especially disillusioned Vietnam veterans whose entire childhood *Weltanschauung*, shaped in constricted, parochial neighborhoods, had been shattered—taught us as much as we could teach them. Vast numbers of blue-collar students and an increasing influx of minority students began to populate classrooms earlier restricted to a younger, more selected student pool. As someone who had graduated from City College in 1957, I could attest to the fact that the newer college generation hardly resembled mine.

Everything was changing from the world of my childhood, schooling, and early professional expectations. I grew up in a confined, privately run housing project in the Bronx, a place called Parkchester, very similar to the neighborhoods my students inhabited a generation later. It looked for all the world like those faceless housing projects designed to warehouse the urban poor after World War II. My father, a modestly prosperous decorator during the 1930s, lost nearly everything in the Second World War and for a time, I believe we were on home relief. I went to a reasonably decent elementary school, spent endless happy hours with my Girl Scout troop in all kinds of interesting projects, including playing with children who had leukemia and children who came to New York City from Europe in 1946 with numbers on their arms from those mysterious "camps" we heard about. I remember long, hot summers in the city streets and playgrounds, watching my little sister, because my family never had vacation money. In the early years of the war, the excitement of community invigorated those desolate patches of Bronx life as we worked on our victory gardens in an abandoned lot near the school, collected rags, tin, and paper on little red carts, and scrimped to buy savings stamps which could become a savings bond. After the war, my father found work and scraped together enough to buy a car; this meant we could go to beaches or parks for barbecues on Sundays.

At 14, around 1950, I began to tire of not having any money. Postwar prosperity never seemed to reach my family. Since I could pass for 16 or 17, I managed to find a way to get working papers and got a job. My mother had taught me touch-typing and I passed myself off as a secretary. Ten dollars a week bought independence. I have supported myself nearly completely since I was 16 or 17.

My immediate family teetered between bourgeois respectability and economic hardship. My father came to the US from Rumania at the end of the first World War, equipped with a fourth-grade education, a capacity for hard work, a terror of starvation (his mother died at the war's end, largely from hunger and weakness), and a very handsome face. One of his older sisters, an earlier immigrant, was married and living in a rural Connecticut town where my father and his kid brother went—initially, to pick tobacco. One day, he bought a car, learned to drive it on the highway to New York City, and never returned to the fields. At the end of the 1920s, he met my mother at a St. Valentine's Day dance and married her six months later.

My mother grew up in Philadelphia and New York City and left high school to work as an executive secretary so that her brothers could go to college. One dropped out; the other became a professor, a historian, and the social science librarian at City College, and eventually the author of *Marriage, Morals and Sex in American History*. My mother went to City College at night for years but never completed a degree—mainly out of fear of the math requirement! Not until I was grown up did I realize how privately unhappy she was about not becoming a teacher, her personal dream.

My family was constrained by financial difficulties. Ordinarily my father worked about 72 hours a week, so he was usually exhausted on Sunday afternoons. When he had any energy, he would talk about European politics, which he seemed to learn osmotically.

During the 1940s, public school education in New York City was considered excellent. The school script was neither innovative nor intellectually challenging—educating a pupil meant stuffing his or her head with unequivocal facts that passed for universal truths. Since my elementary school years coincided with World War II, school was also a place where you learned patriotism, to duck under the desk when the bells rang for a make-believe air raid, and were taught—until 1946—"Uncle Joe (Stalin) is our friend."

By the end of junior high school, however, by 1948, not only was Uncle Joe a demon, the entire Soviet state was our personal enemy. Quickly the textbooks in social studies moved from explaining Soviet shortages sympathetically to presenting them as the result of vicious governmental oppression. And just as swiftly, Germans were suddenly transformed into human beings, a sleight of hand that never ceased to amaze me.

After a year at a nondescript Bronx high school, I was allowed to transfer into the Bronx High School of Science as a junior and thus managed to get one of the best secondary school educations available in New York City. During the senior year hysteria about college applications, I got carried away and thought I might try Cornell. When I realized that my parents would have had to borrow thousands for this, I tore up the application and applied to City. The enraged Bronx High School of Science college counselor called my mother and harangued her for an hour about "letting such a bright child go to a Communist school." When she finished, my mother responded, "Funny, my brother has been teaching there for decades and he never told us it was a Communist school." The counselor hung up. I went to City College.

In 1953, female students (then known as girls) needed a higher average to enter City than male students. Women were newcomers in the liberal arts at City; they usually had been in the School of Education. Two years later, with a nearly straight A average, I was a candidate for a City College fellowship to study abroad. The administration stood on its head in an effort to give it to a male student. (This was really awkward for them since I worked as a receptionist in the Dean's office, one of my three part-time jobs, and I knew what they were doing.) In May 1955, the male winner got cold feet about going away and the College had no more boys up its sleeve. Reluctantly, they awarded me the fellowship. Going to Edinburgh in 1955 changed my life forever.

When I left on the Queen Mary, a provincial nineteen-year-old, I did not realize I was saying goodbye to my fiancé for good and leaving behind my limited notions of the world. A year later—having hitchhiked in six countries, eaten foods I could barely pronounce, discovered resourcefulness I never knew existed in me, studied history from the viewpoint of a culture which considered the US lost colonies, developed friendships with people whose parents had been resistance heroes, visited sites of destruction from two world wars that no written text could ever evoke, and stood in awe of a continent whose cultural artifacts could be counted in centuries—I returned to finish my bachelor's degree and find a life. Two history professors, Louis Snyder and Michael Kraus, suggested I consider graduate school. I had never HEARD the words before.

I had no idea what graduate school was. It sounded right and I applied. The problem, of course, was money.

City College had two teaching fellowships, which would have enabled me to attend Columbia. The history chair, however, became hysterical at the idea of a woman at his department meetings. "How," he asked someone in my hearing, "can we curse if she is around? Who will carry our books to the library?" He gave the money to a man with a B-minus average who became a junior high school teacher. I was given the college's history medal as a consolation. Even pawned, it would not cover a down payment in graduate school.

In 1956, graduate liberal arts departments were very blunt about not offering scholarships for women. Moreover, City College graduates then carried the onus of the McCarthyite period—even the least political of us were suspect as "reds." Several famous eastern schools politely wrote to tell me that they might give me money in a second year. I could never figure out how I was supposed to get to that second year, lacking the means for the first year. One famous upstate New York Ivy rescinded its offer of a fellowship when someone realized that "Sandi" was not male. New York University and the University of Michigan came through with partial help, enough to get started. Since my mother was not well, I stayed in New York. In 1956, New York University was willing to provide a full tuition fellowship; in the following years, they added living monies and finally a teaching assistantship in 1959. They were nervous about their investment, worrying that a "girl" would leave to get married. I swore to one professor that I would finish and not have babies until I finished.

Thus, I kind of slid into my career as a college professor; it was hardly a tradition in the fifties—neither in my family nor in the world at large. My closest friends at undergraduate graduation were all parading around with large hunks of diamond on a certain finger, visiting department stores to compare avocado-colored refrigerators with mustard gold ones. My college friends bluntly warned me that I was courting spinsterhood. One by one they married, fled to suburban housing, abandoned New Deal values, and embraced Republican life-styles. I stayed in touch only with one college friend—our lives remain intertwined; we are the godparents of each other's children—she ended up in New York City. I lost myself in the immense challenge of full-time graduate study, working when and where I could to pick up money to buy a few extras—such as a dress or coat. By 1959, I finished a long master's essay under Leo Gershoy and was awarded a degree. Then began the doctoral research with A. William Salomone and full-time college teaching.

In graduate school I knew I wanted to work in European history. After writing a master's thesis on the transatlantic impact of the French Revolution in Massachusetts, I moved on to a study of the origins of the First World War. The more I read about the unleashing of that catastrophe, so patently against the fundamental interests of reigning regimes, the more I wondered about the suicidal behavior of people willing to believe that war among technologically sophisticated states was winnable.

The bloody history of the twentieth century had totally obscured the existence of peace groups, national and international, whose membership fully grasped what a modern war would do. I decided to do a dissertation on the efforts of private citizen peace lobbyists to persuade national and international political leaders to institutionalize nonviolent forms of conflict resolution in Europe. The Fels Foundation offered me a stipend sufficient to support my proposal. I was able to launch my dissertation in 1959 with the grand sum of $3,000 a year, to cover all expenses.[1]

Between 1959 and 1961, I taught my first college classes and became increasingly enamored of the work, after the initial jitters passed. I loved teaching and student feedback was wonderfully supportive. Some of the students from the early sixties remain my friends—I was, after all, barely six years older than most of them. It was not easy, however, to establish authority. In 1959 I met my first class—mainly boys at the uptown campus of New York University. That semester the university had admitted about eighty young women into the uptown campus and when I showed up the first day, the enthusiastic fraternity greeting party, standing at the entry gates with paddles, whacked every freshman that passed through. Since I was female, they assumed I was a new student (I was 23 at this time) and therefore, they paddywhacked me—to my total astonishment. I shall never forget the face of one of them who showed up in my History 100 tutorial.

In 1961 I was lucky to land a lecturer's job at Douglass College, then the women's college of Rutgers, where Margaret Judson, department chair, followed an unheard-of policy for those days—hiring one woman for every man that she appointed. With my new husband, I moved to New Brunswick, became part of the social and intellectual life of the university, taught, and worked on my dissertation. By the mid-sixties, the civil rights movement, followed by the antiwar movement, hit the campus. The Rutgers history department included several young men who would become eminent in their fields—Eugene D. Genovese, Rudolf Vecoli, Carter Jefferson, Lloyd Gardner, Warren Susman, and John M. Cammett. The Eagleton Institute of Politics at Rutgers also had an exciting staff, including Paul Tillett and Don Riddle. Together we formed support committees for civil rights and participated in the (in)famous Teach-In against the War in Vietnam (1965). I worked very closely with them, despite warnings from the Douglass dean. Don Harris, an African-American alumnus of Rutgers, had been arrested and was being held in an old Civil War jail, incommunicado, with no lawyer, no habeas corpus, because Georgia had charged him with treason against the state, under a Civil

War statute. We mounted a public relations campaign to get him out; we went to senators, congressmen, the press, and the governors of several states. We organized speak-outs on campus—the first time many of us had ever seen or done such things. We broke the silence of the 1950s. I discovered that when a reason existed to do something you learned how to do it. Those years at Douglass ended complicity with unexamined values and institutions.

But none of this was helping me to complete my dissertation. In 1965 I applied for fellowship aid, won a Ford, a Fulbright, and an American Association of University Women (AAUW) award and went off to Europe to finish my research on the AAUW. My husband came along to do his . . . which then was to be on the Greek Resistance in World War II. Travelling with him around Greece, meeting people and learning about the entire resistance, was a marvelous intellectual bonus. At the end of 1966, I had most of my work done, had written all but the last chapter, and returned to Douglass to teach. I was richer by a dissertation but my marriage was over. I took my own apartment in New York City and resumed the life of a single woman.

Academia began to change dramatically in the late 1960s. Suddenly a significant number of positions appeared as colleges expanded and new campuses opened to accommodate a more generous view of who should go to college. As much as I loved Douglass, I decided to return to New York City to teach in the kind of urban institution that I had known as an undergraduate.

Among the new campuses in the City University of New York was Richmond College, to be interdisciplinary, upper division, innovative, and initially, nonhierarchical. In 1967, armed with a brand-new PhD, I was attracted to this brew and was lucky to be picked to serve as one of the founding forty faculty in 1967. Sadly for me—amid the excitement of finishing my degree and launching my new life in New York City—my mother became very ill, dying at 61. She had lived long enough to see me get my PhD and for a gift, bought me academic robes that I still wear, thirty years later. My father, staggered, was at a total loss and needed a lot of attention.

But professionally and politically, we were at the cutting edge in those days. It was impossible to draw the line between the classroom and the streets; one minute you were teaching the anatomies of revolutions and the next minute you were helping students get to Canada. Some of us became as expert on the draft law as we were in our disciplines. You hardly bothered reading the text of the petitions you signed—as long as a friend put them under your nose. At least as much time was spent on picket lines or occupying buildings as was spent on syllabi and library research. Students formed communes, created food co-ops, experimented with all manner of illegal substances right before your eyes in class, demanded the right to vote their own grades, transformed the college newspaper into an underground press, and could be counted on to protest everything and everyone. Young men from traditional, mainly white ethnic backgrounds, lower or working class—immensely patriotic, initially convinced of the Red Menace—returned from southeast Asia as deeply wounded spirits. They stumbled into college, the first in their families, as if seeking the peace of the ashram. For many, college allowed them to understand what had happened to their self-definitions and cultural images and move on to newer lives. It often meant the end of their childhood sweetheart marriages to women who could not follow them along new paths. I can say in all honesty that as a young faculty member, I was not "trained" to cope with this new world.

I remarried (much to my astonishment) in 1967 and am still married to John Cammett, whom I had met at Rutgers in those many civil rights and antiwar committees we both attended. Our friendship changed into a deep attraction, which kept us glued together through nearly thirty years of challenges. He left Rutgers after the political upheavals of the Vietnam Teach-in to join the CUNY faculty at another new campus—John Jay. John was in the full flush of success in 1967 despite the somewhat nasty treatment he had from conservative Rutgers colleagues. His book, *Antonio Gramsci and the Origins of Italian Communism,* garnered front-page rave reviews, including *The Times Literary Supplement*, which established it as a classic. At John Jay, he rose to be dean of faculty and provost in 1969, the year that our daughter, Melani, was born. His other daughters, Lisa and Anni, came to live with us. So did my widowed father. An instant family of so many moveable parts required a certain amount of acrobatics, which was not always easy.

In the late 1960s I also began to connect with colleagues who became lifelong collaborators and friends. I had known Berenice Carroll from Douglass before she went to Illinois. In the late sixties, I met Blanche Wiesen Cook and other people in the Conference on Peace Research in History (now the Peace History Society). Blanche proposed that we, along with Charles Chatfield of Wittenberg, produce a huge reprint series on war/peace titles and the three of us embarked on a six-year project which ended up reprinting over 370 titles—with new introductions for each. The Garland Library of War/Peace[2] remains one of the most significant contributions to establishing the field of peace research in history, itself an effort to integrate alternate visions into diplomatic and political history.

At meetings of the Conference on Peace Research in History, which blossomed in the years following the Kennedy assassination and the Vietnam War, often Berenice Carroll, Blanche Cook, and I were the only women (we were joined occasionally by Mollie Davis from Georgia). What was originally amusing and then irritating was how the "boys" frequently confused Berenice, Blanche, and Sandi (Cook, Carroll, and Cooper—too many shared initials among "the girls," as someone put it once). However, we all overcame difficulties and worked collaboratively on newsletters, the journal *Peace and Change* (still published), conferences, proceedings, books, articles, and the task of opening up minds to a study of the meaning and role of violence in human history. Participants examined issues ranging from multinational corporations and the nation-state to whether or not the atomic bomb was crucial to ending World War II. Peace historians recovered the lost history of peace movements and activists, ordinarily ignored by historians for whom state power is the only significant variable.

In New York City, in the early 1970s, women's groups also cemented new ties and friendships. The Marxist-Feminist circles and the consciousness-raising groups which knit us together—Joan Kelly (Gadol), Alice Kessler-Harris, Renate Bridenthal, Joanne McNamara, Blanche Wiesen Cook, and dozens more—helped us all launch new scholarly projects, newspapers, and journals, and energized work in projects as diverse as opposition to forced sterilization, the legalization of abortion, a woman's right to her own name and credit, home ownership, and medical self-help. I will never forget the excitement as we sat around someone's living room floor when Joan Kelly first described the argument that became the classic, "Did Women Have a Renaissance?"[3] The close kinship was crucial in helping our friends who discovered their homosexuality to emerge from shadowy closets, knowing full well they could depend on our love and support. We organized visits to a young woman historian whose pregnancy was troubled, to amuse her and to discuss her work as she lay in bed for several months. When she finally delivered successfully, one of us helped her secure a major appointment at an Ivy League college. We used our small meetings of the local CCWHP to help young scholars overcome stage fright, and we always shared information about job openings. There was a real effort to introduce a noncombative atmosphere and transform professional relationships into human(e) relationships. We attended seminars to learn about a new idea called "affirmative action" and how it could be applied to enrich and open opportunity. We wanted feminism to shape a new ethos of personal and professional relationships. To have lived through those years is to have been enriched beyond words.

My early education in feminism became the foundation on which I have been able to sustain an activist campaign on behalf of public higher education in New York City. The City University of New York was formalized in 1961–62 by federating a series of independent senior colleges (the oldest, City, my alma mater, was founded in 1847) with a group of newer community colleges, a graduate center, and by 1967, five new senior colleges. Following the tradition of the original City College, tuition was free and costs were minimal, but in 1969, a radical new policy departure was embraced—open admissions.

Suddenly, the campuses were flooded with students—with greatly varying degrees of readiness for college work. By 1974, the system had about 250,000 students in it—and, for the first time, a significant minority representation.

At that moment, the world's money managers decided that the City of New York was bankrupt. Its credit rating slid into negative numbers. From the White House down, the presumed profligate character of the city fueled conservative high dudgeon. Free tuition was featured as a prime reason for the city's troubles. CUNY's trustees were faced with proposals to introduce tuition and close campuses. Both my campus and my husband's were targeted for closure.

My experience in antiwar and women's groups came in handy as I began to organize with colleagues to counter the combined personal and social threat. CUNY's student body had become increasingly female, minority, and older. At the College of Staten Island, for instance, growing numbers of older women, deserted by husbands and left with children and mortgages, timidly knocked on our doors looking for a usable education.

In 1975–76, the struggle to save the university dragged on for an exhausting year. We marched, took radio advertisements, deluged newspapers with letters and op-ed pieces, lobbied politicians, and pushed our faces in front of TV cameras. At the end, we saved most of our campuses but were forced, often, to cut liberal arts and emphasize education as "training" for the job market. I became increasingly angered at what seemed to me to be a radical departure from the educational mission of the urban institution that has served me so well. In 1976, the practical political price of salvation also was the end of free tuition, retrenchment of about 1,400 people (including most of the women and minority appointments made in the seventies) and the abolition of hundreds of programs, mainly liberal arts.

Angered, I ran for the university-wide faculty senate from my college, won, was elected to its executive committee, and have served on it since 1978. In 1991 I was elected vice-chair and in 1994 and 1996, I became the chair of the CUNY University Faculty Senate. It has enabled me to speak out on the social and political implications of public policy on higher education for the poorest college-going cohort in the United States.

In the past two decades, the university has been battered repeatedly by fiscal crises, drastic enrollment swings, inept management, and declining faculty morale. The anti-CUNY barrage merges complaints about costs with attacks on our students and standards by conservative tabloids, trustees, and think tanks. CUNY students are often treated as the academic equivalent of welfare queens. I am often a lobbyist for our students and faculty.

Intellectually, any assessment of nearly thirty years of feminism in American life, particularly in the life of organized academic enterprises, is decidedly a success story. While women have attained far more visible positions of influence and representation in European ministries and parliaments, nowhere have they attained the impact in academic, intellectual, publishing, and media life that they have in the US. I do not claim to have been among the original mothers of the movement launched over three decades ago, but I am grateful that I was able to play a part. We have witnessed a real revolution in male/female relationships, however much we continue to read about lingering oppressive patriarchal practices.

What remains is to transform the spirit of that feminist communalism and mutual support into the worlds of work and power; to weave the web of peace and nonviolence from the individual to the macrocosm; to find the essentials that undergird the multiplicities of feminism found around the globe.

NOTES

1. "Peace and Internationalism: European Ideological Movements Behind the Two Hague Conferences (1899 to 1907)," Department of History, New York University, 1967. My dissertation served as the start of my larger study of European peace movements, *Patriotic Pacifism: Waging War on War in Europe, 1815–1914* (New York: Oxford Univ. Press, 1991).

2. Published in New York, 1972–76, including reprints of classical works with new introductions as well as original anthologies of European and US peace documentation.

3. This essay was the earliest to challenge traditional periodization as it applied to women in history. Published in *Becoming Visible: Women in European History*, ed. R. Bridenthal, C. Koonz, S. Stuard (Houghton Mifflin, 1987, 2nd ed.), it also appeared in *Women, History and Theory: The Essays of Joan Kelly* (Chicago, 1984), a posthumous collection of Kelly's work.

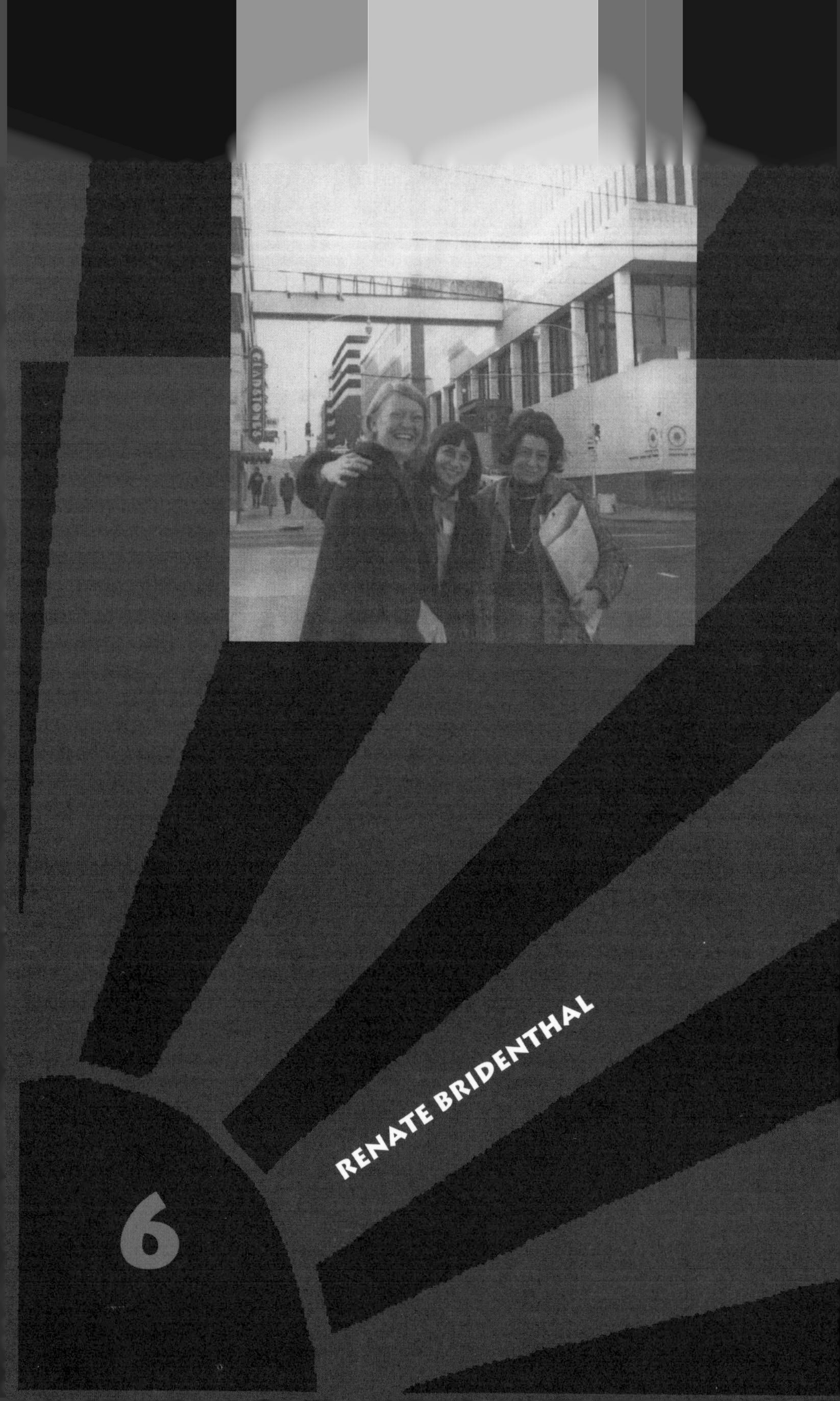
RENATE BRIDENTHAL
6

MAKING AND WRITING HISTORY TOGETHER

I was probably destined to be a Marxist-feminist historian: a Marxist, because I was raised single-handedly by a mother who had been radicalized as a young worker in Leipzig by the German revolution of 1918; a feminist, because she had aspirations for me that I be "someone," not "no-one" like herself; and a historian, because she told me many stories on a long time-line going back to her own grandmother's time in Slovakia. Knowing the history of feminism now, I can see her bridging the complex and contradictory "first wave" for my own lucky experience of the "second wave." Indelible remembrances of my childhood in New York City also include watching her sew sometimes late at night for extra pay, and hearing about her experiences as a fur finisher: the insecurity, the small humiliations, the sexual harassment, the costs of defiance, the value of unionization. I also remember the Cold War, which resonated chillingly in my public high school, where my questioning of the Korean War led a teacher to note her concern on my permanent record that I might become a Russian spy—I was all of sixteen. But it was a fiercely competitive all girls' high school (Julia Richman) and we never had to hide our lights under bushels to please boys. We didn't know the word "feminism," but its seeds were planted.

My refugee experience was certainly formative in itself, and I attribute to it a heightened sensitivity to political change. My parents, brother (age 15), and I (age 3) fled Nazi Germany in 1938, first to Czechoslovakia, and then,

Joan Kelly, Renate Bridenthal, and Sandi Cooper at the American Historical Association, Atlanta, December 1975.

just before the Nazi invasion there, to France. Proceeds from my father's fur business, collected from a sale abroad since Germany prohibited Jews from taking money out, enabled our escape. In Paris, masses of refugees were running from one consulate to another seeking visas abroad, since the French only offered temporary refuge. We got one to Panama, where we arrived in early 1939, finally penniless and still not entirely safe. Faced with the possibility of "repatriation" as "enemy aliens," we were fortunate to be admitted to the United States by a special act of Congress in 1940, and were placed in a furnished apartment in Manhattan by the Hebrew Immigrant Aid Society. And that's where I grew up. My father did not survive the transplantation; he committed suicide in 1941, just before his fortieth birthday and after my sixth.

My mother resumed her earlier work as a fur finisher (sewing linings into coats) and I worked hard at school and at piano. We shared a glamorous dream of my becoming a concert pianist, that being our best hope for a route out of poverty. But my mother didn't transplant well, either. She was always homesick. So, when I graduated from high school at the age of sixteen, we tried to go "home." It was impossible to get to Leipzig, which was now in the German Democratic Republic (East Germany), so we settled for almost two years in Frankfurt on the Main. She sewed even longer hours there, at home, and I attended the music conservatory. She found that "you can't go home again"; I recognized the limits on my talent and my preference for reading Descartes rather than music theory. A failed suicide attempt on my mother's part settled the matter. We came back to New York.

Now I was eighteen and I yearned to be independent. I got a full-time job at Time-Life Inc. and enrolled in City College (flagship of The City University of New York) evening session, getting my BA seven years later, in 1960. CCNY's education was superb, and free to boot, easily equivalent to the elite education at the time enjoyed by some of my contemporary colleagues. I then became the lucky beneficiary of a spurt of educational funding, prompted by concerns that the Soviet-launched Sputnik (the first satellite in space) might put the United States to shame. This windfall subsidized my first four years at Columbia University, whence I emerged with a PhD in history in 1970. The dissertation research took me to Germany for a second time; with each stay, I culturally felt less German. I also took the opportunity to visit my uncle in Czechoslovakia and from his telling finally grasped the endless Jewish diasporic traveling of my family, which had moved through so many lands and whose survivors of the Holocaust were now scattered among so many more.

Reflecting now upon my experience at Columbia University, I know that it was then—and still is—a tough, competitive, relatively unfriendly place. Although we few women graduate students were viewed as oddities, I didn't recognize sex discrimination at the time. My advisors, Professors Rudolph Binion and Peter Gay, accorded me respect and encouragement and supported me for fellowships. Retrospectively, though, I can see some inequalities: not getting insider information about the history profession or being sponsored like a protégé for a career, as some of the male graduate students were. But the times were on my side: in the mid-sixties, The City University of New York was expanding, and I had no trouble at all finding a job, first at the Borough of Manhattan Community College and a year later, in 1967, at Brooklyn College, where I have remained ever since. It saddens me now to see CUNY so viciously cut back in funding, relegating many equally deserving new PhDs to underpaid work as adjunct professors.

While I felt fortunate to be hired at Brooklyn College, there I felt, for the first time, a clear difference in the way women and men were treated. The history department had many women in it, who seemed determined to keep some gender balance (though they would never have called it that), but men predominated. Although I developed good friendships with the two men hired with me, I was soon made to feel the lesser of the three new appointees. That was my first "Click!"[1]

Actually, the very first "Click!" came when my first husband, whom I had met in college and who joined me in graduate school, suddenly announced that I couldn't be a historian after all, because as a woman I couldn't possibly understand diplomacy and war. I think it was the first time in our marriage that I was rendered absolutely speechless with astonishment. But I never for a moment believed him. (We were divorced a few years later.) The teaching job was another matter entirely; there I *had* to take those attitudes seriously.

It was the sixties, after all. Passionately engaged in the antiwar movement, I was soon labeled as a "dangerous radical." A campus strike over the bombing of Cambodia closed our campus, along with 400 others nation-wide, and bitterly divided our department. Both my tenure and that of my second husband, whom I had met in the department, were endangered. The faculty union saved us, but each promotion afterward involved a battle.

With all that furor, I was stunned when one day, a secretary confided: "They're much angrier at you over the feminist organizing than over the antiwar activity." What was my crime? I had brought together women faculty at Brooklyn College to discuss our situation there. Why? Because I had heard too many "Clicks!"—on my job, in my second marriage, in the antiwar movement itself. And the second wave of feminism had brought them all together in one major insight: SEXISM was in my life and in the world.

Thanks to a consciousness-raising group organized by New York Radical Feminists, my consciousness had become so high that I aimed to raise the roof at Brooklyn College. I stuffed the mailboxes of all female faculty with a call to meet and soon we had a group of about 100, all raring to go and make change.

We divided into four task forces: one to develop a Women's Studies Program, another to create a service-oriented Women's Center, a third to set up an accessible daycare center, and a fourth to address job discrimination. Lilia Melani of the English Department came to these meetings and took on the last issue by organizing the CUNY Women's Coalition (CWC). That group shepherded a sex discrimination case through the courts for ten long years until we won a $7 million settlement and a three-year access to the courts via a Special Master who could subpoena records if necessary, to collect evidence of sex discrimination in promotions. Lilia still teaches at Brooklyn College and, with a loyal core contingent, has kept CWC going through scholarships, honorary awards, and intellectual "salons." CWC also has retained a watchdog function. Of course, the halving of full-time faculty at CUNY in recent years has not helped future generations of women scholars. Nor has financial starvation done much good for the Women's Studies Program and Women's Center, which had thrived for their first twenty years. And daycare is again undersupplied. It is time for a "third wave" of feminism to wash over academe. Still, we have made a difference. Thousands of women students have taken courses over the years in our Women's Studies program and in related electives in other departments; many of them have gone on to make a further difference in the world.

The same awakened feminist rage energized my historical work. Like so many others at the time, I suddenly wondered: *where* have the *women* been in history? Where have they been in German history, my field of specialization? I had written a Master's thesis on a nineteenth-century male utopian socialist and a PhD dissertation on a nineteenth-century male German historian. Now my mother's stories came to the forefront of my mind. Where was *she* in German history? I remembered "her" revolution, which had inaugurated the Weimar Republic, so quickly destroyed by Hitler. What changes had it brought? Those questions led me to research the history of women in the Weimar Republic, especially their work roles, looking for signs of emancipation and equality deeper than the well-known image of flappers. I found that the "new woman" was part myth, that a democratic constitution and female suffrage were insufficient, and that a more encompassing revolution—economic, social, and cultural—would have been necessary for women's emancipation. Feminism was a continuing revolution, not only in Germany. I saw *myself* in the flow of time.

Growing numbers of women historians simultaneously were exploring women's history in other countries, where they were finding the powerful and the victimized, individual leaders and mass actors, pioneers and keepers of tradition. I was in marvelous company. After a long childhood and youth of political isolation, I suddenly was surrounded by like-minded people. What a relief! Enter Gerda Lerner and Joan Kelly and Sandi Cooper and Blanche Cook. Gerda generously gave a free seminar at the Graduate Center of CUNY in which she taught some of us the ropes: how to create a panel for the American Historical Association (AHA), how to get published—the sorts of things our graduate school mentors should have taught us. In 1972, coming out of that seminar, Claudia Koonz, Sheila Tobias, and I gave possibly the first women's history panel at AHA, to a crowd of about 200, which fiercely debated our sobering findings. One thing led to another: Sandi took the three of us to a meeting of the original Berkshire Conference, where we presented the same material to a small group of about a dozen mostly retired women historians. We noticed an age gap between ourselves, then in our thirties, and members of the audience, in their seventies. The missing generation was an absent presence, making a statement about the historical profession! Out of this mini-Berks emerged a whole conference in women's history, which was held at Douglass College in 1971, with about 700 people attending. And so "the Berks" was born, which has since drawn thousands to its meetings, more than some annual meetings of AHA itself, though not surprisingly it always feels more intimate than the AHA.

About that time, Sandi and Blanche initiated me into the New York branch of the Coordinating Committee on Women in the Historical Profession (CCWHP). From there I entered the national, and became co-president in the year that the Conference Group on Women's History (CGWH) emerged as a separate organization. Now the two groups have merged again. But the really heady sensation of working with CCWHP came from transforming AHA: bringing more women onto panels, into its leadership (including the presidency), and winning acknowledgment of Women's History as a field. For me, it is personally rewarding now to chair the Committee on International Historical Activities, which prepares AHA's contribution to the quinquennial program of the International Congress of Historical Sciences, planned for Oslo in 2000.

Those early days were exhilarating! I would say, with Betty Friedan, they "changed my life." Feminist solidarity, if not always sisterly affection, was powerful! We felt the world was becoming ours. Becoming. . . .

Becoming Visible: Women in European History was born out of that feeling and out of the movements of the sixties and seventies. Specifically, it was born on the sidewalk in front of the Honeywell Corporation, where I was part of a group of antiwar faculty protesting the manufacture of antipersonnel bombs. These were particularly brutal weapons that targeted bodies to fill them with shrapnel, intending to wound rather than to kill, so that "the enemy" would be tied up with caretaking. The police left us sitting there for hours and I found myself chatting with Ruth Graham, one of the Queens College history faculty.

Both of us were developing courses in women's history and deploring the lack of a usable book. I had an idea for an anthology. Three days later, she had connected me with an interested publisher: Houghton Mifflin. Ruth was not interested in editing such a volume, so I persuaded my friend Claudia Koonz to join me. Together we rounded up innovative historians of women who could create a creditable chronological treatment. The first edition, which appeared in 1977, was a breathtaking adventure, but we expected to be overtaken soon. To our great surprise, no major competitor appeared and so the publisher requested a second revised edition, which came in 1987. Now a third, further revised edition has been published, co-edited by Susan Mosher Stuard, Merry Wiesner-Hanks, and myself. Claudia had other irons in the fire. But we are pleased and proud: we had no idea that the book would be so long in demand; we thought we were "only" pioneering.

All through the seventies, when this exciting research was going on, Joan Kelly was a beacon of light and encouragement to many of us: in CCWHP, both local and national, in study groups, and in friendship. Her essay in *Becoming Visible* was the one most frequently cited and reprinted. Late in the seventies, Joan and I joined forces with Amy Swerdlow to produce a book, *Families in Flux* (Feminist Press, 1980, 1989), which brought a feminist perspective to family history. The research for my chapter showed how much the literature on American families had slighted social class and how the anticommunist hysteria of the fifties had crippled intellectual work. Here my Marxist and my feminist perspectives merged in a quest for deeper understanding. I also joined the fifth subgroup of a mushrooming Marxist-Feminist study group, and then a smaller group that emerged out of it to read Marx's writings, especially *Capital.* Rosalind Petchesky has written eloquently about the difficulties we had in reconciling a class with a gender analysis,[2] but the discussions were very fruitful and led to a spate of published theorizing. However, in our enthusiastic hubris, we erred about the timing: we thought that both transformations could be realized in our very own lifetimes. I admit shamefacedly that at the time we did not pay enough attention to the ways in which race intersects with class and gender.

From the mid-seventies to the mid-eighties, I was also on the board of editors of *Science and Society*, the oldest independent Marxist journal in the world. My first published article, on a utopian socialist footnoted in Marx's *Communist Manifesto*, secured me an invitation to join the editorial board. There I got a second graduate education from probably the last of the Renaissance-like, well-rounded Marxists, an education based more on analysis and less on memorization than my first official one at Columbia University. One of my "mentors" was Annette Rubinstein, over twenty years my senior, whose lifelong ongoing political and intellectual engagement gives me even now the kind of perspective that sponsors optimism. Conversely, Annette credits me with bringing feminist perspectives to her and the journal. When the managing editor, David Goldway, a brilliant and generous man, introduced new editors to a fund-raising meeting of subscribers, he described me as working on "the woman question." I responded: "We're calling it the 'man question' now. It depends on who's asking the question." And soon the journal was publishing many more articles on women than before.

I also continued researching and writing in my area of specialization with another group I had co-founded in the early eighties with Atina Grossmann and Marion Kaplan, now formally recognized as the German Women's History Group. In this group, we meet monthly to read and critique each other's works in progress, with the result that it is cited in many of its members' publications. We have also rejuvenated ourselves with recent PhDs, some of whom we brought together in a conference years ago when they were still graduate students. At about the same time, we organized a conference with some of the male historians of German history, in the hope that they would integrate women's history into their work, and indeed, the younger ones have done so. We have also networked with women historians in Germany itself through international conferences on both sides of the Atlantic. Finally, we keep contact with feminist critics of German literature in annual interdisciplinary conferences.

Among the publications that emerged from this group was *When Biology Became Destiny: Women in Weimar and Nazi Germany* (Monthly Review Press, 1984), still a widely used anthology, which I co-edited with Atina Grossmann and Marion Kaplan. The contributors found alarming connections between attitudes and official positions toward women's issues, on the one hand, and the potential and reality of fascism, on the other. As we noted in our introduction, by the eighties, the tide had turned against the liberatory movements of the sixties and seventies, and the backlash gave cause for concern about right-wing reactionary trends.

One of the things I remember most fondly is the experience of working together on projects. I was no longer a political loner. In the sixties and seventies and early eighties, we were aware that scholarship is, after all, a group effort, no matter how many hours we spent alone writing. We knew that we built on each other's work, which we developed intellectually through argument and collective brainstorming, and that we shared the goal of bringing our hidden history to light. However, there was a personal price to pay for the wonderful world of women I had discovered and for the success that we enjoyed. My marriage slowly crumbled; by 1986 I was divorced again. This time, old friendships buoyed me through the process and have since been joined by wonderful new friendships. My partner now is a woman. I would never have been so free to make that change and that statement were it not for the Gay Liberation movement, of which I was not a part when it was mobilizing, though I certainly understood and appreciated its work.

The nineties remind me in some unfortunate ways of the privatistic, conventional, self-censoring, apolitical fifties, with the addition of a disempowering fin-de-siècle cynicism. While Women's Studies is hanging on by its fingernails at my home institution, Women's History is ensconced as a field and has attracted more historians than departments can employ nationwide. History, along with other liberal arts and social sciences, shrinks alongside business and technical fields. The corporate discourse afflicting academe, of bottom lines and downsizing, of productivity and student-"customers" is having a corrosive effect on good scholarship and good teaching, which may have a negative effect on the next generation. The harsh dog-eat-dog atmosphere has shaken feminist solidarity and sometimes masks the truth that scholarship *is* a collective cultural endeavor: "No woman is an island. . . ." And finally, the disarray of this century's socialist project has lamed Marxist movements. It is a bleak time, indeed, and not only for Marxist-feminist historians.

Still, as Susan B. Anthony insisted, "Failure is impossible." People do not surrender hard-won gains easily. Everywhere, there are signs of renewed mobilization against nearly daily assaults on human dignity. While LIBERATION was a word of promise for a seemingly near new world in the sixties and early seventies, it still remains a word of hope for the future. It is a goal, a process, and a historical agenda. Eduardo Galeano said it best in "Window on Utopia": "She's on the horizon. I go two steps closer, she moves two steps away. I walk ten steps and the horizon runs ten steps ahead. No matter how much I walk, I'll never reach her. What good is utopia? That's what: it's good for walking."

NOTES

1. "Click!" as a moment of truth was popularized by Jane O'Reilly in "The Housewife's Moment of Truth," in the first issue of *MS. Magazine*, Spring 1972, 54–59.

2. Rosalind Petchesky, "Dissolving the Hyphen: A Report on Marxist-Feminist Groups 1–5," in *Capitalist Patriarchy and the Case for Socialist Feminism*, ed. Zillah R. Eisenstein (New York: Monthly Review Press, 1979), 373–389.

KAREN OFFEN
7

GOING AGAINST THE GRAIN: THE MAKING OF AN INDEPENDENT SCHOLAR

Southern Idaho, where I was born and grew to adulthood, is a still sparsely settled frontier region on the western slopes of the Rockies. Until the twentieth century, the passage of humans had not much marked this land; lacking much of a recorded past, it was mostly known as a stopping place on the road to elsewhere. It boasts instead a magnificent, expansive landscape, with views of mountains nearly a hundred miles distant on a clear day. The town where I was raised, named after a local Indian chief, sits in a valley near the edge of a high semi-arid desert ringed by mountains and traversed by ancient lava flows, its fields of wheat and potatoes irrigated by water diverted from the sinewy Snake River as it descends from the Tetons to the Columbia River basin. It still seems an unlikely place to have spawned a historian.

As a young person I had no apparent vested interest in history, let alone European history, which has since become my lifelong passion. For years I have puzzled about how my life evolved as it did, and in particular about how its course ran against the grain, even of the profession I eventually entered. But until recently I never took the time to investigate it with the same care I gave to my historical research. When I did begin to evaluate it, however, I recognized that—as Carolyn Steedman has pointed out—"specificity of place and politics has to be reckoned with in making an account of anybody's life, and their use of their own past."[1]

Only in retrospect has it become clear that in this place without a past I was

Karen Offen. Photo by Carol Ivie.

searching for a context. Only in retrospect did I discover that despite—or perhaps because of—my Idaho origins, historical scholarship was meant to be my vocation and exploring European women's history my life work. Only in hindsight does it make sense that "gendering" European history, or undertaking a comparative historical analysis of European feminisms, would become my destiny. The centrality of French culture to my interests, however, seems even more unpredictable than my overall fascination with things European.

My family of birth, though of very mixed northern "European" background, has no French roots whatsoever. Despite a degree of superficial homogeneity, problems of identity puzzled me, and at one point I became quite interested in genealogy and ancestor tracking. What I discovered was a long series of displacements, of wanderlust and searches for opportunity, accompanied by sporadic changes of religion and occupation. My ancestors came from England, Scotland, Germany, Norway, and Sweden. My male forebears included farmers, preachers, artisans and craftsmen, bakers, cooks, and lawyers—not a factory worker or a union member among them. My female forebears were, almost without exception, homemakers and, sometimes, teachers.

Especially significant, however, is the fact that my mother and father both were raised by women born in Scandinavia. Their families subsequently migrated to America. My grandmothers had a very limited formal education, but each determined to shed her old culture, do what it took to acquire the proverbial American "melting-pot" identity, and provide unprecedented opportunities to her children. Amid today's concerns about identities and subalternity in a postcolonial, ostensibly postmodern world, it is worth considering the effect of this marginally Americanized heritage, even within the boundaries of "white" European provenance, on a young person growing up in a nuclear family during the 1940s and 1950s in the sprawling, sparsely and recently populated state of Idaho. There women had voted since 1896 and self-made men abounded. Few individuals in Idaho could have afforded Freudian analysis, had the opportunity been available. In Idaho, what Betty Friedan referred to in 1963 as "the problem that had no name" had little meaning for most women. There were all too many demands on women's time and energy to allow them to contemplate, much less confront, their dissatisfaction.

Even before I had discovered these aspects of my own background, and had concluded that such a heritage effectively freed me to claim whatever identity I chose, I had become fascinated by things European. Why Europe? Because for so long Europe had been "Continent No. 1" (as a recent *New York Times Book Review* title put it), the shaper of the destiny of the modern world. Born just after the outbreak of World War II, as a child I was steeped in the reflected turbulence of European politics. I was particularly intrigued by France and French culture, which I discovered through maps, picture-books, and

Life magazine; in 1944, following the Allied forces' invasion of Normandy, I found out that France was the country shaped like a teapot; Italy was a boot. I followed the news of Allied military efforts to stop Nazi aggression even as I learned about my own uncle's participation in US Navy efforts to combat the Japanese in the faraway islands of the Pacific. My European focus was enriched by fascinating fairy tales, storybook illustrations of castles and Burgundian princesses, and reinforced by eight years of ballet classes (all that strange terminology—jeté, plié, sauté, pirouette), accompanied by the evocative music of the nineteenth century (roughly Mozart to Mahler), to which I danced and which I later played on the piano. On my bedroom wall hung a reproduction of an 1896 painting of a young girl by the French artist William Bouguereau, the significance of which I only recognized years later when I encountered the original in a museum. This girl's eyes directly engaged the viewer—though young, she seemed confident, sure of herself. I liked looking back at her and I hoped that someday she would share her secrets with me.

As a child of wartime, I also became intrigued by geopolitics and "government," by how the great abstractions of "America" and "nation" and "victory" related to my life. My hometown was a transportation center located strategically at the mouth of a valley that led from Utah and the Great Salt Lake to the Snake River plain. The Union Pacific railroad, in particular, had attracted a considerable number of immigrant workers and their families from southern Europe and the American south and midwest. This influx, plus the nearby Bannock-Shoshone inhabitants of the Fort Hall Indian reservation and our local Chinese restaurateurs, provided a rich sense of what we now call "diversity." The local culture was dominantly Mormon (and benevolently patriarchal), but since my father resisted the Church's efforts to reclaim him and us, I was never really part of it; like my Greek Orthodox, Irish Catholic, and Jewish friends (a smattering of each), I learned what it meant to be part of a minority. Even "mainstream" Protestants were a minority in my hometown. Consequently, many of us banded together across denominational and cultural lines. In a town that had only one high school, where everyone was more or less "new," and where socioeconomic differences were not that great, "class" did not seem to be a particularly relevant concern. Social mobility was fluid, except with respect to the small settlement of Black families (railroad porters and waiters) and reservation Indians, though efforts were made by groups such as the Camp Fire Girls and Girl Scouts, as well as in the schools, to draw them in. My "little sister" in junior high school was a talented Black girl and we tried to welcome others like her at summer camp. Ethnicity, religion, work ethic, and most importantly, behavior (i.e., for girls, whether one was "fast" or not) were the significant factors in our social structure. Education was demonstrably the route to social advancement—and to moving on to more cosmopolitan environs. Southern Idaho held few professional opportunities for young women or young men; indeed, Idaho in those days exported much of its best young talent. Many college graduates moved out of state, to Salt Lake City, to Denver, to Seattle, to Portland, to San Francisco or Los Angeles.

In my family, daughters were considered wonderful; it was an article of faith that my younger sister and I should go to college. My father (though not his brothers) was college-educated and my mother, my aunt, and their two aunts held college degrees. I never had any notion that because I was a girl I could not accomplish anything I set out to do. I had, after all, become an avid reader of Wonder Woman comics and of Nancy Drew mysteries. I recognized from a very early age that it was silly to hide one's talent or sacrifice one's aspirations in order to attract local guys who were no more accomplished (often less so) than oneself. As my aunt used to say (with some sarcasm), "It's easy to get married—unless you're particular!" I learned to have faith in myself and my abilities; I was "grounded" and I had big plans. I cultivated excellence. I became more interested in succeeding within the system than in attempting to topple it—I learned that significant change was possible by working from within.

That self-confidence and grounding, combined with hard work, paid off by the time I was seventeen. I signed up for the hardest courses, reveled in over-achievement, and had a good time. I gained recognition as high school co-valedictorian in a class of nearly 400, a National Merit and General Motors Scholar, Betty Crocker Future Homemaker of the Year (based on a multiple-choice exam, not on course work), an accomplished seamstress and pianist, as well as a highly competitive golfer. I had also earned distinction as a Torchbearer in Social Leadership, the highest rank in the Camp Fire Girls. This organization significantly reinforced my notion that womanhood was a worthy state, that one should become the best woman one could be, without becoming a counterfeit man, as in the Girl Scout vision of that time. (This was the 1950s girls' organization version of the more recent debate over "equality vs. difference" and "equality-in-difference.") It may have been the fifties, but I did not share Wini Breines's sense of being "young, white, and miserable."[2] Even in retrospect, the fifties in southern Idaho remain in memory a mostly positive experience. Although some local residents viewed kindergarten programs and school lunches as part of a Communist plot to destroy the American way of life (this puzzled me greatly), I didn't find the local environment or culture overwhelmingly oppressive. Perhaps I didn't really believe it was relevant to my future. Besides, I could always take off on my bicycle or escape, with the help of an automobile, to the forest or take the train to some other interesting place. I had a driver's license (though not the keys to the car) at the age of fourteen, and that license brought freedom of a sort. Primarily refusing to learn either to play bridge or to conjugate Latin verbs marked my adolescent rebellion. Bridge, I concluded (observing my mother and her friends), sucked up too much valuable time. Latin, I insisted, was a dead language, and I wanted to learn languages—languages like Spanish, French, Italian, and maybe even German—that other people actually spoke. I sought out the several European exchange students that came to our high school; one of them became a lifelong friend.

Unlike some other gifted young Idahoans, I did not go east to college on a scholarship, nor did I accept (much to the consternation of the guidance counselors) admission to Stanford as an undergraduate; I replied to the effect that I might still like to come for graduate school (which I eventually did). Instead, I went north—as had my mother and father—to the University of Idaho, in Moscow, intending to major in math and science and to join a sorority. It was 1957, the era of Sputnik; America needed good scientists. After two years of feeling alienated by being one of the very few young women in chemistry and in engineering physics, and having in the meantime studied French and taken a stimulating elective course in the history of western civilization taught by Charles LeGuin, the husband of feminist science fiction writer Ursula LeGuin, I abruptly changed my major to history. This choice I have never regretted (even though the LeGuins left Moscow for Portland) because Professors Robert Harris and Fred Winkler provided a thorough introduction to the intricacies of European political, intellectual, diplomatic, and cultural history, and William S. Greever provided the necessary American history background. To me history seemed to be the queen of the sciences, inviting, encompassing, infinite . . . and potentially useful. Like a ravenous puppy, I devoured historical knowledge as it was then constituted. I didn't realize at the time that it was a field of knowledge that included few women in its accounts, or that boasted even fewer women experts; in fact, I never thought to ask.

Looking back on that experience, I realize that nowhere in the history curriculum did I encounter women's history, much less works by women historians. During my senior year, however, a friend introduced me to J. Christopher Herold's *Mistress to an Age: A Life of Madame de Staël* (1958), which I found electrifying (in retrospect I like the book far less than more recent feminist interpretations). As an undergraduate, I did encounter women's issues, notably when I discovered in the university library a copy of a 1920s dual edition of Mary Wollstonecraft's *Vindication of the Rights of Woman* (1791) and John Stuart Mill's *The Subjection of Women* (1869). I also purchased in the bookstore the now-notorious antifeminist classic, Lundberg and Farnham's *Modern Woman: The Lost Sex* (1947). It had not occurred to me that "women" might be "one of modern civilization's major unsolved problems," and I found that book extremely puzzling.[3] Not long after, I encountered Margaret Mead, who came to speak at our university during my senior year. She made an enormous impression on me; she was vigorous, she was intellectually sharp, but more importantly, she seemed wise. She had carved out an unorthodox though highly successful career in anthropology. She was one of those people who had taken charge of her own life and made it work. Although I don't even remember whether I spoke to her afterwards, she became a silent mentor and a role model.

Whereas many of my classmates graduated, married, and bore children (not always in that order), I left Idaho in 1961 for France on a Fulbright scholarship. Although I had once been briefly in New York, I never set foot in Boston or Washington, DC, or any other Atlantic seaboard city, until after I had been thoroughly and profoundly marked by Europe. In later years, when I discovered that so many of my colleagues in history had attended eastern women's colleges, or had dense undergraduate networks from other prestigious eastern schools to draw on, or had friendships that dated back to their joint involvement in Students for a Democratic Society (SDS was considered extremely subversive on our campus), I was a bit envious. With the notable exception of Laurel Thatcher Ulrich, who is also from southern Idaho but whom I met only decades later, very few Idahoans have become professional historians, much less of societies outside the US. There was no local network to rely on for emotional or intellectual support; it seemed clear that I would have to build my own.

After a year of study in France and travel throughout Europe (in the course of which I read Simone de Beauvoir's *The Second Sex*, finding it nearly as puzzling as *Modern Woman: The Lost Sex*), I returned by sea through the Panama Canal to northern California. Then I entered graduate school in history at Stanford University, with the support of a few small fellowships and part-time employment as a residence assistant in a small, all-woman dorm. Some of the undergraduates from that dorm went off to Mississippi to work for the civil rights movement; another spent the summer in Vietnam. They were a worldly, well-connected, yet amazingly starry-eyed crew. I wondered why it was that they didn't deploy their energies on behalf of justice and freedom locally.

The Stanford history department experience quickly issued a wake-up call to my already pronounced but unnamed feminist sensibilities. There I learned more than I cared to know about sexism in the historical profession, about the faculty bathroom that was exclusively male terrain, and about the departmental expectation that women were not supposed to finish their PhDs or teach in universities. Instead, the graduate advisor, the distinguished diplomatic historian Thomas A. Bailey, recommended to us master's degrees and possibly junior college teaching. Then I decided, a mere master's degree candidate, to challenge this fate by applying for the PhD program and, somewhat to my surprise, I was accepted and later accorded a small fellowship.

After meeting (on a ski-lift at Squaw Valley) and marrying George Offen (who found smart women attractive) in 1965, I learned first-hand about hiring discrimination against married women. I applied for a Western Civ teaching position at Stanford while finishing my dissertation and was turned down because—it was argued—both the female applicants that year were married, and presumably didn't "need" the jobs. During an interview for a one-year fill-in position at a state college, when I was expecting our first child, I learned of the extent to which one's personal life could become one's potential employer's business. "Having it all"—both career and family, that is—was turning out to be a problem. Little did I know what lay ahead.

How does a woman historian with family obligations organize a career? That was my dilemma in 1971, when women constituted only 13 percent of PhDs in history nationally and the "second wave" women's movement was just getting underway. I actually finished my degree in the fall of 1970, after typing my own dissertation—following five years' work researching and writing up "The Political Career of Paul de Cassagnac." My husband, a former Air Force officer who had returned to graduate school at Stanford while I worked on my thesis, got active in protests against the war in Vietnam: I was too preoccupied. When *Time* magazine published its cover story on Kate Millett's *Sexual Politics* in July 1970, I was recovering from morning sickness; in late August, when New York City threw a grand parade honoring the fiftieth anniversary of women's suffrage in America, I was attempting to finish typing my thesis in California. In September or October, George and I threw a party to celebrate my degree and also announce that we were expecting a child. You can guess which event our guests found most compelling. I was miffed about that for months. I insisted on taking the baby to the graduation ceremonies in June 1971. When, some months later, the Stanford chapter of NOW began to organize, nobody thought it was funny when as a fund-raising idea, I suggested we should bake and sell "gender rolls."

By the mid-1970s I was the mother of two delightful and demanding preschool daughters. In terms of "career opportunities," I was geographically restricted due partly to my husband's graduate study and subsequent employment and partly to our mutual decision to remain together in the highly desirable San Francisco Bay Area, blessed as it was not only with a fine climate and great cultural advantages but also with two outstanding research libraries. We did not view commuter marriage as a desirable option. I did not "have" to work, since my husband had exchanged his post-PhD options in academic engineering for a very good job in industry. This was fortunate indeed, given that in the early 1970s there were virtually no entry-level history teaching positions available in our area. Even poorly paid part-time positions were few and far between. In contrast to some of my committed socialist colleagues, I never believed that paid employment was the only "real" work this world offered, nor was it the only means by which a woman could maintain a degree of independence in marriage. After all, California was and is a community property state, and there was so much other important work to be done. George and I saw our marriage as a partnership, to which each brought special qualities. I did become active as a parent volunteer in the schools as well as on behalf of women in the historical profession, through my work with the Coordinating Committee on Women in the Historical Profession (CCWHP) and the Western Association of Women Historians (WAWH), both of which—thanks to Linda Kerber's fortuitous introduction—threw me a professional lifeline when I needed one most.

Throughout the 1970s (1972 through 1977) I was especially active in CCWHP, both as membership secretary and then as secretary-treasurer, and began to get acquainted with many other wonderful women historians at regional and national meetings. Taking over from Berenice Carroll and Hilda Smith, and collaborating closely with Jordy Bell and Sandi Cooper, I labored tirelessly to keep the growing membership list up to date (George and I keypunched every line in those early days of computerized mailing labels), the dues coming into the treasury to pay for printing the newsletters, and the newsletter sent speedily to members by first-class mail. We kept a watchful eye on the status of women in the historical profession, pushed for more women presenters at conferences, and promoted women's history whenever and however we could, working both with the regional associations and pressuring the American Historical Association (AHA) through its Committee on the Status of Women. When I became a member of that committee in 1983–86, I grew to appreciate the important role of CCWHP and the Conference Group on Women's History (CGWH) in advancing women's visibility within AHA. Further assignments, as chair of the AHA Committee on International Historical Activities and American representative to the International Committee on the Historical Sciences (ICHS), as a founder and officer of the International Federation for Research in Women's History (IFRWH) (1987–95), and as president of the WAWH (1991–93) meant that I devoted countless hours during nearly twenty years to professional service activities on behalf of women historians and women's history and for the advancement of historical understanding.[4] Working with scholar-activists such as Linda Levy Peck, Alice Kessler-Harris, Mary Beth Norton, Nancy Lyman Roelker, Natalie Zemon Davis, and Noralee Frankel provided invigorating stimulation and collegiality.

Although I have never held a full-time or tenured faculty appointment, I had already begun in the early 1970s to explore women's and gender history. With Doris Meadows, I developed and taught (without pay) the first course offered at Stanford (1972) on women in western civilization; we covered the Greeks to the twentieth century in ten weeks! The new women's movement was underway, and women's issues were at the forefront of my consciousness; no "consciousness-raising group" seemed necessary, and I certainly didn't have the time to attend one. Trained in the political and intellectual history of Europe, after my PhD I moved laterally into women's history, the comparative history of feminism, and gender analysis, retraining myself as I went along but still retaining my initial interests, even while formulating new approaches to them. In contrast to many of my contemporaries, I came to women's history neither through social history nor through socialist politics, but through a more traditional historical training, coupled with real-life issues. Indeed, the "fit" that developed in my career as a historian between my own life choices and my historical and current interests became increasingly seamless. I found historical knowledge about women's lives exceedingly useful for addressing contemporary problems, both personal and political. The merger felt intellectually and emotionally satisfying; as I learned more, I felt less and less alone and increasingly confident that I had made appropriate choices.

Thus, perhaps with more courage than good sense, I decided to continue with my research, taking things a year at a time. Women's history became my means of addressing women's issues and women historians became my extended network. I finally was finding a context that "fit." I retrained myself in demographic and family history, developed expertise in the politics of population and nationalism, and slowly carved out an unorthodox but highly satisfying career as an independent scholar, exploring new opportunities as they arose. Many of these opportunities emerged in consequence of my affiliation, since 1978, with the Institute for Research on Women and Gender (founded as the Center for Research on Women) at Stanford University, where I am now a Senior Scholar.

No one was speaking of alternative careers in the early 1970s, but only of "unemployment" for scholar-teachers. But, truth be told, with a whole set of new interests, a husband, a household to manage, and two little children, I did not feel "unemployed." "Overwhelmed" might have been a more appropriate descriptor. Though I did try briefly to interest publishers in my dissertation, I did not succeed in publishing it in book form for nearly twenty years; indeed, I collected rejection letters from some of the most distinguished university presses in America.[5] Nor indeed did I publish much of anything else for nearly ten years after completing the PhD. For most historians on an academic career ladder—"inside the clockwork of male careers," as Arlie Hochschild put it so eloquently in 1975—this behavior would doubtless have provided the proverbial "kiss of death" in a fight for tenure.[6] It was probably a good thing that I wasn't on the tenure track, since I had inadvertently violated the unwritten rules of professional sequencing.

Having the flexibility to design one's own trajectory can, however, be advantageous, and this was particularly true with regard to publishing. I solicited, edited, and published in 1977 an early path-breaking collection of articles on French women's history as part of a little-known French history journal on microfiche, *Third Republic/Troisième République*. My first two "real" books were not only about women, but were co-authored, co-edited, collaborative, woman-centered interpretative documentary works: *Victorian Women: A Documentary Account of Women's Lives in Nineteenth-Century England, France, and the United States* (Stanford University Press, 1981), with an initial team of six co-author/editors, including my two co-editors, Erna Olafson Hellerstein and Leslie Parker Hume, and original team members Estelle Freedman, Barbara Gelpi, and Marilyn Yalom; and *Women, the Family, and Freedom: The Debate in Documents, 1750–1950* (2 vols., Stanford University Press, 1983), with my colleague at Stanford, Susan Groag Bell. These documentary volumes developed in response to pressing educational needs and to unusual opportunities. The National Endowment for the Humanities (NEH) had provided the first with substantial funding as part of a Stanford course-development initiative, while the second, a pioneering work in developing a dialogical, comparative feminist history, was entirely Susan's and my joint venture, funded from our own pockets and drawing on the voluntary contributions of documents and suggestions from many colleagues. Both collections are still used extensively for college teaching and, in the case of *Women, the Family, and Freedom*, have gained wide visibility as core texts for a series of four Summer Seminars for College Teachers, funded by the NEH, and held at Stanford in the 1980s and 1990s in cooperation with the history department. I think Susan and I were among the first independent scholars to receive a grant from NEH, but we would not even have known about the opportunity to direct such seminars had we not been fortuitously team-teaching a one-quarter long undergraduate course in the Stanford history department.

In 1987 I published a second collection of articles on women's history by other scholars, this time as a special issue of the *History of European Ideas* (vol. 8, nos. 4–5). My more "conventional" solo articles and monograph (based on the 1971 dissertation) only appeared in the interstices of these works, and my other two "solo" book manuscripts only now are reaching completion because of massive interruptions.[7] In the late 1980s, following our founding conference at Bellagio for the International Federation for Research in Women's History, I turned again to co-editing a historiographical collection, *Writing Women's History: International Perspectives* (co-published by Macmillan and Indiana University Press, 1991), which because of the rapid growth in the field needed to be completed and published quickly, while the assessments were fresh and could be of most use to others.

With respect to publication choices, questions of "what is marketable" for one's personal career advancement do not always generate the same answers as questions of "what is needed" for the field, or what is most useful for readers. I never will forget the wonderful moment when a reader of *Victorian Women*, who had obtained my telephone number from our publisher, called to tell me that our collection had changed her life! From that moment on, she had decided to leave her office job, to go back to school, and dedicate herself to women's studies. What an affirmation of the power of those remarkable texts, transmitted to this reader by our historical project! How many authors of learned monographs or scholarly articles have ever experienced such validating feedback?

There is also the question of how to attribute credit. Unless one adopts a joint pseudonym, usually authorship is attributed according to alphabetical order, and the last names get abbreviated to "et al." In co-edited or multi-authored volumes, it is thus often difficult for outsiders to evaluate individual contributions, or to distinguish who did what, a question that is ultimately unanswerable when the joint authorial collaboration has been tight, as it was in both documentary volumes, where multiple minds did, in fact, become one. And in edited collections of articles, it is often impossible for anyone other than the editor and individual authors to know just how much effort each put into refining and producing the final versions. Editorial work, another form of collaborative work, is a highly necessary yet virtually invisible and unappreciated form of intellectual endeavor.

This somewhat inadvertent publication sequence has had consequences for my own career and my one-time hopes of reentering academic life as a teacher and trainer of younger historians, consequences that I now am only beginning to acknowledge. In the late 1990s, competition for the few senior academic positions that do materialize from time to time has been so tight and so bound by conventional expectations and the perversities of committee compromises that my path, which followed its own logic at each turning point, looks retrospectively maverick, if not downright foolhardy. In a system that wants in lockstep "the book" and the big articles published in the "right places," with the expectation that every contribution should "alter the paradigm" and that one should have a lengthy track record in teaching and/or academic administration, my resumé does not conform—which is not to say that my contributions have not made a difference in shifting scholarly paradigms and, indeed, in expanding our overall comprehension of European history from a gendered perspective.

Nearly thirty years have passed since I obtained the PhD in history. Since then I have enjoyed an NEH fellowship, a Rockefeller, and a Guggenheim, as well as other honors and awards, invitations to join advisory editorial boards throughout the world, and opportunities to referee book and article manuscripts and to review published works. I have perhaps helped to redefine what it means to be a professional historian, one who has not taken the conventional route. My current projects, which build out of everything I have done to date, aim both to reformulate the writing of French history by placing the woman question at the core of political, intellectual, and cultural history, and to produce a comprehensive history of European feminism from 1700 to 1950. I have acquired a wonderful set of friends and colleagues, with similar interests. I have been blessed with opportunities to travel the world telling of the new insights that we owe to women's history and to the application of gender analysis to all historical events. But the intellectual trajectory itself is perhaps more interesting than any mere list of achievements. To trace this trajectory requires returning again to the early 1970s, when, seeking a new project after Cassagnac, I began to revisit the place and period I knew best, late-nineteenth-century France, asking whether the French had ever experienced a movement for women's emancipation.

What I found was "the woman question" and material for a life's investigative work. Since that time I totally reoriented my research focus by posing questions seldom raised in academia before the 1970s: namely, how does our understanding of history differ when we include the experiences of women as well as those of men? What happens to our vision of the past when gender becomes a central concern for historical analysis? Such questions—I am certainly not the only one who has posed them—must be asked not solely in the domain of social history, where they were posed initially, but in political and intellectual history as well. I found personal empowerment in searching for answers to these questions. Women's history and gender analysis, it seemed, could actually make a difference in people's lives.

Surprising as it may seem, my earlier work on Cassagnac enhanced my ability to grapple successfully with these new issues. He was a nineteenth-century Catholic authoritarian monarchist, whose self-appointed political mission was to save France from liberals and secular republicans. By the norms of republican historiography, his story was that of an adversary and a "loser." As I painstakingly reconstructed Cassagnac's story and familiarized myself with his mental world, entering the debate between him and his adversaries, I learned to understand both the authoritarian and liberal perspectives on a deeper level and to appreciate how they mutually constructed one another. I began to see how such a dialogic understanding of the unfolding conflict between these two camps could be useful for addressing other issues, in particular, the debate over the relationship between the sexes.

What else have I learned? Perhaps this question can best be answered by a statement of my aims and goals as an historian. It is my conviction that the careful historical investigation can illuminate and help resolve some of our current perplexities concerning gender and equality. My 1988 article, "Defining Feminism: A Comparative Historical Approach," and a 1998 article, "Reclaiming the Enlightenment for Feminism," offer proof of this claim.[8] Even as we ask new questions of the past and seek new documentation with which to answer them, however, the challenge to historians and to the historical profession remains constant: to make the past come alive—to the extent that evidence and interpretation will permit, and it is important to insist that we *can* know a great deal, especially regarding the last few centuries, and especially about the European past (which furnishes us with extremely rich source material)—and to alert readers to the relevance of past debates and choices to our present and our future.

As historians, our dialogue is not only with the past per se but with competing discourses and choices made within the past, with roads not taken as well as those that were. To give new life to these past debates, and to draw wisdom and insight from them, we must not allow the biases or fads of our own times or the theory of the moment to obscure evidence. My new motto is: Ask not what feminist theory can do for history but what history can do for feminist theory. We must deliberately try to transcend present-mindedness. That means listening attentively to what new evidence (and re-readings of old evidence and interpretations of that evidence) can tell us. We must immerse ourselves in the worldview of our subjects and relive events from our subjects' perspective. We must appreciate the context of their daily struggles and concerns, even as we attempt to evaluate and judge their activities and ideas with benefit of hindsight. My goal as a historian is to meet this challenge, and to communicate my findings to readers in a manner that stimulates them both intellectually and emotionally. By incorporating both sexes and gender analysis into historical inquiry, and by carefully practicing the craft of historical research, I seek to transform and revitalize our vision of European history and to transmit a richer, more useable historical memory to future generations.

One of my favorite nineteenth-century French feminists, Jenny P. d'Héricourt, wrote in 1860 that "I cannot write otherwise than as a woman, since I have the honor to be a woman."[9] I heartily adhere to her view. Far from wishing to "deconstruct" the category "woman" (or, for that matter, to devalue the significance of "sex") I seek to reclaim it and to insist upon its rich complexity and value, both in contemporary life and in matters historical. It is also important to insist on the potential for partnership between women and men—restoring a balance of power between the sexes—as a historic and ever relevant feminist goal. Partnership between the sexes is, after all, the *real* revolution.

"Like man, woman is called to explore the domain of history," wrote another of my nineteenth-century favorites, "Henriette, artiste," during the French revolution of 1848. "As in all other things, there is room for both [sexes] and both also have differing and specific attributes. . . . For women, history is a lie . . . the truth will only appear once feminine observation and intelligence enter into it and, specifically, link it to women's interests."[10] Without knowing about Henriette, our generation of women historians has been able to bring this "observation and intelligence" into the practice and teaching of history since the 1970s, thus realizing and institutionalizing a perspective that in 1848 was still visionary. I am pleased to have been part of this effort, and particularly to have been able to contribute to the important work of CCWHP. I trust that our successors will be able to build even more extensively and astutely on the sturdy foundations that are now in place. I hope, too, that they will succeed in assuring that our findings and publications are not consigned to library storage facilities but are passed on lovingly to young women and men not only in the US and Europe, but throughout the world.

NOTES

1. Carolyn Kay Steedman, *Landscape for a Good Woman* (New Brunswick: Rutgers Univ. Press, 1987), 6.

2. Wini Breines, *Young, White and Miserable: Growing Up Female in the Fifties* (Boston: Beacon Press, 1992); but see also Myra Dinnerstein, *Women Between Two Worlds: Midlife Reflections on Work and Family* (Philadelphia: Temple Univ. Press, 1992).

3. Ferdinand Lundberg and Marynia F. Farnham, MD, *Modern Woman: The Lost Sex* (New York: Grosset and Dunlap, 1947), 1.

4. The activities of these groups, and the contributions of a multitude of individuals to their functioning, are best grasped through the range of essays in this book, through the series of published organizational newsletters, and through the pertinent commemorative publications assembled by Hilda Smith (for CCWHP-CGWH). For WAWH, see the accounts compiled by Peggy Renner in 1995. Judith P. Zinsser's account in *History and Feminism: A Glass Half Full* (New York: Twayne Publishers, 1993) does not do justice to the contributions of either organization. For IFRWH, see especially *Writing Women's History: International Perspectives*, ed. Karen Offen, Ruth Roach Pierson, and Jane Rendall (Bloomington: Indiana Univ. Press, 1991) and the IFRWH newsletters, which are available by subscription through national representatives. For additional comments, see my short articles "Independent Scholarship and Women's History," *The Forum* (The Official Publication of Mortar Board, Inc.), vol. 24, no. 1 (1993), and in *The CCWH Newsletter*, vol. 27, no. 2 (May 1996), 9–13.

5. It finally appeared as *Paul de Cassagnac and the Authoritarian Tradition in Nineteenth-Century France* (New York and London: Garland Publishing, Inc., 1991).

6. Arlie Russell Hochschild, "Inside the Clockwork of Male Careers," in *Women and the Power to Change*, ed. Florence Howe (New York: McGraw-Hill, 1975), 47–80.

7. In particular, "Depopulation, Nationalism, and Feminism in Fin-de-siècle France," *American Historical Review,* 89, no. 3 (1984), 648–76, and "Liberty, Equality, and Justice for Women: The Theory and Practice of Feminism in Nineteenth-Century Europe," in *Becoming Visible: Women in European History*, ed. Renate Bridenthal, Claudia Koonz, and Susan Mosher Stuard (Boston: Houghton-Mifflin, 1987), 335–73. The first of the two books, *European Feminism(s), 1700–1950*, will be published in 1999 by Stanford University Press. The second, "The Woman Question in Modern France," is still underway.

8. "Defining Feminism: A Comparative Historical Approach" was first published in *Signs: Journal of Women in Culture and Society*, 14 (Fall 1988), 119–57. Since then it has been translated into French, German, Spanish, Italian, and Japanese and anthologized in *Beyond Equality and Difference*, ed. Gisela Bock and Susan James (London: Routledge, 1992). In this article I proposed the notions of "relational" and "individualist" feminisms, seen as distinct argumentative approaches that point to differing sociopolitical solutions to the "woman question." For further discussion of the issues raised, see my subsequent articles, "Feminism and Sexual Difference in Historical Perspective," in *Theoretical Perspectives on Sexual Difference*, ed. Deborah Rhode (New Haven: Yale University Press, 1990), 13–20, 266–67, and "Reflections on National Specificities in Continental European Feminisms," *U(niversity) C(ollege) Galway Women's Studies Centre Review*, III (1995), 53–61. "Reclaiming the Enlightenment for Feminism" appears in *Perspectives on Feminist Political Thought in European History: From the Middle Ages to the Present*, ed. Tjitske Akkerman and Siep Stuurman (London and New York: Routledge, 1998), 85–103.

9. Jenny P. d'Héricourt, *A Woman's Philosophy of Woman, or Woman Affranchised: An Answer to Michelet, Proudhon, Girardin, Legouvé, Comte and Other Modern Innovators* (New York: Carleton, 1864; originally published in French, 1860. Reprinted 1981 by Hyperion Press, Westport, Conn.).

10. Henriette, artiste, in *La Voix des femmes*, no. 28 (20 April 1848), 2–3; as translated by Karen Offen in "'What! Such Things Have Happened and No Women Were Taught about Them': A Nineteenth-Century French Woman's View of the Importance of Women's History," *Journal of Women's History* 9 (Summer 1997), 147–53.

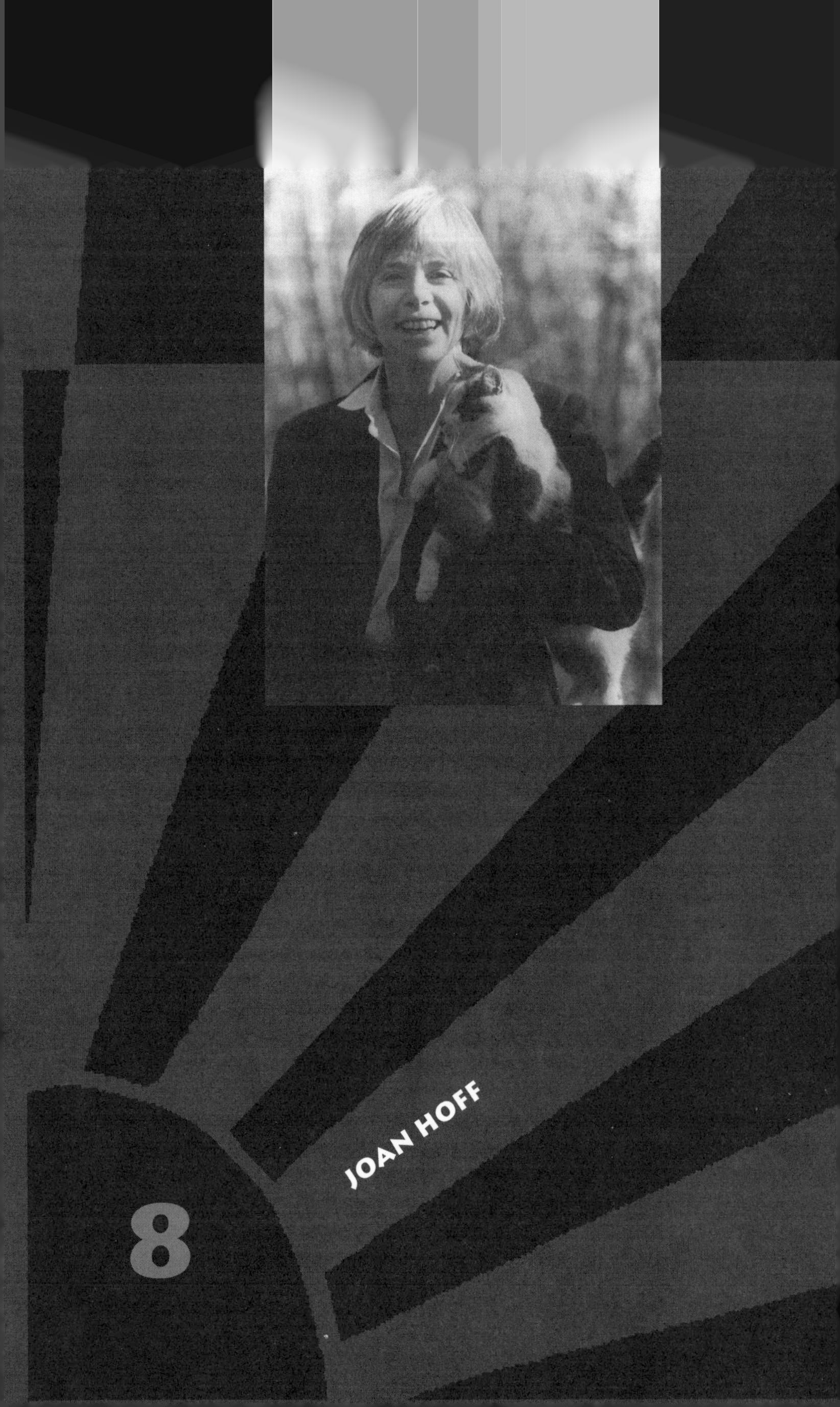
JOAN HOFF
8

REASSERTION OF PATRIARCHY AT THE END OF THE TWENTIETH CENTURY

BUTTE IS IN THE EYE OF THE BEHOLDER

Some of my earliest memories from grade school are walking the mile or so from home and seeing ransacked houses with broken windows and furniture strewn in their yards. Yet I did not grow up in an urban ghetto. This was Butte, Montana—a mining town that suffered from union strikes again and again after World War II, even as the membership in the mining unions declined.[1] In the 1950s this was especially true, as the underground mines were petering out and the Anaconda Copper Mining Company began closing them down as it invested in cheaper open-pit mining. This endeavor finally devoured vast ethnic segments of the city and became known as the Berkeley Pit. Unlike coal mine strikes, where nonstriking workers went home at night, nonstriking copper mining workers or scabs stayed in the mine yards for the duration of each labor/management dispute. This left the homes of the nonstriking workers vulnerable to attack by striking union members, who wreaked havoc upon the unguarded homes of the scabs.

I grew up taking this twice-scarred landscape for granted: scarred once by the Anaconda Company's pollution of the environment, and scarred again by its abuse of the human environment ravaged by unhealthy working conditions and low pay. We didn't feel sorry for those in the ransacked homes of the scabs. In fact, we didn't play with the kids from those houses; my parents didn't speak to their parents—even when they were relatives. Scabs were at risk in bars and

Joan Hoff. Photo by Marian Yeates.

public gatherings for years after they refused to strike. To make matters worse, those of us who lived in the poor section of town called the Flats disliked each other. The Flats spread out along the valley floor below the foothills of the Continental Divide. Everything of value was situated in the foothills, i.e., the mines, the business district, and mansions of the wealthy. Sharing the heights were early immigrant groups. The leftovers and latecomer emigrants spilled out onto the Flats. There was no place for us on the hill and so we hated the hill and we hated each other. In contrast to many middle-class historians (and movie directors) who deal with working-class life, as I reflect on my childhood from the perspective of 1998, I do not think that such an experience is particularly enlightening except in harshest terms of the survival of the fittest. And I believe that is why no Butte native with a working-class, immigrant background has written about growing up on the Flats.[2]

Unlike the separate ethnic groups on the hill—consisting of German, Italian, Jewish, Irish, English, Chinese, Finnish and other early immigrants who had carved out their own separate neighborhoods—those of us on the Flats represented a mix of turn-of-the-century migration from Eastern Europe: largely Croats and Serbs, with a smattering of Poles, Russians, Czechs, and last, but not least, a few Native Americans. We all lived next to each other in small shack houses without sidewalks, rather than in clearly marked ghettos, and we battled each other when we weren't united fighting scab children. The street I grew up on in Butte still doesn't have sidewalks, even though there are fully improved lots all around with sidewalks that were built after the city on the hill began to crumble into the abandoned mine tunnels. Lack of sidewalks still separates rich from poor in Butte.

Life on the Flats was a no-win situation, for it was defined by poverty, hatred, and cultural and language barriers, but we accepted all of this as natural and normal. It wasn't until years later that I even thought about the vicious class, ethnic, and cultural divisions that permeated my early life and memories. The only thing that temporarily overcame our hatred for each other was our common hatred for the Anaconda Company. Ironically, every summer the kids in my neighborhood emulated both the company and the miners by digging our own underground "play" mines using corrugated iron scraps to cover the winding tunnels which ended symbolically in circular dead ends. Like moles, we crawled in our underground tunnels just like our fathers, who spent their time in the mile-deep labyrinth under the Butte hill. To this day, I still can't hear or see the name Anaconda without the hair on the back of my neck rising in anger over what this company did to my hometown. When in 1967–68 my brother led the last and longest strike in Montana history against Arco, which had bought the Anaconda interests in the Berkeley Pit, I dropped out of graduate school to go back and write the press releases on the strike, which the eastern national press ignored even though it went on for eight-and-a-half months. Coal, not copper, strikes were the scoop de jour back then.

Butte now enjoys the largest superfund appropriation in the country because it is hopelessly polluted from both underground and open-pit mining. Despite the superfund and various historical restoration projects, the town waits almost impassively for the putrid waters of abandoned Berkeley Pit to overflow in the first decade of the next century to complete the environmental destruction begun in the name of industrial progress a little over a century ago.

I start with this because I think my background as a second-generation immigrant growing up in a poor union family in a strike-ridden, ethnically diverse town has profoundly affected my historical work and obviously my politics in two basic ways: it gave me a peculiarly reverential (by today's standards, at least) view of education, and a profound sense of "outsidedness" (to say nothing of insecurity) even as I succeeded in becoming educated and blending in with middle-class life in the United States.

The only escape from the harshness of conditions on the Flats was education. Education became my savior, the only way off the Flats, so I hurried through elementary and high school, skipping grades along the way, as though there were a time limit on education—not realizing then that my education would continue a lifetime. Education was my way out of the hatred, the hopelessness, and the wrecked neighborhood of ramshackle dwellings and no sidewalks. But more education allowed the acquisition of knowledge, cultivation, and skills needed "to pass" into the middle class. Into each course I took with me respect and craving for learning without having to be entertained or having a guarantee that what I was learning must inevitably translate into immediate monetary satisfaction. Now when I confront middle-class students who need to escape nothing and have so little respect for education, I am sad and bewildered. I still believe that education is the "great leveler" of society—with the potential to bring all classes and races together—but only when students are at least to some degree motivated to learn for reasons that have no intrinsic value beyond knowledge itself.

At all levels education was a revelation because I knew I knew so little, so I wanted to know everything. Thus, I am increasingly suspicious of students who are interested in learning only what they already think they know from thirty-second sound bites or thirty-minute sitcoms. Obviously, this is not a good attitude to have in an age of consumer education, in which entertainment and fun have increasingly replaced substance in order to meet enrollment requirements and to obtain positive reviews from student evaluations and, of course, to meet the productivity standards demanded by administrators who have discovered that higher educational institutions are businesses—not centers of learning. Rather than dumb down my undergraduate lecture classes in keeping with current trends, I now only teach graduate student colloquia and seminars or teach undergraduates abroad, where you can still find what I call an "immigrant mentality" and adequate reading and writing skills.[3]

Obviously my background continues to affect my views as an instructor. But long before I realized that my Butte background would color my views about education, it influenced my extracurricular activities, politics and ultimately my scholarship. In the eighth grade and as a high school senior I led two minor student revolts in opposition to what my underaged peers and I considered arbitrary rules. The first instance arose when a one-eyed music teacher denied recess breaks during her classes; the second occurred when the administration canceled the traditional Halloween festivities at school on the grounds that these led to drinking and vandalism (which they did). Now, granted, these were not political issues per se, but they were issues involving the misuse of arbitrary authority, which I associated then and now with the past influence of the Anaconda Company over the city of Butte and the state of Montana. Curiously, the response of school administrators in both cases was to give me an IQ test on the assumption, I suppose, that only a mental retard would do such a thing. Instead, the results of such exams simply propelled my fast-track approach to education forward. Rather than being demoted, I just skipped another grade.

I did well in school because I realized early on that education was my ticket out of the Flats. Yet the success of my frantic and almost desperate march out of the Flats has left me with an insecurity caused by jumping several socioeconomic classes in a short time. This feeling of insecurity is common with many that leave their indigenous roots in a hurry without taking time to say "goodbye." I didn't know I would have to live indefinitely with this feeling of "outsidedness"; I only know that had I not used education as a means of escape, I would have remained in Butte, Montana. Moreover, as I look back, I see how many other women didn't make it out and still wonder why I did. Recently I talked with my best friend from grade school about this—a woman who dropped out of school to marry at the age of fifteen. Her life and mine could not be more different, and yet we have come together after years of separation to talk about our common Butte bond and basic similarities with a closeness I have seldom had with most of my professional women friends.

Seeing so many still trapped, but not necessarily unhappy or less fulfilled than those of us who did escape the Flats, has increased my sense of "outsidedness" over the years. At the same time, the male-dominated world of reason, facts, and linear knowledge always seemed foreign to me. To this day when I really want to analyze a subject or take some action, I naturally resort to a commonsense, intuitive, circular thought process that is not only female, but also "Butte." This outsider, nonlinear approach often does not make for efficient thinking, but it has always made me feel "right" about decisions involving political action or research projects.

To resist this feeling of "outsidedness," I usually try to project what my father would have thought or done under similar circumstances. It was, after all, my eighth-grade-educated father who encouraged me to go on to school, not because of the money or fame it might bring, but because, as he said over and over again, "So you won't have to work as hard as I have." And it was only in those terms that he appreciated my later success as a historian. While my father's understanding was limited, his lack of education didn't stop him from dreaming dreams and imaging a more sensible world. Yet he never did understand what I did as an educated person. When I was a TA at Berkeley, I once made the mistake of telling him, when he asked how many hours a week I worked, that it was a total of six. Even years later, I was never able to convince him, as he bragged on me to his friends, that those hours in the classroom did not include preparation time.

My father had wanted to be an artist and apparently demonstrated enough talent to be encouraged by the priests and nuns with whom he came in contact in grade school. The accidental death of his father forced him to drop out, as the eldest of seven children, to support his mother and siblings. His early instructors not only taught him English, making him the first one in the family to speak American, they also instilled in him the ability to dream—an ability that poverty never killed, even though as a teenager he initially worked in the deplorable conditions of the Butte mines. Then, when the strikes became too frequent to allow him to maintain his family during the Great Depression, he became a self-trained auto-mechanic. His artistic dreams led him to make from spare parts the first and only "new" car he ever owned, modeled after the early racecars of the 1920s. It was his dreamer side that, in retrospect, makes him seem more female to me than my loving, but nervous, always anxious, mother. He also seemed more comfortable in the company of women than most men did, even though his various skilled and unskilled jobs kept him surrounded with macho men of the worst and best kind. Despite the fact that my father taught me to shoot and hunt, it was his soft, non-macho qualities that I looked for in other men as I grew up. While this has always made me susceptible to passive-aggressive academic men (of whom there are way too many because they are such experts at killing women slowly), my uneducated father remains to my way of thinking the best model of the "sensitive" male.

Ironically, education allowed me to cover up my multifold sense of insecure outsidedness based on sex as well as class. It led me first to deny my proletarian background and commonsense inclinations in favor of middle-class sophistry; then, in spite of this denial, to choose research topics that were "outside" mainstream historiography using a variety of innovative methodologies; and finally to criticize in no uncertain terms what I consider to be the paralysis of gender analysis afflicting the fields of women's history and women's studies. While education could "cover" for class deficiencies and allow me to tackle offbeat topics, it could never completely "cover" for the endemic marginality that all women professionals face because of their sex.

Early in my professional career I decided that it had been a mistake to ever deny my background or commonsense intuitiveness. Once again, it was my father who was instrumental in this realization. While he was visiting Berkeley during the student and antiwar demonstrations, he noticed in my radical literature collection material about the International Workers of the World (IWW). Much to my amazement he said that as a teenager in Butte he had joined the IWW just before federal troops were sent in to run the copper mines during US participation in the First World War. Because of the 100 percent Americanism atmosphere which prevailed after the war, my father had been shamed by government and local propaganda into thinking that what he had done was unpatriotic. I knew that he had joined the Mine Mill and Smelter Union in the 1920s, but I did not learn about his IWW background until I was a graduate student.

After I explained that his wartime IWW membership had been a logical choice of action at the time and, moreover, was currently "in" on Berkeley campus, we began to talk about what we would do when the revolution finally came. We decided that I would return to Butte and my brother and father and I would blow up the Arco/Anaconda installation. My brother had been blackballed by Arco after leading the strike and so was more than eager to join our dream. We shared this dream for almost a dozen years, until it became clear that there would be no revolution over civil rights, the war, feminism, or anything else. But our conspiratorial fantasy convinced me that my background was responsible for my political activism and my nontraditional scholarship. Realizing this, I became less motivated to embrace middle-class values as wholeheartedly as I once did. Butte is, indeed, in the eye of the beholder, and looking back, the Flats take on a value now that I didn't appreciate while growing up there.

Instead of participating in a bona fide revolution, I ended up a member of SDS, participating in multiple antiwar, Vietnam Day moratorium demonstrations, in a variety of student demonstrations ranging from the Free Speech Movement to People's Park in Berkeley, and in the founding convention of the Peace and Freedom Party in Oakland, California in 1967, ending up in France during the 1968 student demonstrations and general strike. The most enduring legacy of these activities is that I have not voted for a major party presidential candidate since 1968, when I supported Eldridge Cleaver, despite the fact he was ineligible because of his age and status as a convicted felon. Unfortunately, his sexism did not concern us at the time.

In the mid-1970s, this dramatic change in my politics—because I happened to be from Butte, in Berkeley in the 1960s—allowed me to take a new, hard look at what happened to women during the American Revolution. To this day those experiences affect the way I teach politics and foreign policy. Another influence on my thinking was my then-husband's self-imposed exile in Canada over the War in Vietnam after Nixon came to office and abolished most student draft exemptions. While this was a most politically correct and romantic separation at the time, it ultimately marked the beginning of the end of our marriage and my metamorphosis into a more woman-centered woman.

REVISIONIST INTERPRETATIONS AND METHODOLOGY

So Berkeley set my professional career in motion with leftist leanings and interest in innovative methodologies. During my last year there, 1968, I also joined the Women's Sociology Caucus, one of the earliest consciousness-raising (and interdisciplinary) groups. Feminism provided the first and most lasting rationale for having left my roots and having become a professionally trained historian. Aided by what I had learned from the Berkeley consciousness-raising group, a few years later I established one of the first women's studies programs in the country at Sacramento State. Like my early education, feminism took on revelatory proportions in my life; it was not simply a middle-class plaything until something better came along. Feminism also finally and unalterably pushed me into being honest about my background. When I was leaving Berkeley with my PhD in hand for a junior college job, my male colleagues, most of them still ABD, were going on to first jobs in major research universities. Thus I learned the hard way that no phony middle-class identity was going to get me an entry-level tenure-track job at an institution commensurate with my qualifications. The problem was my sex, not my class. Even the first article I published was rejected until I sent it out under initials instead of my first name. And the rest, as they say, is history.

Aside from these early employment and publishing problems, I cannot say that the bulk of my academic career has been difficult or unpleasant. Teaching at second-tier institutions early in my career allowed me to branch out into women's legal history rather than simply staying in twentieth-century politics and foreign policy. It also freed me to become president of the Coordinating Committee on Women in the Historical Profession (CCWHP) (1977–79), during which time CCWHP attempted to bankrupt the American Historical Association (AHA) by obtaining a thousand pledges from members to support putting their annual fees into an escrow fund until the organization stopped meeting in anti-ERA states. I called it the MIFT campaign, referring to "Money in Friendly Territory." CCWHP did not have to implement its plan to introduce an ERA boycott resolution at the business meeting in San Francisco in 1978 because the AHA Council reversed itself, in part because of the financial disaster posed by the MIFT campaign. Later, when I interviewed for the job of executive director of AHA in the early 1980s, this CCWHP campaign came up again and again in the interview, even though I kept reminding members of the hiring committee that my actions should be viewed as those of the loyal opposition. Needless to say, I did not get the job. Instead, I became executive secretary of the Organization of American Historians (OAH) for most of that decade—a decade in which women came into their own on committees and elected positions for the first time.

During those years, OAH also passed a resolution opposing sexual harassment on college and university campuses that several liberal male members of the Executive Board opposed until Nell Painter and other women on the board prevailed. It also passed an anti-Apartheid resolution requiring someone to demonstrate in front of the South African embassy in Washington, DC and be arrested. Surprisingly, no one else on the board had an arrest record, and so the assignment fell to me. And, of course, OAH took exception to the entire Iran/Contra affair by publicly condemning Ronald Reagan for comparing the Contras to the Founding Fathers. Under my direction OAH began to promote public history and a number of high school history projects, such as the *Magazine of History*, which I started with the help of a Rockefeller grant to meet the specific needs of secondary school history teachers. I also directed the editing of four NEH-funded curriculum packets, *Restoring Women to History*, used to integrate women's history into US and western civilization courses. Although I integrated the OAH staff, left the organization in sound financial condition, and gained important administrative and policy experience from being executive secretary, I obviously managed to ruffle more than a few feathers, because I have not been asked to serve on any committee or run for any office of either the OAH or AHA in the decade since I resigned from that position to return to full-time teaching. So I co-founded and co-edited the *Journal of Women's History* from 1988 to 1996 and became CEO and president of the Center for the Study of the Presidency and editor of *Presidential Studies Quarterly*—both largely political-science oriented—from 1995 to 1997. Now, as director of the Contemporary History Institute at Ohio University, I am promoting a critical reevaluation of Cold War policies and peace making in the post–Cold War world.

My initial publication record in women's history, foreign policy, and the modern presidency easily gained me early tenure because revisionism, especially economic revisionism, was not the anathema in the 1970s that it has become. This freed me to pursue a number of revisionist projects and a variety of methodologies in all the subfields in which I chose to specialize. In fact, the topics or my interpretation of them have been unpopular, in part, because the methodologies turned them into revisionist studies—until deconstruction came on the academic scene.

I started with structural functionalism, which led to a corporatist interpretation in my first two books on foreign policy. Then I turned briefly to cliometrics, statistically analyzing colonial women's dower rights in South Carolina. I combined this with modernization theories to come up with a reinterpretation of women during the American Revolution, to which I added selectively from critical legal studies to write a full-scale legal history of US women to the present. I applied all of these methodologies to write revisionist accounts of two unpopular, Republican, Quaker presidents—Herbert Hoover and Richard Nixon. In between, I wrote about the depressing subject of women and US foreign policy, and took a radical feminist stand against pornography and against the harm I believe unintelligible and indiscriminate application of deconstruction was having on US women's history and women's studies. All of these methodologies, including low doses of deconstruction, were useful in writing women's legal history and economic, political, and diplomatic history over the last thirty years.

Currently I am working on a revisionist critique of the way in which the United States fought and won the Cold War at the expense of its soul, and an interdisciplinary study of what has been labeled the last witch-burning in the western world—the torture murder of an Irish woman in 1895 by her loving husband, father, and relatives because they believed she had been turned into a changeling by the fairies. Both will take controversial positions. In the foreign policy book I question not only the way the United States adopted the methods of the enemy to fight the Cold War, but also the brand of primitive capitalism known as the global economy and the "Ferengi democracy" that this country is currently practicing and exporting abroad. ("Ferengi" refers to a species of supremely acquisitive capitalists who live in a no-holds-barred society depicted in a recent Star Trek series.) In the second instance, my coauthor Marian Yeates and I argue that the burning of Bridget Cleary represented a microcosm of socioeconomic and political conditions in Ireland in 1895 and that in this murder case the fairies ultimately had to be accommodated by English colonial law. To say the least, my type of scholarship has not been in the mainstream of US history, except for a brief time in the 1970s when "revisionism" was not a dirty word. This is why I always cringe when I read in tenure and promotion guidelines that books should be well received. Mine have been widely reviewed, but with one or two exceptions, not well received. My only consolation is that some of them have sold well. Both of these latest projects also reinforced my long-standing belief that patriarchy, like capitalism, is endlessly self-correcting. And I believe that we are seeing both regroup and reassert themselves at the end of the twentieth century.

Thus, my sense of "outsidedness," combined with an intuitive, nonlinear approach to understanding history, has influenced my choice of these topics and experimental use of a variety of methodologies. This combination of socioeconomic and intellectual factors account in large measure for my innovative interpretations in the fields of economic foreign policy, colonial women, legal history, and modern presidents. This same accidental combination reinforced my left-of-center politics, as did my ex-husband's exodus to Canada during the war in Vietnam. As a result, I naively concluded that my political beliefs would prevent me from ever experiencing a generation gap with students or younger colleagues. But I was wrong. Instead of each generation entering academe as at least liberal, if not radical, they have become postmodern and neo-conservative. Probably I could have accommodated myself to their politics if it had not often been accompanied in recent years by a return of patriarchy, exhibited in the continuation of second-class citizenship for women in this country and abroad, and the institutionalization of poststructuralism masquerading in academe and the media as feminism behind the rhetoric of gender and masculinity studies.

What do I mean by this—and why have I stopped my methodological sojourn by critiquing poststructuralism, which I am convinced has a pernicious impact on women's history and separates women academics from the politics of the second wave of feminism, where the subfield began? In a circuitous way, I have come to this conclusion by analyzing the relationship between concepts of nationalism, citizenship, and women's rights in the newly emerging nations of Eastern Europe and in Ireland—places where I lived and taught from 1992 to 1994.

CITIZENSHIP, NATIONALITY, AND THE GLOBAL ECONOMY

The year I taught in Dublin forced me to reconsider what citizenship means for women outside the United States. But more importantly, the disintegration of Yugoslavia (and later the peace in Northern Ireland) also made me think about the meaning of nationalism for women and the connection between citizenship and nationalism. Historians of women have not given either subject enough consideration in the last thirty years. I had not been aware of this particular omission in the otherwise enormously productive field of women's history before living in Poland and Ireland.

I have argued for a number of years that women in the United States and most other western democracies remain second-class citizens because they continue to lack three basic freedoms enjoyed by men under most constitutional or other forms of government. The three basic freedoms that women citizens do not possess are: 1) freedom from inferior legislative, constitutional, or juridical status (usually meaning the denial of economic and legal privileges enjoyed by mainstream men, and the fact that sex is still not considered a suspect classification under the Fourteenth Amendment); 2) freedom from fertility and family discrimination (denial of reproductive rights, reflected in restricted access to abortion and an inferior position within traditional family hierarchies, otherwise known today as the return to family values); and 3) freedom from fear (denial of full protection from the violence against women in this country and throughout the world, in part because lawyers refuse to define pornography in order to regulate the harmful effects of the combination of sex and violence on American women).[4] In other words, a common inferior or second-class citizenship has been imposed on women throughout the world, from Athenian Greece to the present.

Why is it that women in most democratic western nations still don't have these three essential rights of citizenship at the end of the twentieth century? The major reason, I argue, stems from the male origins of definitions of democratic citizenship and in the continuation of male-defined citizenship in the newly emerging democracies in Eastern Europe and Russia and most of the Third World.[5] Feminists and historians of women usually have championed certain aspects of male citizenship, such as equal treatment under the law, rather than trying to transform traditional definitions of citizenship to meet the societal requirements of women. This is why we need a feminist approach to international law—to make sure that human rights include women's rights. This means rethinking the definition of national and global citizenship based on equality of rights, so that it includes equitable rights which correspond to women's experiences and needs, as they are reflected in different countries all over the world. The history of citizenship for women in the States and under United Nations' covenants thus proves that equal rights alone, while a necessary starting point for obtaining first-class citizenship for women, is not enough because such equality is typically based on male standards. Women do not exist on an equal footing with men in either postindustrial or less developed nations. Unless women simply want to aspire to act as and be treated as men (despite the odds against achieving this status), equitable, not simply equal, treatment of women must be included in any definition of national or global citizenship in the future.[6]

Nationalism, be it after the American Revolution or the Irish Rising or in the former Yugoslavia and other recently liberated communist nations, is usually not favorably disposed toward the needs or rights of women. Throughout the nineteenth and twentieth centuries the introduction of democratization and modernization in developing nations lowered the socioeconomic and legal status of most women. It was naive to think that history would not repeat itself with the much-touted triumph of capitalism and democracy over communism and totalitarianism.[7] Current criticism of the failure of communism to provide equality for women through a combination of paid work and subsidized motherhood should not blind us to how unequal women remain in the western industrialized countries—for the same reasons: a sex-segregated labor market, a dual work load for most married women, and male-dominated families which discriminate against females on a daily and fundamental basis. Democratization may be an inexorable trend (or end) of history, according to writers on both the left and right, but they usually do not point out that this "relentless progress" has always been at either the expense or neglect of women. Worldwide, half of the "democratizing" countries that the United States so indiscriminately supports today are, in fact, democracies which do not accord the freedom of constitutional liberalism to their peoples, but especially not to their female citizens.[8] In other words political liberties necessary for free elections do not necessarily result in civil liberties. Such illiberal democratic nationalism after the end of the Cold War is but one example of the return of patriarchy at the end of the twentieth century, contrary to the claims of postmodern feminists and mainstream global economists who either deny the existence of patriarchy in the past, or predict that postmodern society has (or shortly will) eliminate the negative material impact of free trade on the American worker and its promotion of patriarchy from within the structure of multinational corporations down to the poorest families within nation states.[9] The other most blatant example of the return of patriarchy in the United States today is the resurgence of the myth of beneficent fatherhood and deification of the perfect, equally mythical, nuclear family of the past.

POSTMODERNISM AND PHALLIC DRIFT

Another example of the return of patriarchy can be found in academe in the form of postmodernism. In the same way that Carole Pateman's book *The Sexual Contract,* in 1988, exposed the androcentric and misogynistic qualities of modern liberalism present in the political theories of John Locke and other "fathers" of the Enlightenment, Somer Brodribb, in her 1992 *Nothing Mat(t)ers: a feminist critique of post-modernism*, similarly critiqued the "fathers" of poststructuralism. Brodribb analyzed and dissected the evolution of various definitions and examples of postmodern, poststructural, deconstructionist, and semiotic theory, demonstrating that the misogynist message of postmodernism is even more subtle than Locke's,[10] making it "the cultural capital of late patriarchy." Instead of substituting a new political vision for an old one, male postmodernists since the 1960s have been disguising their failure as revolutionaries to change the post–World War II world by devising a patriarchal ideology for the end of the twentieth century in which, to use Simone de Beauvoir's words, "appearances are everything . . . [and] the whole real world disappears into thin air."[11]

American poststructuralism specifically defers feminism in two primary ways. In the latest "academencia" game, to use Mary Daly's term, male and female postfeminists now tell academic women that they can avoid being silenced by writing and talking (and reading texts) like the postmodern boys who have rightly been referred to as "TOOTSIES."[12] This process inevitably results in female silence, fear or, at the very least, anxiety, by denying that women's experiences can be used to create feminist theory. As a result, male poststructuralists (and their female followers) are becoming part of the backlash against both radical and mainstream feminism in the United States. It is not surprising that this has happened since some of the French intellectuals who were the "fathers" of postmodernism exhibited such misogynist views that at times they seemed to claim that only men could speak for women.

The irony of all this, according to Tania Modleski, is that various postmodern theories are being "carried out not against feminism but in its very name," and are undermining the political effectiveness of the second wave of feminism. After all, how effective can female postfeminists be as political activists, Jane Gallop has asked, "wearing the hand-me-downs of men-in-drag, [and] writing a feminine which has become a male transvestite style?" Many poststructuralists use feminism as a pretense to enter the field of gender studies, where their fascination with masculinity is leading to more emphasis on men than women and more emphasis on difference or diversity among women rather than on commonalties they may share.[13]

As a sophisticated linguistic technique, postmodernism is a logical and useful methodology for purely textual analysis, but as French feminist Christine Delphy has pointed out, it is irrelevant for analyzing the material reality of gendered relationships because as a linguistic tool it was not designed to discern the existence of socioeconomic hierarchies that give meaning to gender differences.[14] When this pitfall is not recognized, it can lead poststructuralists to deconstruct gender relations in a socioeconomic void. In this way gender can become a postmodern category of paralysis, destroying any collective concept of woman or women through the fragmentation of female subjects. By ignoring that difference and dominance go hand-in-hand and clouding dominance with rhetoric about multiple and indeterminate identities or consciousnesses, poststructuralism can be used to deny or mask the fact that gender analysis is, after all, about the authority of men over women.

The increasing emphasis on masculinity in the study and public discussions of gender have led Kathleen B. Jones and Anna G. Jónasdóttir to conclude that poststructuralism prides itself on asserting that neither feminism nor female culture constitutes a coherent philosophy or ideology. It therefore follows that feminist politics (and the female experiences that drive it) is no more meaningful than any other kind of constructed politics. Feminism no longer can be used to alleviate conditions of female oppression because "identity is not an objectively determined sense of self defined by needs" any more than "politics is . . . the collective coming to consciousness of similarly situated individual subjects."[15] In a word, postmodernism depoliticizes gender.

As a methodology for textual analysis, poststructuralism can be a useful tool for historians of women. As I have already noted, I have employed a variety of methodologies since the 1960s and found all of them useful in writing women's history and economic, political, and diplomatic history over the last twenty-five years. But none of these post-1960s methodologies claimed the status of an epistemology even among its most enthusiastic adherents. The time female poststructuralists have spent trying to include women as a gender into theories that basically ignored them as a sex and as a postmodern category of analysis reminds me of the same attempts several decades ago by so many socialist and Marxist feminists and by female psychoanalysts to put women into the theories of Marx and Freud, instead of developing a feminist version of materialism or psychology. After all, original feminist thinking is always harder than spending endless time adapting male thinking to fit women badly. In other disciplines or professions, poststructuralism has been carried to illogical and unintelligible extremes by a small elite: English, film criticism, critical rights theory, cultural studies, and even, surprisingly enough, architecture, where it is referred to as postmodernism.

Under the influence of feminist movements in far-flung parts of the world in the 1970s, historians of women began challenging patriarchal stereotypes of women and then interpreting a set of common female experiences to explain how women sought to coordinate their private lives with their public ones. The methodological sophistication and growing number of practitioners and publications in women's history occurred long before the appearance of poststructuralism. Its explosion in the last quarter century has led some historians to suggest that women's history is on its way to becoming an *alternative*, rather than merely a subfield, of the discipline. And there is no doubt that feminist historical scholarship has dramatically altered two subfields within the discipline of history—the new social history and the new legal history.

THE FUTURE IS NOT WHAT IT WAS

As the world enters a post–Cold War era and the twenty-first century, women's history in the United States (and other countries) is alive and well, despite the extremes to which some want to carry postfeminist and poststructural arguments. Interestingly, commentators on the 1995 international women's conference in China wrote negatively about this same elitism of many western women from richer nations of "the North" who were bickering over "history as theory," and the question of whether it was demeaning even to talk about women's rights separate from human rights. In contrast, women of "the South" or Third World were organizing for pragmatic goals such as access to capital, the right of inheritance, basic education for girls, and a voice in the political establishment and medical systems so that they could make practical choices about their reproductive health.[16]

Yet even in the United States, where the study of women's history is widespread, women continue to be studied and taught primarily as a separate group rather than integrated into general history classes or other fields. This makes the study and teaching of women within academic settings vulnerable to staffing and funding cutbacks, as well as attacks by neoconservatives for being too "politically correct." Now poststructuralists maintain that feminist history has more to lose than gain in exempting itself from poststructuralism because contemporary intellectual culture has irretrievably lost faith in objective, knowable reality. They tell us to concentrate on *how* we know what we know rather than *what* needs to be known and *why* because that is in keeping with the demands of academic trendiness.

What feminist historians of women are offered instead is a return to invisibility and silence, but with the approval of our poststructural male colleagues. This price is too high to pay, at least in the United States, because thirty productive and successful years for the field of women's history do not deserve to be sacrificed on the unstable altar of poststructuralist relativism. The writing of women's history in any country almost always ends up threatening traditional patriarchal history, with its criteria of power, prestige, and standard periodization; postmodern gender historians' attack in the name of overturning false universal concepts of "truth" has been unnecessary from the beginning.

This is not the first time that theories from Europe have disrupted certain American academic disciplines. If fact, this has happened so often since World War II that it is often said European theories come to the United States to die—meaning that they are not adopted across the Atlantic until they are on their way out abroad. Women's history will survive its predicted demise by postmodernism, despite the latter's current reign as the most destructive imported intellectual trend to hit the United States since World War II. The impact and implications of women's history have been too important and are too embedded in our hearts and minds to vanish when faced with the trendiness of yet another tired academic import.

So, I now contemplate early retirement because I no longer find my "outsidedness" comfortable or rewarding in the current political or academic atmosphere, so strongly influenced by global psychobabble and poststructuralism. In anticipating retirement, I am reminded of Carolyn Heilbrun's leave-taking from Columbia University in 1992. At that time her views about female community and feminism were considered obsolete by those in gender and popular culture studies who believed in multiple identities and many feminisms and who viewed women *qua* women as fiction, a pose, a performance. Since that time we have entered an even more passive political era of psychobabble, in which a privileged few think that women have more than their rights or that the category of "woman" is obsolete: masculinity studies are in and feminism is out; womanizing is in and "the personal is political" is out. The motivating principle behind radical feminism in the 1970s was that we were going to change, not simply reform, the political economy of the United States. Now we must concentrate with the same fervor to prevent poststructuralism from prevailing in academe and politics.

In retirement I plan to (re)conceptualize women's current position in the United States from personal, political, socioeconomic, educational, and sexual points of views. While this sounds overly ambitious on the surface, I think that my diverse immigrant background and diverse personal and professional experiences, and the diverse historical fields in which I have worked, will allow me to produce a controversial and frank synthesis about the reasons for the reassertion of patriarchy at the end of the twentieth century, abroad and in the United States, and what radical feminists can do once again to expose and thwart this phallic drift under the guise of postmodernism and the global economy. I also hope that at the same time we begin to move beyond equal to equitable treatment as citizens and women. In this ambition, I also am encouraged every time I recall Heilbrun quoting Dorothy L. Sayers on her retirement: "Time and trouble will tame an advanced young woman, but an advanced old woman is uncontrollable by any earthly force."[17]

NOTES

1. Michael P. Malone, et al., *Montana: A History of Two Centuries* (Seattle: Univ. of Washington Press, rev. ed., 1991), 329.

2. The Storytellers Project, recently formed in Butte, encourages those of us who survived the Flats and left for successful careers to write about their experiences growing up there.

3. Joan Hoff, "The National History Standards: Let's Go Back to Basics," *Journal of Women's History* 9 (Autumn 1997), 164–71; Glynn Custred, "Academic Rights," *National Review*, Sept. 15, 1997, 44–48; Peter Schrag, "The Near-Myth of Our Failing Schools," *The Atlantic Monthly*, Oct. 1997, 72–80.

4. Joan Hoff, "Why Is There No History of Pornography?" *For Adult Readers Only: The Dilemma of Violent Pornography*, Susan Gubar and Hoff, eds. (Bloomington, IN: Indiana Univ. Press, 1989), 17–46; Hoff, *Law, Gender, and Injustice* (New York Univ. Press, rev. ed., 1994), 33.

5. Nicole Loraux, *Citizenship and Women: The Children of Athena: Athenian Ideas about Citizenship and the Division of Labor between the Sexes,* trans. by Caroline Levine (Princeton, NJ: Princeton Univ. Press, 1993), 6–21.

6. For example, Hilary Charlesworth, Christine Chinkin, and Shelley Wright, "Feminist Approaches to International Law," *American Journal of International Law* 85 (October 1991), 637–43.

7. Joan Hoff, "Liberation Hurts: Polish Women after Communism," *The Warsaw Voice*, July 5, 1992, 10.

8. Fareed Zakaria, "Democracies That Take Liberties," *New York Times*, Nov. 2, 1997, 15.

9. Ibid.; Lawrence Osborne, "The Women Warriors," and Eyal Press, "The Free Trade Faith," *Lingua Franca* 7 (Dec./Jan. 1998), 56, 39.

10. Carole Pateman, *The Sexual Contract* (Cambridge: Polity Press, 1988), 19–117, especially 82–100; and Somer Brodribb, *Nothing Mat(t)ers: a feminist critique of postmodernism* (North Melbourne, Australia: Spinifex Press, 1992), 19, 21, 138.

11. Simone de Beauvoir, *The Force of Circumstance* (Harmondsworth: Penguin, 1968, trans.), 636.

12. See Kathleen Barry, "'TOOTSIE Syndrome,' or 'We Have Met the Enemy and They Are Us,'" *Women's Studies International Forum* 12 (1989), 487–93.

13. Tania Modleski, *Feminism without Women: Culture and Criticism in a "Postfeminist" Age* (New York: Routledge, 1991), x; Jane Gallop, *Thinking Through the Body* (New York: Columbia Univ. Press, 1988), 100.

14. Christine Delphy, "Rethinking Sex and Gender," *Women's Studies International Forum* 16 (1993), 1–9.

15. Kathleen B. Jones and Anna G. Jónasdóttir, *The Political Interests of Gender: Developing Theory and Research with a Feminist Face* (London: Sage, 1988); Joan Wallach Scott, *Gender and the Politics of History* (New York: Columbia Univ. Press, 1988), 5.

16. "The Second Sex in the Third World," *New York Times*, Sept. 10, 1995, "Week in Review," 1.

17. Anne Matthews, "Rage in a Tenured Position," *New York Times Magazine*, Nov. 8, 1992, 47ff.

NUPUR CHAUDHURI
9

BAHUPATH PERIE: THE LONG TREK

In 1963, when I was twenty years old, I left the shores of India to come to the United States. When I landed, I felt like a fragile plant uprooted and transplanted to a completely alien environment. I am a product of educated, middle-class, nationalist Bengali culture. My own desire to leave Calcutta was at best tepid, but my parents desired to send their daughter to the US for a higher education. Various Calcutta periodicals, such as *Prabasi* and *Bharatbarsa* in Bengali and *Modern Review* in English, would periodically contain articles on the benefits of an American education as a counterpoint to a colonial British one. They sharpened my parents' hopes for their daughter's education. When I came to the US, an older brother was already a resident at the Sloan Kettering Institute for Cancer. I came here for an education, not for a job or a husband, but the US Immigration and Naturalization Service is wary of granting visas to single women from developing countries for fear they seek entry with the sole desire of finding a husband. As it turned out, after completing a master's program and moving to another part of the country for a doctorate, I did marry an American citizen, also an immigrant from India who came here initially for higher education. After living in this country for over thirty years, I have found that my experiences with emigration, immigration, and racism are the forces that have dominated my life. Feminism, in turn, has shaped my life. Like many foreign students and immigrant feminists, I still continue to negotiate the different cultural values and historical experiences. These have helped to shape my own feminist perspective and influence my academic interests. A casual

Nupur Chaudhuri in August 1963, just before leaving Calcutta for the United States.

look at my varied professional activities might well create an impression that I hold incoherent professional and academic goals. But a careful reflection would reveal that they are stitched together in a congruous manner by threads of experience in India and this country.

I spent formative years first in Delhi and later in Calcutta. As my father was a very high-ranking civil servant working in Delhi under the British Raj, early childhood had the trappings that came to a man of such status. One of my first memories goes back to August 15, 1947. In the early morning from the yard of my home, father and I watched planes taking officials of the Raj and their families back to Britain. My father remarked that the low-flying biggest plane was carrying the last Viceroy of India, Lord Mountbatten, and his family. One of my earliest personal memories, then, is of a major event in the history of India, and my evolution as a woman and as a scholar has reflected an interest in understanding the historical context of my life.

My home environment fostered political and social activism. When I was about three years old, my teenage brother helped me to memorize children's rhymes in Bengali satirizing the British administration in India and inspiring children to be involved in the "Quit India" movement, which demanded that the British leave India. My brothers aided my memorization of other popular poems and rhymes about exploitation of the have-nots by the haves. An older brother was one of the organizers of the jute workers' strike in 1946; his other activities helped create civil unrest in Calcutta before the departure of the British—while his father was working for the Raj.

The long line of our generations felt that a woman's life also should include both private and public spheres. My mother was active in *Mahila Samiti* (a women's association) in New Delhi, and as a toddler, I went with her to their meetings, where members invited different women leaders of the Congress Party to deliver lectures about the nonviolence movement and nationalism. This association actively raised funds for orphans and underclass women and found shelter and jobs for the homeless among them who became victims of the partition of India.[1] My aunts have long been active in various organizations with the goals of helping women improve the quality of their lives. One of my aunts, now in her mid-eighties, is the president of a home for women and orphan children, promoting educational and vocational training for them through private and state support. My activist family, thus, had a tradition of volunteerism and a strong belief that the state must take responsibility to improve the condition of people who are unable to take care of themselves.

In November 1952, as my father retired, my parents left New Delhi to settle in Calcutta. In New Delhi, I had spoken Bengali at home but English and Hindi with my friends. When we moved to Calcutta, I had to reorient to a totally new environment since Bengali is the state language and none of my friends spoke any other.

I went through grade school and college in Calcutta. My mother first inspired me to study literature. Like many of my generation in postcolonial India, I was attracted to literature by Shakespeare, Charlotte Brontë, Jane Austen, Shelly, Keats, Byron, E. M. Forster, Hardy, and Dickens. My attachment to reading English literature grew out of the intrinsic appeal of the works themselves; it did not result from the application of any plan like that proposed in the nineteenth century by Thomas Babington Macaulay for creating a special class of Indians. In his celebrated 1835 speech to the British Parliament on Indian education, Macaulay had advocated creating a "class who may be interpreters between us and the millions whom we govern; a class of persons, Indian in blood and colour, but English in taste, in opinions, in morals and in intellect."[2] Nor did my interest include the ulterior motive of becoming part of such a special class. I realized at a young age that the English language and its literature transcended space and history and belonged to all of us.[3] In "Pro/(Con)fessing Otherness," Lavina Dhingra Shankar has maintained that if culture is transmitted by education and not by racial heritage, then a postcolonial person from India is also a product of "western" civilization.[4] Like Dhingra Shankar, I do not see an attachment to western literature as a form of cultural imperialism, or "colonizing the mind." I have great affinities for both Sanskrit and Bengali literature.[5] My initial exposures to many European works came as a result of my mother's reading of Bengali translations of late-nineteenth- and early-twentieth-century British, Continental, and Russian literature. I read translations of Somerset Maugham, Victor Hugo, Alexandre Dumas, Anatole France, André Gide, Erich Maria Remarque, Turgenev, Chekov, Maxim Gorky, and Trotsky. These readings helped create a picture of Europe outside Great Britain.

After graduating from high school at the age of fifteen, I entered Sri Shikshayatan College and later Jogomaya Devi College with majors in history and Sanskrit literature. I completed my BA degree in history at the age of nineteen. My father had encouraged the study of history, his field. I read Indian, British, and generic modern western European history, but emphasized Indian history. Two teachers in Calcutta were major influences: Nilima Sanyal, a junior and senior high school teacher, and Amita Ckarvarti, a faculty member in Bengali literature. They taught me to love literature and history and also instilled a willingness to accept the challenges of activism. Interests in history and literature grew together within me and influenced the fields in which I would become an activist.

While studying for an MA in modern Indian history in September 1963, I received a fellowship to Smith College to study for an MA degree in history. My first major shock in the new country came that November with the assassination of President Kennedy. Although I remembered the assassination of Gandhi, the partition of India, and religious violence, with accompanying mass movements of population from one area to another, the violent political climate in this supposedly advanced country shocked me.

At the age of twenty, I gained an additional layer of identity: foreign student. I was now "the other of the family, the clan, the tribes. . . ."[6] Post-modernists argue that identity is not a thing; it is "the subject in process." I believe that all identities are socially constructed, whether based on class, ethnicity, religion, nation, or all of these.[7] In the ongoing construction of one's own identity, what is not clear is how much influence one's family, friends, and cultural heritage continue to have even after transplantation to another country and culture. In writing this account, I could best define my identity as multilayered; the subject evolves by accretion during the process.

Early at Smith, a course on the French Enlightenment introduced the ideas of Voltaire, Diderot, and other Philosophes. The course whetted my interest in eighteenth-century French history and culture; I sought out English translations of writings by Philosophes and others of the time. These seeds flowered a few years later when I undertook a study of Beaumarchais' *Marriage of Figaro* and other writings, eventually making this the subject of my dissertation research.

In 1965, I moved to Manhattan, Kansas to work on a PhD in a young graduate program in history. I love to travel; if I went to the middle of the country, I believed, then I would be able to travel easily. Kansas is in the middle of the country. At that time I did not have anyone in the US to turn to for advice about advanced studies in this country, for my brother was in London teaching at the Guy's Hospital.

A new world opened as I began my academic life in a new institution. I was one of only a few single graduate students in the College of Arts and Sciences. Both professors and peers subjected a single woman, particularly one from a Third World country, to a different kind of scrutiny from that directed at others. Many who had power to exert academic control questioned her motivation. This notion generally complicated my own situation as I strove to earn the ultimate degree. Having extremely limited alternatives, I had to tolerate many slights from professors and colleagues. My academic experiences from my arrival in 1965 until 1974, when I finally received my PhD, are still vivid but remain too painful to narrate. I would rather not have learned all the lessons that I did from the history department, though they did intensify my resolve to reach my own goals.

I struggled to understand my relationship to the history department. In 1966, university librarian Pansy Washington, an African American, suggested that my non-European/nonwhite background made me "invisible." She explained that this country practices racism in various forms. Since I had been shielded from exposure to racism during my formative years in postcolonial India, her elaboration raised my consciousness about various expressions of racial attitudes. I discovered another layer to my identity: for others, skin color and national origin had marked me as a person from an inferior race. I became a "nether" person in the College of Arts and Sciences at Kansas State University.

In the early seventies, I inquired about a teaching assistantship in the South Asian Program. The director, a political scientist who later died in the 1980s, explained that since I had not taken an Indian history course in the US, I would be unfit to assist, let alone teach, any course. His denial of the value of my Indian education resembled the attitudes toward India displayed by many nineteenth-century British women travel writers.[8] He not only denied the significance of my degree in history from an Indian university, but also implied that Indians are not capable of teaching their own history to others.

My gender also made me invisible. Yet academic pursuits yielded precious rewards in broadening my intellectual horizon and deepening self-definition. While working for a PhD degree, I discovered the academic ground relating to western feminism. In a British history seminar, I read Mary Wollstonecraft's *Vindication of the Rights of Women*, which heightened my interest in women's history and feminism. But the timing was not right to begin research on feminism because at that time faculty members were not engaged in such research, and I was unready to make my own way. In the department, where I served merely as an item in the valuable head count of graduate program enrollment, I designed my own program of study, knowing that one day the department head would have to assign an advisor for the work which I would ultimately do. Not having a true mentor in the early years of my PhD program, I chose an apparently nonconfrontational dissertation topic, putting my ambition to work on women's history on the back burner. I finally picked a topic on the French Revolution; this stemmed from my liking a course taught by Steve Golin. Steve's inspired teaching turned the French Revolution into one of the most exciting periods in history. Blending my interest in literature with that in history, I chose to work on Beaumarchais' plays and his various business ventures during the French Revolution, an interest first awakened at Smith. I examined his role in the revolution, his beliefs and attitudes, and those of the Philosophes and other revolutionaries toward slavery and, indirectly, toward race issues. Steve was teaching French history, so naturally he became my dissertation advisor. (In this respect, my experience is somewhat different from that of many Indian women who came here for higher studies in the 1970s and '80s, since they are usually expected and encouraged to work on Indian history.)

Steve was denied tenure in the early 1970s, a casualty of honest expression of his political views, especially against the Vietnam War. In spite of this setback, Steve still is teaching and publishing. His tenure decision came at a time when I was in the middle of my dissertation. Because of his position, the department head, an Americanist, became my thesis advisor. Steve Golin's departure added another layer of complexity to my struggle, intensifying the department's negative feelings toward me. Throughout this turbulent period Cary Wintz, a fellow graduate student (now department chair at Texas Southern University), remained my only friend in the department. After a series of long, strenuous, sometimes bizarre struggles, I finally received my PhD in 1974. After twenty-three years, I remain convinced that my experiences in the department stemmed from racism and sexism.

My personal life provided solace to my stressful academic life. In 1969, I got married, and this provided an opportunity to create a home and not to feel so much uprooted. I changed my student status to "alien resident" status. I thus acquired two new identities: I became a faculty wife and an immigrant. I could have had an uncomplicated, less stressful life as a faculty wife, but I do not like to fly on borrowed wings. So, I continued to strive to achieve my goal and create my own identity.

The year 1974 was an important turning point. I had earned freedom from a stifling academic climate. I could now move ahead in search of professional attainments. I never had an illusion that my institutional connection would be of any professional help. This was an unranked history department whose faculty members, with some exceptions, possessed very limited professional connections or reputations. Against such heavy odds, what I could do best was to depend totally on my own drives and abilities. I needed to create a professional world for myself. [My election to the American Historical Association (AHA) Teaching Division in 1997 indicates success in that endeavor.]

At my first AHA conference in 1974, I attended the Coordinating Committee on Women in the Historical Profession (CCWHP) business meeting, where I met a group of activist feminist historians. There I discovered a new confidence in my own professional goals. I felt a sense of belonging to the organization because CCWHP presented an "imagined community" with goals of advancing the field of women's history and dismantling existing barriers to the advancement of women in the historical profession. To share these common objectives, I joined CCWHP. In 1975, I volunteered to give time to its *Research Bulletin*; the next year I became its editor. That chance marked the beginning of my long association with the organization. Soon, I became the newsletter editor for the Conference Group on Women's History (CGWH), a post I held until 1980. In 1981, I became the executive secretary and treasurer and served in that capacity until 1987. In 1995, I was elected co-president for a three-year term.

At a Western Association of French Historians' meeting in 1975, I met Frances Richardson Keller. This marked the beginning of a long friendship. Soon I joined the Western Association of Women Historians (WAWH), where I came into contact with Peg Strobel, Penny Kanner, and Betsy Perry. Frances,

Peg, Penny, and Betsy have been constant supports for my professional life. I have been professionally rewarded through my association with a great number of feminist activist historians, among them Joan Hoff, Kitty Prelinger, Mollie Davis, Phyllis Stock, Claire Moses, Nancy Hewitt, Judith Bennett, Dorothy Helly, Lynn Weiner, Eileen Boris, Peggy Pascoe, Barbara Winslow, Peggy Renner, Karen Offen, and Antoinette Burton. All of them have helped me to maintain my own identity and at the same time negotiate with different cultural values and historical experiences.

Attaining my PhD enabled me to concentrate on subjects meaningful to both the private and public spheres of my own life. I began exploring the writings of Olympe de Gouges, whose feminism I presented at the first WHOM (Women Historians of the Midwest) conference. Karen Offen and Susan Bell published my translation of "Les Droits de la Femme" in *Women, the Family, and Freedom*.[9] I presented another paper on Olympe de Gouges, analyzing her perception of marriage and motherhood at the Consortium on Revolutionary France in 1989.[10] I chose to work on de Gouges because she defied all cultural and social pressures of the time. But equally importantly, she criticized the practice of slavery.[11] I have published short entries on several Jacobins, including Chabot and Chaumette, for the *Biographical Dictionary of Modern European Radicals and Socialists*. The list of my activities in the field of French history also includes an article, "The Salons, the Shops, the Street: Scenes of Early Feminism in Eighteenth-Century France."[12]

To avoid becoming both the object and the subject of study, I had concentrated research on European and less on Indian women. However, while I was researching Beaumarchais, I had come across the *Englishwoman's Domestic Magazine*, which contained numerous articles on British women (memsahibs) in India. A Newberry Library grant in 1977 set the ground for my study of memsahibs in India. Catherine Hall has asserted that racism, imperialism, and colonialism are the issues for white women in Britain because these issues have shaped their histories, structured their stories, formed their identities.[13] The same forces are equally applicable to postcolonial women of Indian heritage. British domination of India is also part of my history and my identity. By doing research on European women, I have been writing what Darlene Clark Hine has called "crossover history" and others have called "border crossing."[14] This work has provided me the opportunity to produce, reinforce, recreate, resist, and transform ideas about race, gender, and class and has given me the power to raise questions not previously asked.[15]

Hardly any scholarship on memsahibs existed before I began. Pat Barr's book and Alan Greenburg's article were the only publications available.[16] Memsahibs or western women and colonialism were not then fashionable topics. My article on memsahibs and motherhood in India[17] was one of the first based solely on primary sources and not on anecdotal evidence. There I showed how British wives replaced kinship with a network of female friends to cope with life in India. This observation reflected my own personal situation, in which I have replaced female kin with female friends. In 1990, Peg Strobel and I co-edited a special issue on "Western Women and Imperialism" for *Women's Studies International Forum*. This special issue introduced gender as a category to the study of western imperialism. Later, Peg and I co-edited *Western Women and Imperialism: Complicity and Resistance*, the first collection to analyze the various complex roles that British women played in the colonies. It has become one of the standard works on gender and imperialism. Women can contribute significantly to the development of an undercurrent flowing from a dominated to a dominant group, so that a colonized culture makes a permanent mark on the culture of a metropolitan society. I illustrate this phenomenon in "Shawl, Jewelry, Curry, and Rice in Victorian Britain." Other historians are now examining this aspect of cross-cultural trends through food preparation.[18]

Sensitivity to racism prompted my search for characteristics of British women's racism in India. In "Memsahibs and Their Servants in Nineteenth-Century India,"[19] I described the landscape of racism of the nineteenth-century memsahibs. India created a new identity for British women. Often, these women used the situation of Indian women to claim their own superiority.[20] My work on colonialism continues to explore the degree to which British women, especially wives, served as experts in giving information about India to others at home, creating a colonial subculture at home, and perpetuating an imperial mind-set within the metropolitan society. Further, I am considering the extent to which these women were gender-defined in a class-driven society and the ways these women, influencing both the British and Indian economies, contributed to the economic principles of imperialism. These interests led me to serve as the program co-chair of the International Federation of Research on Women's History (IFRWH) conference on colonialism, imperialism, and nationalism, which met at the Congress of Historical Sciences in Montreal in 1995. I am co-editor of the papers from this meeting.[21] From 1995 to 1998 I was the US representative to IFRWH.

Today the issue of immigration is hotly debated in both the US and Western Europe. Again, personal identity has sparked scholarly investigation. My own immigration led to the history of Maria Rye, which yielded the article "Who Will Help the Girls? Maria Rye and Victorian Juvenile Emigration to Canada, 1869–1895."[22] Rye (1829–1903), the daughter of a London solicitor, was one of the founders of the Society for Promoting Women's Employment.

In the 1970s, academic women pioneered bringing women's issues to national attention by creating the National Women's Studies Association (NWSA). Activism propelled attendance at its first conference in Lawrence, Kansas. Here, to my surprise, were many feminists who were creating an organization stamped with their own racism and xenophobia.[23] At that meeting, women of color became outraged by the insensitive attitudes of white feminists toward "others," causing the women of color to threaten to walk out. Active in organizing that "revolt," I was elected to the Third World Caucus, which later became the Women of Color Caucus. At the insistence of our caucus, a resolution was passed stating that the Executive Board could not make a final decision on any issue without the approval of the Third World Caucus. The following year, I organized a panel and a workshop that discussed whether sisterhood is at all possible in the present context of racism and xenophobia. Perhaps as an indication of some progress within the organization, I was reelected in 1993 to the NWSA Council to serve a three-year term as chair of the Continuing Education Committee.

Experience with NWSA brought new insights into race struggles. I realized that NWSA was a creation to serve almost exclusively the interests of white middle-class women. Even now, Women's Studies programs in some universities and colleges remain the preserves of white bourgeois women. My own experiences taught that feminists can be racists and xenophobic. Historical documents of such cases are abundant. I hoped to capture such racism in "Bloomsbury Ancestry: Jane Maria Strachey, Feminism and Younger Strachey Women." Lady Strachey was a feminist by any standard, but she also exemplified negative attitudes toward Indians.[24]

Since 1992, I have been serving on the editorial board of the *National Women's Studies Journal*, the official publication of NWSA. My own academic and professional experiences convinced me that many western feminists have taken for granted that feminism was monolithic and have defined it by the standards of western feminism. To contest these beliefs, Cheryl Johnson-Odim and I co-edited a special issue of the *NWSA Journal* on global feminism, which focused largely on non-European feminist movements.[25] As feminist movements develop on many grounds, I have sought to relate nationalism to feminism in the context of the early twentieth century as expressed in the writings of Bengali women. Recently, I have published my first article on this topic.[26]

I am interested in the political climates of the lands in which I have resided or visited. Although I was deeply disturbed, as were my friends in graduate school, by US policies on the war in Vietnam, my foreign-student status prevented me from public protest. When I gained resident status in 1974, I volunteered to work at the local office of the newly elected US Representative, the liberal Martha Keyes. I worked in her office for about six years while she served in the Congress. In later years, I volunteered for several Democratic candidates for local and state offices.

In 1985, the officers of Kansas Extension Homemakers Units (EHU) wanted to compile the past activities of their various organizations and contacted the director of Women's Studies and faculty teaching American history at the Kansas State University history department. But EHU found no interest in this project from academics at this land grant university. The president of the EHU approached me for the task. Knowing that the groups' activities touched on the lives of many Kansas communities, many far removed from urban centers, I agreed to write their history. I thought that the Kansas Committee for the Humanities would support such a project and was right. In 1986 I published "Good Homemakers Make Good Neighbors: A History of Kansas Homemakers Units, 1914–1982," in *Kansas Quarterly*.[27]

Manhattan, Kansas is a small university town where job opportunities for people with advanced degrees are almost solely limited to the university. My job search in academia has clearly shown my "otherness" in this country. The hiring authorities never have accepted me either as white or as a member of a "domestic" minority in spite of my US citizenship. Consequently, until 1998 I never found a regular academic job, remaining the quintessential "other," the alien. Repeatedly unsuccessful in cracking the stone wall erected against the entry of an Asian woman into the newly established Women's Studies Program, I began to look for any job opportunity in the city, so that I could have some resources to carry out my research on British colonial history. While working as a volunteer in Congresswoman Keyes's office in the mid-seventies, I encountered Mr. Lawrence P. Nicholson. He was then the assistant director of the Douglass Community Center that served, and continues to serve, primarily the African-American population of the town. In 1978, he hired me on an hourly wage as an activity leader for the community center to work afternoon and evening shifts until 11:00 at night, supervising people who came to play basketball at the center. Later, Larry made me an assistant director for the center to coordinate Head Start, the low-income Senior Citizens' Program, the WIC Program, and various other activities. In 1991, I was appointed to the Douglass Center Advisory Board, whose job is to advise and counsel the mayor and other city commissioners about the needs of this community. The board members are appointed from the black community. In 1995, the board elected me as its chair. During my tenure as advisory board chair, I established a volunteer tutorial program in all subjects for the children of low-income families.

My work at the Douglass Community Center opened an opportunity to write an oral history of African-American women and men whose descendants settled in Manhattan as far back as 1870. Larry Nicholson's encouragement and his strong support were invaluable in undertaking such a project, for which I received a grant from the Kansas Committee for the Humanities. Two years' work resulted in "We All Seem Like Brothers and Sisters: The African-American Community in Manhattan, Kansas, 1865–1940," published in

Kansas History (1991–92) and reprinted in *We Specialize in the Wholly Impossible*.[28] This experience led to valuable insight into American history and the many faces of overt and covert racism in the lives of individuals in the African-American community, gained from the perspective of the "internal others."[29] These insights helped remove the scales from my eyes regarding my own situation in some circles within the university community. And I discovered that the project served a valuable function for those I interviewed; it allowed them to clarify their memories, and demonstrated that their memories were valuable to the community. The making (that is, the recording) of history affirms the value and importance of the persons who made (that is, lived and acted out) the history. My role as historian was my entree into a community; even my long journey to the present shaped that role and my self-perception.

My long trek to the United States—family heritage, experiences with immigration and racism, and my own political beliefs—firmly instilled a respect for all people and the need to know, understand, and record a history that affirms one's own identity.

NOTES

I would like to thank Eileen Boris, Frances Richardson Keller, Betsy Perry, Peg Strobel, and Lynn Weiner for readings of this essay.

1. For more information on women's fate after the partition of India, see Aparna Basu, "Uprooted Women: Partition of Punjab, 1947," in *Nation, Empire, Colony: Critical Categories of Gender and Race Analysis*, ed. Ruth Roach Pierson and Nupur Chaudhuri (Bloomington: Indiana Univ. Press, 1998).

2. Deirdre David, *Rule Britannia: Women, Empire, and Victorian Writing* (Ithaca: Cornell Univ. Press, 1995), 32.

3. See Himani Banerji, *Thinking Through: Essays on Feminism, Marxism, and Anti-Racism* (Toronto: Women's Press, 1995), 56.

4. Lavina Dhingra Shankar, "Pro/(Con)fessing Otherness," in *Teaching What You're Not: Identity Politics in Higher Education* (New York: New York Univ. Press, 1996), 201–02.

5. Dhingra Shankar, "Pro(Con)fessing Otherness," 202.

6. Julia Kristeva, *Strangers to Ourselves* (London: Harvester Wheatsheaf, 1991), 95, also quoted by Madan Sarup, *Identity, Culture and the Postmodern World* (Athens: University of Georgia Press, 1996), 7.

7. Sarup, *Identity, Culture and the Postmodern World*, 48.

8. Nupur Chaudhuri, "British Nationalism: A Common Strand in Women's Travel Writings on India During the Late Nineteenth Century," circulating.

9. Susan Groag Bell and Karen M. Offen, *Women, the Family, and Freedom*, vol. 1, 1750–1880 (Stanford: Stanford Univ. Press, 1983), 104–09. This has been reprinted in Marlene Legate's *Making Waves: A History of Feminism in Western Society* (Toronto: Copp Clark Ltd., 1996), 138–42.

10. Nupur Chaudhuri, "Olympe de Gouges' Perception of Marriage and Motherhood," *Consortium on Revolutionary Europe, 1750–1850: Proceedings, 1989*, ed. Donald D. Howard and John C. Horgan (Tallahassee, Florida State University, 1990), 815–21.

11. See Olympe de Gouges, *Zamore et Mirza ou L'heureux Naufrage, Drame Indien* (Paris: n.p., 1788). She republished this in 1789 under the title *L'esclavage des noirs, ou l'heoreux naufrage* and again in 1792 under the title *L'esclavage des noirs*. I have used the 1788 edition.

12. *Biographical Dictionary of Modern European Radicals and Socialists*, David Nicholls and Peter Marsh, eds. (Sussex: The Harvester Press, 1987), vol. 1, 51–54, 107–10, 174–76, 255–58; *Views of Women's Lives in Western Tradition: Frontiers of the Past and the Future*, Frances Richardson Keller, ed. (New York: Edwin Mellen Press, 1990), 264–96.

13. Catherine Hall, *White, Male and Middle Class: Explorations in Feminism and History* (Oxford: Polity Press, 1992), 20.

14. Darlene Clark Hine, "Black Women's History, White Women's History: The Juncture of Race and Class," presented at the AHA Committee on Women Historians' Breakfast, Chicago, December 1991; printed in *CGWH Newsletter* 23 (May–June 1992), 17; see Henry Giroux's *Border Crossings: Cultural Workers and the Politics of Education* (New York and London: Routledge, 1992).

15. Sucheta Mazumdar, "Colonial Legacies, Neocolonial Paradigms: Negotiating the Mean from the Margins," presented at the American Historical Association Annual meeting, 1996.

16. Pat Barr, *The Memsahibs: The Women of Victorian India* (1976; rpt. Bombay: Allied Publishers, 1978); Allen G. Grennberger, "Englishwomen in India," *British History Illustrated* 4 (1978), 42–51.

17. "Memsahibs and Motherhood in Nineteenth Century Colonial India," *Victorian Studies* (Summer 1988), 517–32.

18. See Carol Gold's current research on food preparation and Danish Nationalism.

19. "Memsahibs and Their Servants in Nineteenth Century India," *Women's History Review* 3 (1994), 549–62.

20. "British Women's Periodicals and Advice Columns about Trips to India and Sojourn There, 1860–1900," the 1995 North American Conference on British Studies annual meeting; "The Indian Other in the Travel Narratives of Eliza Fay and A.U.," Pacific Coast Conference on British Studies, April 22, 1994.

21. Pierson and Chaudhuri, eds., *Nation, Empire, Colony*.

22. This appears in *Imperial Objects: Essays on Victorian Women's Emigration and the Unauthorized Imperial Experience*, ed. Rita S. Kranidis (Twayne Press, 1997), 10–42.

23. Nupur Chaudhuri, "Confronting Racism—and Indebtedness: Growing Up: It's a Lot of Work, But Mother and Daughter Are Doing O.K.," in *Re-Membering*

National Women's Studies Association, 1977–1987, compiled by Kathryn Towns with Caroline Cupo and Phylis Hageman (University of Maryland: National Women's Studies Association, 1994), 83–87.

24. This appears in *Women in the Milieu of Leonard and Virginia Woolf: Peace, Politics and Education*, Wayne Chapman and Marilyn Manson, eds. (New York: Pace University Press, 1998), 58–75.

25. "Gender, Race, Class and Sexuality: National and Global Perspectives," a special issue of the *National Women's Studies Journal* 25 (Spring 1996), 31–43.

26. "Nationalism and Feminism in the Writings of Santa Devi and Sita Devi," *Interventions: Feminist Dialogues on Third-World Women's Literature and Film*, Bishnupriya Ghosh et al., eds. (New York: Garland Press, 1997).

27. "Good Homemakers Make Good Neighbors: A History of Kansas Homemakers Units, 1914–1982," *Kansas Quarterly* 18 (Summer 1986), 53–63.

28. "We All Seem Like Brothers and Sisters: The African-American Community in Manhattan, Kansas, 1865–1940," *Kansas History* 24 (Winter 1991–92), 270–88, reprinted in *"We Specialize in the Wholly Impossible": A Reader in Black History*, Darlene Clark Hine, Wilma King, and Linda Reed, eds. (New York: Carlson Publishing, Inc., 1994), 543–60.

29. Here I am using "internal other" in the same sense Edward Said has used the term in "Identity, Authority, and Freedom: The Potentate and the Traveler," *Transition* 54 (1991), 4–55.

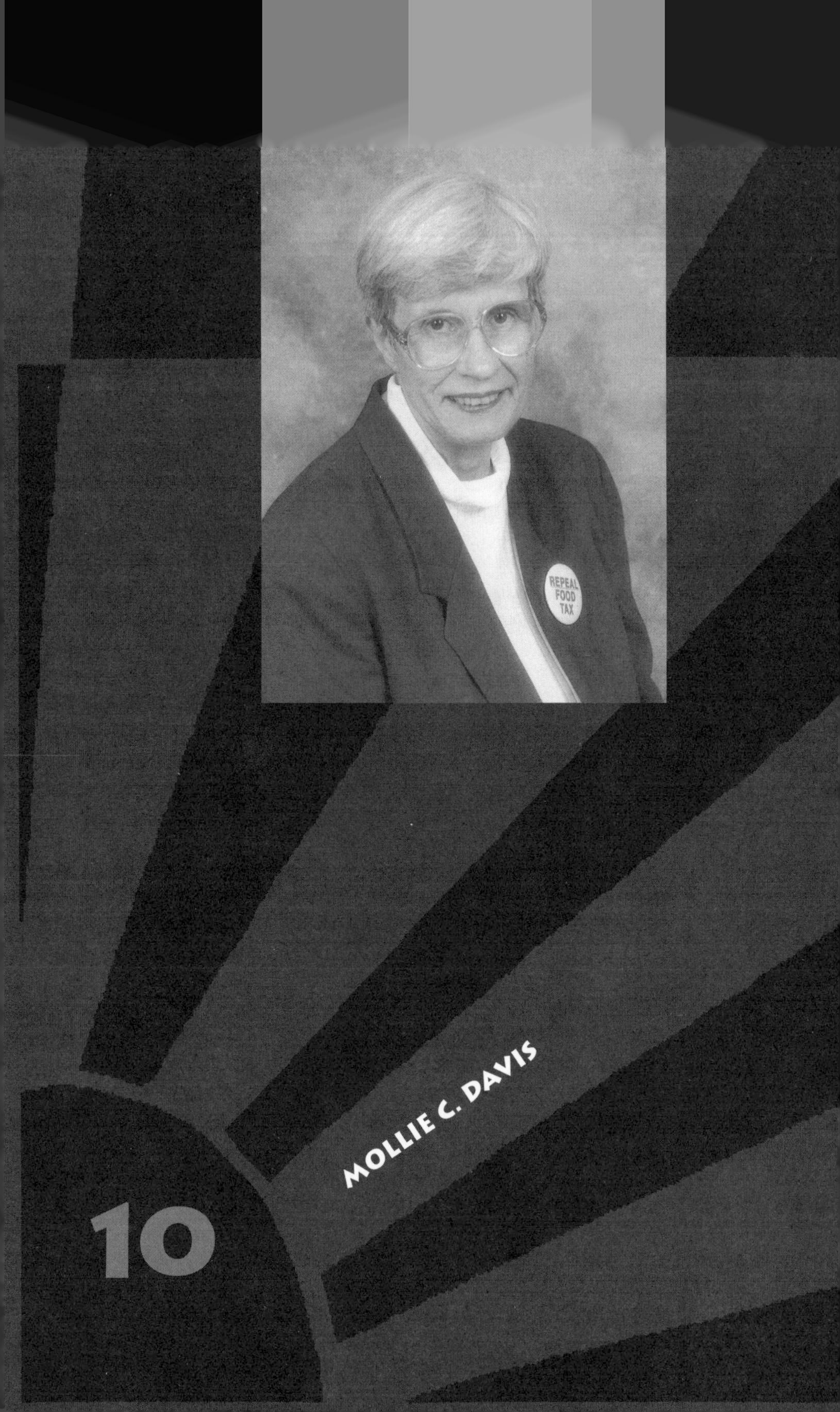

MOLLIE C. DAVIS

10

TWO CATALYSTS IN MY LIFE: VOTER REGISTRATION DRIVES AND CCWHP

As a grassroots activist since my youth, I have accepted the fact that speaking out defines my identity. It has made me a rather good storyteller, students inform me, and it has developed me into a defender of the First Amendment, my colleagues occasionally tell me at faculty meetings. Although I, like Dan Carter wrote in a recent essay, hesitate to rely upon memory to analyze my past,[1] I relish the opportunity to speak out as I reflect upon the personal, political, and professional links in my life, how they intertwined and impacted upon decisions that launched me first as a political and civil rights activist, then as a professional activist and a feminist at work in all that I do.[2]

At the outset, I want to point out my firm conviction that all politics is local and personal, and it is in this sense that politics has affected my professional decisions as it has my whole life. It is difficult to separate local and personal influences from any reflections regarding what propelled me into political activity and in turn promoted my decisions regarding professional life. Local and personal matters informed my youth, my work on Capitol Hill before my marriage, and my housewifery days, as they did my work in the very early 1960s in voter registration drives before and after Georgia abolished the discriminatory county unit system.[3] They transformed me into an academic and finally an instructor in 1965—just as the Vietnam War heated up. Local and personal events brought me to active endeavor for passage of the Voting Rights Act and to political work that included a testing of voter registration

Mollie C. Davis.

during Democratic reformer Ellis Arnall's campaign for governor in 1966. Politics then expanded to promote equality of opportunity within the historical profession, and propelled me to seek out the new Coordinating Committee on Women in the Historical Profession (CCWHP) for its help in forming a caucus of women within the Southern Historical Association in November, 1970. This paper addresses two catalysts in my life—voter registration drives in the early 1960s, and the CCWHP in the early 1970s, but I like to think that one is defined by life in its entirety.

I grew up believing that education was the hope for a better world, and that colleges and universities, along with the church, the press, and organizations like labor unions and academic associations, should encourage their members to speak out in the hope that they would empower politicians and impact the political process. Power can be abused, but an inactive and powerless government legitimizes corporate abuse in our country; I also think that inactivity by faculty and professional historians promotes control of ideas by those who seek to control our culture and our minds. As long as I can remember, I have believed in the positive role of government, and have viewed its power as a tool to bring equitable changes. There is another side of the coin, but I have thought that those who were educated and those who were students could work together effectively for social justice and human rights. My belief in activism with this vision is rooted in my past.

My career trajectory is broken into several legs of a journey.[4] The first segment of my journey to the women's movement and to women's history derives from the circumstances of my birth. Born in March 1932, in the small town of Newnan, Georgia, I was a child of parents who were both veterans of the Great War. Coweta County was unusual for the South of that day, in that its economy was balanced between industry and agriculture, and many and not just one or two families owned its industry. Newnan was an hour's drive from Atlanta, to the northeast; it was the same distance to the southeast to Warm Springs, where Franklin D. Roosevelt went to bathe in the waters. My father was both a lawyer and a farmer; neither profession fared well in the depression.

By the time that I can remember day-to-day activities, my father was enmeshed in New Deal politics. He had a following of veterans and outspoken professionals of the type whom historian John Egerton calls the intelligentsia. The activists plotted the revolution that permitted one ideological southern elite to supplant the older elite.[5] Their networking among differing groups helped agitate for effective change.

I learned about sisterhood from my elderly maternal grandmother, who reared me in her large frame house on the corner of two main highways. She believed in the expansion of suffrage and women's rights, and taught me that each generation has a duty to go beyond the reform efforts of the previous one. She had a social conscience, stemming from the social gospel, and so did my

African-American nursemaid, whose boyfriend was serving time as a "trusty" at the model county farm. We waved at him as the truck carrying convicts in striped suits, balls, and chains passed our house. My family, as did many women's groups, promoted penal reform.

My father ran for Congress in 1938 and was defeated, but the next year, when the incumbent died, he ran and won. The Fourth District Executive Committee opted, as was its privilege, not to use the county unit system subsequently. His election began the era wherein I lived in two worlds, Georgia and Washington, DC. In the capital we lived at first in a brownstone boarding house that served excellent southern food; there, I overheard dignitaries discuss politics. By day I read at the Library of Congress by arrangement. It was hard to balance this world with the Georgia one, but the task became easier when Georgia became more progressive under Governor Arnall (1942–46). Under his administration, the poll tax was abolished, the charter of the Ku Klux Klan was revoked, and suffrage was variously extended; his enemies located in powerful rural counties never forgave him, and he was denounced as a scalawag. Many of his reforms were undone after the war, and he and his followers paid a price.[6] As a young girl, I realized that any fight for human rights is costly to one's family.

The formative years helped make me into an activist. In 1948 one more event was influential. While working as a cub reporter on our weekly newspaper after school, a murder occurred in Coweta County, that of a tenant farmer by a landlord who owned nearly all of an adjacent county. The trial of this near-feudal lord was the first in Georgia where a white man was convicted on the testimony of black witnesses.[7] I learned firsthand, sitting at the press table, about race relations and the law; and a sheriff who was determined to "right the wrongs" convinced me of the power of an individual in the search for justice.

While being schooled in Virginia in Danville and Roanoke, I was a misfit in that I was appalled at the usual Virginia politics, and I came under the wing of professors who nurtured this inclination; Professors Ida Fitzgerald and Cary White taught me about race and labor relations. I spent as much time as possible with my father, who was going blind, and I became his eyes on many occasions. I became politicized watching the House Un-American Activities Committee in action. Finishing college in 1953, I worked on the Hill, where I admired "moderates" like Brooks Hays (D-AR), whose office was next to my father's.[8] My father died in 1954, the summer of the Brown decision, and while I worked briefly for his successor, I gave up my desire for an MA, and returned to the home district, where I married a cotton broker from Newnan. Eventually, I stopped gainful employment and tried to adjust to having just one world and no other to balance it. In a sense, I had completed the first leg of my career trajectory; I thought that my career would be housewifery and volunteer work in politics.

After the birth of two children, I was diagnosed as having had problems related to an undiagnosed case of polio many years before; I was put into a brace and treated by a doctor who frequented the area en route to Warm Springs. On occasions, I went there, too. Since we needed funds to help pay for the household and medical bills, I tried to work for the Democratic party on the local level. Neither my husband nor his father, on whom we greatly depended, would permit this. Newnan, easily connected to Montgomery, was aflame with issues involving race and voting, and I did work for various political candidates anyway.

In 1961, after the birth of my third son, this work began to include church groups and organizations that were preparing for Georgia's abolition of the county unit system, which would give urban counties more clout (rather than just the one or two units accorded these areas). We hoped to elect a moderate governor so that he and the urban areas would lead the state into peaceful school integration. (The university had accepted two African Americans in 1961.) I joined with a woman of my mother's age and others from the Methodist Church and the National Council of Churches to canvass south Atlanta urban areas of African Americans and low income whites; during these visits, we offered rides at specific times to the place of registration. (We were keenly aware that it was hopeless in rural county seats to register African Americans; it would take the Voting Rights Act and then some to achieve this goal.) In 1962 the federal court ruled that Georgia's county unit system was unconstitutional and that, further, the state would have to redistrict according to population. Numan V. Bartley has correctly stated that these changes, which wiped out the bases for political control, were "of such epic proportions that it required a further decade of strife to consolidate."[9] It is miraculous that there was so little bloodshed when one considers that the political changes came at the time of white reaction to the civil rights movement. I can vouch that Georgia was in turmoil the whole decade.

In 1962 I worked diligently to elect Governor Carl Sanders, the young progressive advocating a New Georgia against the segregationist, former Governor Marvin Griffin. My older friend who had been active in the 1930s in the Association for the Southern Women for the Prevention of Lynching also provided transportation in her luxurious touring car to go into Atlanta and under the auspices of a churchwomen's group, with her African-American chauffeur, to register voters and then return on voting day to take many to their urban polling places. Since about half of those I talked with were white, and did not want to register to vote, I began to see the county unit system in an even newer light, as a scheme to disenfranchise workers, and I vowed to try to make it easier for those African Americans who wanted to vote to do so, and to use good offices to try to educate the fearful whites in south Atlanta.

That personal vow was easier to say than to do. While these first bouts of registering whites and a few blacks in Atlanta were nonviolent, and while I was well protected and cared for, I was not dealing with rural meanness. Since Atlanta was not my home, few Newnan people knew any of this, and those who did just thought I was crazy.

From 1963–65 I pursued an MAT degree from Emory University, where the Ford Foundation funded me. A required internship placed me in a newly integrated school in Fulton County (Atlanta) Georgia. There, my homeroom had a very young African-American seventh-grader whose parents taught at the Atlanta University complex. Also in my homeroom was the nephew of the Grand Dragon of the Ku Klux Klan. Many incidents occurred, and I must admit that I lectured frequently on tolerance to this homeroom and to the tenth-graders to whom I taught history. One day in the spring of 1965 I smelled an odor in my car on the way home, and I wheeled into a filling station and jumped out just in time to hear a bang and to see my car afire. The station manger told me the car had been tampered with. I got another car, and determined to leave high school teaching in Atlanta. The summer of 1965 was a fork in the road for me; I graduated just as the Vietnam War accelerated, and I decided to accept a job at West Georgia College.

That fall at West Georgia College, about twenty miles westward, I began my professional career teaching history. Soon after, I became a key worker in the Arnall for Governor campaign of 1966 and the subsequent Write-In Georgia (WIG) effort that drew me into voter education, voter registration, and feminist efforts. Arnall's Republican opponent, Howard Callaway, had served in Congress, where he had opposed federal aid to education, the minimum wage, Medicare, veterans benefits, and of course, civil rights. During the WIG effort, I worked in voter education and registration with Gordon E. Finnie, a delightful nonconformist and agitator, and Ross and Anna Ruth Clark, who taught me the meaning of beloved community. (We were trying to teach how to write in candidates correctly.) On one occasion, however, I was nearly frightened out of my wits when the car I was in was chased out of Barnesville, Georgia and followed closely by a car filled with men. They may have meant us harm, we always thought, until we reached Coweta County, where we still had a sheriff who cared. The WIG effort strengthened my resolve, and it taught me that women were discriminated against in the colleges and sometimes in the day-to-day politics. Finnie helped me figure this out. The unsuccessful WIG campaign and its successful voter registration/education drives were a catalyst in my life.

When I was refused funding for the doctorate at several institutions, a feminist state senator persuaded the Board of Regents to open its scholarship fund to me, despite West Georgia's disinclination to fund a woman. I never forgot that great leap forward from an unexpected source. In my case, the personal had moved to the political, which had propelled me into the career of teaching in higher education. It was only natural that I was transformed into an advocate for equity action issues.

In 1969, while at Swarthmore College researching my dissertation on campus dissent in the 1920s, I was transformed further, from a hawk to a dove, and was convinced that racism and sexism and the war effort were neatly intertwined. I took part in the October peace march of 1969, and I attended only briefly the annual meeting of the American Historical Association that year. A day after the first CCWHP meeting, I was told to sign up and that I would hear from a regional coordinator, who was most likely to be Connie Myers. I did not hear, and I wrote this Connie Myers at Augusta College for information. After many unsuccessful attempts (no letters were returned), I called Augusta, only to be told that no Connie Myers was there. We know now that there was a problem at Augusta College and that Myers was in California, and that her mail was never forwarded. Nor was it sent back, I add.[10] I finally saw a newsletter and found a name, that of Berenice Carroll. When I reached Berenice she had plans to organize a regional affiliate in the South at the meeting of the Southern Historical Association (SHA) in Louisville, Kentucky that November. Berenice came to SHA, and that is a story in itself, for I am positive that she saw what women in the South were against!

There, I became a founding officer and later co-president of the Caucus of Women in History, loosely organized around members of SHA. We thought of ourselves as an affiliate of CCWHP. It was at the AHA meeting in Boston that year that I met most of the early activists in CCWHP and felt the wonderful sisterhood of those early days. Further, I began to work on women's history and to research some of the southern female journalists and leaders in public health.

The early 1970s were crucial years in the women's professional movement, and they had a profound effect on me. Sandi Cooper and the formation of regional affiliates of CCWHP brought me into a web of associates with whom I had treasured friendships that helped sustain me during some hard periods. The personal, political, and professional merged at this juncture of my life and I deeply valued the network, which provided sisterhood for those of us who were isolated. We worked together to make changes in AHA, and I laugh to remember how carefully we orchestrated who was to speak in favor of motions. Sometimes, we had to tell those in the west who had New York accents that their voices would not portray the proper region! We did work together. I remember that Dorothy Ross helped me find the job at Queens College; she was holding the position at AHA that we as a group had lobbied for and won, and she was running an informal employment matching service for women out of the AHA office. The sisterhood of those in the New York Area CCWHP, the West Coast Association, and the Berkshire Conference, plus other groups, were vital to my development as a teacher of women's history at Queens College and as a political activist for the Equal Rights Amendment and other women's issues in North Carolina.

CCWHP and its sisterly network helped open up positions for many of us, including me. In 1973, when Adele Simmons took a position at Tufts, I became chair for Women's History, probably because it was known that I was not going to urge separation of Women's History and women's activity,[11] and I am fairly certain that CCWHP advocates promoted my appointment to the Organization of American Historians' Committee on Women. When I was in Chicago in 1978 working on scholarly activity, Adade Wheeler and I surveyed the most popular American history textbooks to monitor their inclusion of women, and we spent hours visiting publishers' booths at conventions and writing editors to express out dismay. We used precious time to promote the general female welfare. We had to seize the moment before it passed. One of my deepest concerns is that unselfish sisterhood may not be quite so universal today, as it seemed to be then.

At the Newberry Library in 1977 and 1978, I formed strong bonds with Catherine Prelinger, Joan Hoff, Jo Ann Carrigan, and others, including Carol Bleser. Those friendships are deeply rooted. There were many more sisters in my web, including Joan Kelly, who gave me a special push in working for grassroots activities, Sandi Cooper, Joanna Zangrando, and the other early officers of CCWHP. Later on, Nupur Chaudhuri helped encourage my work.

In 1979 I went to the National Endowment for the Humanities, under the Intergovernmental Personnel Act, to work in two NEH programs in the Fellowship Division, the Program for College Fellowships and Summer Stipends. I was to help broaden the base from which the panel of reviewers was to be chosen, to convene and chair peer review panels that judged grant applications. The process had been rather exclusive and mystifying, and the Carter Administration and Joe Duffey, the new NEH chair, wanted to open up the agency to a broader base of grants recipients. I was there for three years and eventually became the program officer for Summer Stipends. After the election of Ronald Reagan, a backlash set in.

In Nupur Chaudhuri's "CCWHP-CGWH: The Second Decade," I am reminded of the very hard work that we all did during those backlash years that increased in their sting each year (1979–1982) that I was in Washington at the NEH.[12] I am aware now of the importance of that period during the 1980s when Kitty Prelinger set the stage for our hard work. I also know the significance of Nupur's own work to bringing order to our finances and to our record keeping. We owe her a special thank you. During this period I served on the

Nominating Committee of AHA (1980–82) and did my best to prevent the backlash from affecting AHA choice of nominees.

I worked hard in the effort begun by Joan Hoff to hold back dues from AHA if it met in states that had not ratified the Equal Rights Amendment, and I supported efforts for passage of the ERA. When approached about the CCWHP presidency, I was grateful for my friends who feared that the isolation back in North Carolina would be hard after the excitement of Washington. Had I known how contentious and vicious the extremists were to be, I am not sure that I would have said yes. Most of my CCWHP presidency will have to stand on its defensive, preventative actions, which I decided would need to be put ahead of everything. The two cardinal points that I wanted to make during the era of 1982–85 were that we needed to bond together in a community to combat these onslaughts against social justice and inclusion, and that we needed to reach out to broaden our constituency so that we ourselves would include others in the battle. My service to the professional community of women was mainly in the form of getting in position for the funding and civil rights battles that were certain to come. One rather large and long-lasting fight was to regain an Independent Civil Rights Commission, on which our member Mary Frances Berry served. Others included our struggles to keep the National Historical and Publications Commission (NHPRC) funded and not abolished. The pace of defense was frenetic.

One positive thing, however, stands out as I recall those days: the establishment and funding of the Joan Kelly Prize. Many valiant efforts, in two stages, combined to produce a substantial prize fund. Conference Group on Women's History (CGWH) president Penny Kanner also strengthened the women's history arm and reached out to have others include commentary and essays in the newsletter.

In chairing the Civil Rights Zap Action Committee (CRZAC) at the request of Frances Keller, I had extremely able committee members: Bob Zangrando, June Patton, and Elizabeth Balanoff. In addition, the officers and key persons in the regionals helped carry out our work of 1986 and 1987. None of it was easy, as civil rights issues never are.

Today, from the vantage point of an outsider, I am fearful that we are not using enough of our energies in promoting the status of women on the political front. These are perilous times, and we need leadership from the top of our profession. There are enormous battles to wage, and we should consider fighting them as sisters, beginning at our local levels. In this way we could grab the chance to move the slow universe of our vision forward. In short, the low status of women on the bottom, both young and old, affects even the grandiose members of our profession. We should be reminded of that occasionally by a sympathetic but jaded activist like myself, who represents a certain segment of rank-and-file women in historical circles—perhaps transitional persons who reentered academe when it was opening up, at a time that was perhaps too late in one way and too early in another, but who value sisterhood and work to maintain it.

NOTES

1. Dan T. Carter, "Reflections of a Reconstructed White Southerner," in *Historians and Race: Autobiography and the Writing of History,* Paul A. Cimbala and Robert F. Himmelberg, eds. (Bloomington: Indiana Univ. Press, 1996), 35.

2. Most of what I do is teach four courses each semester for about six preparations, and then summer school courses. I volunteer to teach in our weekend college, as it is stimulating and carries an extra stipend. It is here that I hear about the ongoing discrimination against women and minorities and other targeted groups by the corporations and by the so-called Christian right, and the need for the "intelligentsia" to speak out about it all.

3. The County Unit System was the device used in the Democratic party primary to elect its candidates. Each county voted by units allotted it, and three smaller counties with one unit each could outvote large counties with two units. Obviously, the system discriminated against cities with more industrial workers and African Americans.

4. My degrees came in three separate decades (1953, 1965, and 1972). I left high school in 1949.

5. John Egerton, *Speak Now Against the Day: The Generation Before the Civil Rights Movement in the South* (New York: Alfred A. Knopf, 1992), 121; see also 120.

6. See Harold Paulk Henderson, *The Politics of Change in Georgia: A Political Biography of Ellis Arnall* (Athens: Univ. of Georgia Press, 1991), 241–45, and campaign literature in possession of author.

7. Margaret Anne Barnes, *Murder in Coweta County* (New York: Reader's Digest Press, 1976).

8. See Brooks Hays, *A Southern Moderate Speaks* (Chapel Hill: Univ. of North Carolina Press, 1959).

9. Numan V. Bartley, *The Creation of Modern Georgia* (Athens: Univ. of Georgia Press, 1983), 196 and 200. See also *The New South, 1945–1980* (Baton Rouge: Louisiana State Univ. Press and the Littlefield Fund for Southern History, the University of Texas, 1995).

10. Constance Ashton Myers has related this to me several times, and she remains a sister in spirit to CCWH. She has reached out in a special way to many in the profession.

11. See Berenice Carroll's excellent piece, "The Twenty-Fifth Anniversary of CCWHP: Reflections on Scholarship and Action, Diversity and Difference," 57–85 in Hilda Smith et al., *A History of the Coordinating Committee on Women in the Historical Profession—Conference Group on Women's History* (Chicago: CCWHP/CGWH, 1994).

12. Chaudhuri's piece is in ibid., 21–42.

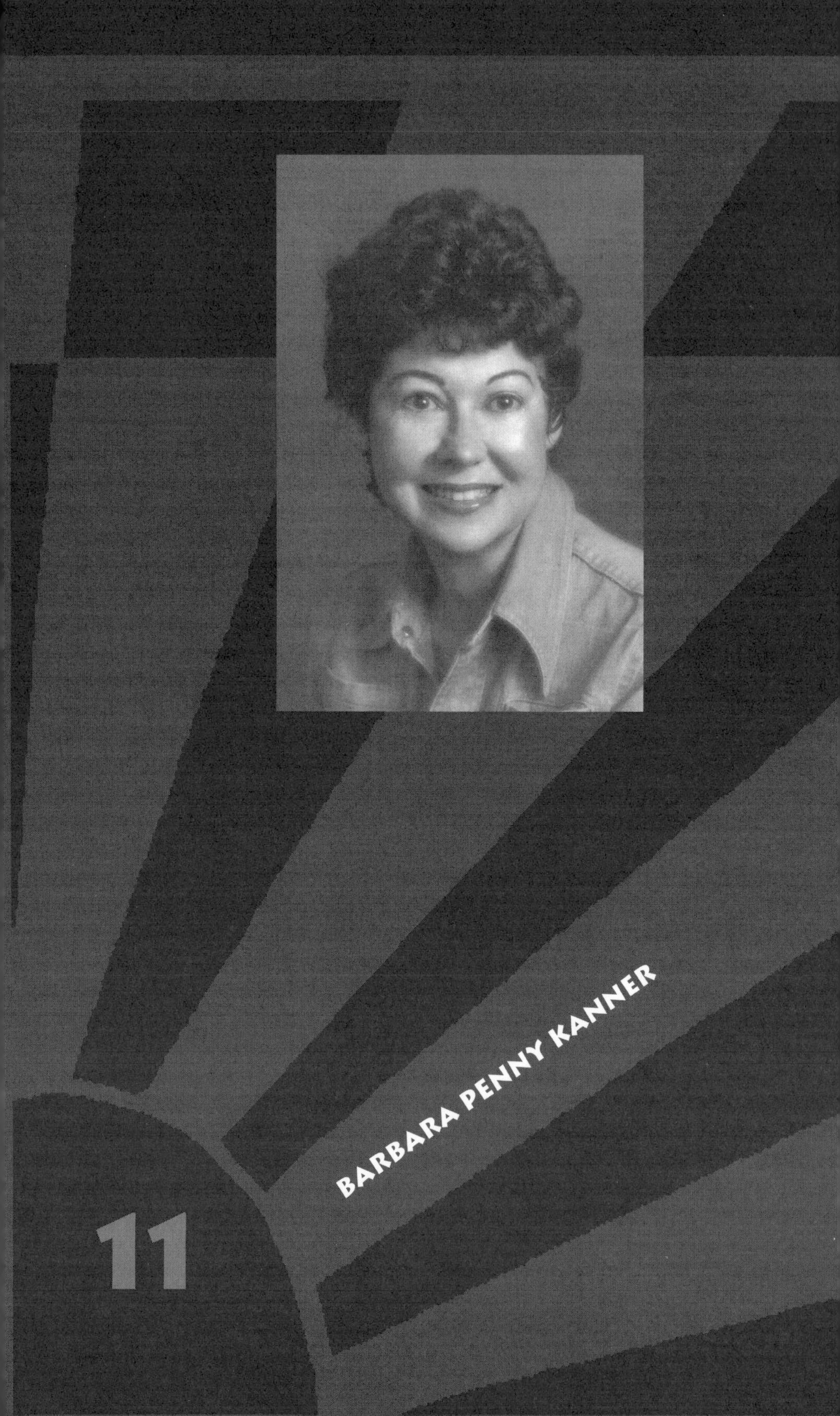

BARBARA PENNY KANNER
11

GROWING INTO HISTORY

> [Upon my return to Oxford University after nursing in WWI], such rationality as I still possessed reasserted itself in a desire to understand how the whole calamity had happened, to know why it had been possible for me and my contemporaries, through our own ignorance and others' ingenuity, to be used, hypnotised, and slaughtered. . . . So, thus portentously, I decided to read History.
> Vera Brittain, *Testament of Youth*, 1933

> In 1972, when the Vietnam War was winding down and the feminist movement was on the rise, I decided to enter the M.A. program in women's history at Sarah Lawrence College. Having been exposed to feminist thinking [by helping to plan] a woman's antiwar demonstration. . . . I was determined to learn more about the historical forces that had shaped my life and dictated the choices I had made as a woman.
> Amy Swerdlow, *Women Strike for Peace*, 1993

Separated by sixty years, the two women historians quoted above give strikingly similar explanations of why they undertook the study of history. Seeing history as a tool for understanding and surmounting adverse circumstances, both of them, in choosing it, declared their self-empowerment. Whatever our experiences as women, we have used the study of history to make sure that

Barbara "Penny" Kanner.

we—not the experiences—gained the upper hand. Still, the specific adversities with which each of us has coped differ from individual to individual. My own feminist "clicks" that made visible the invisible cultural barriers limiting women's opportunities came belatedly, well into adulthood, for I grew up in a household which valued its women as exceptional individuals.

As a child, what I had to contend with was more immediate and personal than a gender bar. I faced the inner conviction that I would grow up to be a self-exposed failure unless I matched or exceeded the accomplishments of my relatives, all self-proclaimed geniuses. In tracing the outlines of my own life, therefore, and in trying to determine to my own satisfaction how the small girl with an inculcated inferiority complex became an established historian, I attempt to pinpoint within my familial environment, educational circumstances, and emotional development those challenging obstacles and intellectual qualities which made historical study for me both a solution and an intense reward.

My family was comprised of ten first- and second-generation central European immigrants who gave me an urban New York upbringing with uncertain financial security. Remarkably, financial limitations had little bearing on the exalted self-identity that the family group enjoyed and ceaselessly praised to my brother and myself. Their specialty—with which they kept me enthralled, in every sense—was collective storytelling about the brilliant artistic gifts, spectacular accomplishments, and supposed blue-blooded origins of our family. My uncle Terry played seven musical instruments professionally; he said he learned them all to compensate for his failure to find work with his favorite: the violin. My mother was celebrated for having shed a sales job as a fancy chocolate dipper to try a theatrical dancing career; several others were nightclub performers; two were career nurses. Furthermore, even women outside the family were made to seem gifted. Because my mother's first child (delivered by a male doctor) had died the day after birth, she would trust only women physicians. Consequently I was delivered and later treated by female physicians only, leading me to believe that women doctors were the norm. (When years later I researched the history of women's entry into medicine, reading the facts of women's struggle to win medical degrees left me dumbfounded.) To a small girl like me, the standards which adults held up seemed fearfully high, and the covert expectation that I would fail haunted my girlhood years.

I was proclaimed the chief beneficiary of the family inheritance of genius due to my early display of gifts in music, dancing, singing, and play-acting. The relatives engaged in a curious mode of praise, however. My dancing would be drawn into comparision with my mother's much-praised talent (she was a "high kicker"), which—they were sure to remind me—was nothing compared with her singing ability, which brought her nightclub audiences to their knees. If they commanded me to sing, my performance would occasion comparison with the musicianship of my mother's sister Sylvia, who was declared able to play "anything" on the piano and who also drew pictures "like a dream." Nor did I escape comparison with the men; my uncle Bert "sang like an angel!" and had found his way into a lustrous thirty-year nightclub career. At odds with their vocal predictions of my success was the covert implication, hanging heavy in the air, that I could never match their accomplishments. Far from reassuring me, my family's celebration of my "gifts" made me a prisoner of their expectations, desperately needing a base of reality upon which to base self-perception.

As I grew older and more experienced, I began to recognize contact points with this needed reality. The first of these was my father. Sitting at the kitchen table with me as the webs of family myth were spun, he did not consume these stories with the same unclouded enthusiasm that I had been conditioned to exhibit. When a relative launched into a particularly entrancing and unlikely memory, my dad would poke me with his elbow, clear his throat loudly, or announce to no one in particular that "There go the Bradleys again!" This was the name—origins unknown—which he used to telegraph to me and my brother that the egregious claims being made were in the service of social snobbery rather than truth. Born not in Europe but in pragmatic Brooklyn, my father had been raised by a cousin while his mother operated a furniture business and his own father passively left the breadwinning to her. As an electrician with a rudimentary education, my father dealt daily with the real world and had enormous common sense. Although our relatives' stories amused him and their performances entertained him, he was too much a realist to let my impressionable mind absorb their grandiose claims without a hefty dollop of salt.

Doubt about the veracity of their stories, however, impacted me less than did the self-doubt these stories raised in me. How could I ever live up to their brand of talent, or fulfill their anticipations? Would they find out and brand me a fraud? Would disappointment lead to withdrawal of their love? Always, they wanted me to memorize things for them, recite for them, perform for them. I complied anxiously in order to meet their expectations, which were of course based on their claims of inborn family genius. In conflicting ways, my fascination with this oral family history inspired, intimidated, and made skepticism bloom within me. It also motivated me to pursue factual research. I needed to find out how much in the family narratives was actually true. I also needed to understand myself, without the gloss of familial wishful thinking. Could I trust family claims about my potential? By what means could I independently learn to recognize my real talents and choose an appropriate life's path?

My attempts at self-discovery were furthered by my reading habits, which gave me another contact point with reality. At age thirteen, I happened one day to see advertised in the newspaper a set of books at a coupon price—$1.85—which was within the range of my modest allowance. Attractive to me as something I could buy for myself, acquiring and reading these books was doubly enticing as an act of rebellion, since my relatives knew and cared nothing about literature. I found myself happily introduced to the magnificently realistic style of the French social novelists: de Maupaussant, Balzac, Zola. When every last page had been read, the reluctant acknowledgment that my allowance would not cover unlimited purchases pointed me toward the New York City public libraries, where a library card allowed periodic escape from the family atmosphere. By the time I turned 16, I had discovered the authorial voice of Dickens and many other British and American novelists. Reading gave me a secret set of mentors, who rivaled the aunts and uncles. More importantly, these authors also showed that there were more truthful, more satisfying ways of telling stories than my relatives knew existed, methods that could turn narration into a valuable tool for preserving past truth.

In the depression of the 1930s everybody had to work, and my parents looked to my potential as a breadwinner. Although the family had highfalutin notions about itself, we were poor. Several relatives had received their music and art training at settlement houses. While my own parents would bridge no charity of this kind and had a wholesale naivete about the need for mentors, contacts, and agents, they dreamed that I would become a highly paid theatrical star bringing them fame and fortune. So, they introduced me at age 12 to the entertainment staffs of country hotels and radio programs, and to singing, dancing, and acting lessons to which each family member contributed 50 cents a week. Although I never reached the stellar heights about which my family fantasized, this show business experience provided valuable lessons. It gave a sense of empowerment, showing me how to turn the director's vision into a vehicle for self-expression. Organizational politics is not too different, with the sense of productive ensemble collaboration being the same whether in a theatrical or a political venue.

My first childhood experience under direction was at radio station WOR on its weekly Sunday radio program, "Rainbow House." With other young singers I performed a solo every week. This experience opened my eyes to the grueling nature of stage training and to the discipline of 6 a.m. studio rehearsals. From WOR I went to CBS to join a company of child performers called "Dolls on Parade." In a group of singers, actors, and full symphony orchestra we learned a repertoire and rehearsed for an entire year, with the management arranging for potential sponsors to come audition us. Another of the "dolls" on perpetual parade was Beverly Sills, who became my subway traveling buddy, homework partner, transliterator of foreign-language lyrics, and confidante. Her parents, as ambitious for their daughter as my own, had chosen the career of operatic diva for her from the time she could carry a tune. They never tired of playing records of the great sopranos they were motivating her to emulate—even before her own talents became evident. I could personally identify with her extraordinary childhood effort to fulfill her family's dreams, although I felt envious of what I imagined was a more knowledgeable and consistent support group than my own. We resumed our friendship in adulthood, recounting experiences and confidences that only people who have similarly labored and struggled, from their earliest days, can share with true empathy.

Coinciding with my high school graduation as an honors student was my departure from "Dolls on Parade," since I had grown too old for the image of the show. I decided to apply to the City University of New York, choosing the only campus that permitted students (after two years of liberal arts) to select a major in education and business administration. This campus came to the top of my priority list at least partly to quiet my parents, who worried ceaselessly about preparing me to earn an income. Another practical reason for its choice was the availability of part-time work opportunities near the campus, so I could have the measure of independence that came with money of my own.

I happily contemplated separating from the family and discovering the world of learning. In my freshman year, however, the drama department discovered me. For the next two years I did my homework in the darkened Pauline Edwards theatre while starring in plays and musicals. By my sophomore year, the tug between theatricals and career preparation became strained; again I chose academics over the stage. Besides, I had just met my future husband: president of both the senior class and student council, he was voted "the man most likely to succeed." We were married in my junior year.

After graduation from CCNY I applied for a high school teaching license in social studies, but (with the next available exam date far in the future) also entered an executive training program sponsored by Orbach's Department Store. That training became my entrée to an assistant buyer's job that paid for rent and groceries until my husband finished business school. With his new MBA, he accepted a job offer on the West Coast, which moved us into a different and exciting ambience. Over the next seven years I had two children and earned a California teaching certificate at the UCLA Extension evening school. It was an interesting period for me, with a double focus. On one hand, to boost my husband's business ambitions I served as a professional corporate wife. On the other hand, I threw myself into UCLA's requried courses for the teaching certificate, which included sociology, psychology, literature, science, and history, which for the first time introduced me to the realm of professional historiography. These thirty hours of cross-disciplinary graduate courses changed my outlook profoundly. Earning the teaching license and spending the next few years teaching high school, I kept remembering the stimulation of an academic environment. Consequently, in 1960, I applied to the graduate program in UCLA's history department and was delighted to be accepted.

Enrolling in graduate school meant that once again I was entering an arena—academia—that for many women has been fraught with sex discrimination. My personal experience as a graduate student helped preserve an ignorance of the academic barriers facing women. In the 1960s, graduate seminars were mainly scheduled in the evening, sparing me a struggle to find day care. I was able to offer room and board to another student in exchange for aiding with childcare, an arrangement that in 1963 helped me survive the simultaneous birth of my third child and exams for the master's degree. Although I worried about my age and status as a returning student, faculty were warm and supportive, convincing me that they overlooked such considerations in favor of students' individual talents and potential. My achievement-oriented husband was also supportive, especially when I won a large dissertation fellowship from the American Association of University Women. That award induced both of us to bend plans to ensure that I could fill the entire term of my research proposal abroad.

It was now 1968, and the women's movement was about to surge into media prominence. Although aware of feminism, I felt little connection to it. However, without consciously intending to write a dissertation in women's history, pre-doctoral research had led me to Urania Cottage, a previously unstudied nineteenth-century philanthropic reformatory for delinquent girls. There they were educated and groomed to undertake respectable work in Australia or South Africa, with the woman founder, Angela Burdett-Coutts, arranging and completely financing their emigration. She had been the richest and most influential philanthropist in Victorian England. That Charles Dickens had agreed to set up and personally manage her girls' reformatory motivated me to research the matter more closely.

I set out for two months of study in England at archives and libraries. Researching the life and writings of Burdett-Coutts became a daily preoccupation. I grew increasingly interested in her and others of the period as real people beyond any functional roles. I also began to pay attention to how their worldviews differed from my own. The differences were weighty and the social implications disturbing. The cumulative weight in their accounts of misunderstandings about women's biology, self-righteous beliefs about women's moral and intellectual inferiority, and of zealous schemes—based on these beliefs—to blame and punish women for their own injuries began to make me see gender as a huge social conundrum more than a century after the fact.

Everything I learned added to my new awareness of women's longstanding victimization. Urania Cottage had been a home for "fallen" women, which meant that many of the texts I studied addressed the issue of how to keep girls "pure" as well as how to help them once the "fatal step" was taken. The majority of nineteenth-century (male) commentators were eager to reform fallen women's "sin" but seemed indifferent to their welfare and future livelihood. Only a few writers seemed sensitive to the compelling finanacial necessity that drove so many women, frantic with either starvation factory wages or unemployment, into the better-paid trade of prostitution.[1] Most writers triumphantly identified the woman as the guilty agent of her own downfall, and it was therefore assumed that females could not begin self-reform unless they were taught to repudiate their vanity through a punitively rigorous course of plain dress, dreary food, and domestic work.

As I read source after source, the aspersions against women and the nearly universal assumption of a need to restrict them zealously assumed the aspect of a gigantic dampening blanket thrown over female ambitions. This disturbing impression lingered after my return to the States, prodding awareness both of the growing women's movement and of gender dynamics within the university environment. When I returned to England two years later to research women's autobiographies, I searched actively for any discussion pertaining to gender. I found oral interviews with working-class women (all in their 70s or older) speaking explicitly and candidly about events sixty years before. Their appraisals of how being girl children impacted these events was impressively insightful. Collectively, the panoramic picture of turn-of-the-century gender attitudes in these narratives was far more complex and nuanced than the new feminist histories being written in the 1960s indicated. These autobiographies were the genuine articles, authentic primary sources, vastly different from the watered-down, secondhand, reductive theories found in textbooks.

In 1970, women's history was beginning to be formally included in the university, but along the way came a politicization process, in which the content and emphasis of the new written histories reflected a covert pressure to serve current feminist agendas. Much of the writing also privileged a simplified outlook and theory, excluding conjecture and debate. Although I had read politicized feminist historical studies, my examination of primary sources suggested that too often the prevailing theories failed to acknowledge many of the qualifying circumstances that real women testified to in their narratives.

In recent years, the opposition between theory and inductive example has fueled debate between proponents of poststructuralism and empiricists in the field of gender studies.[2] To me (then and now) the analysis of gender has serious potential to mislead if it does not take into account the individual experiences of women. In diametric contrast, earlier studies written by historians Ivy Pinchbeck and Alice Clark succeed where theoreticized feminist histories fail, because Pinchbeck and Clark committed their energies to scrupulous empirical research.[3] Their scholarly feminism—after which I would pattern my own—laid evidence bare to speak for itself, showing the inherent complexities that generalization conceals. And although the reductiveness of the broad theories on display in the early feminist histories annoyed me, it also showed me how I might personally contribute to the developing field of women's history by locating and making accessible the wealth of primary sources that remained uninvestigated by and unfamiliar to researchers.

Time in Britain exposed me to the rising tide of feminism in additional ways. I had listened attentively to British female academics complain that rigid bureaucratic categorization of all women as "dependents" had buried important female historical sources in the "Family Assistance Office" or the "Dependent Beneficiary Office," making them virtually unrecoverable. I had listened as young women scholars discussed and developed projects about "sexual divisions in society." At these meetings, I first heard of an archive dedicated to papers by and about women of the British Isles. Ray Strachey had founded this library, named for suffragist Millicent Fawcett. I found it to be maintained by just one professional librarian, on a budget limited to rent and utilities. The lower floors were in disrepair; valuable nineteenth-century journals and pamphlets and documents littered the pavement. I met five or six aged volunteer ladies working near their teapots, trying to preserve rare books and papers in plastic foodwrap. The card file of the cumulative holdings was out of order and out of date. Establishing myself in a nearby hotel, I dug into the Fawcett's holdings and learned more from this direct evidence than from any text or reference work.[4] Such expeditions in libraries and archives enlarged my newly awakened feminist interests. I felt lucky not to have been on the receiving end of discrimination, whether at school, in the theatre, or at home.

My feminist "consciousness-raising" had come at the same time that the century-and-a-half-old women's movement had revived. In the late 1960s women historians in the US formed the Coordinating Committee on Women in the Historical Profession (CCWHP). My own activism complemented its goals. Women's testimonials from the past were inspiring me to disseminate women's historical truths and to work toward enlarging the presence of women's history in universities. This academic project became my activism, both in teaching and in interacting with department faculty. I labored to get undergraduate students thinking about women's history and to win department acceptance of women's history as a legitimate course of study. And I joined the West Coast Association of Women Historians (WAWH), whose aims promised to bring women historians' disparate strengths, resources, and connections together to monitor and improve the stature of both women and women's history within western US academic departments.

Of course, women historians had to discover and map the landscape of women's history at the same time as they fought for its academic legitimization. I knew that it was not enough for any of us simply to proselytize. The years 1969–1975 turned into a detective adventure. What (and especially where) were the most fruitful primary sources for women's history? As I made experimental forays, newly recovered materials provoked new questions that pointed to further research.

In the late stages of my dissertation work I received a morale boost. A California press commissioned me to produce a "women's lib reader." At an academic meeting, I met the editor-in-chief of a publishing house who was putting together a social science series on current issues. They had not yet located an editor for their reader on the women's movement. After telling him (at length) about my own feminist efforts and dissertation, I leaped to accept when he asked if I was interested in taking on the job. Encouraged, I arranged with Kate Millett to reprint the second chapter of her 1970 *Sexual Politics*, won the agreement of feminist writers to waive honoraria and fees for reprints, and even persuaded Gloria Steinem to republish a germinal essay without a fee. And then the parent publishing company reneged, the sort of official repositioning that has forced women's historians for the last thirty years to keep maneuvering to preserve our gains. Corporate headquarters lost confidence in the sales potential of the women's liberation market and stopped the project in its tracks. Frustration seemed the sole result of my expenditure of money and time (with months lost from my dissertation writing).

However, other reactions to my early feminist labors were more gratifying. In 1971, on the recommendation of my mentor D. C. Moore, I contributed "The Women of England in a Century of Social Change" to Martha Vincinus's *Suffer and Be Still*. This guide to research, which urged the integration of women's historical studies into mainstream history, was my first experiment with "bibliomethodology," a method that I developed of exploring historical questions through interpretive bibliography. Bibliomethodology requires setting up historical questions and categories appropriate to current concerns and historical contexts, establishing a historically logical arrangement of the subjects, and integrating the sources within a meaningful discussion that includes debate, documentation of ideas, scholarly beliefs, and critical comment.[5] Bibliomethodology presupposes in the bibliographer a sophisticated grasp both of historical issues and contemporary emphasis, for while useful references under orderly headings attract researchers by offering great accessibility, the chosen set of topics and questions framing the sources will ultimately shape the historical interpretation. In addition, when sources that answer intriguing questions are scanty, it becomes imperative to avoid wishful thinking or conjectural theory to fill in voids which are actually inescapable.[6] I had to learn the pitfalls of this method and how to avoid them as I went along.

A chance to begin enlarging the scope of my classroom work came in 1972 when, armed with my newly earned doctorate, I started teaching both in the UCLA extension system and at Mount St. Mary's College. Another avenue for scholarly activism opened when Peter Stansky, whom I had met that year at the Pacific Coast Conference on British Studies (PCCBS), invited me to give a position paper at a Stanford women's history convention. That 1974 conference, which demonstrated palpably that prestigious universities took women's studies seriously, gave the field an enormous boost and widened my visibility as a feminist historian.

During the same year, the bibliography for that unpublished reader turned into a 300 item foundational reading list for a graduate seminar in women's history at UC Davis. I was thrilled that this would be the first women's studies pre-dissertation seminar there. My own projects reflected the rapidly expanding interest in feminism. These included a second bibliomethodological guide for Martha Vicinus's 1977 *A Widening Sphere*. That year, I formed a panel for the annual PCCBS conference on "What is Women's History? The Case of Britain." PCCBS has held women's panels in every succeeding year. Then, as cho-chair with Cynthia Brantley for the 1975 meeting of WAWH, I put together the first conference that followed the established AHA format.

In retrospect, the political and academic landscape of the early 1970s seems full of triumphs for feminism, with groundbreaking conferences, publications, and employment opportunities making women historians feel that together we could make great strides. I certainly felt that way as I turned to the national CCWHP, where women historians could support each other's research and work effectively toward jointly agreeable goals. At the 1975 AHA I met the CCWHP treasurer Hilda Smith, who was promoting the Conference Group on Women's History (CGWH) as a specialized addition to the existing CCWHP. CGWH would serve as a national clearinghouse for information on the history of women, an immensely appealing plan that confirmed my impulse to join the organization.

At this time I was the busiest I've ever been, juggling teaching and writing with organizational obligations to WAWH, PCCBS, and the Research Society for Victorian Periodicals. By 1979, while researching my first book, *Women of England from Anglo-Saxon Times to the Present: Interpretive Bibliographical Essays*, I was elected to the WAWH presidency.

In 1978–79, both regional and national women's historical associations worked to pass the ERA. When the efforts of then CCWHP president Joan Hoff succeeded in getting AHA to boycott states that had not ratified the amendment, it seemd a tangible endorsement of the effectiveness of women historians' solidarity. This was not lost on any of us; at WAWH's 1981 meeting, Catherine Prelinger urged greater solidarity among all groups to influence professional issues crucial to women historians. As networking became a top regional and national priority—CCWHP President Mollie Davis labeling this effort "Operation Draw Tight"—my election as president of CGWH provided another opening to promote networking. I aimed to strengthen

CCWHP–CGWH as a clearinghouse for scholarly resources as well as for information on jobs and funding. Thus I introduced the "Scholars' Exchange" column to the newsletter so that researchers could share discoveries of primary sources, collections, contact people, and methodologies. Under this rubric, we published syllabi for a broad range of women's history and studies courses.

Flushed with our own successes, women academics often were uneasy that their gains did not extend to their female students, from whom the next generation of women historians would come. Virginia Woolf's tart observations in *A Room of One's Own* regarding the shabby treatment (the word "marginalization" hadn't yet come into use) of women students in a university environment seemed as applicable in the 1980s as they had in the 1920s. When I received a teaching appointment at UCLA in 1980, interaction with female undergraduates and graduate students highlighted how the existing system of rewards and scholarships subtly denigrated women's history by passing it over entirely. Here was an arena where life circumstances led me to endow in 1983 the Marry Ritter Beard Prize at UCLA for the most outstanding history honors thesis or senior paper on women and gender. The many applicants for the prize and the high quality of their dissertation work demonstrated that women's history had an army of superb practitioners on its hands, if only they could be acknowledged and rewarded decently for their efforts. Three years later, seeing that professional encouragement for women graduate students was pitifully inadequate in all disciplines, I endowed the campus-wide Mary Wollstonecraft Prize, administered by the UCLA Center for the Study of Women (CSW), for the most outstanding doctoral dissertation on women and gender in any discipline, providing it uses historical perspective. Last year I set up another annual endowment, the George Eliot Prize for the best literature in history dissertation using a women's history focus.

A 1987 collaboration with Susan Groag Bell generated the research project nearest to my heart, "British Women's Autobiographies, 1750–1950." This won an NEH seed grant administered by Standford University's Institute for Research on Women and Gender. During a second phase on my own, I organized the massive reading and annotation needed for the research guide, which gives scholars access to over 1,000 women's autobiographical narratives. Teaching at both UCLA and Occidental College (as well as serving as PCCBS president in 1995) swamped my daily hours and frazzled my nerves, but the finished guide, *Women in Context* (published in late 1997), has made me wish that my own earlier researches could have had such a resource, bringing together the direct voices and opinions of so many forgotten women for the first time.

I've steadily gravitated toward autobiography as a primary source without equal. I found myself recently reading over a chapter from a women's history anthology and noting with pleasure the number of women's autobiographies the author had used to ground her points. Much of my interest in personal narrative, it seems in retrospect, was first sparked by my relatives holding forth daily on their own life stories in such dramatic and embellished fashion. Yes, they embroidered. They also managed to distill, through their personal perspectives, the essence of what it had been like for their grandfather to have been a Hungarian in the 1890s, or for young people to grow up in eastern Europe within a complex alien cluture whose nuances I could never otherwise have learned. Within academia, the trends that modify how we approach history and what sources we choose to examine—or disregard—succeed each other steadily, significantly altering academic expectations over the years. The present impulse to privilege theory over examination exasperates me. Until this trend passes, I will continue with my empirical researches, trusting that the work will be of use to future generations of academics with priorities we can't begin to predict. Although the place of women's history and womens' historians within academia requires our vigilance lest it be remarginalized, I am not worried. The combined sophistication and motivation of women historians has now attained the "critical mass" necessary to keep women's history central, viable, and vocal.

The young women entering our academic sights are also not like us (much as we would like them to be), for their chronological context, perceived social relevancies, and priorities have shifted them inevitably toward a newly revised feminist outlook. As I had found in reading dusty, forgotten autobiographies at the British Library, the many faces of women's real lives—whether of nineteenth-century philanthropists or twentieth-century historians—defy glib generalizations. And still to be located are an unbelievable number of lost primary documents which can open up to us the lives of previous women even as their discovery nourishes our historical awareness. If women's history thrives in the next century, it will be at least partly due to our efforts to recuperate these forgotten treasure troves of women's sources, to write the books that make the sources accessible, to raise the consciousness of our colleagues, students, and ourselves, and to nurture the coming generations of women historians who will build on the foundations which we have laid.

NOTES

1. Pamphlets by the London City Mission and the London Female Preventive and Reformatory Institution, reprinted in the periodical *The Magdalen's Friend*.

2. For example, Joan Scott, *Gender and the Politics of History* (New York: Columbia Univ. Press, 1988), 6. In contrast, see June Purvis, *Women's History Britain, 1850–*

1945: An Introduction (New York: St. Martin's Press, 1995), 12–13, and Joan Hoff, "Gender as a Postmodern Category of Paralysis," in *Women's History Review* 3 (1994), 159.

3. See Alice Clark's *Working Lives of Women in the 17th Century* (London: Routledge, 1919) and Ivy Pinchbeck's *Women Workers and the Industrial Revolution, 1750–1850* (London: Routledge, 1930).

4. In recent years, with feminist headway having been made in British academia, the Fawcett has fared better. Having moved to City of London Polytechnic, it remains a vital repository for British women's history and social studies, and has recently (1998) recieved a grant from the National Lottery Commission that will establish it as Britain's official, state-funded National Library of Women.

5. Barbara Penny Kanner, "Preface" in *Women in English Social History, 1800–1914*, vol. 1 (New York: Garland, 1990), xii.

6. Kanner, "Introduction" in *Women of England from Anglo-Saxon Times to the Present* (Hamden, CT: Archon Books, 1979), 10.

12

FRANCES RICHARDSON KELLER

A Graduate Student's Odyssey

It happened slowly. My coming into the modern world, I mean.

I came from a remote village of some 3,500 persons. Everyone knew everyone else and everyone knew everything worth remembering about everyone else's family. Not that there weren't distinctions, classic in proportions, as I would say looking back. My family owned the great underground cheese cold-storage plant that constituted the major industry of the village. In a tiny house on Rural Avenue next door to my mother's housekeeper lived the most talented young musician I ever heard. But our paths crossed only in school when we happened to find ourselves in the same music section. All about us, over the gently sloping Adirondack foothills and up Tug Hill itself, stretched the grazing lands where cattle roamed, where they munched grass and supplied milk for making the New York State sharp cheddar cheese so difficult to come by anymore.

When I was very small, I was given great privileges. I heard my mother and my father speak respectfully of books, music, drama, art, languages, accomplishments. Not that anyone said these were the good things of life—just that everyone knew they were. On the shores of Lake Brantingham, in the Adirondacks, my father built a summer lodge; there I would read and wonder about the mysteries of life and love and how had anything really happened. But not until my father became ill did I find the opportunity to listen to the

Frances Richardson Keller celebrating with Linda Kerber and Sondra Herman the 25th anniversary of the Committee on Women of the Organization of American Historians, San Francisco, 1997.

brilliant college student he hired to read for him and to watch that my little sister and I didn't fall into the lake.

He was tall, this young man. His face was pale and his hair was dark. He could raise one eyebrow higher than the other. His family owned a newspaper, the maverick *Lowville Democrat*. He could tell stories. At dusk in summer, we would be sitting in our flat, gray-green rowboat next to the boat house at the edge of Brantingham Lake, waiting for him to tell us a story.

To my mind our storyteller knew every wonderful thing. He could translate Caesar's *Commentaries*, and almost remember a lot of it without looking back. He knew all about where Caesar had been and what Caesar had done. Once I asked him if he knew about the French Revolution. He replied that he knew everything about the French Revolution and most of this he related for me.

He had always been an honor student. I knew that he was headed for graduate school. As I listened to him read and talk, it seemed to me that he was entering an unimaginably magic world. Even then, when I was twelve or so, a large part of me longed to experience that magic. At that time I had not understood that a graduate student's career is only a way station in the search for knowledge and meaning.

In the village, our beautiful red brick home on the corner of Dayan and Easton Streets held eighteen rooms. There were gardens with apple trees and tulips and peonies and a tennis court where children of the village came to play with my sister and me. We were comfortably well off. Looking back, I see that we weren't rich in any sense that wealth is understood these days.

Perhaps because I was a girl, I could early sense a conspiracy in the upstate air: Nobody told me about it, but I knew it well. I would take lessons in everything going, I would do my best in my classes, I would go to college, and then I would marry somebody right away. Not much could go wrong with the world if you did it that way. But vaguely I knew in my head and somewhere in my heart that this wouldn't be the design to accomplish the visions I was coming to cherish.

Then came the Great Depression. My father died. That year, 1929, the world did a tailspin. As I had grown, I had exhibited some fondness for school, and so had become accustomed to approval from the overlordship. But that year I did miserably in all my subjects. When June rolled around, my trust in everybody and everything, especially my trust in myself, had been demolished.

My Aunt Leah, a history teacher, whose full name—Fanny Leah May Bell—suited her large and prepossessing presence, decided to take me, at age fifteen, to Europe. She wanted and tolerated no acquaintance with the abysmal twentieth century. But she possessed a formidable intimacy with the rest of the human experience. I remember that the columns in Napoleon's tomb, Les Invalides, represented each of the conqueror's military engagements. Determined to put an end to my ignorance, Aunt Leah stood me in front of every one of those columns while she recited the details of each battle. I won't listen to her, I told myself. I won't listen to her! But even a cursory familiarity with the events of my life reveals that I heard her.

I knew that somehow, somewhere, even as the depression settled in, and in spite of the cataclysm which had befallen our family fortunes, I would go to college. Nor is there any denying that thoughts of an unending, unfreighted pursuit of truth and knowledge at the most romantic of graduate schools pulsated in the dreams I dreamed by night and by day.

I was fortunate—you might say lucky—to complete a bachelor's degree at Sarah Lawrence College in Bronxville, New York. My teachers there, the first adults I wanted to emulate, brought me to a realization of my lack of knowledge. I had traveled. I knew about castles and cathedrals and great museums. But from those early conferences I learned that I didn't know anything at all about the social and political structure of our nation. I came to realize that I didn't even have more than a nodding acquaintance with American literature or American history, or for that matter with any of the social sciences. But my teachers restored my confidence that I could learn about these fascinating subjects, even as they helped me to realize that I cared deeply about making a contribution of my own.

When I graduated three years later, my psychology instructor, Polly Duffy, arranged a small stipend for me to continue studies at Johns Hopkins University. It didn't begin to be enough. In that year, 1935, the depression dragged on. My sister was ready for college. Still, such was the social climate in which we lived and learned that no one I knew had suggested it would be a good idea to think about supporting myself.

I drifted. I read the news in the *Campus,* our student publication at Sarah Lawrence. "They are going to make up a catalogue of girls interested in getting jobs," an article said. "A tea was suggested—although of course there are problems. . . . There is the problem of girls taking volunteer jobs and thereby making it possible for employers to employ less people with a wage; It is feared that the attitude towards employing Sarah Lawrence girls will be that if they could afford to come here to college they do not need jobs."[1]

For a little while I made some kind of connection with the New York Emergency Rescue Committee, an all-but-volunteer group that was raising money to bring authors and other victims of Hitler's pogroms into this country. I probably learned about the Committee from Max Lerner, one of my teachers. I cared for what they were trying to do. But the job didn't last, probably because I was too unsophisticated to make myself useful.

Rather thoughtlessly, I next found one of those routine, go-nowhere, sales jobs that carried a subsistence wage at Milgrim's on 57th Street in New York City. Although my storyteller had married somebody else and had become an assistant professor at a western university, the most important part of me vividly remembered and in some sense lived with visions of graduate school and a different life. But graduate school would have to wait. I didn't give up the idea. I read *The New York Times* and everything else I could discover.

So began a different kind of education. Until then I hadn't thought much about money. Someone had provided everything, abundantly. One weekend a Sarah Lawrence friend invited me to visit her in Scranton. We went to parties. There I met a handsome broker, the Princeton graduate to whom I became engaged. Although he suited my family and seemed compatible in every outward detail, I soon felt doubts about sharing my life with him, doubts lacking shape or character, doubts indistinct in meaning. But my doubts were persistent enough so that I went to Scranton, intending to withdraw from the engagement.

I must have lacked some measure of confidence in my own voices. In time we returned to my village and married in the gray stone Presbyterian Church at the top of the village green in Lowville. I wore an elegant, ivory satin wedding gown with Brussels and rose-point lace and a long train. There were six bridesmaids. My sister and my best friend Evelyn Segal were maids of honor. Still, I hadn't discovered a path leading any way toward heights I had glimpsed in my childhood.

Then began a life at 55 East 86th Street in New York City. But the honeymoon in Europe and the first of my pregnancies failed to dispel my thoughts about finding myself in graduate school, talking and associating with people who wrote books, people who were spending their lives exclusively—so I believed—in seeking knowledge and truth.

Soon I had a little boy, whom I loved at once, more than my life. Just as I began to realize that I scarcely knew how to take care of myself, I experienced the weight of becoming responsible for another human person. I believe my troubles began about that time. In what must have been an effort to deal with forces pulling in two directions, I registered at Columbia University for a master's degree in psychology. I nearly got the degree. I had come to the end of the course work and had only to write the thesis when I became ill—a curious illness, for the doctor could find nothing wrong. I was, however, almost incapable of functioning when I gave up the effort to do the work at Columbia. Through all the anxiety, I never lost touch with the visions of my girlhood. In the back of my mind I cherished a dream of finding the best of life by going to graduate school, and after that making use of the skills I would learn. It still would have to wait.

But the dilemma intensified. Not too long after the birth of a second beautiful little boy, my symptoms returned. I would tremble and break into a cold sweat for no reason, or my heart would pound furiously. Or I couldn't sleep. I was so haunted by a fear of dying that I could not bear the sight of a hearse or a graveyard or the thought of a funeral. One night these symptoms continued all the night. In those days doctors made house calls, so when the doctor arrived in the morning, he decided again that there was nothing wrong. "Do you ever sit down for a cocktail before dinner?" he asked. And then he prescribed valium for regular use.

This proved a misfortune of great proportions. I did take the valium, regularly, for years. For a long time I couldn't leave the house without knowing it was in my purse. It enabled me to cope with my self and the life I had, even as I knew that it dulled my senses. Two more pregnancies ensued. I loved my children. I felt a total commitment to their welfare. But increased doses of valium proved insufficient to prevent a complete nervous breakdown. Soon a divorce was in the works.

Looking back, I marvel that I escaped the terrifying fates that could have befallen me. My husband, small children, and I moved to Ohio. Somehow I stumbled back toward the University of Toledo, a mile or so from where we lived. It wasn't a good day. My symptoms were present. As I waited for an interview with the director of Graduate Studies, a psychology professor, my eye happened to fall upon an open book on the long, cluttered table in the room outside his office. The top of the page read "Anxiety Neurosis." The article precisely described my condition—every one of my symptoms, the fears I felt. It ended with the heartening news that "These people are experiencing a conflict" and that "they can usually be helped." Strangely, it didn't occur to me to seek professional counsel. I fled. I was unable even to stay for the interview. But I had read and understood that my troubles resulted from a conflict at the very center of my self, and I had realized that my self mattered.

From that day I gradually uncovered the truths about that conflict: I loved my children and had to see to their needs at the same time that I yearned to develop my own possibilities. I started to consider how I could resolve that conflict. I knew that the best way to overcome a fear is to confront it. To conquer the fear of death from which I suffered, I considered looking for a job in a mortuary. I actually got into the car, intending to drive past the cemetery near my house on the way to a funeral home. But I was never quite able to summon the nerve it would have taken to make that trip.

I began, however, to take courses at the university close to where I lived in Ottawa Hills, Ohio. Would it help if I could earn my living? The quickest way would be to get a high school teaching credential. Two electives were allowed. So it happened that for those two electives I walked falteringly into the history department. I've been close to one ever since. I loved every moment of it! I did well in my history classes, and strangely my children seemed to benefit. Slowly my symptoms receded.

Soon I found myself substituting at Sylvania High school for Mrs. Swanson, a kindly, seasoned English teacher who had broken her leg. I can laugh when

I remember that turbulent time. I was teaching Senior Composition over the top of her desk, and on my way to a master's degree in history, studying Chinese history and Russian history under her desk. Those lists of alien names remain somewhere in my consciousness, I am sure, as do the niceties of English sentences I learned with my students, as does the juggling it took to care for my children. I spent the next term teaching and learning at Devilbiss, a high school in the city of Toledo itself.

So it happened that in my late 40s I arrived at a crucial moment. In June of 1964 I got my master's degree. The next month my mother died. After three difficult years, my divorce became final. I learned that I needed some surgery. As one piece of wrenching news followed another, I didn't lose my balance. When I emerged from the hospital I felt emotionally drained, but mentally competent and functional. I made the decision. I would not allow myself to sink into a waiting morass. I would go on to study for a PhD in American history; wherever that resolve might lead, I would take my small children and my middle-sized children with me.

Confident that my academic record could stand scrutiny, I applied to three universities: Harvard, Northwestern, and the University of Chicago. Harvard replied too soon, saying thanks, but no thanks. Polite. No explanations. I heard nothing from Northwestern or the University of Chicago. Time was short, for if either of them took me, I would have to sell my house, move from Ottawa Hills, and then find schools for my children.

Rather than wait and hope I decided to go to Chicago. With one of those over-sized, flower-emblazoned suitcases that turned out to be much too heavy to carry with any degree of comfort, I reached the office of professor Gray, chairman of the history department at Northwestern University. For him, the interview was a routine requirement if someone insisted on showing up. For me, it was crucial to reach a decision; for the first time, I was on my own. I knew there were hazards in selling a house, moving to Chicago, and finding a place to live, especially if you brought children. Then, most importantly, there was locating good, accessible schools. He gave me an answer: "Frankly, Mrs. Keller," he said, "you are over 35 and you are a woman. You would never be able to put back into the profession what it would take to train you."

I was crushed. I remember leaving his office, lugging that suitcase to the curbside, sitting on it, and asking myself, "What am I going to do now?" A taxi rolled by. I summoned it. Though it was too expensive, I rode with the suitcase from Evanston to the Chicago midway and the University of Chicago Social Science building at 1162. It was my last chance. What did I have to lose?

The history department occupied the third floor. In an outer room Professor Richard Wade happened that afternoon to be conducting a seminar in city history. To reach the inner offices you would have to interrupt his seminar.

Again I sat in the hallway on the carpetbag suitcase and I listened. With all my heart I wanted to be there. I knew I could do the work. I waited until the seminar ended to enter Chairman William McNeill's office.

A tall, dignified—and, as I learned, very eminent—gentleman sat therein. I didn't wait for him to speak. "Professor McNeill, are you going to keep me out of here because I am over 35 and a woman?" I asked. "What?" he answered. And then, "Sit down." He talked with me. "You know it is very competitive here?" he asked. "Yes," I answered. "That's why I wanted to come." "I brought some of my papers," I said. "I thought perhaps you would like to look at them?" "Read your papers!" he exclaimed. He was horrified. I told him that I needed an answer and had received no word. I explained about my house and my children. "You will get an answer within a week," he told me. And I did.

Meanwhile I learned in talking with my eastern family that to a person, they thought I was out of my mind. One of them, in a kind attempt to make me see reality, said "Frances, there are fourteen lanes on the Dan Ryan Expressway. You couldn't even drive on it!" I nearly agreed with this assessment when I did find myself driving thereon with three tired children, two lively cats, and many boxes and suitcases. The overpowering trucks and the rush hour slowdown brought us side by side with another motorist. I didn't even know which exit I was supposed to take. I looked at him in his out-of-state car and decided that if he could do it, I could do it.

The rest is literally history. But I want to point out that others shared my longing for the opportunity to study. When I joined the incoming class at the University of Chicago in the fall of 1964 there were eight women in the group. All but two were unable to finish their studies. Yet every one of them brought talent and excitement to the university. But such were the obstacles confronting women seeking advanced degrees that many succumbed.

Once I asked a member of the scholarship committee if women received scholarship aid. He answered that none of them applied! I thought I knew why. Remember, it takes at least eight years and sometimes longer to complete requirements for the PhD degree. Some became pregnant. Some carried other responsibilities, as I did. One can only see becoming a single female parent while undertaking advanced graduate study as a tenuous prospect. Some simply could not find the basic support to pay tuition, buy books and materials, meet living expenses and, if they had children, look after them.

Beyond doubt, for women the road to a PhD in history is lonely; it can be fraught with danger. I believed then, and I believe now, that every one of that entering group at the University of Chicago would have had much to offer the profession of history, and that every one could have made it through with counseling and additional support at critical times. I believe their leaving represented an incalculable loss to society and to the profession. Betty Balanoff, another woman who survived, and I promised each other that if we lasted and if ever we could find ways, we would write and work to improve opportunities and mentoring for young women who wanted to go to graduate schools.

If I had known about every obstacle that I would have to face, I too might have lost the will to confront those obstacles. Now I realize I scarcely looked ahead. I sold my house. This gave me some financial leeway, though divorce and the lack of sufficient, dependable income often thwart the best-laid plans of single parents. That is why the term "single parent," a term I had never heard when I discovered that I was one, has become a frequently noted description. I found an apartment on Ridgeland Street, about eight minutes away from my classes and the children's schools. Each night before I turned out the lights I would hold a consultation with myself: Which readings must I finish tonight? Which books must I find and read tomorrow? Which papers must I start? Which exam will be coming up? Which child needs to be where at what hour? Will my children be safe through the day? At which class must I appear, and when? I scarcely looked beyond the next day's requirements.

I did frequently and wryly recall the romantic notions I once entertained about going to graduate school. As for the opportunity to make friends, I never found leisure. Not until I was leaving in 1972 did I realize that here I had met some of the best, most gifted people I had ever known. Regrettably I had been unable to know them better. I felt gratitude for the friends I discovered in books I read, many times until two or three in the morning.

In 1964, the year I began my studies at Chicago, assignments and classes proceeded smoothly enough. Yet no one could walk about that campus and remain unaware of the turmoil gradually engulfing universities everywhere. As the sixties progressed, crowds of students gathered daily in front of the Administration building, described as "the ugliest building on campus." Students chanted, marched, brandished placards; some shouted through bullhorns. From time to time university police and other police appeared. In that very administration building, ominous confrontations with officials ensued. All of this shocked my notions of right and wrong. I am sure it deeply influenced my children's points of view. Whenever possible, I would bring one of my children along to my classes. I hoped they would better understand their world than I had realized mine.

One day a female protester took my arm and talked to me: "Do you know there is an index card in the Admissions files saying 'Do not admit—Childbearing Age?'" I didn't know about that caveat; knowing, I could never forget it. At that moment, I began to develop a heightened recognition of controls that women face. But in spite of Professor Gray's blunt rejection when I wanted to go to Northwestern, a genuine consciousness-raising about women's disadvantages took longer. Slowly it dawned on me that often enough, women carry disproportionately heavy responsibilities. Slowly I realized that I had been profoundly programmed in the early and middle years of my life. Surely, I had been programmed to my disadvantage.

At that time women's history, black history, and ethnic studies were realms of the future. My professors were eminent scholars, achievers, all of them. Every single one was male. All but one were white. When I came for my first class, I had the good fortune to meet the one black professor just as he came for his first seminar. I signed up, little suspecting that John Hope Franklin's presence, his scholarship, his strength, and the breadth of his humanity would become major influences in my own development.

Only in hindsight can I also realize what it would have done for all of my professors and for their students if women of high caliber and varied backgrounds had been members of the faculty, participants in research and instruction and the making of department policies. One of my revised dreams is that some day women professors will establish themselves in universities in equal numbers.

Meanwhile the turmoil that became part of the campus scene played into the agitation that ensued in Chicago. Significant strikes by garbage collectors and others occurred in various cities. Martin Luther King, Jr., and the Southern Christian Leadership Conference decided to use that combination of circumstances to confront the racial discrimination of the nation. When disturbances occurred in Chicago, they took part. My children had become students at the University of Chicago Laboratory School, which abuts the university campus. Soon they and I and some of their friends and other graduate students from the university found ourselves joining in protest marches through sections of Gage Park on the southwest side of Chicago. There defiant crowds hurled insults and objects as we walked by. My daughter, then a freshman in high school, still bears a scar where a bottle hit her leg.

I remember well Dr. King's wonderful, sonorous voice as he spoke with us in a church on the Sunday after we marched. I remember holding hands and singing in that church. I also remember the tragic day of his assassination. On our way to school the next morning my children and I beheld phalanxes of the notorious Chicago gang, the Blackstone Rangers; silently they occupied the entire mile-long Midway stretch that borders the university. We turned and drove back home. Two days later angry blacks tore asunder the west side of Chicago.

Though women participated in the civil rights movement, all of the leaders were men. This too contributed to the consciousness-raising that had been going on in my life. Prior to coming to Chicago, I had never thought about the disadvantages women and black people confront. Certainly I was perceiving aspects of life entirely new to my experience. Graduate students do not live on oases apart from the rest of life. They live with the complexities of life on each and every day.

About that time I came to the end of my course work. At a gathering to celebrate this milestone and the acceptance of several of us as genuine doctoral candidates, I met a black Chicago attorney. Over the next two years we became friends. During my student time I had become immersed in American history. I had watched it evolve, as Chicago itself had contributed mightily to my education. I had watched my children develop. I had spent two summers doing research at Fisk University in Nashville, Tennessee. It seemed I had experienced every possible graduate-student pitfall, and had somehow emerged. I had the feeling that I couldn't see the forest for the trees, that it was time to move on.

As the youngest of my children left for college, my friend and I decided to marry, then to spend a year in Paris. There my new husband learned the French language while I finished my dissertation at the Centre Universitaire Internationale, a most accommodating institution for scholars on Boulevard St. Germain. In line with interests that had reached the center of my concerns, with the approval of Professor Franklin, now my dissertation director, and with the support of my husband, my dissertation developed into a life study of Charles Waddell Chesnutt, a talented African-American novelist who insisted on his African-American heritage though he appeared white, and who eventually turned to politics.[2]

Upon returning from Paris we decided to settle in California in the Bay Area. My husband prepared for the California attorney-bar examination. I started a search for a teaching job—but just at the moment when cutbacks got underway. I also started to scribble away at a translation I wanted to do. Anna Julia Cooper was an American black woman, born in slavery and raised in North Carolina. Through years of tireless effort she finally got her doctoral degree at the age of 67 at the University of Paris. The Sorbonne published her dissertation, a study in French of relations between the French Revolutionists and their richest colony, San Domingue, now Haiti. The work presented an important, original thesis that slavery in any nation becomes the concern of all nations. But her book had never been published in any language in her native land. I called my translation *Slavery and the French Revolutionists*.[3] Just as I finished my translation and interpretive essay I encountered the difficulties new women PhDs confront. Jobs were scarce. To find one in California you needed to be a young PhD, preferably male, and you needed friends at court. I was female. I was no longer young. I didn't know anybody in California.

But after a number of rejections, I did find a job, and I heard about the West

Coast Association of Women Historians. Now, at the end of the century, this is a greatly expanded organization with a different name: the Western Association of Women Historians (WAWH). I already belonged to the American Historical Association (AHA) and to the Organization of American Historians (OAH); upon joining WAWH, I found colleagues and friendships that were interactive and that mattered. I found a warmth and a welcome that were conspicuously missing in other organizations. I found genuine commitment to the historical profession. I found an important friend in Barbara Penny Kanner, then-president of WAWH. Academically and professionally, she encouraged my efforts.

I treasured these new connections. I began a collection of essays. I wanted to produce an anthology to cover the scope and the consequences of work by feminist historians from prehistoric times to the present. I felt glad to become involved in so fundamental a movement. Thirty-two of those essays, including my own, with my introductions, appeared as *Views of Women's Lives in Western Tradition: Frontiers of the Past and the Future.*[4]

I continued to participate in the large professional organizations. There I also began to form friendships that have grown and flourished. Most of these were with women. I was fortunate to come in contact with Nupur Chaudhuri, an energetic scholar with long black hair. Nupur was born in New Delhi, India. Her fresh insight, her astonishing persistence in the face of difficulty, amazes me to this day. I wonder to myself how many of us could do in her country what she has accomplished in ours. Molly Davis personified the best in southern culture; she seemed, as I thought when I listened to her, a kind of female incarnation of the best of the founding fathers of the old South. Molly and the late Kitty Prelinger became postgraduate mentors for me, generous mentors. I had begun to find my people. With many of my new friends, I also joined the organization that would give us the greatest chance for effective participation on a national level; it was then called the Coordinating Committee on Women in the Historical Profession (CCWHP).

I learned that every one of these members could tell a story about the tribulations of female graduate students, and often about the precarious paths for getting that far. In retrospect, I learned that women graduate students are even more vulnerable than we had realized. They need nourishing and they need encouragement. They need mentors and they need recognition. They often need financial support. The obvious outcome: we had become the people who should be thinking about them. This would be the most important area we could pursue. It became more and more apparent that the voices of women are sorely needed in academia.

As I left the presidency of WAWH a few years later, I believed that we were on the way to meeting some of those needs. Our members showed great good will. My successor, Jess Flemion, started a Western Association fund to encourage graduate students. We were all to raise money by holding pay-parties in our homes, or any other place we could secure. It was a slow but significant beginning.

But it wasn't until later still, as I left the presidency of CCWHP, that we set up a national fund to offer financial assistance to women graduate students. Barbara Penny Kanner was leaving the presidency of the Conference Group on Women's History (CGWH), the other arm of this national organization. She joined me in an effort to raise a substantial sum for an annual award to an outstanding woman student. Our idea then was to expand this fund to the point where we could offer more than one award each year.

Meanwhile, subsequent presidents and board members of the Coordinating Council for Women in History (CCWH) have encouraged graduate students in every way open to us. They have sponsored a graduate student column in our news organ. They have planned annual events to recognize and encourage our female graduate students. Many members have given memberships to their own students. Where once female graduate students were scarcely visible at national conferences, CCWH has included them in presentations, arranged for childcare, and even paid for a lounge and light refreshments, an appreciated detail, as some of them have told me.

Nancy Hewitt particularly realized the hesitations students feel; she became responsible for drawing them into real participation with established scholars. Betsy Perry began workshops for her students and then for everybody's. As she elevated the caliber of the conference group's publication, Claire Moses provided models and included many students. Lynn Weiner not only put our finances in order; she handled arrangements so that our monies escalated. Under Peggy Renner, one of her successors, the fund we started has soared to at least five times the amount with which Penny Kanner and I began it. Gratefully, during the administration of Peg Strobel, we accepted a substantial gift from the Berkshire Conference of Women Historians; now it is possible to offer two graduate awards to promising students. This achievement stands as one top priority of our organization. So many women historians are so generously contributing to these efforts that it is impossible to tell their names. I am sure that they remember well what it was like for them. By conceiving and shepherding this book, Eileen Boris and Nupur Chaudhuri are preserving their stories.

So what are the hazards each graduate student will face? Graduate training costs more than it ever did. So do books. Jobs along the way are scarce. Partly because of increased class size, jobs that do exist consume more time than ever. Housing isn't cheap. Responsibilities are legion. Administrations are under pressure from shortages of funds for department use. Assaults on affirmative action programs mean that no one can tell us that discrimination against women and minorities has ceased to exist. Publication houses have merged as their philosophies stand in question.

But even after thinking about all of this, a woman may want to continue. I believe that one hazard surpasses all the rest. If she fails to listen early and earnestly to her own voices, and if she fails to understand where they are coming from, the costs to her and to society stagger the imagination. Such a risk no one can afford.

For some years I have been writing a book designed to explore the relativities of the histories by which we live; like the rest of my work, this book centers on the fortunes of women and black people. It also explores the luggage historians bring to their craft and the luggage they leave behind when they write in these fields—indeed, when they write in all fields. All this depends on a definition of the concept of a fiction and on my belief that within limits, we can choose what we do. A fiction is not merely an imaginative literary piece. A fiction is a powerful, driving idea that directs the course of a life or a society or the histories historians write. As I muse on this book, for which the title has been *The Fictions of History*, I understand the stakes: If a woman listens early and earnestly to her own voices, she can choose fictions that can contribute to the search to understand the human situation; she surely can learn the sound and the touch and the taste of life itself.

What will it be like? What can women graduate students expect when they do reach their degrees? Aside from threatened attacks on the profession, women PhDs still face an ancient recurring discrimination. They still face the feelings that they are invading male domains, that they may take jobs away from men, that they are too inexperienced or else too old, that they are soft and unable to cope with the realities of corporate worlds, that because of biological concerns, they offer comparatively little, that for various obscure reasons they can't function academically. Few have even suggested that women could bring a new and different caliber of performance to our world.

But with all of this considered, there is much to gain. Many women historians—so many I cannot name them—are at this moment contributing magnificently to dimensions that deeply enhance and even alter the very bases of professional thought.

Despite their achievements, we are sensible of perils that beset all graduate students. Indeed we are sensible of perils all historians face in a time of unequaled technological advance. The danger that our society and the world will be deprived of the experience and the insights historians can furnish is real and more imminent than we would like to envision. I would hope that women historians will find strong voices among those seeking to solve the dilemmas that confront historians. I would like to believe that with effective graduate-student programs, women historians can develop genuine partnerships with their male colleagues, partnerships capable of meeting the daunting challenges ahead.

NOTES

1. Sarah Lawrence *Campus*, June 1, 1935.

2. This work became my first book: Frances Richardson Keller, *An American Crusade: The Life of Charles Waddell Chesnutt* (Provo, Utah: Brigham Young Univ. Press, 1976).

3. Anna Julia Cooper, *Slavery and the French Revolutionists*, Frances Richardson Keller, tr., ed. (Lewiston, New York: Edwin Mellen Press, 1988)

4. Frances Richardson Keller, ed., *Views of Women's Lives in Western Tradition: Frontiers of the Past and the Future* (Lewiston, New York: Edwin Mellen Press, 1990).

13

MARGARET STROBEL

"DROP BY DROP THE BOTTLE FILLS"

Before I became a historian of women, I became an Africanist. And while I was becoming an Africanist, I became a feminist, a historian, and an activist. It is hard for me to sort out how much of the process was mere serendipity. My sense is that I have never had a grand plan of what I wanted to be and do, but rather I took advantage of interesting and compelling notions as opportunities presented themselves to me. These opportunities were, of course, shaped by the period in which I came of age. In many ways, I was rescued from a fairly conventional life by the social movements of the 1960s and '70s.

Although I certainly did not come from an economically privileged background, I have a sense of the privilege that I experienced with others of my generation: the privilege to experiment, travel, develop an international perspective, and follow our interests. Compared to my students today (and my fifteen-year-old daughter), who are fixated on what job they will be able to get, I came of age when the US economy was expanding and the culture at large foresaw few limits to this growth. I don't recall worrying about employment until the year I finished my PhD in 1975. By then, of course, the war in Vietnam had bled the economy dry, and there was little money around to continue to support the federal investment in African Studies that had contributed to my becoming an Africanist. By that time, there were five new jobs in African history advertised in the US.

I had little interest in history, much less in Africa, before I went to Michigan State University as an undergraduate in 1964, although two history

Margaret Strobel, 1997. Photo by Roberta Dupuis-Devlin, University of Illinois at Chicago.

teachers stand out in my memory from the high school in St. Louis Park, Minnesota, where my family had moved in 1958: my tenth-grade American history teacher, Irene Haaskens, was energetic and paid personal attention to some of us. I remember little US history, but I remember very well the attention. In contrast, I remember both the teacher's attention and the content of the course I took as a senior from Marjorie Bingham.

Though it did not seem so at the time, I might have "inherited" an interest in history from my dad, Art Strobel (1906–96). Fathers are known to be very important in the lives of "successful" daughters.[1] Coming from rural North Dakota and having attended country schools and one year of business school in Fargo, he was nonetheless an intellectual. He loved books. While we were living in Grand Forks, he took me to an estate sale of two University of North Dakota professors where, for $1, he purchased all their books, carting them home in several carloads. Interested in family history, he interviewed his grandfather and father about life in the German community near Odessa from which the Strobels migrated in the 1880s. Not until a conversation with my father when I was in my forties did I realize the extent of his influence on me, because he had very rarely offered me advice, and both he and my mother had "let go" when I left home for college. A few years after his retirement, I asked about his own career: Had he ever regretted working for the Standard Oil Company for thirty-seven years, ending up as assistant superintendent of their warehouse? Had he, a man who would read Tolstoy until the wee hours of the morning, been bored at his job? He explained how he was glad to get work in the middle of the Depression. "What would you have liked to do?" I asked. "I think I would have made a good college professor," he responded. I was stunned to discover I had lived out his unarticulated dream, without his ever overtly suggesting it.

On the way to becoming a college professor, I had to choose a field, a convoluted process that took about three years. Although I now see history as a very congenial discipline for me intellectually, my choice of history was based upon less than intellectual factors.

My first year in college was critical, in many ways. I had arrived at Michigan State University (MSU) in 1964, eager to learn—it didn't much matter about what. On my brother-in-law's advice, I took an introductory anthropology class. The professor, Ralph Nicholas, invited me to enroll in his winter and spring quarter upper division seminar on South Asia. Midway through my freshman year, the administrator in charge of National Merit scholars at MSU encouraged me (who had never been east of East Lansing) to go to the University of Nigeria, Nsukka for the summer of 1965. Spending the summer in Nigeria convinced me to take African history courses at MSU from James Hooker. I admired his lucid lectures, delivered without any notes. Nonetheless, much of his appeal was charismatic: he was sexy. He would drink tea with students in the local coffeehouse before class. Excited by the ideas, I also enjoyed this new identity and group of friends. I spent my sophomore year taking courses in African history and anthropology. Since the Africanist anthropologist wasn't sexy and charismatic, however, I became a historian. In the midst of that sophomore year, my art history professor suggested that I go to India on the College Year in India program administered by the University of Wisconsin. I decided to spend my third year of college (1966–67) studying sociology and anthropology at Delhi University, and I prepared by studying first-year Hindi at the University of Chicago during summer 1966.

Complicating these decisions to go to Nigeria and India, but integral to them, was my relationship with my first boyfriend, John Mock. He was interested in history and liked to represent himself as being more sophisticated than me, a hick from North Dakota. I believed him. I now can analyze our intellectual rivalry with feminist insight: neither of us wanted to admit to being influenced by the other; our autonomy as individuals was of utmost importance. It led to a stormy relationship, filled with ambivalence, in the course of which I became a historian, and he an anthropologist. As I formulated my idea for my independent study project in India (professional women juggling career, marriage, and family), I don't recall thinking that these issues were also my issues. In hindsight, it seems obvious. Once again I headed off to an adventure on the other side of the world, leaving John to sort out his feelings and, in the midst of the escalating US war in Southeast Asia, his draft status. From Delhi University I applied for graduate work in African history at schools that John might also attend. Lacking a political vision of how India's economic and population problems might be solved, I had decided that India was too depressing a country to spend my life studying even though I was attracted to the richness of its traditions. I was drawn instead to Africa, sharing the excitement of those heady 1960s years when African nations were shedding their colonial status and African history was being written for the first time with Africans at center stage.

When I returned to MSU in April 1967, John and I found ourselves as ambivalent as ever about commitment. Hence I readily accepted a fellowship from UCLA. Coming from an apolitical family, I was wary of radical politics, the consummate good girl and straight arrow. Consequently, I questioned my California brother-in-law, who reassured me that UCLA was not Berkeley, (in)famous for the Free Speech Movement of 1965. Emotionally exhausted, I finished my BA in 1967, after three years and three summers on three continents, and headed west.

African history was an exciting field in the late 1960s, and UCLA was a great place to study it. As late as 1963, a famous British historian, Hugh Trevor-Roper, had announced that, essentially, African history did not exist, being merely "the unrewarding gyrations of barbarous tribes in picturesque but irrelevant corners of the globe."[2] My generation of graduate students had the chance to refute that view by working with pioneers who uncovered what Africans had done, rather than what white people had done in Africa. Being a white person writing in African history seemed less problematic in 1965, when I began, than in 1975, when I finished my PhD. As I became more politically aware, I believed the issue to be the imbalance of power between myself as a privileged American and the African women I studied, more than the ability of me as an "outsider" to have insights into Africans' experience. And thus, the "solution" was not to have history be written only by members of a group but rather to work to democratize institutions and dismantle the power imbalance. (This remained my perspective in terms of whether men could write insightful women's history, as well.)

Rather cavalierly, I decided to specialize in East Africa, since I had "done" West Africa by studying for a summer in Nigeria and Central Africa by taking courses with Hooker on Rhodesia. This choice reflected both the arrogance of one who knows only a little and a continuation of my tendency to dabble. I studied Swahili during the summer of 1968, in preparation for research in East Africa. During my second year at UCLA, Edward (Ned) Alpers arrived from teaching and doing his research in Tanzania. Although women were still nonexistent in the courses—much less the curriculum—of the history department, Ned's promotion of the "Dar es Salaam/Tanzanian" school of nationalist historiography helped bring some coherence to my sense of what African history was about and what my role in writing this history might be. In place of a narrative about what white people had done in Africa was a narrative (for the nineteenth and twentieth centuries) of how Africans had resisted colonialism and built newly independent nation states. At Ned's suggestion, several of us Africanists took a seminar in early US history with Gary Nash. With Africanists using the intellectual tools of African history to write about American Indians, this seminar proved fruitful for Gary, who went on to write *Red, White, and Black*, which examined the interactions of Indian, Europeans, and Africans.

Although I was intensely lonely during my first year of graduate school, by fall 1968 my personal life was improving. In early 1969, my new boyfriend and I made a fateful move into an old California bungalow in Santa Monica. There my real education began.

The "Third Street house" was a product of late-1960s US politics and culture. Across the country, groups of people were coming together to form intentional communities around some shared ideals and visions. The residents of our house included law-student members of the National Lawyers Guild; a young South African exile; my Africanist roommate, who ended up in medical school; my ex–Peace Corps boyfriend; and a former University of Michigan

Students for a Democratic Society activist turned Africanist and then carpenter.[3]

How did apolitical Peg end up in this house? The answer eludes me (at the time I don't think I wondered why, because I didn't know that we were moving into an intensely political community). In retrospect, I think MSU's Jim Hooker got me into the Third Street house. A political liberal himself, Jim expected us to examine all sides of a question, both the reactions of white settlers in Kenya, and Doris Lessing and Communists in Southern Africa. Consequently, in my first seminar at UCLA, a course on South Africa taught by a very eminent liberal white South African, I blithely questioned the professor about why the syllabus did not include any books by Communists or other leftists. In the silence that followed, the Africanist who was later to become my housemate (and a carpenter) leaned over to me and whispered, "That was very brave of you." I was so unschooled in politics that I did not even consider my question hostile or impudent. Thus a totally undeserved reputation may have proceeded my moving into the Third Street house.

I was pleased to be moving into a house that reminded me of the Midwest (it was made of wood, not Southern California stucco) where we could garden; what I encountered there changed my life. I learned more during dinner table conversations than I was learning in graduate school, through my housemates' discussions of American foreign policy in Vietnam and domestic urban upheavals. Although I had become involved in supporting civil rights activities through my church youth group while in high school, and I participated somewhat in the cultural changes of the 1960s during college, for the most part I had remained unengaged in cultural and antiwar politics. Through the Third Street house came a stream of activists, who slept in our living room, ate our food, lectured at one or another radical event in Los Angeles, and moved on. One of these people was Roxanne Dunbar, who had been a graduate student in US history at UCLA and was at the time (1969) just putting out *No More Fun and Games*, an early radical feminist journal produced in Boston. Over the previous months, I had remembered seeing signs announcing meetings of the Women's Liberation Front (WLF) and thinking I should attend. But I did not do so until the WLF invited Roxanne to speak, along with a Third Street housemate who talked about her experience with the Venceremos Brigade.[4] Shortly thereafter, I started going to WLF meetings. At the same time, 1969–70, the history department decided to allow graduate students to elect eight representatives with voting rights on matters other than promotion and tenure at departmental meetings. I felt that holding such an office was not a very radical thing to pursue, compared to my housemates' activities, but it was an activity familiar to me from my high school days, so I ran and was elected.

Thus my feminist consciousness was formed in the process of developing an overall radical analysis of American society, culture, politics, and history. I had some instincts, too inchoate to be called "feminist." Because I was a very strong student, I experienced little obvious sexist discrimination. I had not been a victim of sexual violence; I had not needed an abortion—I had been spared the very personal experiences that fed a feminist rage in early women's liberationists.

Still, I was aware that there were only a few women professors in universities. Among the books I bought in 1967 was Jessie Bernard's *Academic Women*, but I did not see myself as a feminist. With the cooperation of the graduate advisor, I collected and analyzed statistics on the percentages of females who applied to and were admitted to UCLA's MA and PhD history programs. Around this time, I remember reading, for example, Karen Horney (a feminist psychoanalytic critic of Freud) and various early essays reprinted by the New England Free Press, such as Naomi Weisstein's "Psychology Constructs the Female."[5] My understanding of women's history as a field of study emerged out of my reading US history, specifically an independent study course I did with Gary Nash in the spring of 1970, in which I criticized the sexism of the omission of women in US colonial history. Around the same time, working as Gary's research assistant gave me a better sense of what historians do.

I felt the split between my academic life, taking courses in which women did not appear, and my political life, in which women were part of an evolving radical analysis of reality. I took my oral exam on May 5, 1970, a date I selected so that there would be a party on campus—the Chicano student celebration of Cinco de Mayo to honor the Mexican victory over French forces in 1862. As it turns out, there was a riot. My exams took place the day following National Guard troops' killing students at an antiwar demonstration at Kent State University, and after the shooting of students at Jackson State University in Mississippi. These demonstrations followed revelations of President Nixon's secret bombing of Cambodia. I spent a few days hiking in Yosemite Park to recover from my exams, joined the striking students, and took part in a few incredibly tense history department meetings as an elected graduate student representative.

My actual knowledge of women's history increased enormously the following year (1970–71). I had not received funding to pursue my PhD research, as the number of available federally funded fellowships was reduced by about one-third each year; the war in Southeast Asia was taking its toll in ways other than body counts. Having arrived at UCLA in 1969, Temma Kaplan had become my friend, and I audited a course she offered on women and comparative modernization. As a "reader" for Frank Stricker, who was at UCLA for a year and teaching a course in US women's history, I learned about radical women like Emma Goldman while I attended the trial of Black Panther

Sharon Williams. At a more comical level, I also participated in an "ogle-in," in which several of us whistled and made lewd comments at men from the Girl-Watchers' Club, who were honoring the "Most Watchable Girl."

During this time, as I was learning about women's history, my life as an Africanist was on hold. My unfunded PhD research proposal was a traditional, and uninspired, "trade and politics" topic of the sort that Africanists were doing at the time. It did not occur to me to try to write African women's history until I was heading off to Middlebury College for my first teaching job, a one-year replacement position. As we were discussing how I might find funding to get to Africa, Ned Alpers suggested that I think about writing a dissertation on African women, since I was interested in women's liberation. Driving across the country to Vermont with my dog and almost everything I owned, I pulled together an idea for a Fulbright fellowship proposal.

There was an incredibly small amount of scholarly information about African women in 1971. Relevant information on African women, much less historiographical debate, hardly existed. Mary Smith had done a classic oral history of a Hausa woman, *Baba of Karo*, while accompanying her anthropologist husband M. G. Smith on his fieldwork in Nigeria. But I was going to Kenya, on the other side of the continent. The standard ethnographic source on Swahili-speaking people included one paragraph about women called *makungwi* who ran puberty rituals for young girls. In my proposal, a copy of which I did not keep, I probably said I would use interviews and consult local archival sources to find out what Swahili women on Kenya's coast had been doing during the colonial period. Remarkably, it was funded. I can only believe that it made up in creativity and uniqueness for what it lacked by way of a literature review.

My year at Middlebury College was exciting. I taught courses in African, African-American, and US women's history; my students became my friends. I joined antiwar protests on the East Coast and attended my first college graduation—many Middlebury students were wearing black armbands to protest the war, which made graduation a meaningful ritual event.

September 1972 arrived, and I was off to Kenya and Mombasa, East Africa's largest seaport, with practically no research strategy. In London en route to Nairobi, I found useful material—a dissertation on spirit possession cults in Mombasa and an article describing wedding customs there. In Nairobi, I discovered a newly published work on the twentieth-century history of the Swahili-speaking peoples of Kenya's coast, which contained a few pages about "Arab" girls' education in the 1930s and 1950s in Mombasa. I worked in the Kenya National Archives and found a few—very few—file folders of relevance to women anywhere on the coast. Someone gave me a copy of *Uwongozi* [Guidance], a booklet of reprinted essays from the 1920s and '30s. I recall the excitement of translating Swahili, not as an exercise, but to understand how the Swahili community viewed girls' education and the changing roles of young women in Mombasa.

In mid-November I headed down to Mombasa on the coast, armed with a letter of introduction and accompanied by my friend Fred Cooper, who was in the middle of his research on slavery. My letter brought me into the family of Abusuleiman Mazrui, whose female family members began to introduce me to older women and take me to weddings. My first interview, with the blind and hard-of-hearing Bi Kaje wa Mwenye Matano, was simultaneously rich and disheartening. I had no idea what to ask her (since I had almost no background information on Swahili women), so I said I was interested in how women's lives had changed, what were their customs, what they did at weddings. . . . She launched into a two-hour peroration, beginning with weddings, threading through her slave-owning aunt's household in which she grew up, and ending with her claim that her people were the *real* Swahili and everyone else was a "stranger"—all in Mombasa's dialect of Swahili, which I could barely understand, having learned Tanzanian Swahili. As it turned out, she touched on many of the themes that came to occupy a central place in my dissertation and first book, *Muslim Women in Mombasa, 1890–1975* (1979).[6]

Following Bi Kaje's leads and others, I collected whatever fragments of information I could find in provincial archival documents, records of property transactions, the "Arab Weekly" society page in the *Mombasa Times*, and interviews with women and a few men. Committed to writing about a wide spectrum of Swahili people, I interviewed women from different ethnic backgrounds—descendants of African slaves brought from east central Africa and the area around Mombasa, and African and Arab people of free status. I discovered that the *makungwi* mentioned earlier were typically descendants of slaves who had brought life-cycle rituals from east central Africa and transformed them into Swahili institutions. I found that other women had formed associations that performed a dance called *lelemama*, whose development illuminated the cultural adaptation of a colonized society. Further, I determined that these *lelemama* associations had contributed to the founding of what I called "improvement associations" modeled after British Women's Institutes and aimed at mediating colonial culture in other ways. All in all, I ended up writing about what scholars later referred to as gender, race, and class.

Since I lacked a formal methodology, my research strategy and my vision of what historical study should be about flowed out of my political engagement. I was committed to studying not only elites, but also the disadvantaged. I sought to understand the institutions—Muslim and colonial—that structured women's options and socialized them into particular roles and behaviors. Drawing upon my high school and church youth group organizational experiences, I investigated the organizations that women formed and asked what functions these served. In certain important ways, however, my politics did not help. From my training in African history and my feminism, I was predisposed to look for resistance and, to my frustration, found very little. Upper-class Swahili people had fared better in the colonial period than in a postcolonial Kenya politically dominated by "upcountry" Africans. Even some descendants of slaves talked to me fondly about the good old days of British rule. I wished Swahili women to be subversive and instead found them colluding in their oppression—a wish I felt but largely censored out of my writing. Despite this disjuncture between my political principles and those of my "informants," however, without my political vision guiding me to attend to class and ethnic differences, I would have produced a much less interesting and less accurate social history of Swahili women.

My dissertation research, augmented by a return visit to Mombasa in the summer of 1975, after I received my PhD, formed the basis of a second book, *Three Swahili Women, Life Histories from Mombasa, Kenya* (1989).[7] The book is based on transcripts of interviews that I edited and translated with the help of my Mombasa friend Sarah Mirza. For this volume, I selected three women from vastly different backgrounds. My inspiration for *Three Swahili Women* was Mary Smith's *Baba of Karo*. (Indeed, in its gestation, I called the book Bibi of Mombasa; "Bibi" is a respectful female title.) As an Africanist, I was trained to consider how I could return something to the community I had studied; these life histories were to be my gift to Swahili women. It was a long time in the giving, however—seventeen years—because publisher after publisher was unwilling to publish it in English *and* Swahili, as Sarah and I wished. Finally, Indiana University Press agreed—if we provided camera-ready copy—so I learned the necessary computer skills, and the book appeared in 1989. In the years following my dissertation research, oral history became a standard methodology for feminists seeking to establish women's own views of their lives, with a rich literature about ethics and interpretation.

My study of Swahili women was, in some ways, a dead end. For a variety of personal reasons, I was unable to return to Mombasa to do more research. Upon completing my PhD, I did not find a job teaching African history; instead I was hired as interim director of UCLA's fledgling Women's Studies Program, which was formally approved the month after I filed my dissertation. After me, scholars of African women focused on economic and political activities more than the cultural and social concerns I had highlighted. The growth of Marxist and feminist theory in the 1970s, and postmodern theory in the 1980 and '90s, provided new frameworks for understanding women's lives.[8] Within Swahili history, however, *Muslim Women* had an impact. Laura Fair developed further the history of *lelemama* dance forms, and Susan Geiger revealed the role of *lelemama* associations in mobilizing women in Tanzania's nationalist struggle. As I was writing my dissertation, Natalie Zemon Davis had come to UCLA to talk about "Women on Top," an examination of celebrations and rituals in early modern Europe in which women's subordinate position was reversed. I had discovered similar activities in the celebration of the Swahili New Year. Jonathon Glassman took up my sketchy examination of rituals of status reversal in his prize-winning *Feasts and Riot*.

I developed my ideas about Swahili women's history in the middle and late 1970s in a wonderfully rich period of my life, personally, professionally, and politically. When I returned from my fieldwork in Kenya (and at a point when we no longer had a professor/student relationship), Gary Nash and I lived together for four years as I grappled with, first, how to make sense of the information I had collected and, then, how to teach history and women's studies. Reminiscent of my growth while living in the Third Street house, I learned about doing history and about being a historian, an academic, and an intellectual by knowing Gary and through conversations in our communal household. Our living situation, while not as self-consciously political as was the Third Street house, was nonetheless the site of exploration. There, having finished my PhD, I faced the need to find work. In my thirties and in the most sustained relationship of my life, I struggled to balance autonomy and intimacy, faced wanting to have children, and explored what my feminist and socialist politics meant.[9]

Upon my return to UCLA in 1973, I had joined the socialist feminist New American Movement (NAM), a chapter of which my LA friends had helped found. This political activity broadened my intellectual interests and led me to read the emerging socialist feminist literature. In 1975, I represented NAM in the Coalition to Stop Sterilization Abuse, a leftist coalition that provided political support to law suits against Los Angeles County General Hospital for sterilization without informed consent. Most of my political work involved running NAM's Socialist Community School, in which I taught a course about women in Africa, Asia, and Latin America. My political activity had important personal repercussions as well, because it led to my visiting the People's Republic of China in the summer of 1977 as part of a women's tour planned by the Los Angeles Women's Liberation Union's Media Group. As a result of the tour, I learned a lot about China and met Bill Barclay, whom I married in 1978.

During my three-year stint as interim director of UCLA's Women's Studies Program (1975–78), I became involved in the fledgling West Coast Association of Women Historians (WCAWH). As vice-president and therefore organizer of the annual conference, I was committed to ensuring that the event would include the history of "nonwestern" women. I organized a panel on comparative prostitution, asking Nupur Chaudhuri to comment; this began our longstanding friendship and collaboration on bringing the "Third World" into women's history. During my term of office (president 1977–78), WCAWH supported the proposal that the American Historical Association (AHA) boycott states that refused to ratify the ERA.

These various influences broadened my intellectual interests in women's history. I remained an Africanist, but I read some of what was being written in Latin American women's history. I had studied in India, and I paid attention to developments in recent Chinese women's history. Because I had studied African Muslims, I read some of the work being done on Muslim women. These interests led me, in 1983, to begin work on a joint project to help integrate material on the history of women in Africa, Asia, Latin America and Caribbean, and the Middle East into survey courses. My friend Cheryl Johnson (now Johnson-Odim) and I conceived of the project as an outgrowth of curriculum integration work that the Organization of American Historians (OAH) had undertaken in US and European history. We received funding from the National Endowment for the Humanities (NEH) and the Fund for the Improvement of Postsecondary Education, pulled together four pairs of authors, and produced a "Third World" volume of the OAH's *Restoring Women to History*,[10] which was revised and will reappear in 1999.

This curriculum integration project led to my next major publication direction, work on what has come to be known as "gender and empire." In the mid-1980s, I met Renate Bridenthal at a curriculum integration workshop hosted by Northern Illinois University. I was responsible for covering, as has become usual, the history of women everywhere outside of the US and Europe. Renate mentioned that the European women's history text *Becoming Visible* was being revised. I suggested that they find someone to write about all those European women mucking about the empires. Renate agreed, and like a good editor, convinced me to write the chapter. Such women were precisely the kinds of people about whom I, as an Africanist, had formerly refused to write, rejecting the earlier view of African history as the history of what white people had done in Africa. In this effort, however, I was expanding European women's history to include the Third World, a politically more palatable enterprise. In Mombasa, my friends had told me about Sylvia Gray, the popular principal of the 1950s Arab Girls School, and Miss Anthony, a midwife. Preparing to write my chapter, I discovered many such women—missionaries, travelers, white settlers, nurses and other women seeking employment opportunities, anthropologists (and anthropologists' wives, such as Mary Smith), and wives of colonial administrators. An expanded version of my chapter later appeared as *European Women and the Second British Empire* (1991). This area of scholarship has now expanded dramatically, with significant advances in areas outside the British empire. Indeed, imperial history has been transformed by the addition of gender analysis to what had been a field conceived initially as the political and diplomatic maneuvers of great white men. My work in gender and empire allowed me to revisit and draw upon my study of India and to enrich and develop my friendship with Nupur Chaudhuri. Together we edited first a special issue of *Women's Studies International Forum* (1990), and subsequently *Western Women and Imperialism: Complicity and Resistance* (1992).

Nupur and I had extended our friendship in the 1980s through our work in the Coordinating Committee on Women in the Historical Profession/ Conference Group on Women's History (CCWHP/CGWH). In 1979 Bill and I moved to Chicago when I was offered a tenured associate professorship as the first director of the Women's Studies Program at the University of Illinois at Chicago. Bill gave up his tenure-track position at San Diego State University (such a sacrifice by a partner is uncommon even now, twenty years later) and was elected one of the three national leaders of NAM, headquartered in Chicago. I agreed to become editor of the newsletter of CCWHP/CGWH in 1981–83 and later served as president (1989–91). For our twentieth anniversary, I edited and printed our self-published history.[11] In addition, the entire board worked with former presidents Penny Kanner and Frances Richardson Keller to implement their vision of endowing a graduate student prize in women's history, awarded for the first time in 1991. Probably my visibility in CCWHP/CGWH and my being an Africanist—a rare commodity in the AHA—jointly accounted for my election in 1989–91 to the AHA Council.

In the midst of these developments in my intellectual, personal, and political life, in 1985 I started to research the Chicago Women's Liberation Union (CWLU). Although it seems anomalous at first glance, CWLU was an obvious research choice. In Mombasa, I studied the ideologies and changing structures of women's organizations; I pursued the same with regard to CWLU. (Indeed, I had first heard about CWLU in 1973 while strolling on the Indian Ocean beach with Charlotte Bunch, who had come down to Mombasa to visit me and my roommate Fatma Hussein at the suggestion of friends in Nairobi.) CWLU members had founded my own women's studies program, and many of the women I met in Chicago had been part of it. It was infinitely easier to get to the Chicago Historical Society than to the Kenya National Archives, and so I began reading the documents and interviewing members in CWLU and other, similar women's liberation unions.[12]

That research is still in limbo. It has been pushed aside by the other projects and, most recently, two new ones. *Chicago Women: 1920–1990: A Biographical Dictionary*[13] is a model feminist collaboration between a university center and an independent women's organization. The idea for *Chicago Women* came from the Chicago Area Women's History Conference (CAWHC), an affiliate of CCWHP/CGWH. In the early 1990s, several CAWHC members began to work on the project as volunteers. In fall 1991, I invited them to submit a grant proposal to NEH through UIC's new Center for Research on Women and Gender (CRWG). "Don't Throw It Away! Documenting and Preserving Organizational History" is a project to encourage community-based organizations to create and maintain (or donate) their archives, so that future scholars can include grassroots perspectives when writing the history of issues and movements.[14]

What links all of these parts of my life and work together has been a commitment to uncovering information about little-known women and getting that information into history and women's studies courses. In addition, as a scholar I have studied women's organizations, and as an activist and professor I have tried to build structures inside and outside the university—structures such as CCWHP/CGWH as an outside influence on AHA and the historical profession, and the Women's Studies Program, CRWG, and the Chancellor's Committee on the Status of Women as a power base within my university. My travels and studies in various countries, combined with my political coming-of-age during the Vietnam War, made me an internationalist. Through the social movements of the 1960s and '70s I became interested in the US and committed to working for change here. As part of that process, the women's liberation movement completely reoriented my personal and intellectual life and career.

NOTES

"Drop by drop the bottle fills": *Haba na haba hujaza kibaba*—a Swahili proverb. For their comments, I thank my editors Eileen Boris and Nupur Chaudhuri, as well as Bill Barclay, Jessica Barclay-Strobel, Kathy Clark, Stacey Colwell, Gary Nash, Temma Kaplan, John Mock, Rima Schultz, Shubhra Sharma, Mary Todd, Fran Vavrus, and Lynn Weiner.

1. My mother, Alice (Olson) Strobel (1909–97), was not a strong influence (positive or negative) in terms of my intellectual interests or career. She was a homemaker until I, the youngest of three girls, reached tenth grade. Then she worked as a maid in a motel and, later, in a plastics factory.

2. Quoted in Roland Oliver, *African History for the Outside World* (London: School of Oriental and African Studies, 1964), 1.

3. The NLG is a left-wing organization active in many radical causes; SDS was a prominent New Left student and antiwar organization in the 1960s.

4. These brigades were groups who visited Cuba to work in the sugar fields and learn about Cuban socialism in protest against US isolation and harassment.

5. Weisstein's important article was reprinted many times. Most recently, a special issue of *Feminism and Psychology* [3, n. 2 (1993)] featured a debate on it. Weisstein was one of the founders of the Chicago Women's Liberation Union, whose history I am writing; see later in this chapter.

6. It was co-winner of the African Studies Association Herskovits Award in 1980.

7. The transcripts for the interviews have been deposited in the Herskovits Africana Library at Northwestern University.

8. For bibliographic essays about African women's history, see Margaret Strobel, "Review Essay: African Women," *Signs* 8 (Autumn 1982), 109–31; Claire Robertson, "Developing Economic Awareness: Changing Perspectives in Studies of African Women, 1976–1985," *Feminist Studies* 13 (Spring 1987), 97–135; Nancy Rose Hunt, "Placing Women's History and Locating Gender," *Social History* 14 (October 1989), 359–70.

9. One of our housemates, Constance Coiner, was then just beginning her own personal and intellectual transformation; her life was tragically cut short in a plane crash in 1996.

10. Originally distributed in 1987 (revised slightly in 1989) through the Organization of American Historians; Indiana University Press published the revised version in four volumes in 1999.

11. Hilda Smith, Nupur Chaudhuri, and Gerda Lerner, *A History of the Coordinating Committee on Women in the Historical Profession/Conference Group on Women's History* (Chicago: CCWHP/CGWH, 1989). It was slightly revised and reprinted in 1994.

12. "Women's Liberation Unions," in *The Encyclopedia of the American Left*, ed. Mari Jo Buhle, Paul Buhle, and Dan Georgakas (New York: Garland Publishing, 1990), 841–42; "Organizational Learning in the Chicago Women's Liberation Union," in *Feminist Organizations: Harvest of the New Women's Movement*, Myra Marx Ferree and Patricia Yancey Martin, eds. (Philadelphia: Temple Univ. Press, 1995), 145–64; "Consciousness and Action: Historical Agency in the Chicago Women's Liberation Union," in *Provoking Agents: Theorizing Gender and Agency*, Judith Kegan Gardiner, ed. (Urbana: Univ. of Illinois Press, 1995), 52–68.

13. To be published by Indiana University Press, this work is expected to appear in 2000.

14. For a fuller discussion, see the article by the same title in *CCWH Newsletter* 28 (June 1997), 17–20.

EILEEN BORIS

14

IN CIRCLES COMES CHANGE

During the summer of 1968, as a nineteen-year-old college student, I took the "T" every morning from suburban Newton to Beacon Hill to hang out—to say "worked" would be an exaggeration—as a public service intern at the Massachusetts Commission Against Discrimination (MCAD). A year before, I had labored at a South End settlement house, running the drama class, supervising the playground, and knocking on public housing doors. I was no Jane Addams, my high school heroine whose reformism I then dismissed because she made capitalism work by relieving its pain. Too young to have gone south and too timid to defy my lower-middle-class Jewish family, I was finally contributing to the civil rights movement. Secretly, I was relieved that I didn't have to take the secretarial job at the state insurance bureau that my father arranged through someone he knew and that was more in keeping with his idea of women's proper place. During the previous long hot summer of 1967, while Detroit and Newark burned, mother had worried about the dangers of the slums, especially after a small riot at a Roxbury welfare office. Dressing up to go downtown to the MCAD the next year was more in keeping with her idea of liberalism. I could rise to JFK's thrilling call to public service; government could make a positive difference in fighting racism and ending poverty.

I could say that I made a difference or even an impression, but that would be an exaggeration. The MCAD hadn't figured out what to do with two college interns. I got to follow (Mrs.) Erna Ballantine, the fiery African American

Eileen Boris protesting as part of the Women's Committee of 100 at the White House, November 1995.

woman who chaired the commission. At one point I worked with an African PhD who was negotiating the first black-owned Ford dealership in Boston. But my observations as a sojourner inside the state reinforced lessons offered by the urban rebellions and the police riot at the Democratic National Convention: the state is not to be relied upon; at best it can co-opt or uplift a few into the ruling class. It was whispered that the commission's long-time executive secretary, who ran daily operations, supported the notorious antibusing activist Louise Day Hicks.[1] That hardly surprised my growing New Left cynicism: just like the state to fill an agency with appointees who will subvert its mission. Disillusionment was as naive as my previous enthusiasm, but recognition of the limits of liberalism remains with me yet.

Erna Ballantine didn't stay long at the commission; she resigned sometime the next year. In retrospect that made sense; so did my attraction to her. Ballantine was a fighter. In the MCAD annual report to the governor, she declared that "hope was not dead in 1968, and I was heartened by a country which brought its President to his knees on the issue of war." She further claimed, "Many poverty programs which were ultimately labeled 'failures' did provide the opportunity for the 'poor' to be heard." Her explanation for increased appropriations, as much as her talk of "pervasive racism," suggested what it took to get government to listen to those without money or power: "This country and this state did not act totally out of good will, but to some degree out of fear." Following federal initiatives, under her direction the MCAD established an Affirmative Action division.[2]

From its beginning in 1946, the mandate of the MCAD allowed it to tackle patterns of discrimination and not merely investigate individual complaints; in 1968, it stressed "disparate effects of employment."[3] Race was the burning issue. As a successful student who had not yet recognized differential treatment on account of sex, I considered myself a radical, but was only vaguely aware of feminism. Someone in my dorm had mentioned *The Feminine Mystique*;[4] by the time I read it a few years later, I had bypassed liberal feminism to become an antiracist, socialist feminist. Like others of my generation, I came to politics through the movements of the sixties and early seventies, as refracted in the academy. Only later would I appreciate the potential radicalism of liberal feminism to challenge structural hierarchies by demanding gender equity. Yet even in 1968, I was not going to be the doormat that in my youthful arrogance I perceived my mother, who complained how much she was used without doing anything about it. I wasn't going to invest myself in a spotless house or thankless self-sacrifice. Now I recognize mother's strength; I never had any doubt about her competency. Wanting not to be like my mother, I identified not with my sex, but with the racial "other." This was, I suspect, as much a matter of personal psyche as of political conviction.

Thus I was uninterested in talking with Louise Eckert, the director of the commission's division on sex and age discrimination. Since 1950, Massachusetts had prohibited "economic discrimination" on the basis of age (persons between forty-five and sixty-five). It added the prohibition against sex discrimination in 1965, following Title VII of the Civil Rights Act of 1964. In 1968, sex discrimination complaints made up half the caseload. Most derived from the listing of "male" or "female" in newspaper help-wanted sections.[5] But some came from challenges to exclusionary practices by employers and trade unions alike: I remember attending a formal MCAD hearing against the hotel and restaurant worker's union for barring women from lucrative assignments.

Given that I just have spent a decade writing on women's labor laws,[6] I look back with regret. Why couldn't I have taken "advantage" of being in the midst of the repeal of protective labor legislation? Who was Louise Eckert? In 1968, I dismissed her as a fuddy-duddy with charts and statistics on her office walls. Today I recognize her as a woman of about fifty, now my own age, at the height of her powers. She was one of the first employees of the commission, forced to find work after the war to support an ill husband and a small child. A founding member of the National Organization for Women (NOW), she was an equal rights advocate who challenged labor laws that restricted women's employment. She believed that "as a general rule, *equal* terms, conditions and privileges of employment must be made available for men and women alike." That meant rectifying "situations where men and women are employed in the same or similar classifications but receive disparate compensations"—gaining equal pay—and included opposition to the "requirement for women but not men to resign after marriage"—ending the marriage bar.[7]

When I called Eckert in 1996, she still fumed over Boston Edison's practice after World War II of having women sign a statement that they would resign upon marriage as a condition of employment. She probably had faced such discrimination as a married woman. But the postwar fair employment practice commissions neglected sex just as their model, the President's Committee on Fair Employment Practice (FEPC), had during World War II. Pursuing research on this subject in the mid-1990s,[8] I now heard the stories that in 1968 fell on deaf ears. An Edison employee with twenty years of service captured how gender discrimination remained acceptable, usually unrecognized, when she wrote to the editor of the *Boston Traveler* in 1948: "We have a fair employment act that takes care of color, race and creed, but nothing is done for the fair employment of married women. Are we less than they?"[9] Female difference, which led to differential treatment, appeared natural, while disparities based on race were becoming unacceptable. In 1968, no less than twenty years later, sex discrimination and race discrimination, gender and race, existed on two parallel but separate political tracks—only a small group of African-American women and some white women in the civil rights movement understood what feminist historians by the 1980s would name the holy trinity of gender, race, and class. Title VII had added sex, but many judged that a decidedly unnatural coupling, though its addition was more than an attempt to derail the bill. It was the culmination of a long struggle to bring women into antidiscrimination law. But the categories of law allowed complaints on the basis of race or gender but not race and gender, thus disadvantaging African-American women, who suffered from racism in ways that differed from what their male counterparts experienced.[10]

A lifetime later, I have turned to the issue of fair employment as a scholar. In between, I had married and divorced and remarried and become a mother. I taught in the first women's studies class at Brown and offered my first women's history course in 1974. In the mid-1970s, I had the gumption to teach women in the modern world; now I can barely keep up with the scholarship in US women's history. I had lived the life of an academic gypsy, an ABD who took a series of one-year jobs in a number of states prior to finishing a PhD. I marched against US interventionism in Central America and the Persian Gulf, against violence against women, South African apartheid, punitive welfare reform, and for reproductive rights, trade unionism, the ERA, and gay pride. I participated in the women's liberation movement through Rhode Island Women's Liberation, the Chicago Women's Liberation Union (CWLU) and the DC Area Feminist Alliance. These were as important to my education as any formal class.

In 1976, a work group from the CWLU approached me to be their humanities specialist for public programs on women's labor activism in Chicago. Though still working on my dissertation, I was affiliated with the prestigious Newberry Library. Rather than standing as the elite expert, I became part of the group; that research, along with some I did five years later for Action for Community Organization and Reform Now (ACORN), turned me into a women's labor historian. We premiered the film "Union Maids" and created a slide show used in union organizing drives. Historians, I learned, can facilitate the recovery of memory and connect generations of activists; public history need not be a top-down enterprise but can be forged from the grass roots.

When I moved to DC in 1979, someone suggested calling Claire Moses, editor of *Feminist Studies*, who told me about the DC Area Feminist Alliance. In 1988 Claire, as Conference Group on Women's History (CGWH) president, would bring me onto the board of the Coordinating Committee on Women in the Historical Profession/Conference Group on Women's History (CCWHP/CGWH) as newsletter editor, a post I held for five years. In 1996 I returned to edit the newsletter of the renamed Coordinating Council for Women in History (CCWH). I didn't want to leave "retirement," but commitment to the organization trumped my better judgment.

In 1981–82, I had taken over Claire's teaching and editing duties so she could finish her book[11] and receive tenure. Back in 1979 she had served as my guide to women's organizations in the area, including the Chesapeake Association of Women Historians and the Washington Area Women's Historians, now merged into one group affiliated with the CCWH. From my days in Chicago, the networks of women's historians provided a home. They kept me on track despite the shock of entering professional arenas. In 1970, for instance, I attempted to attend the American Historical Association (AHA). A jean-clad graduate student, I walked into the Sheraton Boston but turned away at the first sight of men in suits, before even inquiring about the program.

My early years in DC continued to merge the academic and the political. I helped organize a local version of the "Economics for Activists" course conducted by the Amherst-based Center for Popular Economics. I again became a humanities specialist, now for forums on "Racism in the Women's Movement." In the nation's capital, race seemed more immediate than class alone as a barrier, especially for women's organizations. Lesbian feminists, who predominated within the DC Area Feminist Alliance, had developed the most cogent critique of racism among white feminists. All women did not have the same interests, apparent every day on the streets and in the neighborhoods of Washington, where race and class sharply divided the population despite the presence of a flourishing black elite. I helped form a DC chapter of the Reproductive Rights National Network, dedicated not only to abortion rights but also to the end of forced sterilization and the right to have healthy, well-fed and well-housed children, issues of particular concern to poor women and women of color. My introduction to this broader reproductive rights agenda actually occurred at a mid-1970s Radical Historian's conference when Joan Kelly asked me to sign a petition against forced sterilization. (CCWH played a major role in fund-raising for the award that AHA gives in Joan's memory; I've fantasized winning it to give it away in her name to advance reproductive rights. In 1998 I began a three-year term on the committee that selects the Joan Kelly Memorial Prize in Women's History.)

In these years, the women's movement divided into various camps. Liberal feminists, who supported women's integration into politics, business, education, and the professions, gained the most media attention. Among feminist scholars, however, the most important divisions existed between socialist feminists, who adhered to some version of more traditional class analysis, and radical feminists, who viewed women as a sex-class. What's the difference between a socialist feminist and a radical feminist? As a socialist feminist I had twice the number of meetings: those of mixed left organizations as well as women's groups. I became active in the New American Movement (NAM) and then went over to Solidarity: A Socialist-Feminist Network when NAM merged into Michael Harrington's Democratic Socialist Organizing Committee to form the Democratic Socialists of America (DSA). We thought DSA too close to the Democratic Party and not feminist enough. But by the mid-1990s, living in the upper South, I find myself a member of DSA and even NOW, whose focus on the Equal Rights Amendment (ERA) had seemed misguided to me in the 1970s. (Adding the ERA to the Constitution was fine, but unless women could control their reproduction and had economic resources, formal equality lacked real meaning.) I've turned into a half-loafer, like the New Deal network of women I've written on. I've even lobbied Congress, the first time with other CCWH members to protest the 1991 gag rule, which restricted doctor discussion of abortion. Reaganism, which trounced the left by removing sources of funding and influence, made feminist revolution less likely; even social democracy would require a constant battle.

The DC Area Marxist-Feminist study group was especially important to my development. This was an offspring of Marxist-Feminist groups based in New York and New Haven and sister to a Baltimore group with whom we met once a year. We belonged to an intellectual position that dominated women's studies prior to the advent of postmodernism and discourse analysis, though some members would go on to pioneer those approaches. Zillah Eisenstein's *Capitalist Patriarchy and the Case for Socialist Feminism*, Lydia Sargent's *Women and Revolution*, and *Feminist Studies* represented our tendency.[12] I had been in study groups before, but this one brought together women who were shaping feminist scholarship.[13] You had to be willing to entertain the validity of psychoanalysis, though some of us humored others in their attachment to object relations theory, if not Freud. We explored the relationship between capitalism and patriarchy, Marxism and radical feminism, production and reproduction. We asked what a feminist social policy would look like; the Institute for Women's Policy Research, founded and directed by Heidi Hartmann, partially emerged from these discussions. But our talk of gender, class, and race never truly integrated white supremacy into the dichotomous framework of capitalism and patriarchy. Some of us gravitated to more unified theories of social life, others to fracturing theory itself.

My intellectual movement from patriarchy to racialized gender seems more like a homecoming than a new direction, facilitated by fourteen years teaching US history at Howard University, the nation's preeminent historically black institution of higher learning. I wasn't going to apply for the job in US women's history at Howard. "It should go to a black woman," I thought. By then, I had a small child and a spouse, the labor historian Nelson Lichtenstein, with tenure at another local university.[14] After two years of small fellowships and part-time appointments, including a full semester at Towson State as the women's history consultant for their curriculum transformation project, I was ready for a real job. But I felt limited to the DC area. "The most they can do is throw away your application," Nelson encouraged me.

I was hired, perhaps because I refused to be bullied by a nationalist colleague who insisted that the Civil War marked the appropriate place to divide a two-semester women's history course, perhaps because I had impressed Mary Frances Berry, always a supportive colleague even when we've disagreed, that I wasn't a gender-only women's historian. Every progressive "white" professor ought to spend at least a term at a black college. I've learned as much from my students as I've taught them. My stay at Howard allowed me to observe, experience, and begin to understand the diversity of black America. I'll always be indebted. In preparing for courses, in interacting with colleagues who pioneered in the study of the African Diaspora, in listening to my students, I've become a better historian. I came back to the study of race and to the history of African Americans because these issues pervaded my life. Knowing my students I couldn't accept essentialist definitions of gender even if I had wanted to. As I move to teach women's studies at the University of Virginia (where my spouse became a faculty member in 1989) and end years of wearing commuting, I hope to live up to the faith that my Howard students placed in me.

This circular path to change reverberates in my return to cultural studies. I received my degree in American Studies; I was a cultural historian who felt that capitalism was too important a force to be left to economic historians alone. My dissertation, which became *Art and Labor*, provided a cultural analysis of material objects.[15] In exploring the influence of John Ruskin and William Morris in the United States, especially through the arts and crafts movement, this work considered the social meaning of design and ended up with the question that has run throughout my scholarship: what is work and who is a worker? As much as I hoped this study would be about socialists and working-class people—Morris's socialism appealed to me, but I was in American Studies, so I couldn't write just on him—the handicraft revival belonged to the history of the white middle class. What began as a critique of art and labor under industrial capitalism turned into a style of art, leisure activity, and personal and social therapy. This was a book nurtured by another aspect of the sixties, the critique of consumer culture and the return to organic and "authentic" ways of living, from "back to the land" and the re-rediscovery of the folk to new attempts at home production and more "honest" design.

I've never been much of a craftswoman, though in high school and college I fancied myself a poet and at one point in grad school knitted through political meetings. My BA at Boston University was in English as well as American Studies, a major chosen for its interdisciplinary tools; I always could learn other histories. Still I've tried to live my life with some aesthetic flair, even when it took a misshapen bohemian form through long skirts, floppy hats, and leotards. Like Ellen Gates Starr, the neglected co-founder of Hull House, I truly felt that the good life demanded beauty, roses as well as good bread. The experiences of a fine arts student from Hawaii whom I met "freshman" year provided a parable of the poverty of left-wing sectarianism. She traded in her muumuu and long hair for a work shirt, short hair, and wire rim glasses, switched to an economics major, and joined the Maoist Progressive Labor Party, whose style was a poor caricature of the factory workers it sought to liberate. When I left New England in 1974 for the Chicago "fellowship" at the Newberry, I went to the Boston Museum of Fine Arts to say goodbye to my favorite paintings. A decade later, I was consulting for a major MFA exhibit on the Arts and Crafts Movement! When I met Nelson in 1978, he owned a working-class version of the Craftsman home in Columbus, Ohio; I coveted his house and he my library. We both cherished Trotsky's *Art and Revolution*.

I was a premature gender historian. Though two chapters of *Art and Labor* considered women in the crafts movement and the textile crafts as women's culture and philanthropy, others offered gendered readings of design, work, and reform, such as the manliness of the Morris chair and the domestic messages of artistic reproductions in the public schools. Personal factors led to this strategy. I left my first marriage shortly before choosing a dissertation topic and felt a "straight" women's history subject would come out too shrill. But the politics of history also entered my decision. Women's history appeared part of cultural and social history; I was unwilling to hand over control of the interpretation of Progressivism or class formation or the labor process to nonwomen historians. Initially I had wanted to write on domestic architecture and domesticity, but felt that the architectural historian at Brown, where I pursued my degree, provided insufficient support to offset venturing into a field for which I lacked technical expertise. Years later I was pleased to learn that my incessant talk had influenced him to add Catharine Beecher to the US architectural history survey. Gwendolyn Wright and Dolores Hayden were researching their fine studies on gender, housing, and architecture, so it turned out for the best that I situated the Craftsman Home and House Beautiful in a different story, one that was more about work than about home.[16] Jack Thomas, a master at intellectual portraiture, proved to be a terrific thesis director, a Tory radical with a playfulness of intellect and a true respect for women students. His support never wavered, even when I took forever; I didn't write a dissertation, I wrote a book.

Crafts production was to save women from both the factory system and home sweatshop, but the line between craftshop and sweatshop blurred, especially when designers separated from makers, who usually were poorer women, often from another ethnic group. This contradiction in the crafts movement sparked an interest in home-based labor. Yet life and politics continued to shape my research. In 1994, I published *Home to Work*, which originated as a response to the Reagan administration's attempt to deregulate industrial homework, or paid labor in the home. It served as a vehicle to historicize the socialist feminist theory in which I was immersed. Though a history of social policy, this work reflected my cultural training: now my texts included social surveys, court cases, and administrative hearings. I had returned to discourse, but found language in multiple forms as I (re)constructed a conversation between opposing social forces and recovered the voices of homeworking women themselves.

Attendance at Martha Fineman's early "Feminism and Legal Theory" conferences expanded my analysis; so did going to India as part of a meeting on home-based labor sponsored by the International Labour Organization (ILO) and the Ford Foundation. There I learned that exploitation or prohibition weren't the only options when it came to homework. For nations where the informal economy generated the most jobs for women, state regulation, producer cooperatives, and homeworker unionization provided alternatives that were stillborn in the United States nearly from the beginning of public debate over homework in the 1880s. Discussions with Renana Jhabvala, Ela Bhatt, and other Indian women in SEWA, the Self-Employed Women's Association of Gurjarit, reinforced a growing feeling that a third way existed. The problem shifted to those elements in wage earning women's lives that turned homework into the best of a set of bad options that led to low wages and long hours. From gatherings of researchers and activists, an international network formed to push the ILO to adopt a convention protecting home-based laborers, which it did in 1996. With political scientist Elisabeth Prügl, I edited a collection whose essays we hoped would aid in the struggle for homeworker recognition and empowerment.[17]

Home to Work took its form because of my experience as a mother, different as that was from the mothers who typed letters, wound coils, or, more commonly, sewed garments at home. Sharing a campus office with others, I too worked at home. I reassessed the implications of maternalist rhetoric and social programs that assumed female difference; the problem of work and home, of the wage-earning woman and the "working" mother (with "work" referring to more than paid labor), became my text because it was my life. (Now that Daniel is sixteen I marvel at how he's embarking on his own journey of self-discovery and critical awareness.) I became caught up in the feminist debate over equality and difference in law and social policy.

Academic women's studies during the 1980s focused on difference, both between women and men and among women. Those who concentrated on women's differences from men advocated female-specific remedies, like maternity leave, that emphasize the unique qualities of women, particularly a nurturing ability that supposedly stems from motherhood. Historians newly appreciated the arguments of turn-of-the century women reformers who found in women's social distinctiveness justification for state intervention in both the family and the labor contract. The success of the "pro-family" right seemed to convince many feminists that maternalism—a position that emphasizes women's primary responsibility for children and justifies female activism on that basis—presented the best strategy for advancing women's status at the end of the twentieth century as it had at its beginning. I agreed that mother-talk and maternalist politics existed, but was leery of their consequences. Motherhood as trope and experience, I argued, could oppress as well as liberate; it depended on which women in what context. African-American activist women, especially from the "better classes," used motherhood to advance community betterment when the referent for mother was "white" and the black woman was to be a worker, not a mother; maternalism for them was far more oppositional than for the native-born, white, Protestant, middle-class reformers who spearheaded drives for mothers' pensions and child welfare.[18] The Clinton years reinforced the pitfalls of arguing for citizenship rights on the basis of children's needs. Calls for universal entitlements and women's rights were not heard and so we found ourselves again "standing by the children."[19]

Long wary of the state's ability to promote change, I had nonetheless turned to the state just as the Reagan administration began to undermine the New Deal order. This initial shredding of the safety net led to further evaluation of the reformism of Progressive Era women like Jane Addams and Florence Kelley. Once, Emma Goldman, Mother Jones, and Margaret Sanger in her IWW days offered historical role models because they rejected state power. Now the women social reformers in settlement houses, state and federal women's and children's bureaus, and throughout the Roosevelt administration looked much more admirable as we sought to maintain the welfare state, however inadequate and discriminatory. Those who fought for economic justice and social protections couldn't be confined to the category of maternalist, even though they often argued for women's rights on the basis of female difference. The rightward drift of US politics, however, generated a dilemma: to critique the racial and gender exclusions of the New Deal further undermined its legitimacy when the right would privatize, if not eliminate, social provision, but the limits of the New Deal and Great Society need analysis in order to reconstruct the welfare state and end racial and gender inequalities.

I co-wrote my first essay on gender and the state with legal historian Peter Bardaglio in 1982; "The Transformation of Patriarchy: The Historic Role of the State" derived from socialist feminist activism. Though its patriarchy paradigm now seems too simple, sociologists and political scientists still find it a useful historical introduction. It stays alive as much from attacks, most notably by sociologist Theda Skocpol, as from its tantalizing generalizations about a shift in the location of men's power from families to larger economic and state structures. Whereas Skocpol saw crude social control (the state as oppressor of women), political scientist Francis Fox Piven—whom I've since gotten to know through welfare rights work—criticized our antipathy to the state. A revised 1987 version reflected my teaching at Howard through a fuller discussion of the differential impact of race.[20]

I've found the interdisciplinary debate over social politics heady, symbolized by the continuous conversation at the annual meeting of the Social Science History Association, on whose Executive Board I served from 1993 to 1996. The Gender, States, and Societies group provided much of the editorial board for *Social Politics*, a journal edited by participants Ann Shoala Orloff, Sonya Michel, and Barbara Hobson. These activities somewhat overlapped with my sitting on the board of managing editors of *American Quarterly*, the journal of the American Studies Association. I've been able to hold together cultural studies and social theory, a tribute to my interdisciplinary training, and thus bring a culturalist analysis to social policy.

Not until the mid-1990s, however, did I even attempt to move beyond a model of gender, race, and class that viewed them as separate, though intersecting, categories of analysis. In "The Racialized Gendered State: Constructions of Citizenship in the United States," I sought to push the international conversation on gender and the state to recognize the centrality of race. A product of lecturing in Europe while holding the Bicentennial Chair in American Studies at the University of Helsinki, this essay argued for the concept "racialized gender" within class societies because each category interacts with the others to transform profoundly the ways in which each stands alone. Influenced by the "whiteness" discussion exemplified by the work of David Roediger,[21] I explored how "Jews Became White," thinking about my own ethnic identity and participating in the Black-Jewish relations committee of the local synagogue. Intervening in the discussion among labor historians on race and class, which only paid lip service to the ways that both were gendered, I considered "the transformation of the economic into the sexual"[22] by reanalyzing racial conflict on the home front during World War II. I turned to the gender of discrimination, revealing the significance of cultural constructions of racialized bodies, understandings of white and black womanhood and manhood, and notions of proper homes and families that pervaded antidiscrimination policy even though sex remained an uncovered category.[23] This series of papers and articles attempted to write about racialized, gendered class and not merely argue for a more wholistic approach.

During the 1995 meeting of the Organization of American Historians (OAH) in Washington, DC, a group[24] who research women and the state met in a downtown restaurant with feminist activists from NOW, the Feminist Majority, the NOW Legal Defense Fund, and the Institute for Women's Policy

Research. Called together by the philosopher Eva Feder Kittay, who had been spending her sabbatical combating the emerging consensus on "welfare reform," we formed the Women's Committee of 100 (named in response to the Gingrich Congress's 100 days of assault against poor women and their children) under the slogan, "A War Against Poor Women Is a War Against All Women." Welfare, we reasoned, should be a women's issue, but despite the demonization of the welfare mother through the image of the unmarried black teenager, women's organizations were not embracing welfare rights. The welfare mother was/is the other, perhaps the object for poverty law and civil rights, but not a subject for middle-class women's activism that grew out of politicizing the personal, that seemed to run away from economic and class concerns in its focus on reproductive rights, sexuality, and violence against women. But such factors were among those that should have compelled all women to worry about restrictive welfare reform. The availability of welfare had allowed some women to leave abusive workplace or family situations; the control over poor women's reproductive decisions through family caps and illegitimacy bonuses—extra monies given by the federal government to states that decrease out-of-wedlock births without increasing abortions—represented just another step toward control over all women's bodies.

Our timing was right: With Clinton's call to "end welfare as we know it" and the Personal Responsibility Act on the congressional agenda, nearly 800 women academics, professionals, and politicians signed on against punitive welfare legislation and for eliminating poverty for women and their children. With political scientist Gwendolyn Mink, social work educator Ruth Brandwein, and political sociologist and welfare rights activist Guida West as the co-chairs, and joined on the steering committee by authors Barbara Ehrenreich and Betty Friedan, Frances Fox Piven, and Welfare Warrior Terri Scofield, we lobbied Congress and the president; ran a full page ad in the *New York Times*; demonstrated in front of the White House; wrote letters to the editor, op-eds, and popular articles; met with other women's groups; and facilitated teach-ins on college campuses by compiling an informational packet. We tried to shift the discourse on welfare away from the dependency of poor solo mothers to the responsibility of state, society, and economy for "poverty as we know it." We didn't stop the end of welfare as we know it, but we did change the conversation on the campuses, if not in Washington.

This political activism represents another riff on the themes that have dominated my scholarship. By listening to the voices of poor single mothers, just as I had industrial homeworkers or black workers during World War II, I am crafting policy history from the bottom up that perhaps will be of some use in future struggles that involve inner-city neighborhoods, no less than commissions of the state. In circles comes change.

NOTES

I would like to thank Nupur Chaudhuri and Nancy Hewitt for readings of this essay and the Women's History Group, Melbourne, Australia for their reactions.

1. Ronald Formisano, *Boston Against Busing: Race, Class, and Ethnicity in the 1960s and 1970s* (Chapel Hill: Univ. of North Carolina Press, 1991).

2. The Commonwealth of Massachusetts, Executive Department, *1968 Annual Report: Massachusetts Commission Against Discrimination*, 3–5, on file at the commission's office, 1 Ashburton Place, Boston, Mass. I thank John A. Hearn for his access to historical files.

3. For affirmative action practices from the start, see "Enforcement Activities," *Annual Report of the Massachusetts Fair Employment Practice Commission*, Nov. 30, 1948 to Nov. 30, 1949, Public Document No. 163, 3.

4. Betty Friedan, *The Feminine Mystique* (New York: Dell, 1963).

5. Louise H. Eckert, "Sex and Age Discrimination," *1968 Annual Report*, 22.

6. Eileen Boris, *Home to Work: Motherhood and the Politics of Industrial Homework in the United States* (New York: Cambridge Univ. Press, 1994). This book received the 1995 Philip Taft Prize in Labor History.

7. Commonwealth of Massachusetts, Executive Department, *1969 Annual Report: Massachusetts Commission Against Discrimination*, 21; telephone interview with Louise Eckert, March 27, 1996.

8. Eileen Boris, "The Gender of Discrimination: Men, Women, and the FEPC," paper presented to the Southern Historical Association, November 1997.

9. Interview with Eckert; M. L. M. Newton, "FEPC Wanted for Married Women," *Boston Traveler*, July 7, 1948, in scrapbook, MCAD offices.

10. Cynthia Harrison, *On Account of Sex: The Politics of Women's Issues, 1945–1968* (Berkeley: Univ. of California Press, 1988); Barbara Omolade, *The Rising Song of African American Women* (New York: Routledge, 1994); Sara Evans, *Personal Politics: The Roots of Women's Liberation in the Civil Rights Movement and the New Left* (New York: Knopf, 1979); Jo Freeman, "How Sex Got into Title VII: Persistent Opportunism as a Maker of Public Policy," *Law and Inequality: A Journal of Theory and Practice* 9 (March 1991), 163–84; Cindy Deitch, "Gender, Race, and Class Politics and the Inclusion of Women in Title VII of the 1964 Civil Rights Act," *Gender and Society* 7 (1993), 183–203; Kimberle Crenshaw, "Demarginalizing the Intersection of Race and Sex: A Black Feminist Critique of Antidiscrimination Doctrine, Feminist Theory and Antiracist Politics," *The University of Chicago Legal Forum* (1989), 139–67.

11. Claire Goldberg Moses, *French Feminism in the Nineteenth Century* (Albany: State Univ. of New York Press, 1984).

12. Zillah R. Eisenstein, *Capitalist Patriarchy and the Case for Socialist Feminism* (New York: Monthly Review Press, 1979), included essays by historians Mary Ryan, Ellen DuBois, and Linda Gordon; Lydia Sargent, *Women and Revolution: A Discussion of the Unhappy Marriage of Marxism and Feminism* (Boston: South End Press, 1981), featured essays responding to a piece by Heidi Hartmann; among the history-minded editors of *Feminist Studies*, first published in 1972, were Hartmann, Ryan, Moses,

Judith Walkowitz, Ruth Milkman, and Alice Kessler-Harris. Later history editors have included Christine Stansall, Ellen Ross, Sara Evans, and Nancy Hewitt.

13. Included were Heidi Hartmann, Jane Flax, Phyllis Palmer, Roberta Spalter-Roth, Karen Brodkin (Sacks), Micaela di Leonardo, Lynn Goldfarb, and Mervat Hatem.

14. He then taught at Catholic University. Having a spouse in a closely related field of US history makes for wonderful conversations, an in-house editor, and wandering around looking for books one of us borrowed from the other. We survived co-editing *Major Problems in the History of American Workers* (Lexington: D. C. Heath, 1991), but generally try to maintain distinct professional identities. So I shouldn't be surprised when other historians don't know we are married to each other. My position at Virginia is a spousal appointment, which came about after a difficult process of negotiation following his receiving a very tempting offer elsewhere.

15. Eileen Boris, *Art and Labor: Ruskin, Morris, and the Craftsman Ideal in America* (Philadelphia: Temple Univ. Press, 1986).

16. Gwendolyn Wright, *Moralism and the Model Home: Domestic Architecture and Cultural Conflict in Chicago, 1873–1913* (Chicago: Univ. of Chicago Press, 1980); Wright, *Building the Dream: A Social History of Housing in America* (New York: Pantheon, 1981); Dolores Hayden, *The Grand Domestic Revolution: A History of Feminist Designs for American Homes, Neighborhoods, and Cities* (Cambridge: MIT Press, 1981); Hayden, *Redesigning the American Dream: The Future of Housing, Work, and Family Life* (New York: Norton, 1984).

17. Eileen Boris and Elisabeth Prügl, eds., *Homeworkers in Global Perspective: Invisible No More* (New York: Routledge, 1996). I previously joined Cynthia Rae Daniels to edit *Homework: Historical Perspectives on Paid Labor at Home* (Urbana: Univ. of Illinois Press, 1989).

18. See *Mothers of a New World: Maternalist Politics and the Origins of Welfare States*, ed. Sonya Michel and Seth Koven (New York: Routledge, 1993), including my essay, "The Power of Motherhood: Black and White Activist Women Redefine the 'Political,'" 213–45, and the forum edited by Lynn Weiner, "Maternalism as a Paradigm," *Journal of Women's History* 5 (Fall 1993), 95–131, in which I asked, "What About the Working of the Working Mother?," 104–9. Today I'd say the wage-earning mother.

19. For a brilliant analysis of this problem, see Linda Gordon, "Putting Children First: Women, Maternalism, and Welfare in the Early Twentieth Century," in *US History as Women's History: New Feminist Essays*, Linda Kerber, Alice Kessler-Harris, and Kathryn Kish Sklar, eds. (Chapel Hill: Univ. of North Carolina Press, 1995), 63–86. The Children's Defense Fund assembled a quarter million people to "stand by the children" on June 1, 1996, but refused a direct attack on the Personal Responsibility Act, which Clinton later signed into law even though it promised to throw a million children into greater poverty.

20. Eileen Boris and Peter Bardaglio, "The Transformations of Patriarchy: The Historic Role of the State," in *Families, Politics, and Public Policy: A Feminist Dialogue on Women and the State*, Irene Diamond, ed. (New York: Longman, 1983), 70–93; Boris and Bardaglio, "Gender, Race, and Class: The Impact of the State on the Family and the Economy, 1790–1945," in *Families and Work*, Naomi Gerstel and Harriet Engel

Gross, eds. (Philadelphia: Temple Univ. Press, 1987), 132–51; Theda Skocpol, *Protecting Soldiers and Mothers: The Political Origins of Social Policy in the United States* (Cambridge: Harvard Univ. Press, 1992), 31; Frances Fox Piven, "Ideology and the State: Women, Power, and the Welfare State," in *Women, the State, and Welfare*, Linda Gordon, ed. (Madison: Univ. of Wisconsin Press, 1990), 261 n.1.

21. David Roediger, *The Wages of Whiteness: Race and the Making of the American Working Class* (New York: Verso, 1991).

22. Robyn Wiegman, *American Anatomies: Theorizing Race and Gender* (Durham: Duke Univ. Press, 1995), 100.

23. Eileen Boris, "'You Wouldn't Want One of 'Em Dancing with Your Wife': Racialized Bodies on the Job in WWII," *American Quarterly* 50 (March 1998), 77–108.

24. Included were Linda Gordon, Alice Kessler-Harris, Sonya Michel, Cynthia Harrison, and myself.

15

LYNN Y. WEINER

DOMESTIC CONSTRAINTS: MOTHERHOOD AS LIFE AND SUBJECT

Like many academics I am not particularly given to introspection. I am also cautious about using memory as evidence for history. While doing oral history, like others I have observed the discrepancy between fact and what others confidently remember as their past.[1] Then there is the problem of selective memory: what we choose to present in a particular order can construct one kind of history, but the same memories cast in a slightly different way lead to a profoundly different interpretation. Yet at the same time there is value in individual social history as part of collective memory.

My story is typical of many. My career has had intermittent stops and starts. I have often chosen to work part-time because it fit my needs at home, but at other times I worked in adjunct teaching or research positions because I had no alternative professional options.[2] Like others in this often tenuous profession I have found intellectual nourishment in networking groups and conference attendance. Like many I have struggled with self-doubt and insecurity, feeling guilty because I was either neglecting matters at home or neglecting my career. Like many, I have produced at a slower rate and worked on a slower "track" than have my colleagues. That I now have a full-time and tenured academic job is as much a matter of luck and timing as anything else.

For much of this century, many academic women thought they could "produce books or babies but not both."[3] My generation, coming of age in the

Lynn Y. Weiner at Roosevelt University.

1960s, thought we could do it all. We were wrong. While a few achieved highly successful careers at prestigious institutions and raised several children, others chose to work but not have children, or to have at most one or two. Others opted for part-time employment or a life as an independent scholar, and lowered expectations for professional productivity. The recent experience of women (and some men) suggests that the traditional male academic model of full-time work begun immediately after graduate school is only one career path among many.

While in some ways the academic profession, with its flexible hours and vacations, seems nicely attuned to the rhythms of family life, powerful domestic constraints remain. These include the lack of day care, long hours at work, the parallel timing of tenure and childbirth "clocks," and the difficulty of travel for research and conference presentations for people with young children. Moreover, the collapse (and restructuring) of the academic job market since the 1970s, combined with the oversupply of PhDs, contributes to the lack of institutional solutions to these dilemmas. For women historians, as for working women generally, the tensions between public and private life have deepened.

I have often made that felt tension between public and private life the very subject of historical study. I try through examination of nineteenth- and twentieth-century US history to extricate the social and cultural meaning of "seemingly insignificant" subjects involving women, labor, and culture. I have written about the history of working mothers, the La Leche League in the context of social change, and constructions of the family. I am currently studying the role of mothers as community activists. I have been a working wife and mother who has directly encountered all the institutions and issues I write about.

As a postwar "baby boomer" born in Detroit, Michigan in 1951, I grew up within a middle-class urban culture where married women did not ideally earn wages. My Eastern European immigrant grandmothers, however, did work; Sarah Allen labored in a New York City shirtwaist factory during the early part of the century, and Bessie Weiner spent much of her life as a caterer and cook. Their children saw women's paid labor as a marker of monetary need and immigrant status, best left behind. Many middle-class women raising children during the 1950s and 1960s, like my mother, instead put their energies into family life and community volunteerism.

My high school guidance counselor shared this view. He suggested in 1967 that I prepare for the only possible jobs available to me—if through some unimaginable disaster I should "need to work": elementary school teaching, nursing, or typing. But as a student at the University of Michigan in the late 1960s, I encountered wonderful teachers who opened up wider vistas, particularly in the area of history. In Ann Arbor I studied with Gerald Linderman, John Higham, William Toll, and Kathryn Kish Sklar, who was one of the few women professors visible in the academic landscape. Kitty Sklar had recently earned her PhD and was teaching in the Residential College at Michigan. She offered a pioneering course in women's history that I took in 1972. This course opened up an entirely new way for me to think about history. "Ordinary" topics like housework and health were taught alongside traditional topics in politics and reform. Because of this course I understood that my grandmothers were part of the historical record. Indeed, for one of my assignments I interviewed my grandmother Sarah, who told me how she heard the anarchist Emma Goldman lecture on a street corner in New York. Wanting to know more, I wrote my senior thesis on Emma Goldman. Through my grandmother's life, I learned how to chase down historical problems.

Perhaps as important, Kitty Sklar exemplified to me a way of life where one could do meaningful work, raise children, and teach others. When she hired me as a research assistant for her biography of Catharine Beecher,[4] I experienced the process and challenge of primary research. Her generous mentorship over the years has been invaluable to me, as well as a model of how a teacher can impact the lives of her students and younger colleagues.

Coming of age during an era of student activism, reemerging feminism, and a sense that the "personal was political" also shaped my future. Ann Arbor was a center of radical student politics in the late 1960s. As did many of my generation, I participated in antiwar, student movement, and civil rights marches and protests.

I also considered a career in journalism, and worked at the student newspaper, *The Michigan Daily*. There I interviewed Gloria Steinem when she founded *Ms.*, covered a meeting with radical feminist Robin Morgan, attended the convening of the National Women's Political Caucus, reported on the enormous antiwar marches in Washington, and worked as an intern at NBC News. My senior year I wrote a weekly column that focused on only three topics: feminism, the peace movement, or student reform. Exhilarated by the apparent inevitability of social change, I was at the same time bothered by the brevity and shallowness of news stories. I decided not to become a journalist. Instead, I wanted to be a professor who studied the historical roots and meanings of the issues then making headlines.

My family was from that segment of the middle class which valued education but found Ivy League education economically out of reach. Financial aid dictated my choice of graduate school. I had to go where I received the most financial support. I applied to American Studies programs, because I wanted to study in an interdisciplinary way. I knew I wanted to learn more about the history of women, reform, and nineteenth- and twentieth-century social history in the US. I was lucky. I landed at Boston University in the fall of 1972, where I found a remarkable community of students in both American Studies and history. My new colleagues were fascinated by social history and by the notion that history mattered. It was a heady time to be in graduate school. While there were no professors doing women's history at that place and time, there were such talented and supportive faculty as Sam Bass Warner, Jr., Richard Bushman, David Hall, Aileen Kraditor, Howard Zinn, Cecilia Tichi, Roslyn Feldberg, and Robert Bruce. There were enthusiastic graduate students, and a larger group of students from throughout New England, who met at regional scholarly conferences and brown-bag lunches. At those lunches we hosted such emerging scholars as Tamara Haraven, Nancy Cott, and Susan Hartmann.

Perhaps a highlight for many of us was carpooling to the first Berkshire Conference on Women's History, which was held at Douglass College of Rutgers University in 1973. If memory serves me, I first met Eileen Boris, then a graduate student at Brown University, on the ride back from New Jersey. Several of us from universities around the region snuck into the conference and slept on dormitory floors. Senior historians were actually friendly to us lowly graduate students. The contrast in ambiance between this lively, informal, and enthusiastic conference and the very staid and hierarchical American Historical Association (AHA) meeting, which I had attended previously, was staggering.

For my graduate assistantship I was assigned to work with undergraduates operating the Boston University Women's Center. At one point some of the students were summoned along with me to meet with the university president, conservative philosopher John Silber. We were very young (I was the oldest, at twenty-one) and he was very imposing. He was very sarcastic and dismissive of the very notion of feminism and especially of the Women's Center. He challenged me, "Why not have a center for people who like horses, or people with red hair?" He wasn't interested in my stuttering counterarguments, and this meeting was soon over.

He didn't, however, derail my growing interest in women's history. While seeking a dissertation topic, I stumbled onto some dusty nineteenth-century studies of women workers. At that time, there was still very little written on the subject, and with the support of my advisor—Sam Bass Warner, Jr., an urban historian with eclectic interests—I had a topic and was on my way. There had been no general study yet of the history of US working women (I was unaware of Alice Kessler-Harris's yet-unpublished survey),[5] so I determined to do a synthesis and overview. I also had the opportunity to work as a teaching assistant for Nancy Cott, who was then finishing up *The Bonds of Womanhood* and teaching a course on the history of family life at the Boston Public Library.

Her commitment to and passion for women's history reinforced my own growing interest in the field.

Here life intervened again; I married. My husband had delayed his own career preparation in Boston while I completed my course work, but he also wanted to go to graduate school. So this time I followed him over a thousand miles west. While he studied for his degree at the University of Minnesota in another emerging field, computer science, I wrote my dissertation. This was a slow process, for during these years I gave birth to our first son, and participated in various community and political organizations.

But still I chipped away at the dissertation. I shaped the thesis around the framework "from working girl to working mother," looking at the degree to which the female labor force changed over time because of demographic and cultural forces. I wanted to see how the working mother came to be viewed as normal after a period of being considered deviant. Actually, I had begun the project in 1975 by looking at the "working girl" alone, intrigued by references to "women adrift" in police and labor department records. I thought these were homeless women, bag ladies of a century earlier. When I realized the term was used to describe single, unattached women who worked in cities—much like myself when I began graduate school—I wanted to find out more. By the time the dissertation took shape, though, and with the prompting of my advisor, I increased the range and scope of the study to include the later twentieth century. That in turn forced me to consider married women and mothers as changing characters in the dynamic tale of the working woman in the US. Although I didn't yet use the term, in this work I began to see that historical experiences are "constructed" in complex ways.

At Minnesota I joined the Women Historians of the Midwest (WHOM). There, through meetings and some local conferences, I met other graduate students and historians and joined a dissertation support group, which proved critical for the completion of my thesis. I met wonderful colleagues, including Heather Huyck, now with the National Park Service, and the late Winifred Wandersee. For someone like me, who for a long period worked as an itinerant teacher and independent historian, networking groups like WHOM have provided important personal and professional support.

By the late 1970s the academic job market had collapsed. There were so few history positions available nationally that my husband chose a position in a large city (Chicago) where we thought I could eventually find a job. I did, but only after ten years of part-time and temporary employment. Because of these circumstances, I never tested the national job market.

Instead, I spent some ten years helping to raise my children (our second son was born in 1984) and chasing part-time work. I taught as an adjunct professor at local universities, teaching mostly at night and on Saturdays. I did free-lance writing and research. I worked part-time for a year on the Jane Addams Papers Project at Hull House, putting together such "personal documents" of Addams as medical and legal records, business card collections, and telephone logs. I wrote encyclopedia articles for ten cents a word on any topic assigned me, from "Air Forces of the World" to "chopsticks." I felt very successful when I convinced a major encyclopedia publisher to let me write a series of entries on famous women in history.[6]

By this time I thought of myself as an historian even though I didn't have the cachet of a "real" position. I attended meetings of another local women's history group, the Chicago Area Women's History Conference. I was given "associate" status at the Northwestern University history department, and through that generous program obtained an all-important library carrel and library card. I published my dissertation in 1985.[7] I wrote several articles. I won a fellowship from the National Endowment for the Humanities, which allowed me to buy a computer and spend a year researching another project. This was to be a book on the history of motherhood in the twentieth century —taking the study of working mothers to another level. It's a work still in progress.

Since graduate school I have attended both local and national academic conferences where I've found a sense of professional identity and perspective. At one notable dinner at an AHA convention in the late 1980s, I found myself at a table with women whose work I had long admired. Yet the conversation revealed to the surprise of almost everyone present that only a few of the ten or so women had "real jobs." Most had temporary or part-time work, masked by the university affiliations listed on their books and articles. Some chose to be employed off the fast track, because of their particular family needs. Others would have preferred a traditional or more prestigious job, but the weak market limited options.

Through meetings of groups like the Coordinating Council for Women in History (CCWH), I met other women historians and increasingly felt connected to an academic community. While I was still under-employed in 1989, historian Peg Strobel encouraged me to serve as executive director of CCWH [then the Coordinating Committee on Women in the Historical Profession/ Conference Group on Women's History (CCWHP/CGWH)] while she served as CCWHP president. There I worked with other officers to establish new ties with graduate students, organize a graduate student award, strengthen the network of affiliated local and international societies, and build the finances of a growing organization. Through this organization I met a remarkable group of historians from around the country. Some were affiliated with institutions, but just as many were working independently.[8]

Meanwhile, I had become interested in the history of the La Leche League, a breastfeeding advocacy organization founded in 1956. This organization held an essentialist vision of women as primarily wives and mothers, but also saw women as empowered within those roles. I had begun thinking about the organization when I was first pregnant in 1978, and was puzzled by the militancy and commitment of league supporters. Equally puzzling to me were the strong reactions of people toward the league—they seemed to either love or hate it. It seemed that the tensions within and surrounding this organization reflected larger issues regarding motherhood, work, and the family. At the same time, there was very little published on "motherhood" as a historical topic. Again it felt like I was working a bit in the dark. I decided to use the league as a way to explore how motherhood was constructed within the context of a specific time and place.

I was surprised to find how many people thought this an embarrassingly trivial topic. Many colleagues, both men and women, who were unfamiliar with infant feeding were baffled by the assertion that this organization had any significance at all. But I located the league archives, interviewed the "founding mothers," and began to present my interpretations of their story at conferences. There were often league members, babes in arms, in attendance and vocally correcting my misunderstandings of their history. I finally published this article in the *Journal of American History* in 1994,[9] and was gratified when it won the Binkley-Stephenson Prize of the Organization of American Historians (OAH). The prize citation noted the "seemingly insignificant" subject of the essay—a phrase that seems apt for much of my work.

"Motherhood" has in the meantime become much more "significant" as a topic of historical inquiry, thanks to the recent publications of scholars such as Rima Apple, Eileen Boris, Janet Golden, and many others. Until about twenty years ago, little attention was paid to the historical dimensions of mothering. Since about 1990, there has been a tremendous increase in interest in the field. Motherhood has been examined in myriad ways, ranging from colonial child rearing and nineteenth-century industrial home work, to slave families, day care, wet nursing, and birth control. Sometimes these works grapple with the concept of "maternalism," a variously defined term exploring political dimensions of motherhood. Some of the best new work is comparative and interdisciplinary, as well.[10]

My own work on gender and the family has focused primarily on the history of white, heterosexual, middle-class culture in the US. I have taken some criticism for not spending more attention on other populations of women. I feel, however, that all of women's history has value. Given the diversity of women and the complexity of factors affecting family and work history, it seems to me that the more varied the perspectives on the past, the richer the history that emerges.

By the late 1980s I had chosen a life away from the "fast track" of our profession, one more consonant with what I perceived as a holistic life with my family and in my community. I spoke to squirming third-graders at elementary school career days on topics like "What is a historian?" I introduced women's history to groups at the local high school, area colleges, the public library, local churches, and the League of Women Voters. I spoke about social history to nurses studying gerontology. I was a room mother, a chauffeur, and a field trip chaperone. I became active in school politics.

Some of us are capable of great productivity as well as a full family life but some, myself included, can't do it all, or at least at the pace of others. We are slowed down by the effort to balance both private and public lives. When I was invited to compete for a prestigious fellowship requiring residence at a campus halfway across the country, I chose not to apply, to the dismay of many of my colleagues. How could I turn down such an opportunity? But for me, to ask my husband, then seeking tenure at his institution, and my school-aged children to uproot and follow me was unthinkable. Equally unthinkable for me was the notion of commuting away from my family. Residential fellowships have never been geared for scholars with domestic constraints.

Like so many of my generation, I have seen the academic labor market from several vantage points. I was a teaching fellow during graduate school. I spent years working as an adjunct instructor for low pay at local universities. In 1990, I was offered a half-time appointment with Northwestern University's Women's Studies program. This was an opportunity to teach excellent students at a major institution and meet colleagues in a variety of fields. It was also a chance to observe again the differences between high-powered academics and the often invisible "second tier" of faculty who populate most research universities in non–tenure-track positions. The part-time teaching positions I held for years, of course, were part and parcel of the same restructuring of the American university system which at the same time reduced full-time tenure-track job opportunities.

But I was lucky. Finally, I was offered a full-time tenure-track job at one of the institutions where I taught part time. Roosevelt University is not an elite or research-oriented university. With campuses in Chicago and its suburbs, the student body is unusually diverse, and includes working-class and first-generation students as well as students of varying races, ages, abilities, incomes, and ethnicity. Over half of our students are women, many with children. At our downtown campus, a majority of students are African American.

Ironically, at Roosevelt the job I took had been opened because of the retirement of the only woman in the department: a historian who also specialized in social history. Betty Balanoff had followed another career path typical of women: she had returned to graduate school at the University of Chicago and earned her PhD in 1974, after her children had grown older. A remarkable teacher, she left as a legacy a series of oral histories of labor activists from the 1930s and 1940s.

By 1991 when I began full-time teaching, I was one of the few professors with young children, a consequence of university demographics. I resisted late-afternoon meetings, night and weekend events. There was no daycare, and the needs of our working students meant that evening and weekend courses were necessary for the mission of the university.[11] I was teaching seven separate courses a year. When I was asked to become an associate dean, I took on that half-time administrative task in order to do more of my workload during the day so that I could be home more often at night.

My work continues to reflect my life. As my younger son recently graduated from elementary school, and I was sitting at the last PTA meeting I would attend as a parent, I was struck with a thought: what about the history of the PTA? I had watched for years as women with little confidence in their own abilities gained remarkable self-esteem and leadership skills in these school meetings. To my surprise a library search revealed that there was a very thin secondary literature, especially after the late-nineteenth- and early twentieth-century period of the National Congress of Mothers.[12] Thus began my current project: a study of the history of the PTA. In this I am looking at issues of race, class, and politics in the development of parent–school groups over the past century, particularly with regard to changing constructions and practices of motherhood.

As I've noted elsewhere,[13] the model I've followed in my own life is not the traditional (male) model of rapid, ambitious, and highly focused career advancement. Instead it is a model of sequential steps of work and family life with a concomitant slower career path. I believe this to be a common path for women, and some men, who choose to try and balance the disparate parts of their lives. It is not to my mind less successful than the more conventional route, just different, and it reflects a combination of personal choice and structural constraints.

The balance is delicate, and obviously not the choice for everyone. For me, however, the balancing act seems to work. While some of my generation produced both books and babies, the *number* of both books and babies were perhaps often less than for previous generations, accompanied by more flexible expectations for what constitutes "success." Perhaps the key is not to think of personal and professional life as dichotomous, but rather as equally compelling parts of a whole.

NOTES

1. See, for example, Dan Carter, "Reflections of a Reconstructed White Southerner," in Paul A. Cimbala and Robert Himmelberg, eds., *Historians and Race: Autobiography and the Writing of History* (Bloomington: Indiana Univ. Press, 1996), 35.

2. This mixed motivation of part-time professors still seems to be the case. See Barbara N. Ramusack, "Good Practices and Common Goals: The Conference on Part-Time and Adjunct Faculty," *Perspectives* (American Historical Association Newsletter) 36 (January 1998), 22.

3. Alicia Ostriker, "Silent Parenting in the Academy," cited in Lynn Weiner, "Working Lives of Women in the Historical Profession," *Newsletter of the CCWHP* 24 (December 1993), 33–35.

4. Kathryn Kish Sklar, *Catharine Beecher: A Study in American Domesticity* (New Haven: Yale Univ. Press, 1973).

5. Alice Kessler-Harris, *Out to Work: A History of Wage-Earning Women in the United States* (NY: Oxford Univ. Press, 1982).

6. See, for example, "chopsticks," *Encyclopaedia Britannica* (Chicago: 15th Edition, 1994), vol. 3, p. 265 and "Florence Kelley," vol. 6, 788–89.

7. Lynn Y. Weiner, *From Working Girl to Working Mother: The Female Labor Force in the United States, 1820–1980* (Univ. of North Carolina Press, 1985).

8. A discussion of the importance of professional networking for academic women can be found in Mariam K. Chamberlain, ed., *Women in Academe: Progress and Prospects* (NY: Russell Sage Foundation, 1988), chapters 11 and 12.

9. Weiner, "Reconstructing Motherhood: The La Leche League in Postwar America," *Journal of American History* (March 1994), 1357–1381.

10. See, for example, the essays in Rima D. Apple and Janet Golden, *Mothers and Motherhood: Readings in American History* (Columbus: Ohio State Univ. Press, 1997).

11. A good discussion of the tensions between academic parents and their institutions is Lizabeth Cohen, "Balancing Work and Family in the Historical Profession," *Journal of Women's History* 4 (Winter 1993), 147–51.

12. The best overview of this period of the National Congress of Mothers is Molly Ladd-Taylor, *Mother-Work: Women, Child Welfare, and the State, 1890–1930* (Urbana: Univ. of Illinois, 1994), chapter 2.

13. Weiner, "Working Lives of Women in the Historical Profession," 35. For further discussion of changing expectations for work and family life, see Women's Committee of the American Studies Association, *Personal Lives and Professional Careers: The Uneasy Balance* (N.P.: American Studies Association, 1988).

INTERNATIONAL W

16

BARBARA WINSLOW

ACTIVISM AND THE ACADEMY

I credit my love of history to my father's influence. Around the dinner table every Sunday night we played a guessing game about US presidents. When I was eleven, I dedicated to him my first collection of historical essays, an illustrated "book" entitled *Maybe I'll Be Famous Too!!* Looking back, it is somewhat remarkable that of the twenty-five people I wrote about, ten were women (and not all presidents' wives): Jane Addams, Louisa May Alcott, Susan B Anthony, Amelia Earhart, Barbara Freitchie, Juliette Low, Dolly Madison, Betsy Ross, and Martha Washington. Also included was the only African American studied by sixth graders—George Washington Carver. My father also instilled a love for involved and activist history, taking us on trips to sites of US history: Gettysburg, Washington, DC, Monticello, and Harper's Ferry.

One trip made a lasting impression. In 1959, my father, who was in the hosiery business, brought us to North Carolina and Tennessee, where we visited a number of factories. This was the first time I came face to face with "Whites Only" and "Colored Only" signs and, as a New York teenager, I was horrified by such segregation. I began to argue with my parents and their southern friends about segregation as well as about the working conditions in the factories. That part of the trip began to stir my political consciousness. We also visited Dayton, Tennessee, the home of the famous "Monkey Trial," in which Clarence Darrow battled William Jennings Bryan over Tennessee's anti-evolutionist laws. The 1925 spectacle came alive as I went to the drugstore

At the March 8, 1974 celebration of International Women's Day in Seattle, Barbara Winslow shares a platform with Elaine Espanza of the United Farmworkers Organizing Committee and Dolores Robinson of the Domestic Workers of America.

where the idea for the court case was developed, sat in the actual courthouse and met people who had been at the trial, had known biology teacher John Scopes, and had heard Darrow speak. Even in the sixth grade, I knew I wanted to teach history, but not in a traditional classroom setting.

I was a history major at Antioch, then a leading radical activist college. There, Professor Louis Filler profoundly influenced me. His history courses were both thrilling and challenging. His two major books, *The Crusade Against Slavery: 1830–1860* (a history of the abolitionist movement) and *Crusaders for American Liberalism*, were calls to action. He responded to Antioch student participation in the civil rights movement by challenging us to understand the past, and in particular the history of the abolitionists. Otherwise, we would never be able to fully develop a perspective on activism and racial justice.[1] Despite the progressivism of this liberal arts college, however, the history department was not particularly supportive of female students, giving the men better grades and awarding them history assistantships.

I continued my education at the University of Washington, receiving a BA, MA, and later a PhD there. I also was active in almost every aspect of radical politics: antiwar, antidraft and GI organizing, Indian Rights, the United Farm Workers' Union, and the Black liberation movement, including support for a Black Studies program. I was a founding member of the Seattle women's liberation movement. At the University of Washington my political and academic activism began to merge.

Political activity in Seattle included both "old" left (that is, activists from the pre-1960s Communist, Trotskyist, and anarchist movements) and "new" left (later political radicals not involved in these organizations), centered mainly, but not entirely, at the university. Beginning in 1966, the Trotskyist Freedom Socialist Party (FSP) conducted a series on "Women in US Society" at the alternative Free University. The FSP had broken from orthodox Trotskyist positions on a number of questions; it was the only "old" left group that considered the "Woman Question" (as it was called prior to 1968) of paramount importance. Mostly young New Left radicals attended these classes, including Judith Shapiro, an assistant professor of economics, and Susan Stern, a graduate student in social work. In November 1967, they invited me to a meeting to discuss the formation of an activist women's group, which became Seattle Radical Women—one of the first women's liberation groups in the US. Seattle Radical Women brought together women from both the old and new left. A wide cultural, generational, experiential, political, and geographic divide existed within the membership, with ages ranging from 18 to 51. The group did little during its first five months—aside from thrashing out the relationship between feminism and Marxism.

We did protest the presence of a Playboy bunny on campus, during which I not only was thrust into the role of spokesperson, but found that I had to rely on my limited knowledge of women's history to explain our actions. In April 1968, the antiwar movement had scheduled a week of protests against the Vietnam War. At the same time, the fraternity-controlled Men's Commission announced that the traditional Men's Day would include an appearance by a Playboy bunny. For Women's Day, the wife of the governor presided over a sorority tea. While many in the antiwar movement viewed the Playboy bunny as a diversion from antiwar activities, others in Radical Women argued that she represented the sexual exploitation of women. Members of Radical Women stormed the stage where the "bunny," Reagan Wilson, was speaking before 450 women. They were dragged off the stage, kicked, beaten, and even bitten. I jumped on the stage to explain the purpose of the demonstration. Later we engaged in hours of arguments with other students over the purpose and goals of women's liberation.

In my course on twentieth-century English history, I had just read George Dangerfield's *The Strange Death of Liberal England,* which discussed the militant women's suffragettes. On stage, I discussed how the Pankhurst women initiated mass nonviolent civil disobedience for the vote; how one day English suffragettes broke every window in downtown London; how they went to jail *en masse* and endured forcible feedings. Since I knew very little about feminism, I drew upon what I had learned about the English suffragettes to make points about feminism and activism.

During the summer of 1968, I began studying women's history in a nonacademic context because, of course, there were no courses offered in the subject. Instead, Seattle Radical Women embarked on a very ambitious six-week educational series on "The Woman Question in America." Topics included "The Origins of Female Oppression," "Women's History from the Mayflower to the Civil War," and "Freud and Women." I volunteered to teach the class on women in the US labor movement. For this I began with the one required reading for our study group, Eleanor Flexner's *A Century of Struggle*, a book which stood by itself in those days. While Flexner focused on suffrage, she also integrated material about African American women as well as women in the labor movement.[2]

I also relied extensively on Philip Foner's *History of the US Labor Movement.* Foner's history was one of the few labor histories that sympathized not just with organized labor but with the most radical element of the labor movement: unorganized and immigrant workers, the Knights of Labor, the Industrial Workers of the World (IWW), socialists, and anarchists. Foner's history was both "sectional" and "inclusionary," for each historical period included separate sections on "Negro Workers" and on "Women Workers." Building on this work, a later generation of radical historians began to integrate class, race, gender, ethnicity, and sexuality.

The history in my formal graduate education had little relevance to my political activities. I was learning more history *outside* graduate school. In February 1969, the local chapter of SDS (Students for a Democratic Society) commemorated the fiftieth anniversary of the Seattle General Strike. We featured participant Harvey O'Connor—a long-time political radical, leading opponent of the House Un-American Activities Committee, and author of *Revolution in Seattle.* Also speaking was participant Jack Wright—former member of the IWW, the Communist Party, the Socialist Workers' Party, and then a member of the Freedom Socialist Party. Our SDS chapter wanted a woman to speak about women during the strike. The major female figure alive from the period was Anna Louise Strong, but she lived in China. Since I was writing my MA thesis on the Socialist Party in Washington State, I agreed to "represent" Anna Louise Strong. Until then I saw her as just another figure hidden from history. She certainly was not someone I had read about, let alone written on for my father's day collection. Nor did graduate seminars on the Progressive Era consider her.

Strong's life spanned Progressivism to Maoism. Born in 1885, in 1908 she became the youngest person to earn a PhD in philosophy from the University of Chicago. Experiences working on children's welfare for the Russell Sage Foundation and the US Children's Bureau moved her to socialism. When she relocated in Seattle, she became active in that city's vibrant radical politics. She found the Russian revolution inspiring; in 1919 she had a column in the city's first and only labor paper, *Seattle Union Record*, detailing news about the new Soviet state. During the general strike, opponents characterized her subsequently famous editorial, "No One Knows Where," as a clarion call for revolution. With the defeat of the strike, and the growing antiradical climate, Strong left Seattle for Russia, where she became a journalist for the revolution. She was the first western correspondent to interview Chinese Communist Mao Tse-tung (Mao Ze-dong), who asserted to her that western imperialism was "a paper tiger." In 1949 Russia expelled Strong for pro-Chinese sympathies. She then went to China to champion the Chinese revolution, dying there in 1970.[3]

Anna Louise Strong fascinated me. At that time no full biography of her life existed. She did not fit into any neat category. She was never a heroine for the Progressives, like Jane Addams; or for the Wobblies, like Elizabeth Gurley Flynn; or for the Communists, like "Mother" Bloor. Neither did Maoists or feminists claim her. Her life spanned the twentieth century and raised issues of class, gender, race, nationality, and revolution. This small project sparked my interest in women's biography, which led eventually to work on Sylvia Pankhurst.

Since the 1970s, March has been designated Women's History Month. This celebration originated from the women's liberation movement's discovery of International Women's Day. In January 1969, Judith Shapiro, who was a red-diaper baby (daughter of communists), excitedly asked me if I had ever heard about International Women's Day. She shoved a page from Leon Trotsky's *History of the Russian Revolution* in my face in which I read about the active role of women, how on "International Woman's Day . . . the revolution was begun from below, overcoming the resistance of its own revolutionary organization, the initiative being taken by their own accord by the most oppressed and downtrodden of the proletariat—the women textile workers, among them, no doubt, many soldiers' wives."[4]

This paragraph excited me. Two years earlier, I had read Trotsky's *History* for a course on twentieth-century Russia, but in the mid-1960s, the role of women in Tsarist, revolutionary, and Communist Russia was not worthy of study. On our own, members of Women's Liberation Seattle researched the history of International Women's Day. We learned about Clara Zetkin, Alexandra Kollontai, the Second International, and socialist garment workers in the US. In March 1969, we celebrated International Women's Day with a day-long meeting that included sessions on the importance of childcare and the historical origins of women's liberation. We screened *Salt of the Earth,* the now-classic movie made in 1954 about the confluence of race, gender, class, and ethnicity during a Mine Mill and Smelter Workers' strike in Arizona. While showing the film, we also discovered that we were discussing US politics, because the film, its director, and most of the actors had been blacklisted during the McCarthy era. After 1969, women's liberation organizations regularly celebrated International Women's Day in Seattle.[5]

Most of my education came from outside political activity. I was quite alienated from academic life, preferring the excitement of radical politics. However, my graduate experiences helped forge my feminism. While many history faculty were somewhat sympathetic to the student movement, none were actively involved. Nor were they supportive when I faced disciplinary charges, or was briefly expelled for political activities. When an undergraduate, I constantly fought with the graduate students who taught the large survey courses. One in particular was most contemptuous of my political beliefs; I always (and successfully) contested his grading policies. By the time I entered graduate school in 1969, I wanted to study (the then unknown discipline of) women's history. However, I had to do it all alone, without any mentoring and without other graduate students sharing my interest. I wrote my seminar papers on women in courses devoted to standard topics, like the frontier in US history, for professors who were most disinterested. In a seminar on the Progressive Movement, I continuously argued about the role of women in history. It seems amazing that there would even have been such debate. The literature available even at the time contained a wealth of information about women and women's struggles, protective labor legislation, women's suffrage, and women and social welfare. As we discussed the meaning of democracy, I asked a fellow graduate student how he could describe the US as a political democracy when all women and black men in the South couldn't vote. "What does that have to do with anything?" he sneered. Our professor said nothing. Like most female graduate students in that period, I got little direction from the graduate faculty.

In 1969–70, I went to work with E. P. Thompson at the Centre for the Study of Social History at the University of Warwick in Coventry, England. I was accepted in the MA Program in Comparative British/US Labor History. Like many historians of my generation, Thompson's *The Making of the English Working Class* changed the way I looked at history. Its passionate, involved, activist historical and theoretical approach transformed the study of the formation of working-class identity in England in the late eighteenth and early nineteenth century and then elsewhere. Those trying to develop a new way of looking at history—history from the bottom up—embraced Thompson's now much-quoted declaration of intent: "I am seeking to rescue the poor stockinger, the Luddite cropper, the 'obsolete' hand-loom weaver, the 'utopian' artisan and even the deluded followers of Joanna Southcott, from the enormous condescension of posterity."[6]

But the part of the book that made the greatest impression on me was Thompson's acknowledgment to his wife, Dorothy, "an historian to whom I am related by the accident of marriage." Unlike most men's book dedications at the time, Thompson did not thank Dorothy Thompson for having his children or keeping his children from bothering him so he could write his masterpiece. Neither did he thank her for cooking his meals or keeping his house. Instead, he explained how he had discussed each chapter with her and declared that he had "been well placed to borrow not only her ideas, but material from her notebooks. Her collaboration is to be found not in this or that, but in the way the whole problem is stated."[7] This dedication was a revelation, for I was painfully aware of the bad treatment accorded "faculty wives" (yes, there was such a term) and wives of graduate students. The academy was as unfair to women as was the rest of society. I would never be relegated to typing my spouse's notes or thanked for housewifely tasks in a book dedication.

Thompson was the most important academic influence on my life, as both professor and mentor. He encouraged my interest in researching and writing women's history. I was constantly amazed at his wealth of knowledge about European and US women's history. He knew every place to look for original material. While he was not politically sympathetic to the women's liberation movement, he was not hostile. Unlike other graduate professors, he called upon women in seminars, listened to them, argued with them and mentored them. While he remained somewhat skeptical about issues of gender and history, he never created obstacles for further study. When I began research on Sylvia Pankhurst, he held the belief shared by orthodox labor and Marxist historians that Pankhurst was simply an ultra-left gadfly, irrelevant to the labor and communist movements. By the time I finished my MA dissertation on Pankhurst and the East London Federation of the Suffragettes, I had convinced him of her significant contributions to suffrage and social history.

The other great influence on my work and politics was Sheila Rowbotham, often regarded as the foremother of the new women's history. While at Warwick, I continued to be politically active, joining the University Socialist Society, the International Socialists, and with other socialist women founding Coventry Women's Liberation. Our women's group consisted of women from the university as well as working class women from the area. We held weekly meetings, leafleted the college and Hillfields, the nearby working-class housing development. In fall 1969, our women's group invited Rowbotham to give the first public lecture. A close friend of the Thompsons, Rowbotham had just published an article in the Socialist newspaper *Black Dwarf* on "Women's Liberation and the New Politics." She was researching her first three books—*Women, Resistance and Revolution: A History of Women and Revolution in the Modern World; Hidden from History;* and *Woman's Consciousness: Man's World.* At the Warwick meeting, she spoke on the women of the 1871 Paris Commune, women's history, and revolutionary movements. She was as interested in the US women's movement as I was in English women's history.

So we began our political and personal collaboration and friendship. We picketed together, as at the first demonstration against the Miss World Contest. At the annual History Workshop meetings, Rowbotham announced she was working on women's history and wanted to meet with others interested in the subject. A group of women historians—including June Hannam, Anna Davin, and myself—met separately to discuss women's issues. After considerable debate, we agreed to organize a conference on women's liberation. In February 1970, Ruskin College hosted the first women's liberation conference since the suffragette days. Over five hundred women, including Juliet Mitchell, Selma James, Sally Alexander, and Labour MP Audrey Wise, poured into the small college town of Oxford, forcing us to move the conference to the very prestigious and, until very recently, exclusively male Oxford Union. This conference marked the beginning of the women's liberation movement in Britain.[8]

In England I easily could combine political and academic activism. I was studying with Marxist and other left-wing historians, who shared a common understanding about a point of view. My professors and other students accepted leafleting factories, selling socialist newspapers, going on demonstrations, and organizing meetings. In my MA group of eleven students, ten identified as socialists, and all participated in student demonstrations. Debates about issues of race, gender, and ethnicity, however, persisted. So many of the male historians privileged class over race and gender, relying on the classic "Wait until socialism" response to the demands of women or people of color.

I spent months researching US and European women's history, writing papers on the relationship of the US and English women's suffrage movement to working-class women and on the Women's Trade Union League. Following Virginia Woolf's advice in *A Room of One's Own,* I read in the British Museum as much as I could on contemporary European and US women's history, including biographies, autobiographies, newspapers, journals, novels, and poetry. I went to the Trades Union Congress for women in the labor movement, the Marx Memorial Library for communist women's history, the London School of Economics Library for social democratic women, the Fawcett library for suffrage history, and the Public Record Office for what the police had to say about women. This was a particularly exciting time for me; it was the only time when I was immersed totally in research and study in an environment where our work was critiqued in an atmosphere of collegiality and comradeship.

By the time I left England, I was fairly confident that I wanted to combine political involvement, especially working-class activity, with teaching at a college or university. But I faced what I considered a serious political problem. In the 1970s a number of socialist groups, including the International Socialists, sent middle-class students to work in factories, not just to give them the experience of factory life, but rather to try and transform them into industrial workers. Such cadres then would organize workers into unions, or rank and file groups within unions, and finally into their particular socialist organizations. While supporting these policies, I did not want to "industrialize." I was not afraid of hard work, but rather was convinced that workers would not believe I was working-class and that I would be discovered as a fraud. Though considering myself a dedicated revolutionary, I also had desired to be a history teacher since the sixth grade. To add to my confusion, I did not want to be an academic. I loved doing research, but not writing; I was uninterested in publishing. I did not know how to resolve this dilemma.

Right before leaving for the United States, I had a long talk with Thompson. Despite his academic support, we were never really personally close. He was somewhat ambivalent toward Americans and not particularly enamored with US radicals, particularly those from the New Left. While he was no longer a member of the Communist party, he retained a residual dislike of Trotskyists. But my work on Pankhurst convinced him that I had some redeeming intellectual, political, and academic qualities. He talked to me about his life as both an activist and academic, explaining that workers are not necessarily put off by middle-class intellectuals. He had taught courses on Blake's poetry to factory workers; he had gained many insights from political discussions with workers in his adult education classes. If I wanted to have relationships with working-class people and with labor struggles, he advised, I could be more politically effective as a teacher in a working-class or adult education setting. He convinced me not to take a factory job. His encouragement enabled me to pursue the political activism that disappointed and embarrassed my parents. (They wanted me to be a history professor at a small northeastern liberal arts college; my father regarded my teaching at a community college as not really working.)

Once back in Seattle, I found myself in a vortex of political activity. Women's Liberation Seattle was involved in a myriad of activities, including organizing women workers on and off campus and working on the successful referendum to liberalize Washington State's abortion laws. We produced a monthly newsletter, *Aint I a Woman,* for which I wrote a regular column on women in history. I also gave women's history talks at the university, community colleges and high schools. With a number of graduate students, particularly Mary Rothschild, I helped establish women's studies. In 1971 and 1973, I taught courses for that developing program. But I continued to focus on political rather than academic activism.

In 1971, my teaching career at working-class community colleges began when members of the Seattle Community College Women's Liberation asked if I could develop a women's studies program. My classes were models of diversity in terms of age, race, class, gender, sexuality, ethnicity, and politics. Such students taught me how to place these concepts into my curriculum.

In 1973, my husband and I moved to Cleveland Ohio to be full-time political activists in the labor and socialist movements. For ten years I taught the women's studies, black studies and labor studies courses at Cuyahoga Community College in Cleveland, Ohio (with a brief stint at the University of Michigan at Dearborn). Teaching represented a way in which to earn money, be a member of the American Federation of Teachers (AFT), and have an ongoing relationship with working-class students, especially students of color.

During this ten-year period, I had little to do with the academic life. I abandoned my dissertation on Sylvia Pankhurst. I knew about the developing organization of women historians, but never attended a meeting of the American Historical Association (AHA) or the Berkshire Conference on Women's History. I once went to the Cleveland Council of Women Historians, then chaired by Lois Scharf. Regrettably, I never came back. On my own, and as best as possible, I tried to keep up with the literature. But I had little relationship to the debates within the new women's history and, with the exception of Sheila Rowbotham, I did not have any personal or political relationships with feminist historians.

Instead, I was involved with women workers, choosing to write about women's struggles in socialist and feminist journals and newspapers. So when Rowbotham came to visit in 1973, we took a four-day trip to Harlan County to meet with and interview members of the Brookside Women's Club, an auxiliary of the United Mine Workers Union. Rowbotham's *Women's Resistance and Revolution* had just appeared in the US and she gave copies to the women in this striking mining community. I joined the Cleveland Council of Union Women (CCUW), trade-union women organizing around equality issues within the Cleveland labor movement.

In March 1974, CCUW traveled to the founding convention of the Coalition of Labor Union Women (CLUW). There I found myself with Rosalyn Baxandall, a sister historian as well as radical and socialist feminist, in an AFT caucus battling women AFT officials. Here we learned firsthand that gender united women, but politics and privilege divided us. In opposition to the leadership, radicals demanded that CLUW open its doors to *all* working women regardless of trade union affiliation, including members of the United Farm Workers Organizing Committee and its vice-president, Dolores Huerta. Further, we wanted inclusion of women who were members of working-class communities like the Brookside Women's Club. We wanted CLUW to be an independent organization of working women, one which could challenge not only the discriminatory practices of employers, but also the racism and sexism of the AFL-CIO leadership. Though we failed, this was the first real opportunity for women like myself to connect feminism with the goals and aspirations of working-class women.

As an officer of the Cleveland CLUW, I traveled throughout the state trying to help organize chapters. I often gave talks on working women's history. I spoke at a United Automobile Workers (UAW) union meeting in Lordstown, Ohio, then notorious for its young workers, who emulated the sixties lifestyle with drugs, sex, long hair, and rock 'n' roll. With United Steel Workers Union women in Youngstown, Ohio I discussed job discrimination. Under a consent degree, an aluminum company was forced to hire women on the same basis as men. The company, the union, and the men in the plant weren't happy to have women around. So, in the name of "equality," they made women lift seventy-five-pound aluminum bars for which men could use machinery or work in tandem. The union local refused to intercede. For several months we met to develop a strategy to win over the union and to establish a legal strategy that could combine issues of women's equality with female difference. Such cases anticipated the theoretical and policy debates that raged among feminists in the 1980s.

I also became involved in February 1979 with striking Laurel, Mississippi poultry workers, which introduced me to southern working-class politics, and challenged many assumptions I held about the South. The 200 strikers, most of whom were women and all of whom were black, demanded a change in absentee policy, overtime pay, and toilet breaks. The union contract allowed only three bathroom breaks *a week*—and then the workers had to explain their situation to a supervisor. The plant supervisor was Charles Noble, an open Klansman accused but acquitted by an all-white jury of murdering a local NAACP leader. Laurel was the home of Sam Bowers, one of the murderers of civil rights workers James Cheney, Andrew Goodman, and Michael Schwerner. After two years of heroic struggle and sacrifice, the strikers, abandoned by union leadership, returned to work without a union contract. During the strike, I began reading southern working-class history, but it was strike support work, not history or theory, which provided insights into debates taking place among feminist historians. After working with these strikers, how could I privilege class over race or accept an essentialist perspective on gender?

In 1983, my political and personal life shattered. After fifteen years, I was no longer a member of a socialist organization and my almost twenty-year-old marriage ended. I was academically disoriented as well. Without a PhD, I could not find a full time-teaching job in New York City's tight job market. For nearly ten years, I was an adjunct at five different colleges, including two years teaching women's studies at Rikers' Island prison. I ruefully joked that I held office hours on the D train. Yet I was confident and positive about my teaching. I developed innovative interdisciplinary courses—one on immigrant women in New York City, another on "Woman as Subject, Woman as Object: The Female Nude in the Western Tradition."

During this extraordinarily difficult period, I was raising two daughters. From the beginning of the women's liberation movement in the sixties, we studied motherhood and the family as agents of women's oppression. During the first few years of the radical women's liberation movement, we read countless books about the family, from Engel's *Origins of the Family, Private Property and the State* to Shulamith Firestone's *Dialectic of Sex.* Contrary to today's antifeminist pundits, the early women's liberation movement was never antimotherhood or children. First, many of the women *were* mothers. Second, one of the main demands was for parent- and staff-controlled, 24-hour-a-day childcare. Once I started teaching, I understood issues of the family and motherhood even better. At both Seattle and Cuyahoga Community Colleges, half the students were women, and a good percentage of them were mothers. The CUNY system is majority female; there always were a significant number of mothers—single and dual parents.

Whatever my theoretical or academic knowledge of the subject of motherhood and the family, my own experiences as a single mother enabled me to become more empathetic toward students. I learned firsthand the difficulties of finding good childcare and the exorbitant cost of babysitting. During Reagan's presidency, the tax law changed, cutting down on deductions for childcare, but not business luncheons. Mother's Day, a holiday I never liked, seemed even more hypocritical. The government, the private sector, and individual men seemingly conspired to make motherhood difficult for women and almost impossible for those of the working class, the unemployed, and mothers of color. Lesbian mothers could lose custody of their children, and poor women, especially women of color, ran high risks of coercive sterilization.

Single motherhood was even more daunting. I was the parent called out of a class because one of my girls took sick at school. I was the cliché of the mother juggling adjunct jobs, finding babysitters (a lengthy routine for a comedy club), writing, and performing as a gymnastics-ballet-soccer-volleyball-swimming-basket-softball-and-lacrosse mom (don't forget classroom mom). Like many of my students, when my daughters' school holidays did not coincide with mine, they accompanied me to class. When I had to travel, I brought my daughters to conferences.

But I'm not complaining. This experience only enriched my understanding of the complexity of family life and personal relationships, as well as the real needs of my students. Like my father before me, I gave them an interest in history, politics, and feminism. Both my daughters are athletes. My oldest was the president of her high school women's group, Cell 16. My younger considers herself a socialist, is one of the editors of her school paper, and has campaigned against sweatshops.

The academic world remained alien. While I had kept up with feminist literature, I did not understand the language, the debates, or the arguments involved in women's history and theory. I didn't know many women historians, and often felt lonely and left out at women's history meetings. On the few occasions when I participated in a seminar or lectured on my research, I felt frozen in the language and politics of the sixties. My research was on an individual woman at a time when many feminist historians looked down on biography. I even considered going back to graduate school. But after extensive research and revision, I completed my dissertation and, after a struggle, the University of Washington in 1990 awarded me my union card, a PhD in women's history. I turned my dissertation into a book, *Sylvia Pankhurst: Sexual Politics and Political Activism.*

My integration into academia ironically resulted from feminist activism. In 1989, Eileen Boris called to see if I would be interested in becoming the executive director of the Coordinating Committee on Women in the Historical Profession/Conference Group on Women's History (CCWHP/CGWH). Eileen and I had known each other through political work in the Reproductive Rights National Network and shared socialist feminist politics. My four-year tenure as CCWHP/CGWH executive director transformed my attitude toward the academy. I learned about the struggles of a generation of academic women who had not only made history as activists, but also changed the discipline of history through inclusion of gender, race, class, ethnicity, and sexuality as central categories of analysis. CCWHP/CGWH played a significant role in making the AHA more receptive to women historians as well as historians of color.[9] Being active in the Coordinating Council for Women in History (CCWH) connected feminism, activism, and the academy.

I continue to hold a feminist, antiracist, and internationalist perspective. Following Thompson's advice, I have taught at colleges with working-class student bodies, the majority of students being women, immigrants, or students of color.[10] Such settings further enrich my methods of teaching as well as my subject matter. My commitment to radical political activity motivated my book on Sylvia Pankhurst and present scholarship on the women's liberation movement. My association with activist historians, especially younger graduate students, provides a vision for teaching history in the future. As an activist, feminist, antiracist, and internationalist historian, my goal is not to "rescue" the twenty-first century's equivalent to the stockinger, the cropper, the handloom-weaver, and deluded followers of charismatic leaders from the condescension of history, but rather create an academy where they become their own historians.

NOTES

I would like to thank Eileen Boris, Jesse Lemisch, Dan Marsh, Jen Mitas, and Ron Napal for all their help with this essay.

1. I thought of Louis Filler, especially after watching in Stephen Spielberg's *Amistad* the inaccurate portrayal of the abolitionists, and in particular, Louis Tappan, a favorite of Filler.

2. Eleanor Flexner, *A Century of Struggle* (Cambridge: Harvard Univ. Press, 1959). I only wish that at the time I read Flexner's book, I had known about her association with radicals and communists and her insistence, that the history of black women not be edited out of the text. See Ellen Fitzpatrick's foreword to the 1996 edition of *A Century of Struggle,* ix–xxiv.

3. Anna Louise Strong, *I Change Worlds: The Remaking of an American* (New York: Henry Holt and Company, 1954); Harvey O'Connor, *Revolution in Seattle* (New York: Monthly Review Press, 1964); Tracy B. Strong and Helene Keyssar, *Right in Her Soul: The Life of Anna Louise Strong* (New York: Random House, 1983); Barbara Winslow, "Anna Louise Strong: 'I Must Be a Socialist,'" *Western Front* 1 (February 10, 1969), 10.

4. Leon Trotsky, *A History of the Russian Revolution* (London: Victor Gollancz, 1932–33), vol. 1, 109.

5. Temma Kaplan, "Commentary: On the Socialist Origins of International Women's Day," *Feminist Studies* 11 (Spring 1985), 163–71, outlined the origins and history of International Women's Day. She also wrote that "according to one story, it [International Woman's Day] was revived in the United States by a woman's group at the University of Illinois, Chicago Circle, which included daughters of American Communists who remembered having heard of the holiday. Since then, it has become the occasion for a new sense of female consciousness and a new sense of feminist internationalism," 170.

6. E. P. Thompson, *The Making of the English Working Class* (New York: Pantheon, 1964), 14.

7. Ibid., 12.

8. See, for example, *Once a Feminist: Stories of a Generation,* interviews by Michelle Wander (London: Virago, 1990).

9. Hilda Smith, Nupur Chaudhuri, Gerda Lerner, and Berenice Carroll, *The History of the Coordinating Committee of Women Historians/Conference Group on Women's History* (N.P.: CCWHP/CGWH, 1994); Judith Zinsser, *History and Feminism: A Glass Half Full* (New York: Twayne, 1993).

10. Eileen Boris and I share this experience of teaching at a black college. I agree with her statement that "every progressive 'white' professor ought to spend at least a term at a black college." I would only add that perhaps every "white" professor, progressive or otherwise, should have such an experience.

17

NANCY A. HEWITT

THE EMMA THREAD: COMMUNITARIAN VALUES, GLOBAL VISIONS

Twenty-seven years ago, I dropped out of Smith College in my sophomore year, choosing wage-work and activism over higher education. Between 1969 and 1971, I passed through my first personal and political metamorphosis—from small-town, honor-student cheerleader to antiwar radical feminist. The idea of continuing my undergraduate work at an elite women's college seemed impossible. Several more times over the next quarter-century, personal upheavals converged with political or intellectual transformations to induce significant ruptures in my life, and in my relation to scholarship and activism.

The first time I was asked to present my intellectual autobiography to a public audience—in June 1991 at the Southern Conference on Women's History in Chapel Hill, North Carolina—I focused on these crisis-driven leaps in understanding and linked significant changes in my thinking about women and history to moments of personal and professional trauma.[1] Growth by disjuncture seemed the right message—indeed, the only message—in a year which was marked for me by the death of close friends, crises in my most intimate relations, and the proliferation of postmodernist and postcolonialist critiques. Even as I wrote that talk, the everyday realities that had shaped my personal choices and historical interpretations for a decade seemed to be dissolving around me. At least the attacks on grand theory suggested that such dissolutions were inevitable, necessary, and perhaps even creative.

Nancy Hewitt presenting a report on sexual harassment to faculty and reporters, University of South Florida, winter 1987. Photo courtesy of the *Oracle* (Tampa, Florida).

In crafting this essay, I returned to the sources by which I had earlier documented my periodic intellectual permutations—fragmented diaries from my months working at the Women's Herstory Archives in California (WHA) (1974) and from the year I entered graduate school (1975); articles penned for the feminist monthly *New Women's Times* (1975–76); papers written at Smith College (1969–71), SUNY-Brockport (1973–74), and University of Pennsylvania (1975–81); early files of Coordinating Committee on Women in the Historical Profession (CCWHP) newsletters and correspondence (1974–81); and fifteen years of scholarly publications. I was shocked! As I reexamined my personal "archives," I saw evidence everywhere of continuity, common themes, and long-forgotten speculations that prefigured later work. Suddenly it appeared that despite all the apparent ruptures in my life, the same fundamental issues had shaped my thinking for the past twenty-five years.

So, had there been ruptures and paradigm shifts after all, or had the shattered fragments of earlier thought patterns simply been reconfigured within the same general frame, like the glass shards in a kaleidoscope? Had my disparate experiences in distinct times and places really transformed my vision of women, politics, and history, or had the vision of radical feminism that crystallized for me between 1969 and 1971 continued to frame my reading of seemingly discordant moments?

I write this essay at a time when calm prevails. In 1996–97, I spent a year on leave at the Center for Advanced Study in the Behavioral Sciences at Stanford; I have nearly completed my long-overdue book on Latin, Black, and Anglo women in Tampa, Florida; my first dissertation student, Anne Valk, has defended, graduated, and gotten a tenure-track job; my personal relationships seem loving and stable; I feel well-regarded and well-rewarded by colleagues and students. In the last two years, moreover, I have been able to build new links between my scholarly work and women's grassroots politics, thereby helping to create the common ground between activism and academics that I first sought so long ago. And as I began this essay, my friend Judith Bennett sent me the final draft of her article, "Confronting Continuity." It seemed directed not only to women's historians as a whole, but to me personally.[2] This seems like a propitious moment, then, to explore how I constructed myself as a feminist historian, and how political and intellectual ruptures played out in the context of powerful ideological continuities to shape both my sense of self and my body of work.

The threads of this narrative stretch back to fall 1969, when I left my hometown of Spencerport, New York for Northampton, Massachusetts. The Emma thread is the most important of these. I did not encounter the thread's namesake—Emma Goldman—until 1974, when I devoured her two-volume autobiography while living in Berkeley, California. But I had been searching for her from the moment I discovered radical politics, during my first semester at Smith. I became fascinated then by individuals who devoted their lives to challenging dominant truths in hopes of transforming the world. As a convert to antiwar feminism in fall 1969, I wondered how it was that most of the "truths" I had grown up accepting could suddenly seem so wrong. And how was it that many of my new friends had already imbibed understandings of the world that fit so much more neatly with civil rights, antiwar, and feminist politics? Was it wealth, political lineage, more cosmopolitan upbringings? And if leftist political views were so much more jarring for me, then how did I manage to embrace them at all when my friends back in Spencerport continued to reject such challenges? I was interested, that is, in what conditions made radical politics imaginable, and to whom.

These questions intrigued me, haunted me, exhausted me as I joined antiwar demonstrations, vigils for students killed at Kent State and Jackson State, campaign caravans for Allard Lowenstein, draft counseling classes, and, by 1971, the flood of college dropouts. While still at Smith, I wrote papers on Janis Joplin as radical spokeswoman, on the Trail of Tears along which Cherokee Indians were removed to Oklahoma in the 1830s, and on the revolutionary "saints" in Tudor-Stuart England. In a fit of politically induced bravura that now makes me cringe, I taught a student-initiated course with my friend Patrice Nelson on Native American cultures. After leaving school, I spent time in Toronto, Canada trying to combine college courses and political activities, but when the latter took over, I lost my student visa. Back in Rochester, New York I worked nights at Dunkin' Donuts. I also rang door bells for George McGovern, read all I could on the feminist movement, experimented a bit with drugs, and tried to lead an exemplary life despite the fact that I was dressed eight hours a day in a pink and white waitresses' uniform and smelled perpetually of jelly, sugar, and honey glaze.

In fall 1972, I quit the donut business, took a day job selling office supplies, and enrolled in SUNY-Brockport's urban outreach program. Dr. Robert Smith, a French historian and a wonderfully generous teacher, offered a course on "History's Outcasts: Women, Children, and Criminals" in a downtown church. He brought me back into the college fold, and by spring, I had enrolled full-time at Brockport, fitting classes around my job at Scrantom's Book and Stationary Store and, later, a night shift at Eastman Kodak.

I kept searching for the elusive process by which individuals broke with accepted norms and imagined the world in a new light. I wrote papers for a women's history course, team-taught by Professors Bob Smith and Susan Stuard, on Shulamith Firestone and Anaïs Nin, and a senior thesis on Alice Paul and the National Woman's Party. I focused only on the early years of militancy and ignored the period when Paul and her followers wielded sex equality to fend off discussions of racial and class injustice.

When I graduated from Brockport in May 1974, I was torn between going to graduate school and becoming a full-time feminist activist. Susan Stuard had persuaded me to join the CCWHP while an undergraduate, so in 1974 I wrote to membership director Karen Offen, asking advice on graduate programs in women's history. She responded immediately and suggested that I contact Suzanne Lebsock, who was then the graduate student representative on the American Historical Association (AHA) Committee on Women, and Dr. Anne Firor Scott, professor at Duke University. A decade later, Lebsock and Scott would become important mentors and colleagues. At the time, I stuffed Offen's letter in my backpack and headed to Berkeley to work as an intern for Laura X at the WHA.

My "career" as a feminist activist did not last long. Working conditions at WHA were even worse than those in my previous jobs, and the promised training—a how-to course for creating a local women's archives—was nonexistent. Still, knowing no one in Berkeley except the other new interns, I sold my car, house-sat periodically for Laura X, and got a part-time job selling office furniture to make ends meet. I rented a room from a woman who sometimes woke up screaming, and I watched the Watergate hearings on a small black and white TV in a cramped kitchen when I had the time. I had more time after a group of interns tried to organize WHA workers, and I was fired.

My career as a feminist historian benefited from these crises. Not only did the thought of selling office supplies for life inspire me to submit graduate school applications, but a number of events that summer and fall shaped the directions I would take as a scholar. Perhaps most importantly, I fell in love with Emma Goldman. I read *Living My Life*, both volumes, cover-to-cover, and then began inhaling everything I could find on Emma and anarchism, which in Berkeley was considerable. Emma explained, though not as transparently as I thought at the time, how she became a radical. And like so many other feminists of my generation, I somehow found myself identifying with her youthful experiences as a Russian Jew, cheering her on as she emigrated to America, and weeping with her as the Haymarket martyrs were hung, yet recognizing that it was this shock to her sense of justice that led her to devote her life to anarchism. I was amazed that Emma had lived in Rochester for a time—just fifteen miles from where I grew up—and I was moved by the way she combined embeddedness in a very particular community of comrades with an internationalist perspective.

Anarchist critiques of centralized power seemed to keep Goldman from universalizing her own particular sense of truth, yet allowed her to promulgate a global vision of change. She and her comrades took seriously the priorities established by working-class communities across the country even as they sought to draw them into a wider circle. And Goldman, more attuned than her male co-workers to the particular needs of poor women, seemed to maintain an especially fine balance in her work between communal values and global visions. Emma Goldman thus offered me a new way to think about the tensions between local and global perspectives, one that placed them in a creative rather than competitive relation to each other. She also introduced me to communitarian models of change, in which collective needs were valued—in theory if not always in practice—over individual rights.

At the same time I was introduced to Emma, I immersed myself in the history of women's activism. Despite my conflicts with Laura X, she opened up new worlds to me during my stint at WHA. I spent hours in her library reading about women's movements in the US, Russia, England, and France. I filled my spiral notebook with quotes from militant suffragists like Inez Milholland Boissevain and women's historians like Anne Firor Scott, and I compiled lists of woman's rights advocates who had started out as abolitionists. For some reason, I even noted the number of Quakers among this group. The differences I began to see among women activists in the nineteenth century echoed through the struggles within the WHA and among local feminists in Berkeley, though issues of race, class, and sexuality played out somewhat differently in the twentieth century.

I was deluged with competing notions of what constituted women's emancipation and began to realize how race, class, and ideology shaped different conceptions of equality and liberation. My own sense of personal and political identity was undergoing another metamorphosis. Sex and money were the keys. Though I had gotten married during my Dunkin' Donuts days, I was in California on my own, and free to explore women's bars and political lesbianism, that is, the commitment to identify as lesbian for purposes of solidarity whatever your sexual practice. At the same time, I increasingly understood the importance of material conditions in shaping women's choices—my own and those of the women I encountered in Berkeley and Oakland. Though I never fully embraced either lesbian separatism or socialist feminism, I did identify more and more closely with diverse sexualities and materialist perspectives.

In addition, the internationalist bent of anarcho-feminist writings combined with the expanded geographical consciousness that came with antiwar work introduced me to women's movements in China, Vietnam, and Cuba. In these revolutionary strongholds it seemed that women had gained a semblance of equality by struggling alongside men against authoritarian regimes. Such tales of revolutionary camaraderie between the sexes resonated with me—after all I not only had a husband back in Rochester but two brothers to whom I was very close. Still, I found a special energy and comfort in the all-female spaces that were now part of my daily life. For the moment, at least, global and local perspectives, sisterhood and difference, lesbian separatism and social networks that included men seemed deeply intertwined, each incomplete without its counterpart.

As I applied that fall to history graduate programs, I envisioned myself studying the history of radical women in the US or Europe. I applied to Berkeley in hopes of working with Natalie Zemon Davis, whom I had read about in the local student paper. I applied to the University of Pennsylvania because my best friend from the WHA, Valerie Jaworski, was returning to complete her BA there. And I applied to Harvard's American Civilization Program because Professor Barbara Sicherman had written such an enthusiastic response to my letter of inquiry. That was all I could afford, so Duke didn't make the cut.

In December, my brother Will had back surgery, and I returned home to help with his care while my parents worked. The day after I arrived home, my father was taken to intensive care with an embolism. He was soon back home recuperating. I quickly reverted to the dutiful daughter and wife, even returning to my job at Scrantom's. But I knew graduate school might be only nine months away. Biding my time, I joined a circle of local feminists who were starting a newspaper, the *New Women's Times*. The heading noted that Rochester was the home of Susan B. Anthony, but I thought of it more as the home of Emma Goldman. I sold ads, distributed bundles of papers to drugstores and newsstands, and wrote articles on anarcho-feminism and local women's studies programs. I attended endless hours of meetings and dragged along my best friend from Scrantom's, Debbie Drechsler, a talented artist.[3] I went to the University of Rochester library and, in the days before computer searches, painstakingly compiled a list of every book on anarchism in their holdings.

Then, one day at work, I received a call from the director of graduate studies at Penn. He had tracked me down through my work number in Berkeley—I had forgotten to send any of the graduate schools my change of address. Despite that and my slightly erratic undergraduate career, Penn offered me admission and a partial fellowship. I leapt at the chance, since Berkeley had offered me admission but no money, and Harvard had rejected me by return postcard—or at least that's the way I remember it.

After several years of mixing wage work, night school, marriage, and activism, graduate school seemed luxurious. I worked only twenty hours a week at a medical archive; my fellowship was labor-free the first year; my tuition and fees were paid; I shared an apartment with Valerie Jaworski; and my brother Tom lived just north of Philadelphia. The only traumatic part initially was going to class. I was awed by how much the other students seemed to know, and much to my dismay, Carroll Smith-Rosenberg was just heading out the door on leave when I arrived. I floundered but stayed afloat my first semester, mainly by saying very little and thereby covering up what I perceived as my intellectual shortcomings. Over semester break, I filed for a legal separation from my husband, and then returned to Philadelphia determined to write the history of women's activism.

Luck was with me. That spring, Lynn Lees taught a European women's history course and insisted that we use foreign-language sources in our research. I leapt into documents—newspapers and memoirs—on women in the Paris Commune. At the same time, visiting professor Barbara Welter allowed me to write a paper under her direction on Emma Goldman and anarchist contributions to feminist thought. When Smith-Rosenberg returned for the summer, she directed me back to more mainstream topics—nineteenth-century women physicians and antebellum women reformers—and taught me the basics of US women's history. During her second year of leave, I explored American social history, sociolinguistics, and ethnohistory, deepening my interest in community studies and local ethnographies.

That same year, a group of graduate students formed a local chapter of the Mid-Atlantic Radical Historians Organization (MARHO). We met monthly to read and debate classics of leftist history—including the writings of Karl Marx and recent debates on the transition from feudalism to capitalism. We also leapt into newer debates on sexuality and power, pouring over the latest translations of Michel Foucault. Walsh's Tavern became our regular meeting place, allowing us to simultaneously organize protests (usually over graduate student funding), drink beer, debate politics, and share tips on teaching and research, all of which I viewed as extensions of political action.

Thus, as the faculty at Penn worked to gently but firmly transform me from a feminist polemicist into a women's historian, the MARHO crowd sustained—and forced me to defend—my anarchist, feminist, materialist beliefs. The combination proved remarkably productive. And when it became clear that neither Smith-Rosenberg nor my committee was going to approve a dissertation on Emma and anarchism, I was ready with an alternative. I would return to Rochester, pointing out it was the home of Susan B. Anthony, and trace the efforts of women activists to reform, and transform, society in the mid-nineteenth century.[4]

I had visited the University of Rochester archives on a trip home in 1977. There archivist Mary Huth introduced me to an incredible range of activists in the antebellum city, including Amy Post, a Quaker abolitionist and woman's rights advocate whose family papers had just been catalogued. As soon as I began reading the Post papers, I knew I had found Emma's foremother. Here was another woman who embedded her activism in a communitarian vision, insisting on the intertwined character of racial, economic, and gender justice. Along with advocating the emancipation of slaves and women, Post sought to advance the rights of Seneca Indians and free blacks, create links with English and European radicals, abolish capital punishment, organize working women, and promote spiritualism, land reform, and religious freedom. She lived her life in accordance with her political views—refusing to consume slave-produced goods, socializing in mixed-racial company, donning bloomers, and providing a haven for escaped slaves, abused wives, and itinerant activists. Within this circle, women worked side by side with men, yet also retained all-female spaces modeled on the women's meetings in the Society of Friends. And within both mixed-sex and single-sex arenas, Post and her co-workers struggled—sometimes successfully, often not—to overcome the racial and class prejudices they had imbibed as farmers in downstate New York and as members of the lower middle class in Rochester.

The tensions between Post's upbringing in an isolated Quaker farm community and her entrance into a more heterogeneous, urban world fueled her commitment to radical change. The communitarian vision of social order that she embraced as a girl was difficult to maintain in a city marked by class, ethnic, racial, and religious differences and conflicts. Yet instead of abandoning her communal values, Post nurtured them in a variety of activist, free black, and Native American communities and searched for their echo in political movements throughout the US and Europe.

Amy Post only came to see the local character of the truths she had been raised to believe after moving to Rochester. It was the dramatic change in her circumstances, the rupture caused by moving to a non-Quaker city, that forced Post to recognize the particularities of her values. For those of us coming of age in the 1960s, the spell of the familial and communal values we were raised by was more often broken by the televised images of civil rights demonstrations, the news coverage of Vietnam, the killings at Kent State and Jackson State, or the Watergate hearings.

The painful process of coming to terms with difference and with change, then, began when local truths were challenged. There are dangers, however, in recognizing the particularity, and thus the limits, of community-based perspectives. Communal values can too quickly be defined as parochial and irrelevant, and more global visions as the preferred framework by which to formulate political agendas and actions. In the 1970s, the adage "think globally, act locally" reflected activists' faith in solutions that could be readily transferred from one community to another, regardless of cultural differences or material constraints. The feminist counterpart—"sisterhood is powerful"—honored the same capacity for instituting changes that would benefit women as a whole, whatever their race, class, national origin, religion, ideology, or sexual orientation. I embraced both of these slogans for a time, a long time, and identified myself in the early 1970s as a radical feminist, that is, one who viewed sex as the primary source of oppression historically and in the present.

Yet I remained attracted as well to communal and communitarian values, recognizing that so-called global perspectives were also rooted in some place, some particular cultural and material position. There was no outside, no place where one could stand that was not grounded already in historical relations and ideological assumptions. Advocates of standpoint theorizing made a virtue of grounding one's interpretation in the specificity of place, time, and culture.[5] But the locations I seemed to occupy were considered suspicious—white, middle-class, northeastern—since they were the ones too often taken for universal already. And the places I came from—lower middle class, Hungarian, and small town—had been dramatically transformed by antiwar work, radical feminism, graduate education, and employment. My standpoints were multiple and shifting. The best I could do, then, as a scholar or an activist, was to continually test global visions against communal values, and vice versa.

Much of my early writing, for courses and for feminist newspapers, documents my desire to embrace a global vision. But beginning with my dissertation, my scholarly work focused on the particularities of women's activism in specific times and places—mid-nineteenth-century Rochester, New York and turn-of-the-twentieth-century Tampa, Florida—and on differences among women within these local arenas.[6] Like so many other social historians, I embraced the community study as the best means of exploring the larger trajectory of ordinary people's lives.

Still, the question is always asked of those who focus on local histories—how typical is this case? I have long argued that the importance of a community can lie in its atypicality, its dissonance from what is considered the normal (national or global) pattern; and I have denied any interest in creating a grand synthesis from the profusion of case studies. Yet I can now see that over the course of my career, I have crafted—piece by piece and locale by locale—a larger narrative exploring one thread of women's activism, the Emma thread, that embeds a global vision of change in communal and communitarian values.[7]

My attempts to follow this thread were enriched and complicated as I completed the Rochester study, published as *Women's Activism and Social Change* in 1984. A whole new conceptualization of women's history and political action was emerging at the time. Studies of working women, black women, and immigrant women argued that the community values which underwrote their activism were often at odds with the supposedly global visions wielded by middle-class and ruling-class whites. Asked by *Social History* in 1984 to author a review essay on the state of American women's history, I wrote "Beyond the Search for Sisterhood" as a manifesto for incorporating Difference. It now appears a rather moderate proposal.

This transformation in the field of women's history assured the resurgence of the local as a way of developing inclusive histories that recognized not only diversity but also conflict. The change crystallized in the 1980s, during my years of teaching at the University of South Florida in Tampa. The city was deeply marked by racial, ethnic, and class differences, and I began researching the lives of Latin, mainly Cuban and Italian, women cigarworkers who settled in the area at the turn of the twentieth century. At the same time, I worked with a group of progressive faculty and students at USF, organizing symposia on Central America and militarism, protesting the Gulf War, demanding divestment, writing sexual harassment guidelines, sustaining a faculty union, and working with Florida Endowment for the Humanities to promote multicultural history programs.

My local circumstances enriched my historical understanding and sustained my political interests, but from the perspective of my professional identity, I was living on the edge. To build connections to historians with similar interests, I depended on networks created by earlier feminist scholars. The most important of these for me was the Coordinating Committee on Women in the Historical Profession/Conference Group on Women's History (CCWHP/CGWH). The circle of women who founded the organization and those who continued to direct it welcomed new recruits. As a graduate student and young professor, I staffed the CCWHP/CGWH table at conferences, attended business meetings, and stayed connected to developments in the profession and the wider world of women's history through interactions with Karen Offen, Nupur Chaudhuri, Lynn Weiner, Peg Strobel, Claire Moses, Eileen Boris, and others.

When I was asked to serve the organization as chair of the graduate student prize committee, then as CGWH president, and finally as vice-president of the International Federation for Research in Women's History (IFRWH), my links to women's history and women's activism became still more global. Combined with my work as American editor of *Gender & History*, my service to CCWHP/CGWH assured that the forms of community activism I uncovered while researching immigrant women in Tampa would be in continuous conversation with the regional and global efforts analyzed by an array of feminist academics.[8] The Southern Association of Women Historians (SAWH) provided a similar network of US historians whose work on race, gender, and class inspired me to expand the Tampa study to include the stories of Anglo and African-American as well as Latin women activists.

As I explored this new terrain of women's activism, the Emma thread reappeared—in a racially mixed community of Latin workers intent on overthrowing Spanish rule in Cuba and Puerto Rico. This time the rupture was caused by the arrival of thousands of white and Afro-Cuban cigarworkers in the 1890s, just as the institution of Jim Crow laws sought to wipe out the experiments in interracial cooperation and political equality that followed emancipation. Over the next three decades, movements for social change among women would be established and reimagined as Latin anarcho-syndicalists, African-American advocates of racial and economic justice, and native-born white moral reformers crossed paths and crossed swords. The thread that ran from Emma to Amy was woven into the fabric of Tampa activism by the Afro-Cuban advocate of Cuban independence, Paulina Pedroso, and the Puerto Rican feminist labor organizer, Luisa Capetillo. Both offered Tampa residents visions of change that were deeply rooted in community networks and communitarian values, yet profoundly influenced by global concerns that linked the fates of people in Tampa to those in Spain, the Caribbean, Latin America, the Philippines, and elsewhere in the US.[9]

In the midst of writing the history of women's activism in Tampa, I was offered a position at Duke University. It was there in 1995–96 that I directed a Sawyer Seminar on Women's Leadership and Grassroots Activism funded by the Andrew W. Mellon Foundation.[10] A group of area faculty, graduate students, and activists met in a biweekly seminar with grassroots leaders and scholars from Africa, Central America, the Caribbean, and the US. For Monique Mujuwamaliya, Dollie Burwell, Elsa Barkley Brown, Tessa Rouverol, Shirley Sherrod, Chana Kai Lee, Kiki Sedua, Loune Viaud, and the other incredible women who shared their lives and work with us, radical visions of change were most often rooted in communal and communitarian values. Yet such visions resonated with Emma's thread, creating the potential for a network of communitarian politics across time and place.

As this shift in perspective occurred in the seminar, I realized that in my own work I had been struggling to make this case for years. It was precisely those women activists who combined immersion in local communities, communitarian models of change, and internationalist concerns who I had long defined as the model radicals. And it was those communities in which such radicals were able to flourish that most intrigued me.

If Rochester, New York—a Republican city from the time that label signaled emancipation until long after it became a mark of the New Right—and Tampa, Florida—a Sunbelt city that prospered from tobacco and tourism—could provide spaces for women to imagine, voice, and disseminate radical agendas, then there was hope for almost any place. The key was the moment of rupture that challenged local truths, yet allowed certain women to reconfigure rather than reject communal and collective values as the source for global visions. These women, the ones who carry on the Emma thread, inhabit diverse worlds, but seem always, at the moment of rupture, to be living on the margins of new worlds—the Russian Jewish émigré, the Quaker transplant, the Afro-Cuban southerner. Their lives suggest that differences among women—in the past and the present—can serve as a creative catalyst for rather than an unyielding barrier to change. Moments of rupture, then, might indeed be the most fertile time for rethinking our course, causing the kaleidoscope to spin, and offering new ways to look at old images, even as we continue to embrace fundamental commitments to collective action and collective rights.

As I complete this essay, a new period of upheaval has begun, leading to my resignation from Duke and my move to Rutgers University. But the path by which I came now seems to stretch back more than twenty-five years, providing some guidance for where to go next, as an activist and a historian.

NOTES

1. This talk was published as "Multiple Truths: The Personal, the Political and the Postmodernist in Contemporary Feminist Scholarship," Working Paper #5, Memphis State University Center for Research on Women, Series on Southern Women: The Intersections of Race, Class and Gender (January 1992).

2. Judith Bennett's article "Confronting Continuity" has been published in *Journal of Women's History* 9 (Fall 1997), 73–94.

3. Debbie Drechsler now lives in Santa Rosa, California, where she works as a freelance artist and writes feminist comix for Drawn and Quarterly Publishers.

4. Luckily, the professors in the History of Consciousness Program at the University of California at Santa Cruz were more open to Emma, and Candace Falk completed a dissertation on her life which became the basis for her book, *Love, Anarchy and Emma Goldman* and the inspiration for the development of the Emma Goldman Papers Project, which Candace continues to direct.

5. On standpoint theory, see especially Patricia Hill Collins, *Black Feminist Thought: Knowledge, Consciousness, and the Politics of Empowerment*, Perspectives on Gender, Vol. 2 (New York: Routledge, 1990).

6. The primary examples of this work include *Women's Activism and Social Change: Rochester, New York, 1822–1872* (Ithaca: Cornell Univ. Press, 1984); *Women, Families and Communities: Readings in American History* (HarperCollins, 1990); *Visible Women: New Essays on American Activism*, co-edited with Suzanne Lebsock (Urbana: University of Illinois Press, 1993); and a series of articles on Latin, Black, and Anglo women in Tampa, Florida.

7. My work has built upon and challenged the work of dozens of colleagues and students. My debts in this regard can be traced through the acknowledgments and notes in my various publications. In terms of the tensions between global visions and communal values, I have been most frequently inspired and tested by the work of Temma Kaplan, Jacquelyn Dowd Hall, Martha Ackelsberg, Deborah Gray White, Elsa Barkley Brown, Judith Bennett, Ardis Cameron, and the amazing group of graduate students at Duke University.

8. My debt to Leonore Davidoff, founding editor of *Gender & History* in England, is immense. Her willingness to take on a young associate professor from an unknown

university as co-editor and then to incorporate me as her equal partner in the development of the journal opened many doors for me as a scholar, an editor, and an activist.

9. Their stories will be told in the forthcoming book, *Forging Activist Identities: Latin, African American and Anglo Women in Tampa, Florida, 1880–1940* (Urbana: Univ. of Illinois Press).

10. My most important consultants and coworkers in planning and directing the seminar were Temma Kaplan, Robert Korstad, Carol Spruill, Catherine Newbury, Tera Hunter, Jacquelyn Dowd Hall, Alicia Rouverol, Kirsten Delegard, and Anne Valk.

18

MARY ELIZABETH PERRY

CLIO ON THE MARGINS

"Deviant insiders," I called prostitutes in early modern Seville; but the label applies just as well to me, for deviance from the center has played a major role in my professional life, my historical writing, and my political consciousness.[1] Like so many women, I have entered professional life from the margins. After interrupting graduate work to put a husband through law school and two children through a cooperative nursery school, I returned to graduate school as one of those marginalized older "returning women students." The study of women's history was in its infancy then and far from the center of "legitimate" history, but it spoke very directly to me. Choosing to write my dissertation and my first book on criminals in a Spanish city, I consciously aligned myself with those on the margins of respectability and legitimacy. In criminal records from the city of Seville's archives I found prostitutes as a gender-specific form of deviance, and they in turn brought me to consider the marginalized status of all women—deviants from the male norm, but absolutely essential to the male center.

My personal teaching experience made me even more aware of marginality, for I began as a part-time lecturer, euphemistically called a "visiting professor." I was first hired to teach on my fortieth birthday, which seemed to me a wonderful celebration. However, I learned on the first day of class that I had been hired to replace a regular faculty member who had suffered an emotional breakdown and was standing at the door ready to teach. I used other people's offices, except at one university where the department had neglected to find office space for me. There I held office hours beneath a tree next to my class-

Mary Elizabeth Perry.

room building. One year I taught at two institutions many miles apart and became a freeway flyer, trying to remember what day of the week it was so I would not end up on the wrong campus. I filled in for faculty members on leave, taught the large survey courses, and felt happy to be asked to return to teach—but always as a visitor. In those early years the faculty never included me in departmental meetings or decisions. I taught a women's history course only because I got funding for it through a program for developing new courses, and it attracted so many students that history departments were happy to co-sponsor it thereafter for FTE credits.

Yet not all has remained on the margins in my professional life. Although I have never held a tenure-track position, I have published four books and some two dozen essays. One of my books has been translated and published in Spain, and two of the books won the Sierra Prize awarded by the Western Association of Women Historians (WAWH).[2] I am often invited to lecture, participate in professional conferences, and write essays for anthologies. Despite my adjunct status, I have won grants, worked with graduate students, and I have chaired an international conference. For the past ten years I have taught at an institution where my tenured colleagues respect me and invite my participation in most departmental and faculty meetings.

Professional organizations have provided meaningful opportunities for active participation. On the suggestion of Kathryn Kish Sklar, I joined WAWH as I finished graduate work and quickly moved into board positions. Soon after serving as president of WAWH, I participated more actively in the Coordinating Council for Women in History (CCWH) and became co-president. In 1992 I was elected to the Council of the American Historical Association (AHA) and also served on the Professional Division. During all this time women's history has gained wide acceptance, moving into a position of much greater legitimacy within the discipline.

This professional activity has caused me to question marginality in my own life and to re-examine the entire concept of marginality in history. Realizing that my politics, personal story, and professional life are so closely intertwined that it is impossible to consider each separately, I want to examine them together not in a linear chronological pattern, but interweaving them as a tapestry, raising four major questions about marginality. What are basic hegemonic assumptions that lead to marginalization, and how does the very concept of marginalization reinforce hegemony? How do those marginalized use this position for resistance and empowerment, and what do they lose by becoming "mainstreamed"? How does marginality cover up differences, and why do we need to look beyond this cover? What is the role of subjectivity in women's history in particular and in historical studies in general, and how does marginality discourage us from questioning ourselves, our subjects, our relationships with our subjects?

HEGEMONY AND MARGINALIZATION

Many of us in women's history have defined ourselves in terms of a paradigm of center and margins, in which we have developed our identities in opposition to a male-dominated center. In doing so, we have used a model that is not only based on hegemonic assumptions, but is also preserving the whole notion of hegemony—that is, that one elite group dominates through setting standards and controlling institutions to which others are expected to conform. In my own case, I grew up in a small town in Washington state with a strong sense of being different from those in authority and a deep concern about intolerance of difference. As I became a young adult, the civil rights movement, the women's movement, and the antiwar movement provided important opportunities for me to express opposition to structures of power that excluded and intimidated and waged war—all in the name of "our democratic system."

When I returned to graduate school in 1972, it is not surprising that I found myself impatient with the traditional history of elites at the center of power and became much more interested in studying the past from the bottom up or the outside in. Inspired by a short story by Miguel de Cervantes, as well as the historical approaches of George Rudé and E. P. Thompson, I chose to write my dissertation on a criminal underworld in early modern Seville. I knew that I did not want to write a history that pretended to be "objective" while focusing on the usual centers of power. I believe that I was intrigued not only by the study of a subculture so different from my own, but also by the connections—and in fact the interdependence—between criminals and elite structures of power. Yet it was the legitimate power structure that had the power to define who and what were criminal and to create a consciousness in support of its norms.[3]

From its earliest years, women's history has also defined itself in opposition to an established structure of power—in this case, the exclusionary history that saw significance only in elite men who dominated established institutions such as law, religion, economics, and politics. Opposing the universalization of elite men's experience, women's history has insisted on the significance of women and non-elite people in the human past.[4] If this has caused us women historians to uncover the oppression and victimization of women, we have also tried to see women as active agents in history—in opposition to elite male history that has depicted women (if it has recognized them at all) as passive pawns and, less commonly, as the exceptional woman who becomes a patriarchy-confirming "spectacular representation . . . as a lesser male."[5]

A major problem in writing women's history is that so many historical documents reflect an elite male viewpoint from the center, an "imperialist gaze," which construes the other as a mere object and exercises an exclusive subject-defining status for itself.[6] Gayatri Chakravorty Spivak has noted that historians' knowledge of subaltern or insurgent subjects is so dependent on elite or counter-insurgent documentation that they can see subalterns only in contradistinction to the elites.[7] As we seek others than elite males in history, we try to respect them—and this raises the issue of positionality. Where can we stand when we speak of others in a culture so permeated by a dominant viewpoint? Is there, in fact, any position "'outside' that dominance which is uncompromised by it"?[8] Must we become deviant *outsiders* in order to write about women as active agents of the past, or to escape the "otherness" imposed on us by the dominant center?[9]

Catalina de Erauso, the "nun-lieutenant" who ran away from her convent in Spain and became a soldier for the Spanish king in colonial South America, forced me to look at these questions. At first I hoped that this person, who chose and constructed a gender identity, held out the promise of being a woman who resisted the patriarchal order of early modern Spain. But none of the documents that I could find described Catalina de Erauso as resisting gender prescriptions; in fact, the "autobiography" and memorials supposedly written by the nun-lieutenant describe a "lesser man" who supported the gender order, a person born female who then chose to become male and demonstrated bravery—even bravado—in establishing her masculinity. Note, however, that the either/or, male/female pronouns of English and Spanish cannot accurately describe this person.[10] Both marginalized as a man-born-a-woman and absorbed into the center as a female yet patriarchal hero, Catalina de Erauso/Alonso de Erauso demonstrates the difficulties of the center/margins paradigm for women's history.

RESISTANCE, EMPOWERMENT, AND MARGINALITY

Despite the problems of becoming defined only in terms of a dominant center, marginality offers certain advantages for women and other non-elite peoples. It is "much more than a site of deprivation," as cultural critic bell hooks writes; "it is also the site of radical possibility, a space of resistance."[11] Paradoxically, the margin becomes a center itself—a "central location for the production of a counter-hegemonic discourse that is not just found in words but in habits of being and the way one lives."[12] In fact, marginality can become "a site of transformation" where oppressed people can build "communities of resistance."[13] Oppressed peoples meet in the margins and begin to identify not merely in the terms the center elite uses to define them, but also in contrasting terms of resistance to the elite.

Some women historians have found that being on the margins of traditional elite history can be very empowering. Critical of traditional history, they have seized the very considerable power to represent, to name, to write history and shape knowledge, and to "ask questions that have not previously been asked."[14] These powers go well beyond the writing of history. Women's history has brought together feminism and scholarly work so that my politics can infuse my professional life with passion and energy.

Women's history further strengthens my work by providing a community of scholars who together effectively question the assumptions of traditional history. We have formed our own professional organizations, such as WAWH and CCWH, in which we interact and find common interests. In addition, we have developed our own voices for saying what it is we want to change in the historical profession—and we are growing in numbers. When I first entered graduate school in 1961, I did not know another woman historian, nor did I have any female faculty as models, nor were there more than two other women in my classes. Since then, women have been elected as officers of the AHA and as members of its council and divisions. Moreover, the AHA has created a Committee on Women Historians (CWH) to address and advocate some of our interests.

Thanks to the female presence in the AHA, we were able to provide important support for another marginalized group, gay and lesbian historians who in 1994 protested AHA plans to meet in Cincinnati, which had passed anti-gay legislation. I took to the AHA Council a strong letter from CCWH presidents Nancy Hewitt and Judith Bennett, which opposed that location. And in the name of the CCWH board, I told the council that if it proceeded with plans to meet in Cincinnati, we would urge our members to boycott the meeting. Despite concerns of having to pay large penalties for withdrawing from reserved hotels, the council agreed to find a location that would welcome all AHA members regardless of sexual orientation, race, gender, or politics. Numbers, allies, and organization enabled us to resist from the margins.

In my research, I have also found women empowered in their marginality. Perhaps we should clarify here the meaning of power, for feminist scholars have frequently argued that power is not just about holding political office or controlling major portions of wealth. Rather than power as *dominance over* others, as traditional male-centered studies usually assume, women historians study the power of women as *influence with* and *empowerment of others.* I will be forever grateful to Temma Kaplan, my dissertation advisor, who encouraged me to read and think of power in new ways.[15]

One woman empowered by her marginality in early modern Spain is Madre Catalina de Jesús, a *beata*, that is, a woman who dedicated her life to God but did not take the vows of a religious order. Outside the control of the Church or a convent, Madre Catalina preached and taught and prophesied, breaking Church strictures against women.[16] This woman inverted the gender order, assuming leadership over men and calling her male second in command a "spiritual son." Not surprisingly, the Church grew uneasy about her power, and in 1627 the Inquisition effectively silenced her.

Madre Catalina reminds us that the power and resistance developed on the margins have certain limits. If we develop too much power and resist too effectively, those at the center will act forcibly to assert their own ability to dominate and keep us on the margins. On the other hand, the powerful elite may attempt to absorb us into the center, co-opting any resistance or influence into their own program. Some history departments co-opt women's resistance when they agree to hire a female faculty member but make certain that tenure review will be as difficult as possible by disparaging the significance of her work in women's history. One reason that the CCWH is so important is that it consciously guards its independence from AHA leadership and refuses to become another CWH or to be amalgamated into the existing committee. Distance from the center becomes very important to develop power, and resistance on the margins makes an impact on the center, sometimes transforming it and sometimes moving the center to the margins.

Moriscas, baptized Muslim women of early modern Spain, demonstrate very clearly the imperative of distance for marginal groups. Muslims who wanted to remain in Spain after their defeat in 1492 accepted baptism but continued their own cultural practices in *morerías* (urban Moorish quarters) or in isolated mountainous and rural villages where few Christians ventured. If an outsider came to one of these isolated areas, the residents would quickly and secretly warn each other against practicing their forbidden culture. Their strategy for survival became palimpsestic, conforming on the surface to obscure subversion of the dominant order.[17]

Women in their homes played major roles in the cultural resistance of these people.[18] As Christian authorities determined to destroy the hated Muslim culture, however, they sent sheriffs into *morisco* homes unannounced and especially at mealtimes, when they could surprise a family eating food prepared in the Muslim manner, seated on the ground in traditional fashion. Rather than providing a protective distance and a female space safe from intrusion, the home became a primary focus for cultural and religious conflicts.

Many of us on the margins do not recognize the significance of a protective distance, for we have learned to evaluate our success by how closely we approach the center. I rejoiced when I persuaded the Professional Division of the AHA to take on the issues of adjunct and part-time faculty—issues that affect all of us in academe and not merely the growing numbers of part-time and adjunct faculty. However, these issues stalled in a newly elected Professional Division, lost in a series of meetings with other professional organizations that belong to the American Council of Learned Societies. Perhaps we forfeited the advantage that distance gives to those on the margins who want to make changes in the center. It may be that when we approach the center too closely, we lose the strength of our programs and our sense of difference that has empowered us to call for changes.

DIFFERENCE AND MARGINALITY

Marginality has such a great impact on how we define ourselves and develop resistance that it is easy to ignore other major influences in our lives, work, and politics. Too often we assume that "woman" can be universalized, that all marginalized women form a homogeneous group, and that all difference can be reduced to that between center and margin.[19] In the margin/center paradigm, it is too easy to simply define difference as opposition, and to see the opposition as "an undifferentiated mass."[20] Yet not all women are the same, even though patriarchal culture marginalizes them.

Women of color have insisted that race plays a very significant role not only in marginalizing them from an Anglo-male-dominated center, but also in the ways they define themselves and resist domination. These women do not want others to define them, nor do they want others to interpret their experiences.[21] They must resist domination not only from a patriarchal center, but from other marginalized peoples as well, because allowing other people to describe them erases or transforms their differences, reinscribing "patterns of colonial domination, where the 'Other' is always made object, appropriated, interpreted, taken over by those in power, by those who dominate."[22]

As I research the *morisca* minority in early modern Spain, I find myself concerned with becoming lost among several layers of difference. I note the differences between myself and the *moriscas*, between *moriscas* and other minority women of early modern Spain, and between *moriscas* and women of the dominant Christian culture. Moreover, I recognize differences among *moriscas* themselves—whether rural or urban, recent or long-ago immigrants, recent or long-time converts, wealthy or poor, young or old. In fact, respecting all these differences threatens to fragment any attempt to see them as more than a large collection of different individuals. But I could recognize these women as having multiple identities that include sameness as well as difference. As Mae Gwendolyn Henderson found in studying Black women writers, these women "speak from a multiple and complex social, historical and cultural personality" that produces "a multiple *dialogic of differences*," but at the same time they carry out "a *dialectic of identity* with those aspects of self shared with others."[23]

Yet to reduce difference to binary oppositions, such as same/different or center/margins, limits our discussions of race and gender. Instead, we need to map "intermediary spaces where boundaries become effaced and Manichean categories collapse into each other."[24] And we need to move beyond the categories of race, class, and gender, to examine intersections of differences, especially in relation to sexuality.[25] The issue of difference becomes so complex that it seems to defy any theoretical analysis and to make us beat a hasty retreat to the comfortable old center/margins paradigm, where differences exist, but remain well concealed by a simple opposition.

Discussing the problem of writing "the history of difference," Joan Scott has noted that historians often present "experience" as "evidence for the fact of difference, rather than a way of exploring how difference is established, how it operates, how and in what ways it constitutes subjects who see and act in the world."[26] Yet if feminist theorists insist upon the complexity of difference, they also propose some basic principles that we can use in our historical work. Difference, as Toril Moi has pointed out, is constructed, not innate.[27] Moreover, difference is violent and hierarchical, rather than neutral, for it is postulated through opposition in which one term is marked as deviant from the unmarked term assumed to be the norm. Finally, difference is legitimized by an appeal to nature, itself a construct. These three arguments reveal the fallacies of simple explanations of difference: biology (that difference results from the innate essence of a subject), objectivity (that difference can be observed neutrally), and naturalization (that difference occurs within a universal ground unaffected by a particular context).[28] For women historians, this means that we must read our sources to hear "the polyphony of voices, to sort through various truth claims and interpretations."[29] And we must be willing to celebrate difference not only in our subjects, but also in our methodologies for studying them. There is more than one way to study women's history, just as there is more than a single "feminist position."[30]

As a specialist in Spanish history, I have been especially aware of the different ways in which women's history has developed. When I was in graduate school, I could find so few publications that even mentioned women in Spain in the early modern period that I resolved to focus a chapter of my dissertation on women.[31] I like to believe that this chapter in *Crime and Society in Early Modern Seville* and an ensuing essay on prostitutes in the then new and still exciting journal *Feminist Studies* have encouraged many other historians to look for nontraditional approaches to study women in Spanish history and to include women in their broader historical studies.[32]

Historians in both Spain and the US have worked with colleagues in other disciplines to publish essays on women in Spanish history. Literary scholar Anne Cruz and I decided to "mainstream" scholarship on women in two anthologies on Counter-Reformation Spain, and we have participated in multidisciplinary conferences on women's questions that published their proceedings.[33] Since the 1980s, Spanish monographs in women's history have greatly increased, and recently the University of Granada has begun publishing *Arenal: Revista de historia de las mujeres*, a review of women's history for which I am a member of the editorial board. Historians in Spain have borrowed theoretical approaches of women historians from the United States, as well as those of French writers such as Julia Kristeva and Luce Irigaray. However, they have recognized the need for specialized studies within the particular context of Spain's history.[34]

Attempting to develop my own methodology for studying *moriscas* and dissatisfied with the usual research in archival and secondary sources, I have also explored music, dancing, feasting, and traditional costuming. At times I think my book on *moriscas* should contain a compact disc or paper dolls, or that it should be of the scratch-and-sniff variety. At other times, I am overwhelmed by the tragedy of a century of persecution that ended only with expulsion from Spain in 1609. Cool detachment is out of the question, and I write "dialogues" with individual *moriscas* and burn scented candles on my desk to remind me that all is not dark. I turn tearfully from reading a contemporary account of the *morisco* uprising of 1570 to write a poem in which my feelings are as much the subject as the *moriscas* themselves.

MARGINALITY AND SUBJECTIVITY

Recognizing that differences cannot be reduced to a center/margins opposition, we have to ask questions about these differences, not only those that distinguish our subjects, but those that make ourselves, the historians, subjects. Subjectivity is a complex concept, but here it refers both to the position of being subject to study and to the formation of ideology. It includes internal qualities as well as external manifestations of them, and it is the product not only of one's position but also of one's historical context. Subjectivity asks us to look at the construction of meaning and to be aware of our participation in this construction. It includes pluralities of identification as well as interaction as subjects with our historical subjects. Filmmaker and critic Trinh Minh-ha refers to this interaction as endless, a "to-and-fro movement between the written woman and the writing woman."[35]

One of the healthiest signs of the maturation of women's history has come from its growing beyond the single message of women as different from, or victims of, men. It has developed a variety of approaches that emphasize complexities of meaning, seen in books and essays and awards and conference programs of women's professional organizations. The CCWH decision to offer a second graduate student prize acknowledges that eligible women can be carrying out historical work not only in history departments, but also in area programs such as Afro-American, Asian, or Latin American Studies. While we especially value historical research, we recognize in it a plurality of approaches and differences.

A recognition of difference does not have to discourage theorizing, nor does theory have to suppress difference. Trinh Minh-ha proposes "writing the body" as "a way of making theory in gender, of making of theory a politics of everyday life."[36] Viewing the body as a social construct that acts as a metaphor for society, we can see not only the individual differences of our subjects, but also their joining together as a complex society. Trinh further proposes that such an approach provides a way for recognizing, even emphasizing, nondominant identities in our subjects, "thereby rewriting the ethnic female subject as site of differences."[37] To view *moriscas* as a site of differences that explodes into open conflict in Spanish history helps me to understand why I have felt so compelled to study them. And make no mistake: I am a subject in this study, even as I try to focus on *moriscas.*

Acknowledging my own subjectivity, I realize that I, too, have been a member of a social body marked by great diversity and explosive conflicts. I live in a community with the fastest growing immigrant population in the nation and a strongly conservative religious Right. The year that our youngest child entered kindergarten, Pasadena public schools moved to comply with court-ordered integration. I joined many other parents who were determined that the outraged opponents to integration would not force a violent confrontation. We monitored bus stops, and I chaired a project in which parents of our newly integrated school replaced the playground asphalt with gardens and creative play spaces. After the conflict over reproductive rights escalated in response to *Roe v. Wade*, I co-chaired a Pro-Choice Task Force and participated in demonstrations and clinic defenses, once again determined to oppose a vociferous opposition that would not tolerate any difference from its position. The 1992 Los Angeles "riots" after the acquittal of policemen implicated in the beating of Rodney King, the California immigration initiative to withhold services and civil rights from immigrants, and the state initiative to abolish affirmative action make it very clear to me that I cannot escape difference and conflict and oppression—neither in personal life nor in historical studies.

As a subject interacting with my historical subjects, I look at their differences and conflicts, aware of those in my own community, and I realize that we all have multiple identities that make our subjectivities and our interactions even more complex. It is here that Queer theory has been especially helpful. If the body can be seen as a metaphor for society, it is also a metaphor for groups that identify themselves against others. Discussing the notion of the "moral anatomy of the body," Paul Julian Smith points out that what the body sees outside itself is a "chaotic menace of the other." It "seeks to withdraw behind membranes which will secure its internal space from external invasion."[38] Yet these membranes, such as the tympan and the hymen, are permeable and have "the problem of negotiating that perilous transition between inside and outside (same and other) that occurs on the surface of the body."[39]

If the membranes that serve to define our identities are necessarily permeable, they are also subject to "graphesis," or cultural inscription.[40] Here historical context must be considered, for graphesis varies with time, place, and people. The *morisco* culture of early modern Spain may have inscribed identifying membranes very differently than those cultures of present day Los Angeles. *Moriscos* accepted intermarriage with Christians under certain conditions, for example, yet retained a sense of difference from them. And Christians in early modern Spain inscribed these membranes even more differently, usually believing that the danger of permeability was not that *moriscos* would become more like Christians, but that Christians would be forever contaminated by any mixture between the groups.

In contrast with proposals to define otherness in terms of fear or loathing, Queer theorists suggest that otherness can also be eroticized—that is, that we desire what we are not or what we lack. Even more important, we do not have to stay with a paradigm of self/other; we can instead see ourselves "in a vast network of *near-sameness*," in which lack is not inherent in desire and desire is to want to repeat or intensify the same.[41] While I do not want to dilute all differences of *moriscas* in early modern Spain in "a vast network of near-sameness," I realize the importance of asking why the dominant Christians of this period emphasized their differences from these people so much more than their similarities, why the eroticization of their differences led to expulsion rather than assimilation, and how all of this represents a political imperative for a developing state.[42]

None of these questions is easy, particularly because my study of *moriscas* is still in process, "an organic process of interaction and influence," as Nupur Chaudhuri writes, that includes students and writers of history and the people and events studied.[43] Acknowledging the role of historians as subjects interacting with historical subjects leaves us exploring the formation of subjectivity, which Catherine Hall has identified as "an ever-unfinished process, one that inevitably involves psychic conflict and antagonism, and one that is fundamentally unstable, but always has historical conditions of existence."[44]

Whether we see ourselves as marginalized deviants or as collective weavers of a vast tapestry, our historical writing involves a process of self-discovery, even as we study others who lived in different societies in different periods of times. As historians who interact with our subjects, we too must be subject to the scholar's gaze and leave behind the unquestioned assumption of integrated self protected from scrutiny. Writing this essay became so difficult as I scrutinized myself that I tried to explain my discomfort in a poem entitled "Exposure." I include it here not for its literary merit, but simply to illustrate my own subjectivity and attempts to come to terms with it:

> Strange how we scholars hide behind our subjects,
> Turning intense and blazing gaze on them while
> Off in the shadows we keep well-hidden our own
> Subjectivity.
> Yet honesty makes us admit that we as subjects
> Interact with our subjects, shaping representations
> Of them by questions and selections we make, and personal
> Reservations.
> And when we are asked to assess the personal, professional
> And political in our lives, we feel the discomfort of being
> Caught in the blazing gaze that invades the safety of
> Shadows.

NOTES

1. "Deviant Insiders: Prostitution and a Consciousness of Women in Early Modern Seville," *Comparative Studies in Society and History* 27 (January 1985), 138–58.

2. The WAWH established one of the earliest book awards for historical work by and about women, which I received for *Crime and Society in Early Modern Seville* (Hanover: Univ. Press of New England, 1980); and *Gender and Disorder in Early Modern Seville* (Princeton: Princeton Univ. Press, 1990). The latter was translated and published as *Ni espada rota ni mujer que trota* (Barcelona: Crítica, 1993).

3. Sidonie Smith, "Who's Talking/Who's Talking Back? The Subject of Personal Narrative," *Signs* 18 (Winter 1993), discusses the hegemonic construction of consciousness and the compliance of marginalized subjects, 396.

4. Camilla Stivers, "Reflections on the Role of Personal Narrative in Social Science," *Signs* 18 (Winter 1993), notes that universalization of elite male experience and "knowledge" provides the basis for its claim to power, 417.

5. Toril Moi, *Sexual/Textual Politics: Feminist Literary Theory* (London and New York: Methuen, 1985), 135.

6. Lee Edelman, *Homographesis: Essays in Gay Literary and Cultural Theory* (New York and London: Routledge, 1994), 47.

7. Paul Julian Smith, *Representing the Other: "Race," Text, and Gender in Spanish and Spanish American Narrative* (Oxford: Clarendon Press, 1992), 18.

8. Smith, *Representing the Other*, 29.

9. Vinay Bahl, "Cultural Imperialism and Women's Movements," *Gender and History* 9 (April 1997), 5.

10. See my essay "From Convent to Battlefield: Cross-Dressing and Gendering the

Self in the New World of Imperial Spain," that will appear in *Queer Iberia: Crossing Cultures, Crossing Sexualities*, edited by Josiah Blackmore and Gregory S. Hutcheson (Duke Univ. Press, 1998); and Catalina de Erauso, *Lieutenant Nun: Memoir of a Basque Transvestite in the New World*, trans. Michele Stepto and Gabriel Stepto (Boston: Beacon Press, 1996).

11. bell hooks, *Yearning: Race, Gender, and Cultural Politics* (Boston: South End Press, 1990), 149. To Catherine Hall, *White, Male and Middle-Class* (New York: Routledge, 1992), margins are "very productive terrain—a space from which both to challenge establishments and develop our own perspectives, build our own organizations, confirm our own collectivities," 34.

12. hooks, *Yearning*, 149.

13. Ibid., 213.

14. Sucheta Mazumdar, "Colonial Legacies, Neocolonial Paradigms: Negotiating the Mean from the Margins," unpublished paper presented to the AHA January 1996, discussed in Nupur Chaudhuri, "On the Outside Looking in: Writing and Teaching about Groups Not Your Own," *Journal of Women's History* 8 (Fall 1996), 143–45.

15. Especially the early essays of Natalie Zemon Davis, Olwen Hufton, Joan Kelly, and Sheila Rowbotham, as well as Judith Van Allen, "Sitting on a Man," *Canadian Journal of African Studies* 6 (1972), 165–81.

16. Perry, *Gender and Disorder*, 105–17; P. Smith, *Representing the Other*, points out the significance of mysticism, so closely associated with Madre Catalina, as "the discourse of the other *par excellence*," 111.

17. Toril Moi, *Sexual/Textual Politics*, discusses the palimpsestic strategy of women writers, but the strategy certainly applies to other oppressed groups, 59.

18. See my essay, "Beyond the Veil: Moriscas and the Politics of Resistance and Survival," in *Spanish Women in the Golden Age: Images and Realities*, eds. Magdalena S. Sánchez and Alain Saint-Saëns (Westport and London: Greenwood Press, 1996), 37–53.

19. S. Smith, "Who's Talking/Who's Talking Back?" 397; see also Sidonie Smith and Julia Watson, *De/Colonizing the Subject: The Politics of Gender in Women's Autobiography* (Minneapolis: Univ. of Minn. Press, 1992), discussed in Bahl, "Cultural Imperialism," 8.

20. P. Smith, *Representing the Other*, 37.

21. hooks, *Yearning*, 55.

22. Ibid., 125, and 151–52.

23. Mae Gwendolyn Henderson, "Speaking in Tongues: Dialogics, Dialectics, and the Black Woman Writer's Literary Tradition," in *Feminists Theorize the Political*, eds. Judith Butler and Joan W. Scott (New York and London: Routledge, 1992), 147, author's emphasis.

24. Françoise Lionnet, *Autobiographical Voices*, quoted in S. Smith, "Who's Talking/Who's Talking Back?" 406.

25. P. Smith, *Representing the Other*, 15.

26. "Experience," in Butler and Scott, *Feminists Theorize*, 22 and 25.

27. Moi, *Sexual/Textual Politics*, passim; see also Paul Smith's discussion of Moi's theory of difference in *Representing the Other*, 28.

28. P. Smith, *Representing the Other*, 28.

29. S. Smith, "Who's Talking/Who's Talking Back?" 402.

30. Stivers, "Reflections on the Role of Personal Narrative in Social Science," 424.

31. Early publications include Temma Kaplan, "Women and Spanish Anarchism," in *Becoming Visible: Women in European History*, eds. Renate Bridenthal and Claudia Koonz (New York: Houghton Mifflin, 1977); Temma Kaplan, "Spanish Anarchism and Women's Liberation," *Journal of Contemporary History* 6 (1971); Heath Dillard, "Women in Reconquest Castile: The *Fueros* of Sepúlveda and Cuenca," in *Women in Medieval Society*, ed. Susan Mosher Stuard (Univ. of Pennsylvania Press, 1976). Examples of Spanish publications include Mary Nash, *La mujer y los anarquistas* (Tusquets, 1976); María LaFitte, condesa de Campo Alange, *La mujer en España: cien años de historia, 1860–1960* (Aguilar, 1964); and Geraldine M. Scanlon, *La polémica feminista en la España contemporánea (1868–1974)* (Siglo XXI, 1976).

32. The article is entitled "'Lost Women' in Early Modern Seville: The Politics of Prostitution," *Feminist Studies* 4 (1978), reprinted in *Social History of Western Civilization*, ed. Richard M. Golden, vol. I (St. Martin's Press, 1992).

33. The two anthologies that Anne Cruz and I have edited are *Cultural Encounters: The Impact of the Inquisition in Spain and the New World* (Berkeley: Univ. of California Press, 1991) and *Culture and Control in Counter-Reformation Spain* (Minneapolis: Univ. of Minnesota Press, 1992); an example of publications from conferences on women in Spain include *El trabajo de las mujeres: Siglos XVI–XX*, Jornadas de Investigación Interdisciplinaria sobre la Mujer, ed. María Jesús Matilla and Margarita Ortega (Universidad Autónoma, 1987).

34. Two recent and exciting studies include María Helena Sánchez Ortega, *La mujer y la sexualidad en el antiguo régimen: La perspectiva inquisitorial* (Akal, 1992); and Magdalena S. Sánchez and Alain Saint-Saëns, eds., *Spanish Women in the Golden Age: Images and Realities* (Westport: Greenwood, 1996).

35. Trinh Minh-ha, *Woman, Native, Other: Writing Postcoloniality and Feminism* (Bloomington: Indiana Univ. Press, 1989), 30.

36. Ibid., 44.

37. Ibid.

38. P. Smith, *Representing the Other*, 88.

39. Ibid., 90.

40. Edelman, *Homographesis,* 12 and 74.

41. Leo Bersani, *Homos* (Cambridge, MA: Harvard Univ. Press, 1995), 146, author's emphasis.

42. I attempt to answer these questions in "The Politics of Race, Ethnicity, and Gender in the Making of the Spanish State," in *Subjectivity and the Modern State in Spain*, eds. Tom Lewis and Francisco Sánchez (New York: Garland Press, forthcoming).

43. Chaudhuri, "On the Outside Looking In," 145.

44. Hall, *White, Male, and Middle-Class*, 22.

19

NANCY RAQUEL MIRABAL

QUE SÉ YO: A HISTORIAN IN TRAINING

> Qué quiere decir ser de aquí? Pues . . pa' mi 'ser de aquí' es . . . mango y strawberries . . . alcapurrias y pretzels . . . Yemayá y los Yankees . . . Yo no veo la diferencia. What's the big deal? Eso es lo que somos: brunch y burundanga, quiche y arroz con habichuelas, Chase Manhattan y la bolita . . . Todo depende de como empaques tu equipaje. Pero todo es parte de él. Todo es la misma cosa . . . You see, I decide what it means to be from here, porque allá afuera hay muchos que piensan que aunque hayas nacido aquí y te cambies el nombre a Joe o Millie, they think you're not from here anyway. De aquí, de allá . . . que sé yo.[1]

With only a few sentences the Cubana playwright Dolores Prida describes the process invoked to create and reinvent a sense of self and community among many Latina/os in the United States—a process that considers, leaves out, and on the whole crosses language, experience, naming, location, religion, and tradition. It is, as Prida's characters remind us, ultimately about how we choose to pack our suitcases; what we put in and what we leave out. It is about what you name yourself, all the while knowing that you are also being named. It is about finding home in the most unlikely of places. It is about how in the long run, despite the reinventions and the recreations, we are still left with the realization that we simply don't know, "¿que sé yo?"

Nancy Raquel Mirabal with a student, San Francisco State University, 1998.

I begin this essay with a brief discussion of Prida's quote because it has been both a source of inspiration and a reminder of my own constructed sense of place—a place that for all its familiarity is still rooted in contradiction and incongruities. And yet, I find comfort in that contradiction, in having mixed feelings; in being, as Gustavo Pérez-Firmat has written, "vexed, hexed, complexed."[2] These places, while confusing and often painful, also have the power to provide a freedom that is difficult to find elsewhere. I have to admit that I am enamored, in love, head over heels, crazy about any space, any place, spiritual or practical that lets me consistently reinvent and discard. And yet, I know that I have come to love these spaces because it is there that I ended up working as a historian. I say "working," because as the title suggests, I fully believe that I am still in training. There is a lot yet to learn, a lot of lessons that I am waiting to be taught, and even more mistakes I am gearing up to make. I can't wait to make more mistakes.

For me, the mistakes have been the most interesting part of the whole process. Growing up I never once blurted out that I wanted to be a historian to all of the relatives who asked me what I wanted to be when I grow up. I do, however, remember saying that I wanted to be a journalist, a writer, or perhaps even a foreign correspondent who dodged bullets and drove jeeps at neck-breaking speed, all to make sure that the story got in on time. I thought about driving taxis in New York City and harbored a secret desire to be just like the waitresses who worked at Bob's Big Boy on Florence Avenue. I even remember that in the fifth grade I wanted to be a nun. I was about to make my first communion and, as a result of my catechism courses, believed the nuns to have a certain chic quality. But never once did I say or even think that I would become a historian.

In November of 1983 I was beginning my senior year in high school and it was clear that it was time to think about college. Although I never met or knew anyone who had attended the University of California, I wanted to go. Out of curiosity I went to my high school counselor and asked him for an application to attend UC Berkeley. He refused. Not only did he refuse to give me the application, but also he suggested that it would be much more "practical" if I applied to East Los Angeles College. When I suggested that he help me despite his doubts—"You know, just to see what happens"—he still refused. His refusal was so final, so unwavering, that it stirred in me an ever-greater desire to attend a university that I knew nothing about.

I relay this one incident because it was a defining moment. It was the first time that I had been so openly underestimated by a person whose very objective was to encourage and advise. This is not to say, however, that I had never felt underestimated. On the contrary, underestimation was familiar and commonplace. Underestimation was an everyday presence in the faces of our teachers, of the people around us who, without saying a word, wondered what would become of us after high school. I believe that all of the students in one way or another felt the continual underestimation that was part of our school routine. I can't put my finger on it, but it is without a doubt an intuitive energy that marks you from early on. The painful thing is that at that age I didn't have the words to help me point to or even sort out the energy that was being directed to me and to the other students. Yet I am convinced that we were all in one way or another aware of it. I am aware of it still.

Despite the counselor's advice, I applied to UC Berkeley. Sitting around the kitchen table, my cousin, aunt, and mother helped me fill out the application and write the statement of purpose. The day I received my acceptance letter my mother and I danced, yelled, and hugged each other real tight. I learned more than I could ever imagine during my four years at Berkeley. The university, however, did not make me a historian. I studied United States history because I had "heard" that a degree in history would help me get into law school, journalism school, and public policy school. In other words, my degree would help me get another degree.

What I did learn was the role that history as document and voice could play in the reimagination of a people and community. I was hungry to learn more about how race, gender, class, location, ethnicity, affected the parameters of United States history, or better, one's *own* sense of history. As I learned more about different histories, I became increasingly fascinated with literature. I took a number of literature courses and in the process was introduced to writers like Toni Morrison, Ana Castillo, Leslie Marmon Silko, Paule Marshall, Jean Toomer, Rosario Ferré, and Jessie Fauset. These writers rendered voice and texture to the histories I was reading and studying. Their stories reminded me of all that was missing and of all that needed to be told. Like a trickster who cajoles, fools, and in the end teaches a powerful lesson, these stories forever changed my historical thinking. They forced me to rethink my own concepts of telling and the role that power played in the production of history. As the anthropologist Michel-Rolph Trouillot has written, "History is the fruit of power, but power itself is never so transparent that its analysis becomes superfluous. The ultimate mark of power may be its invisibility; the ultimate challenge, the exposition of its roots."[3] I wanted desperately to learn how to expose roots. Yet it would take years of fighting myself and others to get to a point where I could fully understand what it meant to simply take up the challenge.

WE'RE NOT IN KANSAS ANYMORE. . . .

No, I definitely was not in Kansas, but I was in Michigan. In the fall of 1989 I was fortunate enough to be admitted to the history program at the University of Michigan. Yet, outside of the teaching assistants I had encountered while finishing up my bachelor's degree in history, I can honestly say that I knew no one who was in graduate school. No one in my family had ever gone to graduate school and as a result I had no idea what to expect. As I would soon learn, perhaps that was a good thing.

When asked by students or friends about graduate school, I can say very little. I have no real answers or direction. It is difficult for me to offer them information on scholarships or grants because the ones that I was awarded came to me in very strange ways. I cannot suggest how to go about finding a research topic, because I never had to look for one. I cannot offer tips on how to finish a dissertation because I am still writing one. What I can say is that if you decide to go to graduate school do so with one eye open and one eye closed. Keep an eye open to witness, experience, and learn all of the lessons that a graduate training can bring you. Keep an eye, as well as your heart, open to the people who will be there to help you and offer guidance. By the same token, make sure to keep an eye closed to the infighting, unnecessary criticisms, and the energies that may deplete your creativity.

The profession, as many have now revealed, is in crisis. There are not enough jobs to employ the high number of doctoral students graduating from universities. In addition, universities across the country are beginning to question their commitment to people of different racial and ethnic backgrounds. Affirmative Action programs are slowly, but very steadily being dismantled by universities, namely the University of California and the University of Texas. What is further disheartening is that there appears to be little support from white women, who as statistics have shown, benefited most from Affirmative Action policies. Along with the changes in policy, there has also been a move to cut programs, which over the years have helped to fund the high costs of a graduate education. There is no doubt in my mind that these changes will result in only reversing much of the gains made by people of color. I still fail to understand why so many believe that limiting access to education is sound public policy. I refuse to believe that Affirmative Action somehow did not or does not work regardless of the messenger's racial or ethnic background. I will continue to trust my instincts that we as a community are valuable thinkers and writers who are more likely to add to the discourse than to subtract from it. I will continue to subscribe to the notion that, as bell hooks has articulated, the move toward ending Affirmative Action has more to do with that fact that it is successful than with the widespread perception that it is a failure. The changes that have occurred in the last ten years have, unfortunately, made it difficult for me to even suggest graduate schools to my students —who, by the way, are almost all Latina/os. I am never sure whether I am helping them or setting them up to be deeply disappointed. At the same time, I find it hard to not encourage them to be at their absolute best. I never want to be put in a position where I have to tell someone who is thinking about attending graduate school that they should not go, for whatever reasons, especially when I know in my heart they have the same right as everyone else to attend universities and find their place.

I was a miserable student. I didn't like having to jump hoops and I am not good at telling people what they like to hear. But I do love to think. I love to analyze, examine, and rethink. And I am drawn to people who also take thinking seriously. So, while I wasn't very good at the mechanics of graduate school, I did enjoy being around so many people who were just as interested as I was in thinking about issues, topics, and historical processes. The opportunity to think, to be with one's thoughts is—as my mother has told me time and time again—a privilege. I come from a working-class family where much of the thinking was done around the kitchen table in the privacy of our home. It was mainly during these moments that we discussed politics, policy, and legacy. These discussions were intense and deep. You learned to hold your own. These kitchen table discussions were important to my parents because it was the only time that they expressed opinions openly, ruminated publicly, and experimented with ideas. During the day, no one asked them or even cared to know what they were thinking. Their role was to provide a service and to do a good job for the foreman.

As for graduate school, I got through it.

LAS BOTANICAS QUE HABLAN: CREATING AND FINDING COMMUNITY IN SPITE OF THE BAD WEATHER

Growing up, the botanicas were places where the women in my family would go to buy herbs, candles, and statues of Catholic saints. They are found in almost every barrio in the United States, and invariably you will find a group of people gathered together speaking Spanish and relating stories. There was always something mysterious and yet comforting about the botanicas in my neighborhood. Things weren't always what they appeared to be and any "real" knowledge concerning the use of certain herbs, oils, and candles was offered conditionally. It is this sense of conditional knowledge, of the power of the unwritten and the unsaid, that would stay with me and influence how I would come to look at my work and my place in the profession.

An important part in finding my "place" was building a community of women who believed in endurance, strength, and the power of the "spirits." While the atmosphere in graduate school was indeed contentious and at times difficult, I was still nonetheless able to be a part of an exciting, worthwhile, brilliant, nurturing, and at times frightening collective of women of color thinkers, writers, and activists.[4] These women were struggling with many of the same ideas, concepts, and realities that I was facing. We struggled with making ends meet, with finding our way in an institution that did not know what to do with us, with balancing what we knew intellectually and what we believed had to be accomplished politically, but most of all in our own way, we all struggled with finding our individual voices. I thank them for never letting me take the easy way out, for forcing me over and over again to trust voice over silence.

CALABASA, CALABASA CADA UNO PARA SU CASA: GOING HOME

After many years on the academic road, I finally went home. Like the familiar saying heard after most parties and gatherings, I was now the 'calabasa' returning home. It is no coincidence that I was considered 'la gitana' in the family. The gypsy who wandered around the most unglamorous of places conducting research and writing papers that most people would never read. When I did go "home" I was always asked the same questions: When was I going to finish? What was I actually doing? Why did I have to be in school so many years? Did all of these years of schooling translate into a nice, fat salary? At the same time, I was rarely asked whether I actually liked what I was doing, or if I believed that my work would eventually come to mean anything. In a way it didn't matter that those questions were not asked of me, because to put it plainly, those were questions that I had yet to ask myself.

The biggest change took place in 1995, when I was awarded a César Chávez Dissertation Fellowship at Dartmouth College. After six years of living and working in Ann Arbor, Michigan I was now packing my bags and moving further north to a state most in my family had never heard of, let alone knew how to pronounce: New Hampshire. The fellowship was a generous one and it helped me to draft what was increasingly becoming a tedious and difficult dissertation.[5] It was not an easy year, but it served as the necessary springboard for finding a job. I had become so focused on working on my dissertation that I had not given myself enough time to prepare or even think about what I was going to do after the fellowship ended. Luckily a colleague at Dartmouth showed me an e-mail advertising a job at San Francisco State University. It was a bit karmic since I had made the decision to move out west regardless of whether I had a job waiting for me. In the summer of 1996 I was offered a tenure-track position in the La Raza Studies department at San Francisco State University. Without the dissertation in hand, I trekked across country to teach and finally finish. I was now a faculty member in a Latina/o studies department in the *only* College of Ethnic Studies in the country.

Going home meant that I would finally be in a position to do the "work."

For years I had worked with graduate students in developing tutoring programs for homeless students and students of color seeking to go to college. I loved working with these students. For me it represented the opportunity to go back and rewrite the script that I had lived with as a high school student. In the process of rewriting the script, I found my voice as a teacher. I knew that I loved teaching because I never stopped thinking about the work or about my students. I wanted to work harder than usual in making sure that they learned.

My colleagues at the La Raza Studies department understood this type of teaching and gave me full rein to do my work. With few restrictions and much support I taught students of all backgrounds, races, and ethnicities. They are not, on the whole, the privileged, middle- to upper-class students one usually finds at the University of Michigan or Dartmouth. These students are, for the most part, working-class students who are most likely holding down two jobs just to get through school. Many of my students are single mothers, and the majority of them graduated from public schools. Because of this, I understand their drive and their need to prove that they too have a stake in making a life for themselves. These students are on many levels brilliant, judgmental, and intent on teaching me something in return. I thank them for that. Because of them, I have learned some of the most important lessons in my career and, more importantly, in my life. They will not, thank God, let me off easy.

Going home has also meant having to deal with state politics, controversial statewide educational policies, and the dismantling of Affirmative Action programs. It has meant witnessing the impact of anti-immigrant sentiments like Proposition 187 on my students. In June of 1998, millionaire software developer Ron Unz authored a statewide initiative that would further restrict the educational rights of immigrants in California known as the "English for Children" initiative. The aim of Proposition 227 was to do away with bilingual education in California. Despite the protests of many, Proposition 227 was passed.

The steady decrease in the rights of immigrants and the even steadier devaluation of our children is no accident. There is a reason why many of these policies target educational access. I believe that success is frightening to people who do not want to relinquish their own access to privilege and power. The students whom I come across "know" fully what is happening to them and they won't be lied to. I must admit that I was not as ready as I thought I was to handle the barrage of attacks against immigrants, the gentrification of Latina/o and African-American neighborhoods in San Francisco, the difficulty in encouraging students when everything around them is discouraging, the rapid changes in the economy, and the ruthless manner in which technology can leave behind those who "don't keep up." And yet, perhaps these are all my fears. The students I have worked with are survivors and masters of reinvention. Over and over again they remind me of their tenacity, brilliance, and optimism. They insure me that they are here to stay and that what they have to offer is more than anyone can ever imagine.

NOTES

Thank-you to Eileen Boris and Nupur Chaudhuri for their patience and vision. I would also like to give a *super-big* thank-you to Mauricio Palma for his insights and poetic criticisms regarding this essay. I have dedicated this essay to my family, who pushed me with a refined combination of grace and tactlessness, and to my students at San Francisco State University, who as I get to know them and their work, never let me forget the meaning of true brilliance and beauty. Gracias a todos.

1. Dolores Prida, "Botanica," *Beautiful Señoritas and Other Plays* (Arte Publico Press, 1991), 164. A fuerte gracias to Dolores Prida for suggesting this passage to me as I thought about this essay.

Translated, the passage reads: "What does it mean to be from here? Well . . for me 'to be from here' is mango and strawberries . . . alcapurrias and pretzels . . . Yemayá and the Yankees . . . I don't see the difference. What's the big deal? That's what we are: brunch and burundanga, quiche and rice and beans, Chase Manhattan and the bolita . . . It all depends on how you pack your suitcase. But everything is part of it. It's all the same thing . . You see, I decide what it means to be from here, because out there there are many who think that even though you were born here and you change your name to Joe or Millie, they think you're not from here anyway. From here, from there . . . what do I know."

2. Gustavo Pérez-Firmat, *Bilingual Blues: Poems, 1981–1994* (Tempe: Bilingual Press/Editorial Bilingue, 1995).

3. Michel-Rolph Trouillot, *Silencing the Past: Power and the Production of History* (Boston: Beacon Press, 1995), xix.

4. These women include, but are not limited to, Wendy S. Walters, Mercedes Rubio, Reshela DuPuis, Amy Jordan, Tracye Matthews, Michelle Johnson, Kim Smith, Sharon Holland, Brenda Cárdenas, Sandra Martinez, and Dianne Ybarra.

5. While at Dartmouth College I was fortunate enough to have encountered and become part of a group of women scholars and thinkers who influenced me greatly. I would like to thank Agnes Lugo-Ortiz, Diane Meliotis, Annelise Orleck, Alexis Jetter, Brenda Bright, Diana Taylor, Silvia Spitta, Carmen Oquendo, Mattie Richardson, and the unforgettable Dolores Prida for their friendship and support. I would also like to thank Marysa Navarro, who as my advisor at Dartmouth was solely responsible for making the fellowship a reality. I am grateful for her generosity and time. I would also like to thank Rafael "FTFB" Gonzalez, Diana Valle, Wendy Walters, and Jason Hackner for their unflinching love and support during a difficult period in my life.

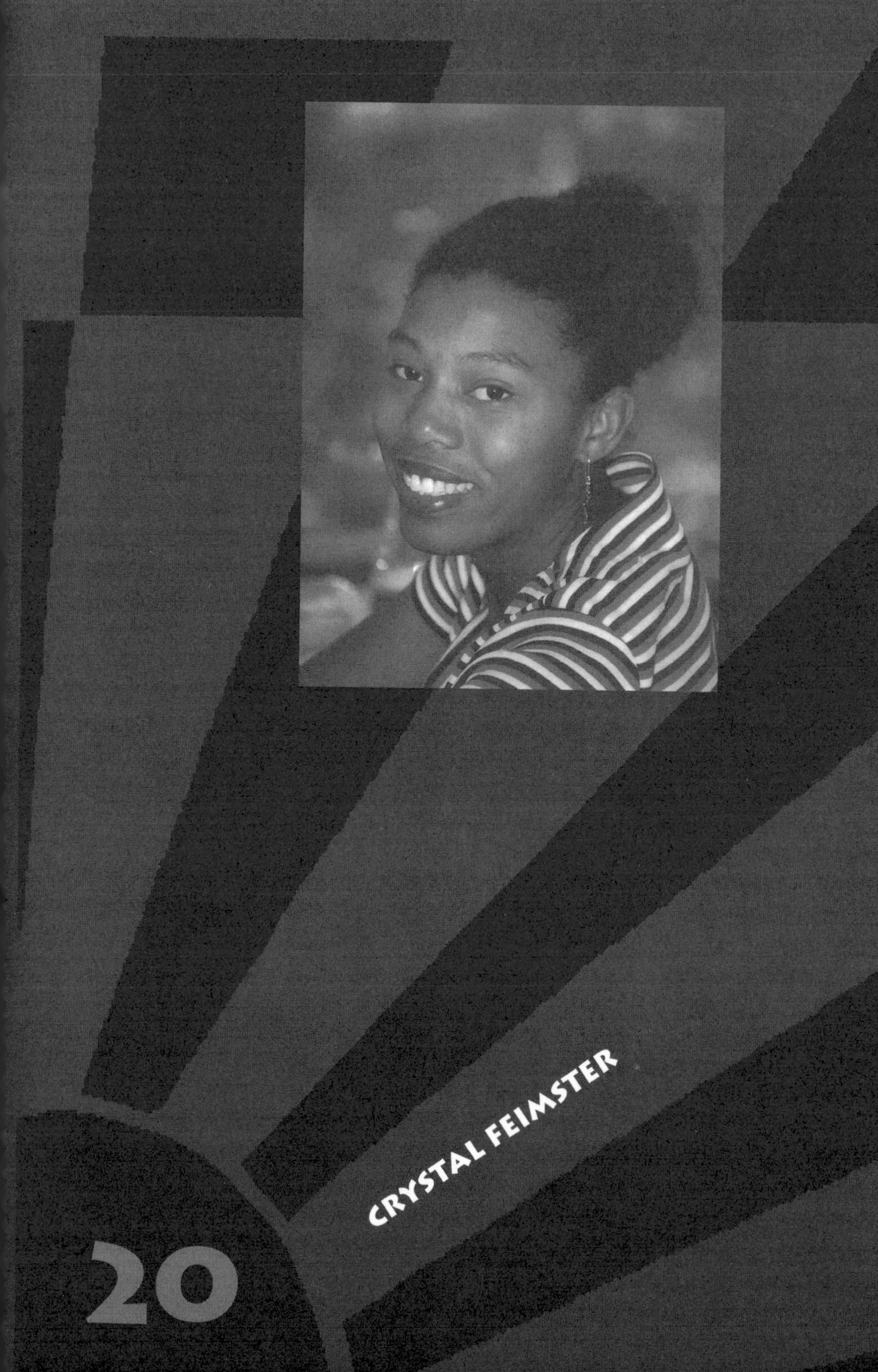

20

CRYSTAL FEIMSTER

A NEW GENERATION OF WOMEN HISTORIANS

The title "A New Generation of Women Historians" suggests something radically different or "new" at the same time that it acknowledges a strong link with what has come before. While my age automatically places me among this new generation, my particular positioning as a young woman of color within this group distinguishes me. Both the increase in the numbers of women of color in the academy and the ways in which we are able to negotiate and define/redefine our collective differences is distinctly new. So are our shared experiences as women from many races, ethnicities, age groups, and social, cultural, and class backgrounds. To use the term "generation" is more than a way of recognizing divisions produced by difference in age and race. It is also a way of highlighting our power to engender a historical profession which allows for "a new generation of women historians."

I first realized that I belonged to a new generation of women historians in 1994 when I graduated from the University of North Carolina at Chapel Hill with a double major in American history and women's studies. From six different women professors I had taken eight of the eleven courses needed for the history major. At the time, four of the professors were senior faculty members, one was chair of Women's Studies, and another was a program director (of the Southern Oral History Program) who held an endowed chair. Two of my history professors were African-American women; of the two male professors I had worked with in the history department, one considered himself a feminist and the other encouraged my interest in women's history. A double major in women's studies allowed enrollment in courses that grounded my interest in women's history and provided me with the opportunity to work with and study under women professors across the disciplines.[1] Even now it is hard to believe such an experience was possible. In an academic world that is predominately white and male, I found women (both black and white) who served as role models, provided me with the skills I would need to engage in the professional study of history, and encouraged my interest in women's history.

My first lessons regarding the realities of women's experiences (particularly women of color) in the academy came from my interaction with these women. The issues we discussed and debated ranged from questions of tokenism to the problems of sexism and racism, the danger of elitism and the place of feminism and activism within the academy. Our discussions were not always on equal terms, but my professors always encouraged my voice. I experienced a freedom that most women and students of color only find at women's colleges or historically black universities. As a women's studies and history double major, I found that many courses served as sites for community building, especially for women and students of color interested in understanding interlocking systems of race, class, and gender.

Through my "womentor" and women's studies advisor, Barbara Harris, I entered the world of female historians. Our pairing seems unlikely considering that Harris is a Jewish woman from Newark, New Jersey working in the field of European women's history, and I am an African-American woman from Statesville, North Carolina working in American history. She had been at UNC-Chapel Hill for only a year when I arrived as a first-year undergraduate, but had been teaching and mentoring undergraduate students for over twenty years. As my advisor and teacher she did not assume the posture of an all-knowing professor. More importantly, she did not pretend to know everything about my experience as a woman of color. However, this did not prevent her from fulfilling her duties as a womentor and preparing me for the professional study of history. A passionate teacher and confident feminist, she was determined to be a womentor who addressed and confronted the realities of what it meant for me to be not only a woman in the academy, but a woman of color in a profession dominated by white men. Harris knew that for me to become a fully self-realized historian, her work—and the work of other feminists—went beyond teaching us knowledge found in books. She would have to teach us an oppositional worldview that differed from that of our exploiters and oppressors. Such a worldview would enable me to see myself not through the lens of sexism or racist stereotypes but to look at myself, at the world around me, critically/analytically—to see myself clearly and succinctly, first and foremost as striving for wholeness, for unity of heart, mind, body, and spirit.

In my first year I took two courses with Harris—Introduction to Women's Studies and Women in Europe since 1750. She encouraged my interest in women's history and introduced me to faculty and graduate students in the history department. As the undergraduate representative on the Women's Studies Advisory Board and the co-chair of the Women's Forum, an organization for undergraduate women on campus, I was able to work with her on several projects. Working together we developed a teacher-student relationship based on mutual respect—not hierarchy. Harris acknowledged her position as one of power and used it in ways that enriched my undergraduate experience. For example, as a representative of the Housekeepers Association—a student/faculty support group for campus service workers who were fighting for fair wages, humane treatment in the workplace, and improved benefits—I asked the Women's Studies Curriculum to provide an open forum for workers to discuss grievances with faculty, students, and administrators. She welcomed the idea. Her choice in many ways humanized our relationship and allowed for a partnership defined by our commitment to improving the position of women and people of color in the academy, regardless of their status.

While I believe our relationship is special, it has much to teach us about negotiating differences in a productive way. Though she is a white woman, I could talk to Harris when I was having a difficult time with issues of racism in one of my classes. While sexism, rather than the combination of racism and sexism, had defined her academic experience in graduate school, nonetheless I gained encouragement from her example of resistance, perseverance, and success. Talking to her made me feel less alone and I was reminded that problems of racism and sexism, while real and with real impact, are not insurmountable.

Harris demonstrated a desire to see more women, particularly women of color, in higher education through commitment to me and other women and students of color in the department. During my time at UNC-Chapel Hill she made sure I had funding to attend the Berkshire Women's History Conference, encouraged the dean to provide me with financial assistance for a GRE course, and introduced me to historians across the country. To list the many things that Harris has done and continues to do for me would not capture the essence of our relationship. More than anything, our relationship teaches that when we confront the realities of sex, race, and class—the ways they divide us, make us different, stand us in opposition—and work to reconcile and resolve these issues, we are able to learn from one another and engender a historical profession that allows for a "new generation of women historians."

Changing hiring practices have meant that there are increasingly more women and professors of color at universities across the country, and our presence mediates in many ways the racism and sexism that exist within the academy. Unlike many of the women and students of color who came before me, I was able to avoid taking courses with racist and sexist professors during my undergraduate career. Chapel Hill was one of the universities in the United States that was attempting to transform the institution both in terms of gender and racial composition of students and faculty and in terms of perspectives on knowledge and reality. Success in continuing and promoting such efforts, however, has become the work of women and people of color. The increase in the number of women and people of color in the academy has had an incredible impact on the historical profession and the isolation from which so many us suffer. My experience as a member of "a new generation of women historians" reflects in some ways the positive changes that have grown out of the call for diversity and the ways in which women and people of color have been sought out, recruited, promoted, and supported like never before. However, it also provides insight into the ways in which the academy continues to devalue and ignore our presence and contributions to the profession.

The problem of inclusion without influence is an issue that women and students of color continue to confront. In classrooms, students continue to point out that though professors are supportive, they are not prepared to be resources for learning about women, people of color, and/or working-class people. The task of working collectively to confront difference, to expand our awareness of sex, race, and class as interlocking systems of domination, of the ways we reinforce and perpetuate these structures, is not an easy one. At many universities we still exist as the "only one"—the token woman/the token person of color. Our battles for tenure and acceptance in departments all over the country are constant reminders of how far we have yet to go. Since entering graduate school at Princeton I have witnessed the increase in the number of women of color in the profession. I have also struggled with the reality that has emerged from what our presence means—the good, the bad, and the ugly.

I entered my graduate program as one of four African Americans. With three African Americans in the year ahead of me, we were the majority in many of our classes. Our presence changed the dynamics of the discourse; as a group we had to be acknowledged. When we arrived in Princeton for minority recruiting weekend, we first encountered the racism and hostility of students who either resented our presence or who were absolutely unprepared for our arrival. I was sitting in the history lounge with the four other recruits when a white female student shocked by our numbers asked, "What are they doing, busing you guys in here?" We all looked at one another as if to say, "Did she really say that?" Having one another, as well as an advisor with whom we could talk about such issues without feeling as if we were being hypersensitive, provided the support and affirmation that so many students of color lack at institutions of higher education. Acknowledgment is one significant way to begin the process of confrontation and transformation. Sharing our personal strategies for negotiating structures of racism is a useful process of intervention. The more familiar we are, the more we communicate with one another, the greater our awareness that we are not isolated, the more we project our concerns so that they impact on the experience of everyone else at Princeton.

My experience at Princeton University can not be understood separate from my relationship with my advisor, Nell Painter. She has created an environment here that has made my survival possible. Her efforts to recruit both faculty and students of color have had a tremendous effect on my graduate experience. Before arriving in Princeton I had no idea about what it meant to be a black woman at a predominately white, Ivy League institution. Sitting through my classes feeling like everyone around me was speaking another language and not being able to relate to the other graduate students and their Ivy League undergraduate experiences, I felt like a foreigner. I was a black woman from the South who had attended a public institution, and so not only were these graduate students and their language foreign to me, I was foreign to them as well. That first semester I felt marginalized in most of my classes even though I was not the only person of color in my courses. However, it was Nell who best understood my intimidation and feelings of discomfort, and it was she who made sure I was fully armed and prepared when I entered into my second semester of course work. I can easily argue that the ways in which Nell has been a wonderful advisor have nothing to do with her racial identity, but I do believe it is her particular experience as a black woman historian that has made my experience at Princeton University a less painful one. As a role model and inspiration, she helped me to deal with the realities of my experiences as a black woman at Princeton.

Even as I write this essay I am confronted with the reality of being a black woman at Princeton. Just this week I was once again mistaken for one of the other women of color in the department. I have been a student in the history department for over three years and students and faculty still have a problem distinguishing me from this other woman of color. Even more frustrating than being "called out my name" are the attempts that are made to justify the mistake. In many cases I am made to feel as if the mistake were my own. One incident typifies this experience. In my first year a professor in the department called me Cheryl (the name of an African-American woman a year ahead of me in the program). He refused to believe me when I told him, "My name is Crystal, not Cheryl." He replied, "Then who is Cheryl?" Even after I told him who Cheryl was and after Marie (another woman of color in the department for whom I often am mistaken) confirmed my identity, it was only after he asked a white male student who happened to be passing by—"What is her name?"—that the professor was finally convinced I was who I said I was. He concluded the conversation by saying, "Oh, I guess you were not lying." It is especially frustrating because I do not look like either of the two women I am often mistaken for. Just this week a faculty member who mistook me for a woman of color whose exam committee he had served on explained, "The resemblance is striking, almost uncanny. You must get that all the time."

For many whites, women of color are interchangeable—the assumption is that because we are black and work with an African-American faculty member, then we must all work on the same thing. After my return to Princeton from a research trip down South, a student asked, "How was your research in Albany?" When I replied that I had been in Mississippi and that Cheryl works in Albany, he responded, "Well, I just assumed you all worked on the same thing." Once again I am forced to reclaim my identity and explain why I am not some other woman of color in the department. The presence of women of color in higher education has meant many things, but the old stereotype—"They all look alike"—still holds true for those who are unprepared or unwilling to accept our presence.

After returning from a graduate student conference in which I was the sole African-American participant, and having had to deal with what that meant—my immediate reaction was to speak out. I talked to all the women and students of color in the historical profession I knew about my experience and, as a graduate student representative of the Coordinating Council for Women in History (CCWH), wrote a column in the newsletter discussing the event. I explained in an open letter to my advisor:

> The first day of the conference I was in a state of profound confusion as I experienced myself as both a participant and not a participant at the conference. The participant was a black female graduate student from Princeton University presenting a paper titled, "The New Southern Woman: The Lynching of Black and White Women in the New South, 1880–1930" and the non-participant was myself trapped at the crossroads of all these identities. What I mean by participating and not participating has to do with the way in which others projected their ideas about what kind of participant I was and my own perception and ideas of what it meant to be a participant. At first I thought that the "multiple personality" problem could be explained away by lack of ease—produced by the reality of being the only one. In my effort to make sense of the ontological confusion I realized that I had experienced a shift from being one person to being a different person. This shift was not willful or even conscious, and yet I was completely aware of being different. I was different because in the eyes and words of the other participants, I represented all of their ideas/stereotypes about their constructions of who they thought I was as a black woman historian at an Ivy League institution in the North using gender theory to talk about violence and white supremacy in the South. I was caught in a web of constructed identities; the conference took on a new meaning as I struggled to free myself and present an identity of my own construction. I wanted to be more than what

> others chose to project upon me. And yet, I may have animated such constructions, even though I did not intend my moves, gestures, and acts in that way.

My experience at this conference appears representative of what many women and students of color experience in history departments across the country. Whether we exist as the only one or as one of many women of color our identities are constantly in flux. Our bodies/identities become sites on which others construct race and gender in ways that allow for both hypervisibility and/or invisibility. We become visible markers of race and gender whose purpose is to exist within those representations. When we attempt to move outside of the constructions/stereotypes that are heaped upon us, we are no longer familiar and therefore become invisible.

The responses I received from women in the profession to my open letter were overwhelmingly supportive, but more than anything they were an opportunity for many to tell me I was not alone. After reading the letter, my advisor welcomed me "to the long-suffering, much-abused community of black women academics." The shock of my treatment at the conference and my continued disbelief in the ways the profession treats women of color testify to the relative success of both my undergraduate and graduate institutions in creating in some ways a welcoming intellectual community of women and people of color.

It is our ability to generate—to bring into existence something "new"—which transforms the academy. More and more, there are university settings where black female graduate students and women students can study in supportive atmospheres. Racism and sexism are always present, yet they do not necessarily shape all areas of our experience. When I talk with black female graduate students working in history departments, I hear that many of the problems women and people of colors faced ten years ago have not changed. We experience the same intense isolation and loneliness that characterized the experience of the many women who came before us. However, I also hear about the communities of support that they/we have been able to create as we attempt to bridge the gap between the old and the new while making way for a new generation of women historians.

NOTE

1. My professors were Barbara Harris, Tera Hunter, Jacquelyn Dowd Hall, Genna Rae McNeil, Suzanne Lebsock, Sarah Chambers, Peter Filene, Gerhard Weinberg, Jane Boxill, Katherine Newberry, Sheryl Kleinman, Soyini Madison, and Valorie Johnson. Both Hunter and McNeil, the two African Americans on the history department faculty, at different times served as my history department advisor.

CONTRIBUTORS

EILEEN BORIS became Professor of Women's Studies at the University of Virginia in the fall of 1998. Previously she was Professor of History at Howard University, where she had taught since 1984. After editing the CGWH newsletter from 1988 to 1993, she emerged out of "retirement" to edit the CCWH newsletter, 1996–98.

RENATE BRIDENTHAL, Professor of History at Brooklyn College, the City University of New York, was co-president of the CCWHP in 1974–75 and has been a member since its inception.

BERENICE A. CARROLL is Director of the Women's Studies Program and Professor of Political Science at Purdue University. She served as Director of the Women's Studies Program at the University of Illinois at Urbana-Champaign from 1983 to 1987. A founder of CCWHP, she served as co-chair in 1970 and as chair in 1970–71.

NUPUR CHAUDHURI, who teaches at Texas Southern University, serves on the editorial boards of *Women's History Review* and *National Women's Studies Journal*. She is also the US representative for the International Federation for Research in Women's History. She has been involved with CCWHP as an officer since 1976.

SANDI E. COOPER served as chair of the University Faculty Senate at the City University of New York (1994–98) and is Professor of History, College of Staten Island and the Graduate School, CUNY. She was chair of

CCWHP from 1972 to 1974 and founding member and co-chair of the Metropolitan New York area chapter, CCWHP, 1969–71.

MOLLIE C. DAVIS is Professor of History at Queens College in Charlotte, North Carolina, where she teaches in the College of Arts and Sciences during the day and in the Pauline Lewis Hayworth College (for working adults) evenings and Saturdays. She also coordinates the Hayworth College American Studies Program. A founder, co-president, then president of the Southern Association of Women Historians (1970–73), she served briefly as CCWHP chair for women's history in 1973 and then president of CCWHP, 1983–85.

CRYSTAL FEIMSTER was CCWH graduate student representative, 1997–99. She plans to receive her PhD in history from Princeton University in 1999.

NANCY HEWITT became Professor of History at Rutgers University in the fall of 1998. Previously she was at Duke University. She served as chair of the Graduate Student Awards Committee in 1989–90 and then as president of CGWH from 1990 to 1993. She currently is completing a five-year term as vice-president of the International Federation for Research in Women's History.

JOAN HOFF served as CCWHP president, 1977–79. Co-founder of *The Journal of Women's History*, she currently is Professor of History and Director of the Contemporary History Institute, Ohio University.

BARBARA PENNY KANNER was CCWH President from 1982 to 1984. She is a visiting scholar in UCLA's history department and a longtime research scholar in UCLA's Center for the Study of Women.

FRANCES RICHARDSON KELLER retired from San Francisco State University, where she was adjunct Professor of American History, 1978–96. She was CCWHP president from 1986 to 1988 and with Barbara Penny Kanner headed up the committee to establish graduate student awards.

LINDA K. KERBER is May Brodbeck Professor in the Liberal Arts and Professor of History at the University of Iowa. From 1970 to 1972, she was editor of the CCWHP Bulletin "Current Research in the History of Women" and its occasional supplement, "Courses Offered in Women's History and Related Fields." She has served as president of the American Studies Association (1988) and the Organization of American Historians (1997).

GERDA LERNER is Robinson-Edwards Professor of History, Emerita, University of Wisconsin–Madison. She was co-chair of CCWHP in 1969–70 and president of OAH in 1981–82.

NANCY RAQUEL MIRABAL is Assistant Professor, La Raza Studies Department, San Francisco State University. She served as CCWH graduate student representative from 1996 to 1998 while pursuing her doctorate at the University of Michigan.

KAREN OFFEN, an independent scholar associated with Stanford's Institute for Research on Women and Gender, held various CCWHP offices—membership secretary, secretary-treasurer, and treasurer—from 1972 to 1977.

MARY ELIZABETH PERRY is Adjunct Professor of History at Occidental College and Research Associate with the UCLA Center for Medieval and Renaissance Studies. She has served on the CCWH Graduate Awards Committee and was CCWHP president from 1992 to 1995.

HILDA L. SMITH is Associate Professor of History at the University of Cincinnati, where she also served as Director of Women's Studies from 1987 to 1993. She was the first secretary-treasurer of CCWHP, 1969–71.

MARGARET (PEG) STROBEL is Professor of Women's Studies and History at the University of Illinois at Chicago. She served as CCWHP newsletter editor in 1981–83 and as CCWHP president from 1989 to 1991.

LYNN WEINER is Professor of History and Associate Dean of Arts and Sciences at Roosevelt University. She was CCWHP/CGWH executive director, 1989–1991.

BARBARA WINSLOW is Professor of Women's Studies at Brooklyn College/CUNY. She has taught both as an adjunct and a full-timer at Baruch, John Jay, Hunter, and Medgar Evers Colleges, all part of the City University of New York. She was CCWHP/CGWH executive director from 1991 to 1995. She became the secretary-treasurer of the Berkshire Conference of Women Historians in 1997.

INDEX